British Foreign and Defence Policy si

Also by Robert Self

Neville Chamberlain: A Biography
The Neville Chamberlain Diary Letters (4 vols)
Britain, America and the War Debt Controversy, 1917–1942
The Evolution of the British Party System, 1885–1940
The Austen Chamberlain Diary Letters, 1916–1937
Tories and Tariffs, 1922–1932

This book is dedicated to Katie – as always

British Foreign and Defence Policy since 1945

Challenges and Dilemmas in a Changing World

Robert Self

First published 2010 by
PALGRAVE MACMILLAN

Palgrave Macmillan in the UK is an imprint of Macmillan Publishers Limited, registered in England, company number 785998, of Houndmills, Basingstoke, Hampshire RG21 6XS.

Palgrave Macmillan in the US is a division of St Martin's Press LLC, 175 Fifth Avenue, New York, NY 10010.

Palgrave Macmillan is the global academic imprint of the above companies and has companies and representatives throughout the world.

Palgrave® and Macmillan® are registered trademarks in the United States, the United Kingdom, Europe and other countries

ISBN 978–0–230–22079–9   hardback
ISBN 978–0–230–22080–5   paperback

This book is printed on paper suitable for recycling and made from fully managed and sustained forest sources. Logging, pulping and manufacturing processes are expected to conform to the environmental regulations of the country of origin.

A catalogue record for this book is available from the British Library.

A catalog record for this book is available from the Library of Congress.

10 9 8 7 6 5 4 3 2 1
19 18 17 16 15 14 13 12 11 10

Printed and bound in China

Contents

List of Tables and Maps

Tables

Maps

List of Abbreviations

ABM	Anti-Ballistic Missile
ANC	African National Congress
AWE	Atomic Weapons Establishment
BAOR	British Army of the Rhine
CAP	Common Agricultural Policy
CDS	Chief of the Defence Staff
CFSP	Common Foreign and Security Policy
CPP	Convention People's Party
CSI	Committee on Security and Intelligence
DEA	Department for Economic Affairs
DEFRA	Department for the Environment, Food and Rural Affairs
DEL	Departmental Expenditure Limit: resource and capital budgets less depreciation
DESO	Defence Export Services Organisation (of the Ministry of Defence)
DfID	Department for International Development
DOPC	Defence and Overseas Policy Committee
DSI	Directorate for Strategy and Innovation (at the FCO)
DTI	Department for Trade and Industry
EC	European Community
ECU	European Currency Unit
ECSC	European Coal and Steel Community
EDC	European Defence Community
EEC	European Economic Community
EFTA	European Free Trade Area
EMS	European Monetary System
EMU	Economic and Monetary Union
EOKA	National Organisation of Cypriot Fighters (Ethniki Organosis Kyprion Agoniston)
ERM	Exchange Rate Mechanism
EU	European Union
EMU	European Monetary Union
FCO	Foreign & Commonwealth Office
FO	Foreign Office
FRES	Future Rapid Effects System (new Army battlefield vehicle)
FY	Financial Year
GCHQ	Government Communications Headquarters

G7	Group of Seven (major industrial economies) – G8 since 1997
GDP	Gross Domestic Product
GNI	Gross National Income
GNP	Gross National Product
GPEX	Gross Public Expenditure
HIPC	Heavily Indebted Poor Countries
ICBM	Intercontinental ballistic missile
IMF	International Monetary Fund
IPPR	Institute for Public Policy Research
IRBM	Intermediate range ballistic missile
JIC	Joint Intelligence Committee
MDG	Millennium Development Goals (of the UN)
MIRV	Multiple independently targetable re-entry vehicle
MoD	Ministry of Defence
NATO	North Atlantic Treaty Organisation
NIC	National Intelligence Council (US)
NIE	National Intelligence Estimate (US)
NPT	Non-proliferation Treaty
NSID	National Security, International Relations and Development Committee
ODA	Overseas Development Agency
OECD	Organisation for Economic Co-operation and Development
OEEC	Organisation for European Economic Cooperation
OSA	Overseas Sterling Area
PAC	Public Accounts Committee
PLP	Parliamentary Labour Party
PRC	People's Republic of China
PUS	Permanent Under-Secretary [for Foreign Affairs]
QMV	Qualified majority voting
SDI	Strategic Defense Initiative – otherwise known as 'Star Wars'
SDR	Strategic Defence Review
SEA	Single European Act
SFO	Serious Fraud Office
SIPRI	Stockholm International Peace Research Institute
TSO	The Stationery Office
UDI	Unilateral Declaration of Independence
UNCLCS	United Nations Commission on the Limits of the Continental Shelf
UOR	Urgent Operational Requirements
WHO	World Health Organization
WEU	Western European Union
WMD	Weapons of Mass Destruction
WTO	World Trade Organisation

Chapter 1

Introduction: Britain's Place in a Changing World

From 'superpower' to 'global hub'

During a period of less than half a century after the end of the Second World War in 1945, Britain divested itself of an empire spanning almost a quarter of the world's landmass and population. It withdrew from far-flung military bases scattered across the globe and engaged in innumerable reviews of its defence commitments in the vain hope of reducing expenditure, while throughout much of this period remaining heavily engaged in military operations in various trouble-spots around the world. Although its economy grew more slowly than most of its major competitors, it continued to spend a larger proportion of its GDP on defence than any of its European NATO allies. Its unwavering quest for an 'independent' nuclear deterrent that it had neither the financial nor infrastructural resources to sustain added to the nation's stature on the world stage, but only at the expense of forcing it to accept a position of almost total dependence on the United States. Feeling the chill wind of relative economic decline and fearing political marginalisation, it promoted the idea of a European free trade area, at least in part, in an attempt to derail the progress of European integration. When this failed, it reluctantly resigned itself to entry into a European Community it often appeared to mistrust as inimical to national interests, and in consequence it rapidly acquired the reputation of being an 'awkward partner'. Above all, it doggedly maintained its faith in a supposedly 'special relationship' with the United States, although this connection always mattered far more to London than it did in Washington, and which fluctuated greatly over time in both its amity and its balance of costs and benefits to Britain. Given a post-war history characterised by an over-extended foreign policy, an overstretched defence capability and an underperforming economy, it is scarcely surprising that many look back and lament the speed with which Britain has declined from its hegemonic position as the world's leading nation in the 1880s 'to its pre-imperial status as an offshore island of a powerful continent' (Alford 1996: 1).

1

This retreat from greatness has overtaken the nation so rapidly that it is easy to forget that when W.T.R Fox coined the term 'superpower' in 1944, Britain was naturally included in this category alongside the United States and the Soviet Union (Fox 1944). Although curious to modern eyes, perhaps, at the time it was no more than an accurate reflection of Britain's perceived position in the world. Churchill had attended the great wartime Allied conferences sitting alongside Roosevelt and Stalin as one of the 'Big Three'. Despite the ravages and dislocation inflicted by five years of total war, by the early 1950s Britain still produced nearly a third of the industrial output of non-Communist Europe, half the world's trade was still denominated in sterling and it possessed more weapons than all the other European members of NATO combined. Moreover, it was still a major centre of the world financial system, the hub of its own highly advantageous Overseas Sterling Area (OSA) and it still presided over the largest empire the world had ever seen. For all of these reasons, Britain occupied a very special position in world diplomacy and few doubted when the war ended in 1945 that it would continue to do so for many years to come.

This mood of post-war confidence was reflected in the enduring potency of Winston Churchill's hypnotic vision of Britain's overseas interests lying within what he described as three 'interlocking circles' of influence. As he variously explained to the Conservative party conference at Llandudno in October 1948 and the Cabinet in November 1951, Britain stood uniquely at the intersection of three circles of influence in the world. First, it was the dominant power in European affairs and was necessarily involved in this arena – albeit only as 'a separate, closely and specially-related ally and friend' rather than a direct participant in continental efforts at closer integration. The second and more important circle of influence concerned Britain's relationship with its Empire and self-governing Dominions. Finally, there was Britain's very 'special relationship' with the United States; an association Churchill had nurtured assiduously through his personal rapport with Roosevelt during the Second World War. More to the point, Churchill intimated that Britain's influence in each circle was increased by the fact that it could draw upon the authority and power conferred by membership of the other two. (McIntyre 1998: 38). For over two decades, this intoxicating doctrine occupied an almost sacrosanct position in British strategic thinking for governments of both parties. Unfortunately, it also acted as a brake upon the necessary adaptation of its global strategy to the unpalatable realities which would become such a prominent feature of British national life in the following decades. As Hugo Young notes, Churchill's vision, while 'represented as the essence of wisdom, could equally well be described as a biblical text for the justification of strategic indecision.' (Young 1998: 32).

The notion of continued special status in an essentially bipolar world proved so attractive that policymakers were reluctant to challenge this tantalising self-image of Britain as a great power and major bridge-builder in international relations. In these circumstances, as Kierkegaard once formulated it, there was a tendency 'to think backwards while living forward'. Above all, critics noted there was the ineffable assumption that no matter how weak Britain's economy and armed forces, it would always somehow continue to enjoy this special influence in the world and would naturally emerge on top (Waltz 1979). In the immediate aftermath of an economically devastating war, Clement Attlee's Labour government (1945–51) confronted what Lord Keynes described as a 'financial Dunkirk' which threatened a serious collapse in the standard of living and welfare. Yet for all that, Ernest Bevin, the Labour Foreign Secretary, declared in the House of Commons in May 1947 that the Labour government did 'not accept the view . . . that we have ceased to be a great Power, or the contention that we had ceased to play that role. We regard ourselves as one of the Powers most vital to the peace of the world, and we still have our historic part to play' (Darby 1973: 18). In private, Bevin was even more confident in predicting that 'if we only pushed on and developed Africa, we could have the United States depending on us, and eating out of our hand, in four or five years' (Gallagher 1982: 146).

Bevin's private dreams proved grossly overoptimistic but the underlying belief that Britain could maintain its former position in the world proved to be extremely deeply rooted in the collective psyche of the Whitehall 'official mind'. Sir Oliver Franks, a senior Foreign Office official and Ambassador to Washington between 1948 and 1952, revealed something of that mind-set at the time when he recalled:

> We assume that our future will be of a piece with our past and that we shall continue as a great power. What is noteworthy is the way that we take this for granted. It is not a policy arrived at after reflection by a conscious decision. It is part of the habit and furniture of our minds: a principle so much at one with our outlook and character that it determines the way we act without emerging itself into clear consciousness. (Darby 1973: 22, cited in Franks 1955)

The Chiefs of Staff certainly reflected this tendency when advocating the development of a British hydrogen bomb in June 1954 with the claim that 'we must maintain and strengthen our position as a world power so that Her Majesty's Government can exercise a powerful influence in the councils of the world'. The possession of such a weapon, they confidently opined, 'puts within our grasp the ability to be on terms with the United States and Russia' (Hennessy 2007: 339–40). Two years later, the 1956 Defence White Paper also declared a firm intention of maintaining a deterrent 'commensurate with our standing as a world power'. Behind the fragile optimism, however, there was the lurking recognition (as Anthony Eden put it in 1952) that 'once the prestige of the country has started to slide, there is no knowing where it will stop' (Greenwood 2000: 105).

As a former Chancellor of the Exchequer himself, when Harold Macmillan became Prime Minister in January 1957 he knew only too well the degree to which foreign and defence policy was constrained by indifferent economic performance but he was equally reluctant to challenge the rhetoric of national greatness. On the contrary, in his first broadcast as Prime Minister in the aftermath of the humiliating Suez debacle, he had explicitly denounced 'defeatist' suggestions that Britain was now 'a second – or third – class power'. 'Britain has been great, is great, and will stay great, providing that we close our ranks and get on with the job' (Wallace 1970: 204, 207–8). During his Far East tour in February 1958, Macmillan now freely acknowledged that Britain would never be able to match the power of the US or the Soviet Union, but it 'still chose to remain a great power' and that although its resources were severely stretched, 'we still had great influence' (McIntyre 1998: 46). In October 1964, Harold Wilson led a Labour government into office with the confident assertion that Britain was 'a world power and a world influence or it is nothing'. As he told the Commons in December 1964, 'I want to make it clear that . . . we cannot afford to relinquish our world role . . . We have always been a world power; we should not be corralled in Europe' (Darby 1973: 284). According to Wilson, Britain's frontiers lay on the Himalayas and in the Indian Ocean. Three years later, the traumatic experience of chronic economic crisis prompted a reluctant withdrawal of British forces from 'East of Suez'. As Michael Stewart, the Labour Foreign Secretary, acknowledged publicly, Britain was now only 'a major power of the second rank' (Zeigler 1993: 219).

Public candour of this sort was not something to which British politicians or their electors adjusted easily. Despite his determination to make the EEC the cornerstone of his foreign policy, even Edward Heath sought to maintain the illusion that Britain was still a leading world power with a contribution to make in Southeast Asia, and he negotiated the Five Power Defence Arrangements with Australia, New Zealand, Singapore and Malaysia in 1970–71 with this in mind (Benvenuti 2009). Margaret Thatcher was less reticent in her glorification of Britain's broader role in the world. In the victorious aftermath of the Falklands War in 1982 she thus rejoiced that the conflict had put the 'Great' back into Britain. 'Once again Britain is not prepared to be pushed around', she declared triumphantly at Cheltenham in July 1982. 'We have ceased to be a nation in retreat' (Jenkins 1987: 164). John Major said much the same in the wake of the Gulf War in 1991, while Tony Blair's 1997 election manifesto, *New Labour Because Britain Deserves Better*, contained more than a dozen references to leadership in foreign policy and in Europe.

In view of Blair's repeated efforts to present Britain as a nation uniquely qualified to bridge the gulf between the United States and the EU, Blair's first annual foreign policy speech at the Lord Mayor's banquet in November 1997 on 'The Principles of Modern British Foreign Policy' reformulated the traditional rhetoric in still more positive terms. 'We cannot in these post-empire days be a superpower in a military sense. But we can make the British presence in the world felt. With our historic alliances, we can be pivotal. . . . We can be powerful in our influence as a nation to whom others listen.' Or, as he put it two years later: 'We have a new role. . . . It is to use the strengths of our history to build our future not as a superpower but as a pivotal power, as a power that is at the crux of the alliances and international politics which shaped the world and its future' (www.fco.gov.uk). As Foreign Secretary, Jack Straw also boasted proudly that Britain was still capable of 'punching above its weight' in international affairs (MccGwire 2006). By 2007, the language had changed. Employing a new metaphor for a new government, David Miliband, Gordon Brown's first Foreign Secretary, declared at Chatham House in July 2007: 'The vision is a Britain that is a global hub.' This was the objective around which the new FCO strategy *Better World, Better Britain* was formulated when it was launched in April 2008 (www.fco.gov.uk).

Trying (and failing) to adjust to harsh realities?

The unwavering persistence of this belief in Britain's special destiny in foreign affairs since 1945 is all the more remarkable in face of the nation's sustained relative economic decline and the limitations this problem has placed upon its ability to perform as an autonomous actor on the international stage. In private, a Cabinet paper for Macmillan's 'Future Policy Study 1960–70' conceded in February 1960 that even if Britain's economy expanded sufficiently to double National Income in 25 years, 'we shall still fall behind . . . [and] our relative position vis-a-vis both the United States and Western Europe will . . . decline'

(Hennessy 2007: 587). But as Chapter 2 demonstrates, in public policy terms the necessary adjustment to these harsh new economic, military and diplomatic realities has proved to be a slow and painful process – not least because it has challenged many previously cherished images about Britain's place in the world. Seventeen years after the end of the war, at West Point in December 1962, the former US Secretary of State, Dean Acheson, delivered a stinging indictment of Britain's failure to adapt to changing international circumstances:

> Great Britain has lost an Empire and has not yet found a role. The attempt to play a separate power role – that is, a role apart from Europe, a role based on a 'special relationship' with the US, a role based on being the head of a 'Commonwealth' which has no political structure, unity, or strength, and enjoys a fragile and precarious economic relationship by means of the Sterling Area and preferences in the British market – this role is about played out. Great Britain, attempting to work alone and to be a broker between United States and Russia, has seemed to conduct a policy as weak as its military power. (Coles 2000: 36)

There was abundant evidence to justify this criticism at the time – not least the consistent failure fundamentally to reappraise British foreign and defence priorities 'East of Suez' after Indian independence had removed much of the original rationale for such a presence. In fairness, as Prime Minister, Attlee combined a belief in Britain's status as a great power with a continued global role with the sceptical recognition that there was still considerable scope for a timely retreat from excessive and superfluous defence and overseas commitments. In March 1946, his Cabinet memorandum pressing for the adoption of a new total global strategy, which achieved a better alignment between economic strength and real needs, has been described as 'one of the most penetrating and perceptive written by any British statesman in the 20th century' (Barnett 1995: 54). In the end, however, he was defeated by Bevin and the Chiefs of Staff, who threatened to resign if Britain pulled out of its bases in the Middle East (Pearce 1991: 162–3). A similar fate awaited subsequent efforts to achieve this realignment between resources and commitments undertaken on several occasions by the Conservative governments of the 1950s, and even when this was partially achieved with the decision to withdraw from 'East of Suez' in the mid-1960s it was the unwilling but ineluctable product of chronic economic crisis rather than a conscious act of political choice (see Chapter 6).

Thirty years after Acheson's famous indictment, many were still arguing that Britain in the 1990s had failed to adjust itself to a rapidly changing world. At this juncture, adjustment was necessary to adapt not only to the changes wrought by the Second World War, but also to those engendered by the dramatic end of the Cold War with the collapse of communism and the Warsaw Pact in eastern Europe culminating in the eventual dissolution of the Soviet Union in 1991. While the first President George Bush (1989–93) optimistically predicted the emergence of a 'New World Order', many concluded this crucial watershed offered the long-awaited opportunity to rethink Britain's place in the world, cut its defence budget and reallocate the 'peace dividend' to some of the less tangible aspects of diplomatic relations – particularly as there was now a greater need than ever before to persuade voters and allies that Britain 'still has a distinctive and valuable contribution to make' (Clarke 1992: 111; Wallace 1992). In the event, this was to be yet another of those great 'missed opportunities' which supposedly litter the history of post-war Britain. John Major's government continued the pretence that Britain was still a great power qualitatively different in influence from its European neighbours, and 'realism' remained the dominant approach to international relations. But, as Wallace concluded, perhaps this 'missed opportunity' was symptomatic of a more fundamental failure as successive governments gradually adjusted to a changing global environment 'without thinking it necessary to re-define national goals or to launch an organised debate about history and identity' (Wallace 1991).

'Traditionalist' versus 'transformationalist' perspectives

This paramount emphasis upon Britain's economic, diplomatic and military decline within the international system reflects what might be called a 'traditionalist' approach. When viewed from this perspective, the story is invariably portrayed as one of unremitting national decline, with faltering economic performance relegating Britain from its position as an imperial and global power in 1945 to that of a disgruntled second-rank island anchored off the European continent; a confused and ambivalent member state consigned to a marginal role as an 'awkward partner' while at the same time belatedly trying to seize the leadership of a European Community/Union it neither likes nor particularly feels at home within. This preoccupation is tellingly reflected in the titles of such classic works as F.S. Northedge's *Descent from Power* (1974), David Dilks's *The Retreat from Power* (1991) and C.J. Bartlett's history of post-war defence policy entitled *The Long Retreat* (1972). At the heart of all these works is the proposition that Britain has contravened what Northedge labels the 'Micawber rule of foreign affairs', in which nations whose resources exceed their commitments enjoy 'happiness' while those whose resources fall short of their commitments must expect 'misery'. From this traditionalist perspective, post-war Britain most definitely falls into the second category and its foreign policy has suffered accordingly (Northedge 1976: 243). As Sir Nicholas Henderson summed up the general perception in his valedictory dispatch as Ambassador in Paris in March 1979, since Ernest Bevin pleaded a generation before for more coal to give weight to British foreign policy, 'our economic decline has been such as to sap the foundations of our diplomacy' (Henderson 1987: 152).

Few would refute the validity of Paul Kennedy's general proposition that when considering the rise and fall of great powers there is 'a very significant correlation *over the longer term* between productive and revenue-raising capacities on the one hand and military strength on the other'. It is equally undeniable that Britain's position in the world system has undergone some fairly fundamental changes in the last 65 years and that even by comparison with 1945 it has declined to the position of being 'just an ordinary, moderately large, not a Great Power' (Kennedy 1989: xvi, 549). But it is important to avoid oversimplification by succumbing to an exaggerated sense of economic determinism. First, it cannot be emphasised too strongly that the measurement of 'decline' is a far more elusive concept than it might first appear and depends greatly upon precisely what is measured, how it is quantified and the chronological benchmarks employed when making such comparisons. Furthermore, as Jim Tomlinson rightly reminds us, historians have too often in the past based their 'declinist' critiques upon highly politicised and polemical contemporary discourses about the existence of more profound social, technological, political and cultural failures in twentieth-century Britain (Tomlinson 2009). Secondly, it needs to be remembered that while Britain has declined sharply *relative* to its international competitors, in absolute terms it is still much more prosperous and technologically advanced than ever before. Finally, as Table 1.1 demonstrates, for all the Cassandra-like cries of doom and gloom, today Britain still remains a formidable economic and military force which controls the world's fifth-largest economy, and since 1945 it has consistently spent more on defence than any country other than the United States. This is a remarkable fact given that Kennedy argues that for a country of its size, population and natural resources the United Kingdom ought to possess some 3–4 per cent of the world's wealth and power. When viewed from this perspective, despite an often uncritical national acceptance of the notion of 'decline', as David Reynolds points out, it was always 'unlikely that a nation with only two per cent of the world's population could control over a fifth of its land surface, maintain half its warships and account for 40 per cent of its trade in manufactured goods for very long' (Reynolds 1991: 33).

While it is undoubtedly true that the persistence of relative economic decline from this artificially high nineteenth-century baseline has been an important factor shaping much of Britain's post-war foreign and defence policy, when viewed from an alternative perspective Thomas Otte is correct in arguing that 'assumptions of an abrupt fall from great power status are misleading. The main theme of post-war British foreign policy is rather one of constant attempts to adapt to the changing international setting' (Otte 2002a: 22). Similarly, David Greenwood

Table 1.1   Britain's place in the world in the 21st century: vital statistics

In the world league tables (for 2007 unless stated) it was ranked as the:	
5th	largest economy in terms of GDP ($2772 billion)
6th	largest economy in purchasing power ($2143 billion)
2nd	largest recipient of foreign direct investment inflows ($224 billion)
2nd	largest source of outflows of foreign direct investment ($266 billion)
4th	largest producer ($1874 billion) and exporter of services (10.76% of world exports)
4th	largest stock market capitalisation ($1852 billion)
5th	largest exporter of goods, services and income (6.1 per cent of world exports in this sector)
5th	largest industrial producer ($569 billion)
6th	largest maritime trader (3.8 per cent of world trade) with the tenth largest merchant fleet (876 vessels)
7th	largest manufacturing output ($270 billion)
8th	in the index for the adoption of technological innovation
9th	largest trader of goods (3.3% of world trade)
14th	highest GDP per capita ($45,404)
14th	largest holder of official gold reserves ($8.3 billion)
21st	in the index for global competitiveness (in 2008)
In addition, it is ranked:	
2nd	largest defence spender ($63.3 billion in 2007)
4th	largest bilateral and multilateral aid donor
	Home of four of the world's top ten universities

Source: The Economist, Pocket World in Figures, 2010 edition.

Table 1.2 British Prime Ministers and Foreign Secretaries since 1945

Prime Minister	Government dates	Foreign Secretary	
Clement Attlee	Jul 1945–Oct 1951	Ernest Bevin, 1945–March 1951	Lab
		Herbert Morrison, Mar–Oct 1951	Lab
Winston Churchill	1951–Apr 1955	Anthony Eden, 1951–Apr 1955	Con
Anthony Eden	1955–Jan 1957	Harold Macmillan, April–Dec 1955	Con
Harold Macmillan	1957–Oct 1963	Selwyn Lloyd, 1955–Jul 1960	Con
		Earl of Home (later Sir Alec Douglas-Home) July–Oct 1963	Con
Sir Alec Douglas-Home	1963–Oct 1964	Richard Austen Butler, 1963–Oct 1964	Con
Harold Wilson	1964–Jun 1970	Patrick Gordon Walker, 1964–Jan 1965	Lab
		Michael Stewart, 1965–Aug 1966	Lab
		George Brown, 1966–Mar 1968	Lab
		Michael Stewart, 1968–Jun 1970	Lab
Edward Heath	1970–Mar 1974	Sir Alec Douglas-Home, 1970–Mar 1974	Con
Harold Wilson	1974–Apr 1976	James Callaghan, 1974–Apr 1976	Lab

Table 1.2 British Prime Ministers and Foreign Secretaries since 1945 – *continued*

Prime Minister	Government dates	Foreign Secretary	
James Callaghan	1976–May 1979	Anthony Crosland, 1976–Feb 1977	Lab
		David Owen, 1977–May 1979	Lab
Margaret Thatcher	1979–Nov 1990	Lord Carrington, 1979–Apr 1982	Con
		Francis Pym, 1982–Jun 1983	Con
		Sir Geoffrey Howe,1983–July 1989	Con
		John Major, July–Oct 1989	Con
John Major	1990–May 1997	Douglas Hurd,1989–July 1995	Con
		Malcolm Rifkind, 1995–May 1997	Con
Tony Blair	1997–June 2007	Robin Cook, 1997–Jun 2001	Lab
		Jack Straw, 2001–May 2006	Lab
		Margaret Beckett, 2006–Jun 2007	Lab
Gordon Brown	2007–	David Miliband, 2007–	Lab

plausibly challenges the established orthodoxy of the 'decline thesis' by arguing that British defence policy during this period can be characterised less as one of decline than a successful process of readjustment and reorientation away from its former world role towards a more credible and realistic European focus (Greenwood 1976).

It is equally important to recognize that the international order in which Britain operates has also changed profoundly since 1945. Not only has there been an enormous increase in the number of sovereign states (from around 50 in 1950 to nearer 200 today) but also international relations have become more complex, with the growth of globalisation, multilateralism, increasing interdependence and the emergence of a challenging new transnational agenda encompassing everything from human rights, climate change, world poverty, Third World debt and drug trafficking to the need to formulate a far broader and more sophisticated understanding of the multifaceted threats to national security. As Smith and Smith argue: 'This transformation does not render the relative decline of British power irrelevant, but it places the decline within the far wider and arguably more significant framework of constraints and opportunities' (Smith and Smith 1988: 19–20). When viewed from this alternative 'transformationalist' approach, it could be argued that Britain has been rather more successful in adapting to the challenges of the twenty-first century than the 'traditionalists' concede – particularly as it has still continued to 'punch above its weight' in international affairs through a combination of resources, determination and skilful footwork. Just as Clement Attlee declared that Britain was not just one of the crowd in 1945, the same sentiment was echoed with almost equal credibility by Margaret Thatcher in the 1980s and Tony Blair in the early years of the new millennium. This volume does not seek to make a contribution to international relations theory or even to apply existing theories to the British case. Rather, its purpose is to explore the central issues, problems and dilemmas of external policy which have confronted British policy-makers since the end of the Second World War.

Chapter 2

British Power and the Burden of History

The rise of British imperial power

The depressing central theme running through most studies of Britain's post-war foreign and defence policy is one of remorseless and unremitting decline. As discussed in Chapter 1, this is a highly contested concept but concerns about 'the decline of Britain' did not begin in 1945 and nor did the problems that accompanied it. On the contrary, to understand the predicament confronting British foreign policymakers in the post-war era, it is necessary to return to the zenith of British power in the last quarter of the nineteenth century because it was ironically during this period that most of the difficulties and agonising dilemmas confronting British policy after the Second World War were already making themselves evident. Not least among these problems were those posed by what Basil Liddell Hart would later call 'imperial overstretch'; a phenomenon characterised by the existence of a vast 'resource gap' between Britain's massive imperial and overseas commitments and its ability to mobilise the diplomatic, financial and military resources needed to defend and extend those interests.

None of these difficulties were foreseen in the first three-quarters of the nineteenth century. On the contrary, in the 60 years after the end of the Napoleonic wars in 1815, Britain rapidly emerged as the dominant world power in a qualitatively different class from all its competitors. As the first to benefit from mass industrialisation, Britain's share of world manufacturing production increased from 1.9 per cent in 1750 to 9.5 per cent in 1830 before spiralling upwards to a peak of 22.9 per cent by 1880. With only 2 per cent of the world's population (and 10 per cent of Europe's population), Britain possessed between 40 per cent and 45 per cent of the world's industrial potential (and 55–60 per cent of that of Europe). Its total exports amounted to 17 per cent of world trade carried across the oceans in a vast British merchant fleet of 6.5 million net tons – some 40 per cent of the world total. In every respect, therefore, by 1870 Britain was the great hegemonic power of the age.

Furthermore, while this ascendancy was increasingly challenged there-after, even in 1900, Britain was still the world's largest banker at the undisputed centre of the global financial system; the world's greatest trading nation; it possessed the world's largest merchant fleet; a healthy balance of payments surplus; and a navy more than equal in size to that of its next two rivals combined – and until the late 1890s it was prob-ably stronger than the next three or four navies combined (Kennedy 1989: 193–8).

Beyond the sheer scale of Britain's ascendancy, its position in the world was characterised by two uniquely distinctive features of its his-torical legacy which have directly influenced policy priorities and pre-occupations through to the present day. First, it possessed more overseas investments than the rest of Europe combined – a source of financial strength both qualitatively and quantitatively different from anything that had gone before and crucial to its prosperity. In the decade after 1815, £6 million had been exported in investments. By the mid-nineteenth century this figure had increased to over £30 million and by 1885 it reached £185 million before peaking at a staggering £4080 million by 1914. This export of capital brought in £200 million annually in interest to cover the growing gap in the visible balance of trade. But, undoubtedly, the most striking feature of this trend was that 95 per cent of this investment was outside Europe and a similar pattern existed with regard to Britain's export trade where 61 per cent was out-side Europe by 1913. On this basis, Bernard Porter argues convincingly that this pattern of capital flows conferred upon Britain a very different perspective on world affairs from that of its continental neighbours. Above all, it encouraged policymakers to look outwards beyond Europe to see the nation's true interests lying overseas in other conti-nents – and in its turn, this meant the preservation of its unfettered ability to trade anywhere and everywhere in the world. This very dis-tinctive feature of British foreign policy provided a persistent legacy well into the later years of the twentieth century (Porter 1987: 66).

Similar consequences followed from the fact that by 1900 Britain presided over the largest Empire the world has ever seen: an Empire which consisted of some 12,000,000 square miles – a fifth of the total world surface area containing 400 million subjects (Hyam 1976: 258). The sheer scale and success of this imperial zeal was attested by the fact that the British Empire grew at an average rate of around 100,000 square miles a year between 1815 and 1865, and it increased in total area by nearly two-and–a-half times between 1870 and 1914, despite fierce imperial rivalry and the marginal economic value of many of these new territories. Furthermore, beyond its formal annexations, Britain enjoyed the benefits of a massive 'informal empire' encom-

Table 2.1 Relative share of world manufacturing output, 1750-1980 (per cent)

	1750	1800	1830	1860	1880	1900	1913	1928	1938	1953	1963	1973	1980
United Kingdom	1.9	4.3	9.5	19.9	22.9	18.5	13.6	9.9	10.7	8.4	6.4	4.9	4.0
United States	0.1	0.8	2.4	7.2	14.7	23.6	32.0	39.4	31.4	44.7	35.1	33.0	31.5
Germany/German States	2.9	3.5	3.5	4.9	8.5	13.2	14.8	11.6	12.7	5.9	6.4	5.9	5.3
France	4.0	4.2	5.2	7.9	7.8	6.8	6.1	6.0	4.4	3.2	3.8	3.5	3.3
Russia/USSR	5.0	5.6	5.6	7.0	7.6	8.0	8.2	5.3	9.0	10.7	14.2	14.4	14.8

Sources: adapted from Kennedy (1989: 190, 259); Reynolds (1991: 12).

passing much of Latin America, China, and the Near East, where it exercised varying degrees of overlordship on the basis of a treaty-based hegemony designed to ensure commercial advantage and the security of its communication routes without the financial and manpower demands imposed by an already overstretched empire.

On the basis of these vast acquisitions, a new imperial myth propagated by works such as Sir John Seeley's *The Expansion of England* (1883) produced a new form of 'pink on the map Empire' national jingoism which intoxicated public and politicians alike throughout the first half of the twentieth century. This pomp and imperial splendour was celebrated before the entire world at Queen Victoria's Diamond Jubilee in 1897, the victory parades of 1918, the British Empire Exhibition of 1923, various imperial conferences between the wars and on the annual Empire Day. Yet, in reality, while this beguiling myth served as a 'necessary psychological crutch' for an increasingly beleaguered nation, it has been argued that 'when measured in terms of economic and strategic advantages balanced against entanglements and obligations, the Empire was not so much an asset as a liability, one of the most remarkable examples of strategic overextension in history' (Barnett 1995: 7–8).

New threats and challengers: the British Empire and the 'resource gap' before 1914

Beneath the lavish display of imperial power at Queen Victoria's Diamond Jubilee, on the eve of the twentieth century, British policymakers fell prey to a new sense of insecurity, uncertainty and increasing vulnerability. Much of this anxiety was engendered by stiff industrial, financial and economic competition from the United States and Germany as the early vigour of Britain's phenomenal economic growth began to slow while its two principal challengers grew at more than twice Britain's rate of 2.1 per cent per annum. Britain's share of world trade fell from 23 per cent in 1880 to 14 per cent by 1913, and its share of world industrial production decreased by a similar amount during this period (see Table 2.1). By the end of the nineteenth century, Britain's industrialists appeared to be complacent, sluggish and conservative when confronted by the challenge of rapidly developing new technologies and new competitors eager to displace the British hegemon. Much debate continues to surround the reasons for this relative decline, but it is tolerably clear that Britain's rise to world dominance after 1815 had been the product of a unique combination of favourable circumstances which were not going to last forever and when the challenge came, Britain's rivals were often better placed to compete with a nation so accustomed to pre-eminence that it failed to develop important new industries, neglected the modernisation of its established industrial base and preferred instead to rely on invisible overseas earnings. In retrospect, economic historians suggest that many of these late nineteenth-century concerns about the nation's industrial and economic decline were misplaced and that, on the whole, Britain's economic performance in the period 1870–1914 was fairly robust, but this was not how it appeared to contemporary policymakers (Floud 1980: 1–26).

In addition to this industrial and commercial challenge, Britain's imperial greatness posed problems of its own and these further intensified the existing sense of anxious vulnerability. The Empire was unquestionably a reflection of British greatness, but in a very tangible sense it was also the foundation for that power, and many agreed with Joseph Chamberlain that without its colonies Britain would soon slide to the rank of 'a fifth rate nation' (Green 1995: 35). Yet as Jan Smuts, a future South African premier, argued in 1899, in reality the Empire was a 'ramshackle structure' spanning the globe but 'largely inhabited by antagonistic peoples, without any adequate military organisation' and in which British dominance rested 'more upon prestige and moral intimidation than upon true military strength' (Howard 1974: 11). There was much truth in this allegation. As a conscious act of policy, during the post-1815 half century of *Pax Britannica* the armed services between them consumed only between 2 per cent and 3 per cent of GNP – or an annual cost to the nation of just £1 per head of population. In fairness, this was sufficient to maintain a Royal Navy which for 60 years after 1815 truly did rule the waves unchallenged and overwhelming. The fleet assembled at Spithead to celebrate the Diamond Jubilee in June 1897 consisted of over 165 British warships, including 21 first-class battleships and 54 cruisers. It was a formidable force, although its predominance had markedly declined since 1883 when it possessed more battleships than all the other great powers combined (Kennedy 1976: 209).

The navy's problems paled into insignificance, however, when compared with those of Britain's army. The Victorian ideal of the laissez faire 'night watchman state' and the discipline imposed by Gladstonian balanced-budget orthodoxy meant that unproductive military spending was low on the list of government priorities. The price to be paid for Gladstonian financial rectitude was that, in stark contrast to the vast conscript armies of its European neighbours, Britain possessed only a small professional volunteer army, largely employed in colonial policing. A dismal military performance in the Crimean War (1854–56) did briefly prompt demands for radical reform but, as Thomas Otte notes, 'in the end Britain lacked the political will to create a European-style standing army. Ambitions to be a European power thus ran counter to an unwillingness to meet the necessary financial costs' (Otte 2002b: 11). Indeed, between the Crimean and Boer (South African) wars, Britain's National Debt fell steadily along with the level of government expenditure – to the marked detriment of an army which by the turn of the century was smaller than that of Switzerland, prompting Bismarck's contemptuous quip that if it landed on the German coast he would call out the local police to arrest them (Kennedy 1976: 207)! Unfortunately, by this juncture there were now far more challengers to Britain's ascendancy than at any time in the preceding century given the emergence of a vigorous new German naval challenge, intensified French imperial rivalry and the omnipresent nightmare of the Russian threat to India and British interests in China, not to mention the newly emerging pretensions of the United States in the western hemisphere.

By 1900, this combination of economic, military and imperial challenges indicated that Britain was already chronically overextended in its commitments. As Joseph Chamberlain encapsulated the increasingly pervasive sense of late-Victorian nervousness in 1902, Britain appeared to be a 'weary Titan staggering under the too vast orb of its fate' (Amery 1951: 421). For a variety of compelling reasons, this lesson was forcefully driven home by the South African War of 1899–1902. First, when it became clear that the war would not be over in a matter of months, Britain was forced to fund the expedition by borrowing on the New York money markets for the first time since the Seven Years' War (1756–63); an expedient which set a disturbing precedent for Britain's far more costly endeavours during the First World War. Secondly, evidence from the recruitment stations at home revealed the appalling physical condition of a large proportion of the working class attempting to enlist to defend the British Empire. This alarming evidence of what was described at the time as 'progressive race deterioration' confirmed the findings of social investigators like Seebohm Rowntree and Charles Booth, the founder of the Salvation Army, who revealed the 'hidden continent' of poverty in 'Darkest England' during the last quarter of the nineteenth century. Such revelations challenged the complacent mid-Victorian assumption about the inherent superiority of the British race while underlining existing fears about the nation's ability to defend its far-flung Empire; a shock to the national consciousness which provoked an obsession with eugenics, 'national efficiency' and social reform during the years leading up to the First World War (Harris 1993: 237–41). Finally, the humiliating defeats of 'Black Week' in December 1899, at the hands of an irregular army of mounted Boer farmers, dealt a severe blow to British confidence in its own military prowess.

The South African war also, alarmingly, highlighted Britain's complete diplomatic isolation from potential allies on the mainland of Europe. Throughout the nineteenth century, the principal foreign policy objective had been to support a harmonious and stable balance of power between the main powers in Europe to ensure that none of them could directly threaten national security. As British Prime Minister and Foreign Secretary, Lord Salisbury dominated British external policy for much of the two closing decades of the nineteenth century. For this pessimistic patrician, peace represented the principal objective for Britain as a satiated imperial power and he believed this could best be achieved through a policy of 'Splendid Isolation', by which Britain maintained a 'free hand' to act in its own interests unencumbered by binding alliances. At the Albert Hall in May 1898, Salisbury had declared confidently: 'We know that we shall maintain against all comers that which we possess, and we know, in spite of the jargon about isolation, that we are amply competent to do so' (Charmley 2007: 132–3). Throughout, however, he was haunted by the conviction that 'whatever happens in the world will be for the worst and therefore it is in our interests that as little should happen as possible' (Otte 2002c: 119). It was a view that would be echoed repeatedly by British foreign policymakers over the next half century.

By revealing the bankruptcy of both the Empire's military and diplomatic arrangements, the South African War compelled British policymakers to recognize the unpalatable truth that only two possible options existed if they were to bridge the vast gulf between Britain's commitments and the resources it possessed to defend them. One possibility was to increase the Empire's military resources, but this was implicitly excluded from the outset on the grounds that it would require higher taxation, compulsory military conscription and the active military participation of the white Dominions in Imperial defence – and none of these crucial requirements was deemed politically practicable. Indeed, although the idea of an 'Imperial Federation' which fused the white Dominions and the 'Mother Country' into a 'Greater Britain' had powerful advocates like Joseph Chamberlain and Lord Milner, after the 1887 Imperial conference the whole concept aroused widespread opposition within the Dominions while the necessary abandonment of free trade to create imperial preferences within an imperial Customs Union encountered equally powerful resistance at home.

If it was impossible to increase the Empire's military resources, the only other option was to limit its imperial liabilities by reducing the number of potential challengers. In order to defend the Empire on the cheap, this policy of 'limited liability' demanded the negotiation of mutually acceptable compromises with the Empire's most threatening potential enemies. In the space of only six years between 1901 and 1907, Britain thus abandoned its 'Splendid Isolation' and forged a series of regional alliances with those rival powers which threatened it most directly. In 1901, under the second Hay-Pauncefote Treaty Britain effectively ceded the western hemisphere to the United States; in 1902, the Anglo-Japanese alliance was designed to secure its Far Eastern interests and colonies by effectively transferring this responsibility to the Japanese navy. More important, after two decades of bitter colonial rivalry, the Anglo-French *Entente Cordiale* came into existence in 1904 and gradually developed into something approaching a military alliance as the price of mutual security against Germany. Finally, in 1907 the Anglo-Russian Convention completed this circle of understandings by removing the looming threat to imperial security along the North-West Frontier of India, Afghanistan, Tibet and Persia; a challenge taken far more seriously in the early years of the twentieth century than even that posed by Germany and which tied up 75,000 British and almost double that number of Indian troops (Nielsen 1995). Ultimately, these diplomatic arrangements resulted in the 'encirclement' of Germany. They also led Britain directly into a 'Continental Commitment' which culminated in the bloodbath of the First World War – but this was the unavoidable price to be paid by an economically faltering state seeking to defend a vast Empire on the cheap.

The First World War and its legacy

Although Britain emerged triumphant from the First World War, victory had been purchased at a ruinous price for its economy and international position. The financial burden alone had been crippling. In the last year of peace, there was a budget surplus of £4.8 million. By 1918 this healthy surplus had been turned into a deficit of £1988.8 million. In the crisis year of 1917 the war was costing the Exchequer some £7 million a day. Britain's total war expenditure amounted to £2579 million. Government expenditure, which had been only one-eighth of the national income (£302 million) in 1913, absorbed more than half of it in the last three years of the war, peaking at 59.3 per cent in 1918. To cover this rapidly escalating cost, domestic taxation spiralled upwards but this still covered only 28 per cent of expenditure, leaving a total deficit of £6942 million. To make up the difference, the Treasury was forced to sell large quantities of overseas assets and investments; a desperate measure which later weakened the interwar balance of payments by removing the dividends on which it had previously relied so heavily.

When all other sources had been exhausted, the cost of the war was covered by heavy borrowing to enable Britain to meet its own war needs and to fulfil its role as the paymaster of the entire Entente. By the end of the war, Britain's overseas debt stood at £1241 million, of which £840 million was owed to the US government. Worse still, while Britain struggled to pay its war debt to the United States until 1934, its Allies repaid singularly little of the £1534 million that Britain had advanced to them during the war (Self 2006b). As a direct result, the United States displaced Britain as the world's greatest financial power while the latter was left with a fourteen-fold increase in its National Debt which by 1919 had risen from £19.9 million to £270 million, the annual interest payments on which absorbed some 40 per cent of total central government expenditure until 1931 after which it slowly declined, although even in 1939 it still accounted for over a quarter of gross public expenditure. War took an equally grim toll on British export trade, as many lucrative markets in Latin America and the Far East were lost permanently to neutral American and Japanese competitors (only adding to the now chronic weakness of its balance of payments), while the necessary dislocation of war severely damaged Britain's industrial capacity and still further impaired its already waning competitiveness.

Table 2.2   The budgetary burden of the First World War (in £ millions)

	Expenditure	Revenue	Surplus/Deficit
1913/14	197.5	198.2	+750.0
1914/15	560.5	226.7	-333.7
1915/16	1559.1	336.8	-1222.4
1916/17	2198.1	573.4	-1624.7
1917/18	2696.2	707.2	-1989.0
1918/19	2579.3	889.0	-1690.3
1919/20	1665.7	1339.6	-326.2
1920/21	1195.4	1425.9	+230.6
1921/22	1079.2	1124.8	+45.7
1922/23	812.5	914.0	+101.5
1923/24	788.8	837.2	+48.3
1924/25	795.7	799.4	+3.7

Source: adapted from Thorpe (1994: 106–7).

In retrospect, the scale and long-term implications of these irreversible economic problems are all too painfully obvious. Yet the fact remains that Britain emerged from the Great War in an ostensibly stronger position than when it had entered it. Certainly Prime Minister Lloyd George thought so when he boasted to a friend in March 1919: 'We have got most of the things we set out to get' (Riddell 1933: 42). He was largely correct in this assessment. Britain's already vast Empire increased significantly in size while it commanded an unprecedented level of military resources. Furthermore, the appearance of power was substantially enhanced by the comparative weakness of its traditional rivals at a time when Germany was defeated, disarmed and economically devastated; Russia was in the throes of revolution and bloody civil war and France was still reeling from the destabilising effects of war. Similarly, although both the US and Japan had grown substantially stronger (to a considerable degree directly at British expense) they did not represent an immediate challenge to its position on the world stage. After the First World War, even more than before it, therefore, Britain was a satiated power which had nothing to gain and everything to lose by further conflict. As a Foreign Office memorandum encapsulated the position in April 1926:

> We . . . have no territorial ambitions nor desire for aggrandisement. We have got all that we want – perhaps more. Our sole object is to keep what we have and live in peace. . . . [S]o manifold and ubiquitous is British trade and finance that, whatever else may be the outcome of a disturbance of the peace, we shall be the losers. (Kennedy 1981: 256)

Such sentiments were the direct lineal descendants of those of Lord Salisbury a quarter of a century earlier – and with good reason because they reflected the same complex reality of superficial power and underlying vulnerability. As the peaceful era ushered in by the Treaty of Locarno (1925) gave way to economic depression and the far more threatening atmosphere of the early 1930s, these prognostications about the dangers of another war became increasingly more alarming.

Foreign and defence policy challenges of the 1930s

During the interwar period, the problems afflicting foreign and defence policy were fundamentally the same as they had been at the turn of the century. The key difference was that they were now infinitely greater in scale because of the conjunction of two crucial developments. First, while most of the industrial world enjoyed a period of rising prosperity during the late 1920s, the British economy remained becalmed in the economic 'doldrums'; a stagnant period of unhealthy quasi-equilibrium characterised most poignantly by the existence of the 'intractable million' – that 10 per cent of the insured workforce permanently surplus to requirements even before Britain crashed into the mass unemployment of the Great Depression of the 1930s. As a result, Britain's relative share of world manufacturing output, which stood at 22.9 per cent in 1880, had fallen to a meagre 9.9 per cent by 1928, while its share of world manufacturing exports fell from 30.4 per cent to 22.4 per cent in the same period (see Table 2.1; and Alford 1996: 118–19). The reality of this economic decline permeated every aspect of British external policy in the interwar period.

The second factor compounding Britain's problems was that, as a direct result of the Treaty of Versailles, an already gigantic Empire was extended by a further 25 per cent through the acquisition of the former German colonies of Tanganyika, South-West Africa, Togoland and the Cameroons, while the collapse of the Ottoman Empire enabled Britain to obtain the mandate over Palestine, Transjordan, Iraq and the sheikdoms in the Persian Gulf. If Britain had been pursuing an 'overextended' foreign policy before the Great War, after 1919 the problem had been magnified to almost insoluble levels (see Map 2.1). As the Prime Minister presiding over an Empire, which by the 1930s encompassed 11.4 million square miles and 525 million people, Neville Chamberlain encapsulated the problem succinctly in January 1938: 'We are a very rich and very vulnerable Empire, and there are plenty of poor adventurers not very far away who look on us with hungry eyes' (Feiling 1946: 323).

British perceptions of the possible policy options after the rise of Hitler in January 1933 were conditioned by two crucial concerns. First, policymakers were rightly obsessed by the nightmare scenario of a war on three fronts against Japan in the Far East, Italy in the Mediterranean and North Africa and Germany in continental Europe; a fear greatly exacerbated by the general belief that war with any one of them would force the diversion of military resources away from other theatres of action and thus encourage the opportunistic aggression of one or both of the other revisionist powers. In this sense, therefore, while these were three quite separate challengers in different parts of the globe, the threat they posed to the British Empire was most definitely cumulative in effect.

The second novel aspect of the challenge to national security related to the development of military air power. For 900 years, Britain had enjoyed an almost total sense of security on the basis of a 22-mile

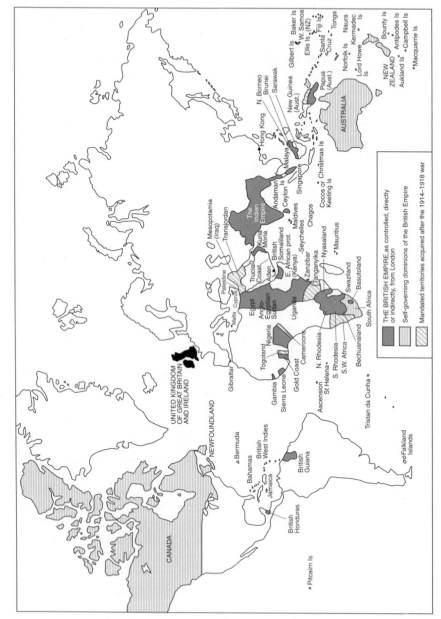

Map 2.1   The British Empire in 1919

stretch of sea cutting the island off from the mainland of Europe and dominated by the overwhelming superiority of the Royal Navy. Yet even during the First World War, German Gotha bombers had brought the war directly to the British mainland with their occasional morale-shattering aerial bombardments during 1917–18. The implications of this development were painfully obvious to all. As Stanley Baldwin memorably declared in 1934, 'the old frontiers have gone. When you think of the defence of England you no longer think of the chalk cliffs of Dover; you think of the Rhine'. Ultimately, what made the advent of air warfare all the more terrifying was the confident belief that (as Baldwin once again put it in 1933), 'the bomber will always get through'. Not only would enemy aircraft rain down unimaginable death and destruction on helpless civilian populations from the sky, but also British policymakers had to reconcile themselves to the chilling conventional wisdom that there was absolutely nothing they could do to prevent it. Certainly this appeared to be the lesson to be learned from the experience of cities like Guernica during the Spanish Civil War (Self 2006a: 237). When seen from this perspective, Harold Macmillan was not exaggerating when he later recalled that 'we thought of the air warfare in 1938 rather as people think of nuclear warfare today' – a threat that was both unstoppable and totally devastating in its effects (Macmillan 1966: 575). To understand the horrifying magnitude of this perceived threat, it should be remembered that British defence planners estimated in 1937 (on the basis of First World War experience) that the expected first devastating 'knockout blow' from the air would leave 20,000 casualties in London in the first 24 hours alone and that the first bombing campaign would end with 600,000 Britons dead and another 1.2 million injured (Self 2006a: 269).

These fears and apprehensions were compounded by the realisation that any effective response to these threats was subject to a variety of fundamental constraints. The budgetary priority on debt reduction, combined with the chronic underperformance of the British economy after 1920, severely limited the amount that could be spent on the defence of Britain and its global Empire. The most notorious illustration of these economic constraints upon defensive capability was the introduction of the 'Ten Year Rule' in 1919. This injunction compelled the armed services to plan on the rolling assumption that Britain would not be engaged in a major war for ten years. On the basis of this convenient proposition, defence expenditure fell dramatically from £766 million in 1919/20 to £299 million in 1921/22, before progressively descending to its lowest point of £103 million in 1932/33. Confronted by the three-pronged threat from Hitler, Mussolini and Japan in widely separated theatres of action, only the existence of overwhelming mili-

Table 2.3　UK public and defence expenditure, 1932–40 (£m)

	Total UK revenue	Total UK expenditure	UK Defence spending	UK Defence expenditure (% GNP)	German defence expenditure (% GNP)
1932	745	777	103.3	3	1
1933	724	693	107.6	3	3
1934	709	701	113.9	3	6
1935	749	746	137.0	3	8
1936	797	803	185.9	4	13
1937	873	844	256.3	6	13
1938	927	940	397.4	7	17
1939	1049	1817	719.0	18	23
1940	1495	3971	2600.0	46	38

Sources: Thorpe (1994: 107); Overy (1999: 368); Peden (1979: 8).

tary and financial strength could have provided any semblance of true imperial security – and by the late 1930s these prerequisites simply did not exist. Worse still, 15 years of chronic neglect of the armed forces had been accompanied by a concomitant deterioration in the industrial infrastructure necessary for rearmament.

In these circumstances, British policymakers were obliged to accept that skilful diplomacy in support of a policy of 'appeasement' designed to redress the legitimate grievances of Germany and the revisionist powers was essential. As Chamberlain argued repeatedly, this was not 'a peace at any price' policy, but 'in the absence of any powerful ally, and until our armaments are completed, we must adjust our foreign policy to our circumstances, and even bear with patience and good humour actions which we should like to treat in a very different fashion'. If diplomacy was successful, the threat of war would be averted; if it failed, it would have still bought the time needed to complete the necessary programme of rearmament. As Chamberlain told his Foreign Secretary in the immediate aftermath of the Munich conference in September 1938, their strategy should be to hope for the best while preparing for the worst (Self 2006a: 267, 271).

Against this background, it is reasonable to argue that 'Appeasement' was not a new policy dreamt up by weak men in the 1930s to excuse their craven timidity in not 'standing up' to Hitler. On the contrary, its roots can be traced back to the mid-nineteenth century as a direct response to the same problems of global overstretch which Neville Chamberlain inherited just as the entire train of thought hit the buffers of Hitler's maniacal desire for world domination in 1939. In the event, Chamberlain failed because the endemic disharmony in British total strategy between foreign policy ambitions and military strength made success a virtual impossibility, but, as Paul Kennedy argues, in the circumstances appeasement was 'the natural policy for a small island state gradually losing its place in world affairs, shouldering the military and economic burdens which are increasingly too great for it' (Kennedy 1981: 301). Any doubts about the truth of this proposition were unequivocally dispelled by the negative long-term impact of the Second World War upon Britain's place in the world.

The Second World War and the consequences of relative economic decline

Although few realised the full extent of the tragedy at the time, Britain had emerged victorious from the Second World War only by accepting the financial, industrial and commercial devastation of its economy. Victory left the nation insolvent for the first time in its history. In total, the war cost Britain a quarter of its national wealth, some £7300 million. Between 1938/39 and 1944/45, defence spending totalled £23,101 million and much of this had been financed by borrowing. The total National Debt trebled from £7130 million in 1939 to £21,366 million by 1945, creating a substantial burden of internal indebtedness to be paid by future taxpayers. The country's gold and currency reserves of £548 million at the beginning of the war were virtually exhausted by the end of 1940. In addition, £1118 million worth of British overseas investments (a quarter of its pre-war total) had been mortgaged or sold as payment for foreign imports and military supplies and this in turn reduced income from interest and dividends by over 70 per cent, from £168 million in 1938 to around £50 million by 1946. A further £500 million of foreign assets was lost through default, confiscation or physical deterioration. Britain also emerged from the war with enormous overseas indebtedness, as its net external liability increased from £476 million in August 1939 to a staggering total of £3355 million – some 81 per cent of which was owed to the Overseas Sterling Area, to be repaid out of unrequited exports after the war, despite the fact that crucial export markets had been sacrificed in the interests of victory.

Beyond the appalling financial state of post-war Britain, the position of the real economy offered no greater cause for optimism. By 1945, exports

Table 2.4   Public revenue, expenditure and debt, 1939-45 (in £millions)

	Expenditure	Revenue	National Debt	National Income
1913/14	197.5	198.2	711.3	2322
1938/39	1018.9	1006.2	7247	4671
1939/40	1408.2	1132.2	8014	5075
1940/41	3970.7	1495.3	10,480	6066
1941/42	4876.3	2174.6	13,153	6978
1942/43	5739.9	2922.4	15,933	7652
1943/44	5909.3	3149.2	18,671	8115
1944/45	6179.5	3354.7	21,473	8310
1945/46	5601.1	3401.2	23,741	8355

Sources: Thorpe (1994: 107); Central Statistical Office, *Annual Abstract of Statistics, 1938–1948* (1949); Hancock and Gowing (1949: 71, 256).

stood at 30 per cent of their 1939 total and import prices had risen 50 per cent. In addition, 18 million gross tonnes of shipping, a quarter of Britain's massive pre-war merchant marine fleet (which contributed an eighth of pre-war import earnings) had been destroyed by enemy action, while the entire economy had been subject to wholesale distortion to maximise the war effort at the expense of capital investment and the needs of civilian and export production. Beyond all of this, the Attlee government faced the problem of demobilising nine million personnel and the reconstruction of the nation's damaged and neglected infrastructure. Of its 4.5 million houses, 210,000 had been totally destroyed and another 250,000 were rendered uninhabitable by bombing, inflicting a total of £1450 million worth of damage to domestic and industrial property at 1945 replacement costs. Beyond this destruction, the deferment of all but the most essential repair and maintenance in industry, transport and housing created a cumulative total cost of industrial disinvestment of another £885 million (Dewey 1997: ch.16).

Against this background, Lord Keynes, the government's chief economic adviser, was scarcely exaggerating when he warned the incoming Labour government in August 1945 that it faced a 'financial Dunkirk' – particularly as total foreign earnings covered only 40 per cent of its expenditure overseas, forcing it to fill the gap with still more borrowing from abroad (Cairncross 1992: 45–52). Without a combination of severe retrenchment, a massive increase in exports and substantial aid from the United States, Keynes warned that Britain faced the grim prospect of severe austerity at home, while abroad it would mean a 'sudden and humiliating withdrawal from our onerous responsibilities with great loss of prestige and the acceptance for the time being of the position as second-class power' (Barnett 1995: 42). It is no surprise that Ernest Bevin entered the Foreign Office in July 1945 declaring jocularly that what he needed most was 30 million more tonnes of coal to export (Northedge 1974: 22). Although few realised it at the time, the devastating impact of the war upon Britain's financial and economic strength would both directly and indirectly influence almost every act of British diplomacy in the world thereafter.

Despite the parlous state of British economy, policymakers were remarkably slow to acknowledge economic decline and even slower to admit it to an electorate fed on a high-fibre diet of British imperial glory and military greatness. Yet in the immediate post-war years this was less extraordinary than it appears with the wisdom of hindsight. As John Kent rightly argues, far from closing their eyes to the problem, 'policymakers were fully aware of the decline in British power produced by the war, but they believed such decline could be reversed' (Kent 1993: x, 214). If there was a problem, it was not the reluctance to confront unpalatable truths but rather an optimistic refusal to accept that these difficulties were anything other than temporary phenomena soon to be resolved as the country resumed its rightful place in the new global order. The fundamental challenge, therefore, was simply to find the most effective means of achieving the transition back to some state of peacetime 'normality'. On this question, policymakers were relatively sanguine – and not without reason at a superficial level. By 1950, Britain's share of world manufactured exports had actually risen from 21.3 per cent in 1937 to 25.5 per cent – a figure equivalent to more than two-and-a-half times that of France and three times that of Germany, while much of the war economy had been translated back to a peace footing without incurring the problems of either mass unemployment or galloping inflation.

Basking in this fragile post-war confidence, external policy reflected a high level of continuity with the past. Above all, there was the reaffirmation of confidence in Britain's self-image of a 'great power'. In large part, this faith stemmed from its status as the only victorious combatant to have fought continuously from 1939 until 1945. More to the point, it rejoiced at having bravely fought on alone and against the odds between June 1940 and July 1941 to uphold the torch of democracy and liberty against Nazi oppression. As such, victory in 1945 was perceived to be a very British victory. In recognition of this fact, its leaders were represented among the 'Big Three' peacemakers at Yalta and Potsdam, playing their rightful part in determining the shape of the peace. Beyond all of this, Britain remained a major participant in world events on every continent, it possessed an impressively extensive network of strategic bases, its military and naval strength was vital throughout much of the world and it sat at the apex of a vast global empire. London was also home to one of the world's reserve currencies, a major financial centre and the hub of the Overseas Sterling Area.

Against this background, as Prime Minister between 1945 and 1951, Clement Attlee encapsulated the prevailing view when he declared with characteristically bland confidence that 'Britain was facing a difficult position as a great power which had temporarily been gravely weakened' (Roberts 1984: 22). Basking in this all-pervading 'illusion of victory', as Jean Monnet described it, it was inevitable that policymakers banished any thought of a permanent retreat from power and dreamed instead of reasserting Britain's former position in the world while traditional rivals like France, Germany and Japan had been shattered by defeat and occupation. Attlee was thus scarcely exaggerating in July 1950 when he told Sir Oliver Franks, the British ambassador in Washington, that Britain was not just 'one of the queue of European countries' but rather it was 'one of two world powers outside Russia' (Morgan 1984: 233). This mood of post-war confidence was reinforced by the enduring potency of Winston Churchill's vision of Britain's position at the intersection of the three 'interlocking circles' consisting of Europe, the Empire and the Atlantic alliance (see Chapter 1). Until overwhelmed by chronic economic crisis in the mid-1960s, this encouraging doctrine dominated strategic thinking to the extent that it was taken as axiomatic that Britain's great power status and global interests demanded it should maintain the necessary diplomatic, military and economic trappings commensurate with its self-image.

In the longer term, a far harsher reality intruded into these dreams of continued greatness. At one level, such fantasies were undermined by the geopolitical changes wrought by the Second World War. Superpower dominance within a new bipolar world order, the threat from nationalist independence movements in the Developing World, the powerful momentum carrying the rest of Europe inexorably towards supranational integration and the prohibitive cost of modern weapons systems made it progressively more difficult to maintain the facade. Moreover, by the mid-1960s British policymakers finally recognized that participation in each of Churchill's three circles did not increase Britain's strength and prestige. On the contrary, this vision was severely overstretching the nation's limited resources and, far from strength in one circle leading to greater power in the other two, the reality was that Britain's weakness in one contributed to its weakness in all three. Perversely, the very attempt to keep all its options open for as long as possible meant that Britain's foreign policy choices were actually circumscribed and curtailed.

Strategic realities of this sort were belatedly reinforced by the grudging recognition of Britain's spectacular post-war economic decline. As Sidney Pollard points out, there is no record in history of a great power falling behind at such startling speed as that of Britain after 1945 (Pollard 1984: 6). In terms of GDP per capita, Britain slipped down the world league table from seventh highest in 1950 to eighteenth place by 1970. By 1981 it occupied a miserable twenty-first position before recovering to fourteenth place again in 2007. Similarly, in 1950, Britain still produced 25.4 per cent of world manufactured output but this had fallen to 14.2 per cent by 1964. Twenty years later the figure stood at a derisory 7.6 per cent, although in 2007 it was still the world's seventh largest manufacturing producer (Jenkins 1987: 32). By making it progressively more difficult to sustain the validity of Churchill's 'three circles' vision, the scale and speed of Britain's post-war decline forced policymakers belatedly to recognize the urgent need to bring ambitions and commitments into closer alignment with the nation's reduced circumstances. In 1945, however, none of this was apparent as Ernest Bevin laid the foundations for a bipartisan foreign and defence policy which has persisted, in very different circumstances, through to the present day.

Continuity and consensus in post-war foreign and defence policy

In assessing the direction, content and tone of British external policy, it is important to recognize that 'consensus' is not synonymous with continuity. Almost by definition, external relations and national defence are spheres in which there is a natural tendency towards a high level of policy continuity. First, foreign policy is invariably defined by long-term national interests rather than the changing needs of party ideology or short-term electoral expediency. In this context, British Foreign Secretaries are prone to quote Lord Palmerston's classic declaration in the House of Commons in March 1848: 'It is a narrow policy to suppose that this country or that is to be marked out as the eternal ally or the perpetual enemy. Our interests are eternal and perpetual, and those interests it is our duty to follow' (Joll 1967: 56). When viewed from this perspective, continuity is an inevitable consequence of the fact that since the mid-nineteenth century Britain had been a satiated status quo power which needed to be left in peace to manage the imperial estates and commercial interests it already possessed. In later years, this preference for the status quo was reinforced by the fact that it had no incentive to change an existing international order from which it derived considerable benefits – such as a seat on the United Nations Security Council, the leading European role in the NATO alliance and the possession of the most up-to-date nuclear weapons.

A second factor conducive to continuity in external policy is that it is generally formulated over long periods and its direction can be extremely difficult to change in response to short-term stimuli. Many foreign policy priorities and relationships are enshrined in treaties and international accords which are not subject to easy or rapid modification. For example, Britain's membership of the EU, United Nations and World Trade Organisation represent significant constraints upon its freedom of manoeuvre – and these are but a few of the vast number of such agreements which limit the government's ability to act autonomously on the international stage. This problem of long time horizons is even more pronounced in relation to defence, where the modern 6–10-year planning cycle for the MoD means that incoming governments inherit the procurement decisions of their predecessors, leaving little scope for radical restructuring. When the Thatcher government entered office in 1979, almost 90 per cent of its defence procurement budget was already committed and, even in 1984, past decisions still accounted for almost 80 per cent of its spending on defence equipment (Freedman 1986). Similarly, in conjunction with the programme to upgrade Trident, the Brown government's decision in 2008 to build two new giant aircraft carriers equipped with advanced (and very expensive) American F35 multiple-role aircraft means that these two commitments will effectively dominate the defence budget for at least two decades and it will be extremely difficult for future governments to change without incurring massive cancellation costs (Rogers 2006: 652).

A third factor which makes foreign and defence policy inherently resistant to rapid change is the power of history and nostalgia. Britain's persistent pursuit of the great power illusion, long after the material base for such perceptions had been eroded, can partially be explained by the nature of the 'official mind' and the assumptions inherited from previous generations. As Sir Oliver Franks explained in 1954, the assumption that Britain should be a great power was 'part of the habit and furniture of our minds' (Darby 1973: 22). The difficulty British foreign policymakers experience in escaping from the intellectual and emotional traditions of the time in which they lived is exemplified by the continuing addiction to the concept of an Anglo-American 'special relationship', the need to maintain an 'independent' nuclear deterrent in increasingly adverse economic and technological circumstances, the commitment to a military presence 'East of Suez' long after Indian independence had undermined much of the supposed rationale, and the efforts of various Prime Ministers from Churchill to Thatcher to act as an 'honest broker' mediating between the superpowers to negotiate an end to the Cold War. The legacy of the past is equally evident in Britain's persistent resistance to the idea of supranational power within the European Community. The existence of these inherited perceptions, prejudices, values, instincts and unspoken assumptions in the collective thought world of policymakers ensures that adjustment and change only come about after a long period of gradual transition rather than as a knee-jerk response to external stimuli.

The power of history as a force militating against rapid policy change, is strengthened still further when pragmatism and gradualism are part of a nation's political culture. These would appear to be defining characteristics of British foreign policy with an accompanying commitment to empiricism and scepticism about abstract principles. Reflecting on his period as Foreign Secretary between 1905 and 1916, in true Palmerstonian language Sir Edward Grey dismissed all talk of 'far-sighted views or large conceptions or grand schemes' guiding the policy of hard-pressed ministers:

> If all secrets were known it would probably be found that British Foreign Ministers have been guided by what seemed to them to be the immediate interest of this country without making elaborate calculations for the future. Their best qualities have been negative rather than positive. They would not execute sharp turns or quick changes of front; they were not disposed to make mischief or stir up strife among other nations, or to fish in troubled waters; for their instinct was that peace and stability in Europe were the conditions best suited to British trade; and they have generally shrunk from committing themselves for future contingencies, from creating expectations that they might not be able to fulfil, and from saying at any time more than they really meant. On the whole, the British Empire has been well served by these methods. (Grey 1925, I: 6)

Over half a century later, Lord Carrington recorded similar sentiments about his experiences at the FCO between 1979 and 1982. 'I am a pragmatist. I have found all my life that the gulf between what is theoretically desirable and what is practically attainable is so wide that it is sensible to concentrate almost exclusively upon the latter' (Carrington 1988: 373). In similar vein, Sir Nicholas Henderson, a senior long-serving diplomat, encapsulated a fundamental truth when he noted that talk of grand designs in diplomacy was 'the sort of idea that was apt to make the British wince' (Henderson 1987: 78). This pragmatism is not necessarily a problem and some even regard it as a virtue. As one Deputy Undersecretary at the FCO told Michael Clarke, 'Our skill is in *not* having a grand strategic concept' (Clarke 1992: 110). This may well be true, but as Sir Edward Grey conceded, reliance on pragmatism and incremental change does tend to encourage the avoidance of major choices and reinforces the desire to stick with well-established patterns of thought.

Notwithstanding the existence of various factors conducive to continuity, it is often argued that a substantive and purposive foreign policy consensus emerged in Britain after 1945 to parallel the so-called 'post-war settlement' on the fundamentals of domestic policy. As with the domestic settlement, the term 'consensus' does not imply that everybody agreed about all aspects of foreign and defence policy all of the time. On the contrary, as Kavanagh and Morris argue, the term is best understood as 'a set of parameters which bounded a set of policy options regarded by senior politicians and civil servants as administratively practicable, economically affordable and politically acceptable'. This is not to deny the continued existence of highly vociferous wings in both major parties which dissented from the ruling orthodoxy. Labour's 'Keep Left' group in the late 1940s, the Bevanites in the 1950s and their left-wing successors in the 1970s and 1980s were profoundly hostile to the United States, NATO, the EEC and Britain's commitment to nuclear weapons. Similarly, many Conservatives on the imperialist right never resigned themselves to the retreat from Empire and others have proved still more fiercely resistant to the idea of a supranational European future. But notwithstanding this dissent, foreign policy disagreements generally occurred within parties rather than between the respective leaderships. Consensus does not suggest either that there were not major differences in the rhetoric employed by party leaders when addressing the faithful during annual party conferences and elections. But, irrespective of the conflicting language, nuance and emphasis, the fact remains that at a front-bench level these differences were often important but not fundamental. More important, *when in office* the continuity of policy invariably stands out far more clearly than the differences (Kavanagh and Morris 1994).

Ernest Bevin and the foundations of the post-war foreign policy consensus

Supporters of the idea of a purposive bipartisan consensus on external policy are also generally agreed that it was firmly established by Ernest

Bevin as Foreign Secretary in the Labour government of 1945–51 on foundations already partially constructed by Anthony Eden, his wartime predecessor (Ovendale 1984: 2; Roberts 1984: 23). Despite Attlee's claim in 1937 that a 'socialist foreign policy' would be wholly different from that of the Conservatives, the transition from Churchill's wartime coalition to a peacetime Labour government in July 1945 was achieved without any significant impact upon the main lines of foreign policy because of the pre-existing cross-party consensus. This agreement was assisted by the warm mutual regard between Bevin and Churchill and his even closer understanding with Eden, with whom Bevin continued to consult after coming to office. As Eden later recalled in his memoirs, 'Bevin and I had been good colleagues during years together in the War Cabinet . . . At that time I was closer to him than to any other member of his party, and the friendship between us lasted until his death' (Eden 1960: 5). Such was the degree of continuity that one Labour MP remarked jocularly after Bevin's first foreign affairs debate, 'How fat Anthony Eden has grown' (Pelling 1984: 121). Little wonder that when the Conservatives returned to power in 1951, Churchill paid tribute to the outgoing Labour government for 'several most important decisions about our foreign policy which . . . form the foundation on which we stand today'. In similar vein, Eden told the Conservative party conference in 1954 that 'I always believed that the more bipartisan foreign policy can be, the stronger the authority of the Foreign Secretary of the day' (Seldon 1981: 15, 414).

Bevin ostensibly appears an unlikely choice for the Foreign Office in July 1945, but he was extraordinarily well qualified for the task. First, having been the most influential trade unionist of his generation, Bevin was such an extremely skilled negotiator that one of his senior officials later recalled: 'No Foreign Secretary ever entered the Foreign Office with greater skills in this field, with greater experience of negotiation from weakness as well as from strength.' Secondly, although Minister of Labour during the War, he was one of the few Cabinet ministers to receive all the key foreign and diplomatic papers. He thus entered office well informed about his new portfolio. Third, while a passionate anti-communist in his trade union role, his attitude towards the Soviet Union was initially 'wary and suspicious but not automatically hostile', but his first words when arriving at the Potsdam conference as Foreign Secretary were that he was 'not going to have Britain barged about'. This pugnacious nationalism remained a central theme of his policy throughout (Morgan 1984: 235; Pearce 1997: 1961). Above all, Bevin's greatest strength was his willingness to accept advice while remaining 'very much his own man' (Roberts 1984: 23–25). His natural style was to lead from the front and in so doing he proved to be 'a dominant, transcendent, creative force', and his principal biographer portrays him as the personal originator of foreign policy in the style of Canning, Palmerston, and Salisbury (Morgan 1984: 235–6; Bullock 1983: 17–18).

Bevin's record as Foreign Secretary has been criticised from both ends of the political spectrum. From the left, the 'Keep Left' group and other advocates of a 'socialist foreign policy' in the late 1940s condemned his slavish subservience to the United States, hostility towards the Soviet Union and conservatism about decolonisation. Critics from the right, like Correlli Barnett, consider him 'an altogether disastrous Foreign Secretary' in that his pursuit of the fatal delusion of Britain's continued world role prevented the necessary economic reconstruction and modernisation upon which future prosperity depended. Yet what these criticisms cannot obscure is the general agreement among his fellow politicians, Foreign Office officials and later scholars that 'history will very probably rate him as one of the greatest Foreign Secretaries this country ever had and the best she could possibly have had at this particular juncture' (Roberts 1984: 21). As Paul Kennedy argues, Ernest Bevin ranks 'among the most successful in the history of British external policy' – not least because his strategy judiciously accorded with the reality of rising challenges and reduced resources (Kennedy 1981: 362). Bevin had ample justification for lamenting that 'all the world is in trouble [and] I have to deal with all these troubles at once', but as Northedge notes, in his defence of British interests 'there were a few tricks which the Foreign Secretary missed during these years' (Northedge 1974: 53).

This post-war consensus on external policy was constructed around four central pillars. The first, and perhaps most important, component was a dominant Atlanticism founded upon the supposed 'special relationship' with the United States initially forged between Churchill and Roosevelt during the Second World War. Although Anglo-American relations cooled markedly in the immediate aftermath of the war, Bevin played a crucial role in forcing the United States to accept a pivotal role in the defence of Western Europe and the 'containment' of Soviet expansionism throughout the world. This strategy culminated in the North Atlantic Treaty in April 1949 and the creation of NATO – the first peacetime defensive treaty in American history. As Chapter 4 demonstrates, despite its vicissitudes and fluctuating fortunes, this Atlantic alliance has remained the cornerstone of British foreign and defence policy for governments of both parties ever since.

A second and related core element in this external policy consensus is the commitment to an independent nuclear deterrent. Here again, Bevin played a crucial role in the Labour Cabinet's acceptance of the need to build an independent nuclear weapon to maintain Britain's rightful place at the 'top table' of world diplomacy, and as an insurance against US unreliability in the event of localised Soviet aggression in Europe. Such was the degree of consensual bipartisanship that in the immediate aftermath of Britain's first atomic bomb test in October 1952, Churchill paid handsome tribute to the Attlee government for initiating the project. Moreover, as Chapter 7 explains, notwithstanding Labour's flirtation with unilateral nuclear disarmament when in opposition during the late 1950s and the early 1980s, the leadership of both parties have remained deeply committed to this option ever since. Even in a post-Cold War environment, Blair's New Labour government had little hesitation when agreeing in December 2006 to upgrade its Trident deterrent in order to maintain British security against any future unspecified potential enemy (Cm. 6994 2006: 5). The relative importance attached to conventional forces also has remained unquestioned throughout this period, and successive governments have been equally united in attempting to evade the question of how to sustain this level of defence capability without bearing the heavy financial burden it entails.

The remaining two elements of the post-war foreign policy consensus are also directly interconnected – but in a largely inverse relationship. It is sometimes argued that on the questions of colonial policy and Britain's retreat from Empire the 'post-war bipartisanship was perhaps at its strongest' (Kavanagh and Morris 1994: 97). Labour's Creech Jones followed in the progressive footsteps of the Conservative Oliver Stanley at the Colonial Office in 1945 and they agreed there was 'a great deal of common ground' between them. As Stanley told the Conservative party conference in 1947, 'I have done everything to keep the Empire out of party politics. There is no hope of a consistent imperial policy if that policy is put upon a partisan basis' (Pelling 1984: 155). Even in a self-proclaimed 'revisionist' volume explicitly designed to refute the idea of a 'post-war consensus', Nicholas Owen concedes that among the policymaking elite 'there was broad agreement on the essentials of colonial policy' even if this vision was the product less of willing bipartisan convergence than a response to the harsh economic and international constraints which confronted all British policymakers in the post-war period (Owen 1991: 160, 176; Seldon 1981: 377).

The final element of the post-war foreign policy consensus concerns Britain's troubled and ambivalent association with the continent of Europe. As in the other areas discussed above, Bevin led the way with his vigorous opposition to the cause of European integration along supranational or federalist lines while simultaneously promoting inter-governmental cooperation through his pivotal role in the creation of the Western European Union, NATO and the Organisation for European Economic Co-operation (OEEC). As Chapter 5 demonstrates, this policy preference has persisted as a central theme in Britain's relations with Europe since the late 1940s and it remains implicitly at the heart of the difficulties the Thatcher and Major Conservative governments encountered in the 1980s and 1990s in dealing with the accelerating pace of the movement towards 'ever closer union' after the Single European Act (1986) and the Maastricht Treaty. The emergence of Tony Blair as Prime Minister in May 1997 signalled a potential watershed in the tone of Britain's interaction with the EU. Two months after coming into office, Blair told a senior official:

> The Germans lost the war and have got over it. The French were humiliated by the war and have got over it. The British won the war and have never got over it. My generation do not have the same hang-ups about Europe as older generations. My job is to establish a lasting relationship and to lead Britain in Europe. (Seldon 2005: 320)

Despite a more positive *communautaire* rhetoric, however, the burden of history lay at the heart of many of New Labour's difficulties with the EU in the early years of the twenty-first century as the preference for structures of intergovernmental cooperation rather than supranational control continues to manifest itself in Britain's position towards European Monetary Union (EMU), the harmonisation of taxation, the adamantine defence of Britain's non-negotiable 'red line' objections to the European constitutional treaty and in many other areas of conflict. As Paul Sharp rightly concludes, 'post-war British policy towards Europe has been distinguished by a remarkable continuity in both preferences and the inability to realise them' (Sharp 2002: 276).

Considerable debate has been provoked by the question of whether this bipartisan consensus on external policy has been a good thing for the nation or (as Correlli Barnett maintains) a bizarre fantasy which has proved fatal to post-war economic recovery, industrial modernisation and subsequent prosperity. Barnett's highly polemical thesis has been subject to considerable criticism, but many scholars would accept the general proposition that there is a direct causal relationship between Britain's relatively indifferent economic performance and its overextended external policy (see Chapter 6). As Stephen Blank puts it, post-war economic problems have arisen because 'British leaders were unable, especially in the first post-war decade, to devise an acceptable international role that the nation could afford' and that the commitment 'to restore and protect Britain's role as an international power dominated domestic economic policies and objectives' and helped 'to lock Britain into a low growth situation' (Blank 1979: 73, 85).

It is certainly true that Bevin's foreign policy implied a high financial burden. In 1946, defence expenditure stood at £1736 million while almost 1.5 million men and women remained in the services and the defence industries were still consuming a fifth of total GNP. Even after the Treasury imposed economies in January 1947, defence expenditure still remained at £700m in 1948 and after the creation of the Brussels Treaty Organisation, NATO, and the outbreak of the Korean War, the defence budget spiralled to £1112 million in 1951/52; increasing its share of the budget from 6 per cent to 10 per cent and committing Britain to a higher expenditure per head on defence than even in the United States. When this burden is combined with the Attlee government's extensive commitment to the promised 'New Jerusalem' of full employment and a comprehensive welfare state, Barnett argues that Britain was distracted from the crucial task of adjusting its economy to address the harsh 'audit of war' (Barnett 1995: 520).

While controversy continues about the wisdom of such a commitment, there is much less doubt either that a purposive external policy consensus actually did exist or that its foundations were robustly laid in the late 1940s. In reality, post-war economic and political history might have been very different had the Prime Minister had his own way. Clement Attlee was profoundly anxious about the parlous state of the domestic economy and his government's capacity to build the promised 'New Jerusalem' while attempting to reassert Britain's great power status in the world. Sceptical about Bevin's quest, early in 1946 he warned the Chiefs of Staff and his Foreign Secretary that 'in the present era we must consider very carefully how to make the most of our limited resources. We must not, for sentimental reasons, give hostages to fortune' (Barnett 1995: 52–3). This radical call for a more realistic alignment between Britain's politico-military commitments and its economic resources was defeated by Ernest Bevin's unshakeable commitment to the vision of Britain's continuing world role and the need for a defence establishment capable of sustaining it. Bevin may not have been correct in his assessment of the future but his vision has been willingly embraced by his successors ever since.

Chapter 3

From Empire to Commonwealth

The imperial legacy and the test of war

During the 1930s, British policymakers were tormented by the fear that another war would destroy the structure of British imperial rule at a time when it was more vulnerable to attack than at any time in its history. The Second World War swiftly vindicated these gloomy apprehensions. There were obvious advantages to be derived from the imperial connection – not least the five million Dominion and colonial troops supporting the British war effort. But, as Bernard Porter reminds us, 'the empire brought Britain some benefits, but as many liabilities' (Porter 1987: 308). The damage inflicted on the British Empire by the Second World War was profound and multifaceted. It undoubtedly weakened still further the familial relationship between the 'Mother Country' and its white Dominions. Some of these ties were already feeble – particularly with Eire, which declared its neutrality during the war before becoming a Republic outside the Commonwealth in 1949. Similarly, the South African Parliament only narrowly voted to join Britain's war effort, and thereafter Afrikaner anti-British sentiment increased sharply. The war had a far more corrosive impact upon Britain's relationship with its other formerly more supportive Dominions. Canada increasingly consolidated its bonds with the United States upon whom it depended for its security after the Ogdensburg Agreement in August 1940, while after the catastrophic fall of Singapore in February 1942 Australia and New Zealand also looked to the United States for defence, their confidence in Britain's promise of a naval shield shattered forever.

Ultimately, however, the Second World War inflicted its most severe damage upon British control over its dependent colonial Empire. At one level, war raised new doubts about Britain's military capacity to restore its authority – particularly in its Far Eastern colonies where local nationalist guerrilla armies formed to fight the Japanese were inevitably reluctant to allow former colonial masters to resume where they had left off after victory had been achieved. Even in those colonies not captured by the enemy, local nationalists in Egypt, Iraq, Palestine and India seized the opportunity provided by war to campaign against British rule. In many respects, they were assisted by British responses to the demands of total war and the radicalising effect these had upon the colonial political consciousness. In the past, the golden rule of British colonial administration had been to let well alone as far as possible to avoid alienating local opinion; a philosophy enshrined in what John Darwin aptly describes as 'a policy of masterly inactivity' (Darwin 1988: 48). But in wartime, Britain's struggle for survival compelled it to intervene actively to force colonial governments into actions they knew to be unpopular but which were vital to mobilise all available imperial resources for the war effort through increasing regulation of agricultural production and prices, the arbitrary use of forced labour to meet production and recruitment targets, and the imposition of higher taxation. As Keith Jeffery puts it, the War 'clearly demonstrated that colonial control depended ultimately on force, albeit applied by Britain in pursuit of national survival' (Jeffery 1999: 326).

At a diplomatic level, the war also fundamentally served to damage the Empire by increasing British dependence upon the United States. From the outset, Roosevelt regarded the 'Old World' colonial empires with profound antipathy as an obstacle to American trade and an affront to its democratic traditions. Yet, while Roosevelt insisted that the Atlantic Charter of August 1941 should specifically include an affirmation of 'the rights of all peoples to choose the form of government under which they live', Churchill's entire career had been dedicated to the defence of the British Empire and he was determined to restore it to its former greatness after the war. As he declared pugnaciously after a row with Roosevelt over the Empire in November 1942: 'We mean to hold our own. I have not become the King's first Minister in order to preside over the liquidation of the British Empire' (MacIntyre 1998: 90). To drive the point home, he threatened to resign from the premiership if Roosevelt demanded concessions to Gandhi – at which point Roosevelt backed away from further confrontation, but 'by 1943–44, . . . the defence of the British imperial system had become, in the eyes of British leaders, almost as much a diplomatic struggle against their ally as a military struggle with their enemies' (Darwin 1988: 39).

Notwithstanding the damaging impact of the Second World War, the fact remains that, in 1945, Britain's ramshackle Empire was still apparently intact and, despite Labour's traditional anti-imperial traditions, both major parties were determined to reassert control over former colonies. Against this background, it is important to avoid the temptation to conceptualise Britain's retreat from empire as a single timely process of planned orderly withdrawal. Not only was it often neither planned nor orderly, but also the process involved a number of quite distinct phases, each characterised by different motivations and responding to different pressures. The Labour governments between 1945 and 1951 certainly inaugurated the first phase, but this was largely in response to overwhelmingly adverse economic and military factors which effectively undermined imperial control in both India and Palestine. Between 1951 and 1955, however, Churchill's determination to defend the Empire with a policy of repression and retrenchment was exemplified by the brutal battle against the Mau Mau in Kenya. Despite this imperial zeal, however, the increasing recognition that Britain no longer possessed either the will or the capability to sustain its imperial role prompted the Macmillan governments to engage in a second phase of wholesale decolonisation after the October 1959 general election. During the ensuing decade, many of its most valuable African colonies attained self-government, when only a few years before this was expected to take a generation or more.

The withdrawal from Empire, phase 1: India and Palestine

British imperial policy after 1945 was characterised by a high degree of pragmatism and very mixed levels of success. Inevitably, in some colonies the existence of overwhelming obstacles to the restoration of British control forced it to withdraw rapidly. This was the case in both India and Palestine in the late 1940s. But these early examples of imperial retreat should not obscure the more fundamental fact that in most other colonies Britain pursued a policy of 'retrenchment' to prevent any further erosion of its influence. In part, this was achieved through repression of domestic dissent and counter-insurgency operations, but these methods were often skilfully combined with well-crafted constitutional concessions designed to sidetrack demands for independence by appeasing moderate pressure and diverting it away from fundamental reform while simultaneously isolating more extreme nationalist opinion and leaving it easier to deal with. As David Sanders puts it, the story of the post-war era 'somewhat paradoxically, is simultaneously one both of "withdrawal" and of "retrenchment"' (Sanders 1990: 74). Ultimately, there can be no better illustration of the operation of this dual policy than the experience of the Indian subcontinent in the twentieth century.

India was always rightly regarded as the jewel in the British imperial crown. With some 400 million people, it was the most populous dependency in the Empire, the largest market and the recipient of the highest proportion of British overseas investment. Little wonder that Lord

Curzon, the Viceroy, had written in 1901 that 'as long as we rule India, we are the greatest power in the world. If we lose it we shall drop straight away to a third rate power' (Howard 1974: 14). Given this pivotal economic and strategic importance, British policy towards Indian nationalism after 1918 fluctuated between two tactical approaches. On one hand, there was a regular resort to repression and detention of Indian political leaders like Jawaharlal Nehru, India's first Prime Minister, who spent nine years in British jails between 1921 and 1947. On the other hand, periodic civil disturbances encouraged Whitehall to combine a carrot with the stick in the form of repeated promises of future constitutional reforms supposedly designed to lead ultimately to self-government. This process began with the Montagu Declaration in December 1917, announcing the intention to introduce 'self-governing institutions with a view to the progressive realisation of responsible government in India'; a goal reaffirmed by the Montagu-Chelmsford reforms, the 1919 India Act, the 'Irwin declaration' in October 1929 and, after much Conservative hand-wringing, finally enacted in the 1935 Government of India Act. In addition, Whitehall exercised considerable ingenuity in consolidating its control between the wars with other reforms variously designed to confer fiscal autonomy on India and advance the 'Indianisation' of its Army and civil service. As David MacIntyre argues, however, British responses to Indian political demands 'always came too little, too late'. Equally importantly, they were invariably unaccompanied by any timetable for the advance towards responsible self-government. In this respect, India offers a classic example of the strategy of retrenchment in action (MacIntyre 1998).

India offers an equally illuminating case study of the adverse effects of the Second World War upon the pace of political change by forcing the British to break their own golden rule of 'masterly inactivity'. This danger was evident from the outset when the Viceroy, Lord Linlithgow, declared India was at war alongside Britain in September 1939 without any consultation with Indian opinion. More damaging, however, was that the need to mobilise India's resources for war purposes produced shortages, inflation, the dislocation of markets, famine and a sharp increase in the scope of government regulation and interference. As a result, the British Raj became an obvious target for popular resentment. Worse still, these necessary wartime decisions had two further negative consequences for the perpetuation of British rule in India. First, in retaliation for these unpopular actions, the Indian National Congress launched an effective campaign of civil disobedience in October 1940, which culminated in August 1942 with Gandhi's 'Quit India' movement. When this was ruthlessly suppressed, with the loss of 900 lives, the grievance only further intensified the determination of Congress to reject any compromise with the imperial power.

A second adverse consequence to flow directly from this intransigence was that Britain was forced to seek allies among the enemies of Congress. In practice, this meant cooperation with the Muslim League led by Mohammed Ali Jinnah and from 1940 onwards this was dedicated to the creation of a separate Muslim state in direct conflict with the ambition of Congress to rule over a free united India under a strong central government. In these highly explosive and polarised circumstances, the incoming Labour government was further handicapped by the fact that its imperial policy suffered from 'a woolliness and illusion about decolonisation which was as strong as that of the Conservatives' (Inder-Singh 1987: 144–5).

This already difficult situation was rendered utterly impossible by the outbreak of uncontrollable communal violence following the massacre of Hindus in the 'Great Calcutta Killing' of August 1946, when some 5000 people died in Calcutta alone. In many ways, this event represented the final nail in the coffin of imperial rule in India and a turning point for British policy. Advised by Lord Wavell, the Viceroy, that he had lost the power to control the incipient civil war and with the domestic economy in the depths of severe financial crisis in February 1947, the Attlee government bowed to the inevitable – but not before taking a final calculated risk. On 18 February 1947, the Cabinet announced that British rule would come to an end by June 1948. Although Attlee had previously deprecated any idea of 'setting paper dates', he was now gambling that this would force Congress leaders to accept partition on the grounds that they would be no more capable of controlling the predominantly Muslim areas than the British had been (Owen 1991: 158). This gamble paid off handsomely. The date for the independence of India and Pakistan was then advanced to 15 August 1947 – even before the new boundaries of the Punjab and Bengal had been established. Ceylon achieved independence in February 1948 and it followed India and Pakistan in joining the Commonwealth. Burma refused to do so when it gained independence in January 1948, largely because the fight against Japanese occupation had completely shattered the foundations of British rule.

Attlee defended the withdrawal from India by declaring that Britain was not so much losing an empire as gaining a multiracial Commonwealth. It was thus rosily presented as 'not the abdication but the fulfilment of Britain's mission in India', occurring 'without external pressure or weariness at the burden of rule'. In so doing, Attlee laid the foundations for the myth that Indian independence was a well-planned and timely act of generosity (Owen 1991: 167). David Fieldhouse is correct in suggesting that the actions of the Labour governments of 1945–51 represented one of only three genuine 'watershed' moments in the long history of the British Empire (Fieldhouse 1984: 82). The old subject colonies were now about to begin their slow and halting progress towards independence as members of a British Commonwealth of Nations: a body confidently expected in Whitehall to grow eventually into a surrogate empire bolstering British prestige on the international stage. In this context, therefore, John Kent is right in emphasising that the Attlee government's decision to grant self-government to India in the late 1940s was 'not seen as part of managing Britain's imperial decline in the sense of projecting less power and influence in the world, than as part of an attempt to rebuild the British Empire as a global system on somewhat different lines' (Kent 1993: x).

In Palestine, the problems were similar to those in India, in that the imperial power confronted irreconcilable communal differences and an escalating pattern of violence against a background of chronic economic crisis at home – and Britain responded to the challenge in much the same way as it had in India. The crucial difference, however, is that while India could be plausibly projected as some sort of triumph for enlightened generosity, the same could never be said of the British scuttle from Palestine. Britain had been the dominant foreign power in the Middle East between the wars, and its objective here, as elsewhere, was to interfere as little as possible to avoid conflict with the indigenous population – and, by the late 1930s, this meant a policy in Palestine designed to be broadly acceptable to other Arab states.

This was easier said than done after Britain's mutually contradictory promises to rival Arab and Jewish communities in Palestine during the First World War. In order to encourage an Arab revolt against their Ottoman masters allied to Germany, the McMahon letter of June 1916 had promised that Britain would 'recognize and support the independence of the Arabs' in Palestine while, to appease Jewish opinion, the Balfour Declaration in November 1917 announced the British government's commitment to the principle of 'a national homeland for Jewish people in Palestine' – with the crucial (often conveniently forgotten) proviso that this must not prejudice the rights of the existing Palestinian Arab community. Confronted by this intractable dilemma, British strategy between the wars was designed principally to conciliate Arab opinion. To this end, Jewish immigration into Palestine was restricted in 1940 and 1944 while further restrictions were placed on land purchase by Jews. This was in the hope that by preventing a mass influx it would be possible to avert conflict in a country of 560,000 Jews and 1.2 million Palestinian Arabs while simultaneously satisfying the other Arab states, enhancing British influence in the region and enabling it to use Palestine as its main Middle Eastern base in peace-time; an ideal outcome which would enable it to withdraw from Suez and thus clear the way for a significant improvement in relations with Egypt.

These strategic objectives were rapidly overwhelmed by a bewildering concatenation of countervailing pressures immediately after the war ended. Firstly, the spectacle of tens of thousands of Jews released from concentration camps being barred entry to Palestine by British troops inevitably created an adverse impression abroad. Secondly, world sympathy and guilt about the Holocaust made the Jewish desire for a homeland even more difficult to resist – particularly in the United States where the Jewish lobby was wealthy, influential and of crucial electoral importance to a president about to seek re-election. Thirdly, Britain now faced a well-armed and well-organised Jewish underground army supported by a number of other Jewish terrorist organisations like the Stern Gang and Irgun in which future Israeli statesmen like Menachim Begin (later Prime Minister) and General Moshe Dayan (Defence Minister) played a leading role. Together, these terrorist forces sustained an escalating spiral of violence which tied down 100,000 British troops, a tenth of the empire's total military man-power.

In the event, powerful US pressure to allow the immediate entry of 100,000 Jewish immigrants and the partition of Palestine between Jews and Arabs placed the British in an utterly impossible position. In part, this was because Whitehall knew that neither side wanted it, but it also feared support for partition would jeopardise its strong position in a region regarded as vital to its Cold War strategy, to the Suez Canal and the Gulf oilfields. On the other hand, the American pressure was extremely difficult to resist at a time when Britain was heavily dependent on US economic aid and cooperation on a wide variety of other international issues. Exasperated by this hopeless 'no-win' situation and in the depths of economic crisis, in late February 1947 the Cabinet referred the issue to the UN with the implicit threat that it would resign the mandate unless some satisfactory agreed solution emerged. When this expedient failed to achieve the desired result, on 30 September 1947 the Cabinet decided to resign the mandate and withdraw its forces by 15 May 1948. In profoundly unpropitious circumstances, the Labour government had adopted a policy of outright 'scuttle' and it received much international opprobrium for a humiliating debacle which effectively abdicated all responsibility and allowed war to determine the political geography of the region (Morgan 1984.) Sixty years later, the Palestinian refugee camps still bear witness to this abject failure of British policy.

Retrenchment and resistance, 1945–57

In both India and Palestine there was no grand plan for British decolonisation; the reality was that the colonial power had simply been forced out. But in Malaya, British policy displayed absolutely no indication of any desire to cut and run. On the contrary, it appeared determined to strengthen its control over the peninsular – and after the murder of three British planters in June 1948 this meant engaging in an expensive 12-year counter-insurgency operation to prevent the emergence of a communist regime hostile to British influence. This willingness to fight in Malaya but not in India or Palestine can be explained by a variety of factors. Firstly, Malaya was absolutely crucial to the British imperial system and the revival of its economy because it produced one third of the world's rubber and half of its total tin production – both products sold to the United States in return for half of all OSA dollar earnings without which the whole edifice would have collapsed. Secondly, Britain's willingness to retrench rather than withdraw in Malaya was based on the belief that British forces could win the military struggle against communist insurgency in Malaya while there was absolutely no prospect of being able to restore law and order in India or Palestine. Finally, in geostrategic terms, control over Malaya and Singapore was crucial to Britain's hopes of re-establishing its old ascendancy in East Asia and China, while the onset of the Cold War made Whitehall extremely reluctant to withdraw from any area of strategic or economic significance for fear that communist influence would replace the departing imperial power – a particularly worrying prospect at a time when Chinese Communists had just won the civil war in October 1949 as a prelude to the outbreak of 'hot war' in Korea in June 1950. For all these reasons, Britain simply could not afford to lose the struggle in Malaya and, in its battle against communist insurgency, military force went hand-in-hand with a rapid acceleration in the pace of constitutional development. Malaya finally achieved independence within the Commonwealth in August 1957.

Although Malaya represented an unequivocal success for Britain, it also fuelled the illusion that it could maintain a global total strategy, blinding British policymakers to the reality that was producing a dangerous overextension of British power which it no longer had the economic capability to sustain. As David Sanders concludes, 'the real paradox of imperial policy in the decade after 1945 was that a string of *tactical* successes could have added up to something approaching *strategic* failure' (Sanders 1990: 98). In the short term, however, victory in Malaya demonstrated that Britain still possessed the military power and the political will to resist local nationalism elsewhere. In these circumstances, it fell back on the traditional policy of retrenchment as a means to delay withdrawal. African representation in the legislative council was extended in the Gold Coast and Nigeria in 1946 and in Sierra Leone in 1948 but they remained firmly under British control. Britain's Caribbean and West Indies possessions were 'a monument to colonial failure: poverty-stricken, politically backward, economically as well as politically fragmented, with a golden past and a leaden future' (Darwin 1988: 217). Yet even here some constitutional reforms occurred. British Guiana acquired a new constitution and adult suffrage in 1943 and there were similar arrangements for Jamaica and Trinidad in 1944 and 1946 respectively. In each case, however, local participation was largely cosmetic and real power remained firmly in the hands of the governor. Another favoured British method of retrenchment involved the creation of federations among neighbouring British colonies to create larger units capable of being self-sufficient and potentially prosperous, a solution adopted in East Africa, Malaysia and the West Indies, but each of these artificial structures collapsed after a relatively short and troubled life.

When concessions failed to defuse the nationalist challenge, Britain was prepared to use force to preserve its colonial presence during the 1950s. In British Guiana, the Marxist-inclined Dr Cheddi Jagan was deposed and the new constitution was suspended in 1953. Similarly, serious rioting in the Gold Coast in February 1948 was vigorously suppressed while Britain engaged in protracted military operations to defeat communist insurgency in Malaya and against EOKA independence fighters in Cyprus (1954–9). Above all, it was prepared to wage a bloody and costly colonial war in Kenya between 1952 and 1956. Kenya was Britain's most valuable African possession and regularly considered as an alternative base for British military and naval power given its location within striking distance of the Middle East and the Gulf region. In addition, it contained Africa's largest and most influential white settler population, controlling 16,700 square miles in the 'White Highlands' exclusively for their use. These factors combined to ensure that when Kikuyu unrest (fuelled by land hunger and fundamental socio-cultural crisis within tribal society) boiled over into the Mau Mau insurrection, the British colonial authorities were prepared to engage in stern repressive measures to defeat the independence movement.

Although the Churchill government entered office in 1951 declaring its desire 'to help the colonial territories to attain self-government under the British Commonwealth', the only state actually to achieve independence before Macmillan became Prime Minister in January 1957 was the Sudan in January 1956, where an army mutiny in 1955 was followed by widespread insurrection. In the midst of this chaos,

Table 3.1   The road to colonial independence - phase I, 1945–59

February 1946	Mutiny in Indian navy and air force
March 1946	Transjordan gains independence (Jordan from 1949)
July 1946	Irgun and Haganah blow up British Army HQ at King David Hotel in Jerusalem
August 1946	'Great Calcutta Killing'
March 1947	British troops withdraw from Egypt to the Canal Zone
April 1947	Palestine mandate referred to UN
August 1947	India and Pakistan gain independence
November 1947	UN vote for partition of Palestine prompts British decision to withdraw
May 1948	British leave Palestine
June 1948	Malaya emergency begins against communist guerrillas; independence for Burma (Myanmar from 1989), Ceylon (Sri Lanka from 1972) and Palestine (Israel)
1949	Ireland withdraws from Commonwealth
1950	India becomes first republic to join Commonwealth
October 1951	Egypt denounces 1936 Anglo-Egyptian Treaty
December 1951	Libya gains independence
October 1952	State of emergency declared in Kenya to suppress Mau Mau uprising
1953	Nyasaland, Northern and Southern Rhodesia form Federation
1954	New Anglo-Egyptian Treaty signed allowing for the evacuation of the Suez base
1955	Start of the Greek Cypriot EOKA terrorist campaign
January 1956	Sudan gains independence; Mau Mau rebellion suppressed
November 1956	Anglo-French military expedition to recapture control of Suez Canal
1957	Gold Coast (Ghana) and Malaya (part of Malaysia from 1963) gain independence
1958	West Indies Federation formed

Sudanese nationalists declared independence and Britain was simply powerless to resist (McIntyre 1998: 38). Relatively rapid progress also occurred in the Gold Coast, where constitutional reforms in 1946 produced a black majority in the Legislative Council, but these concessions failed to prevent either serious rioting in February 1948 or the emergence of Kwame Nkrumah's mass movement, the Convention People's Party (CPP). To a large extent, the success of the CPP and its 'positive action' campaign of strikes and boycotts can be attributed to the efforts of the colonial administration to extract more revenue and production during the war and its immediate aftermath – particularly as these produced food shortages and inflation in the towns, while in the countryside, draconian measures to control a virulent disease in cocoa trees ended in an unpopular campaign of widespread crop destruction.

Perhaps the most significant factor easing the Gold Coast towards independence was Nkrumah's explicit objective of achieving self-government *within* the Commonwealth and the OSA. As independence would make little fundamental difference to Britain's material interests, it was deemed better to have an independent state unified under Nkrumah than to see the fragile unity of the new state collapse into tribal and regional separatism. As John Darwin explains: 'As so often elsewhere, the real nightmare of British policy was not the transfer of power but the disintegration of the administrative unity they had laboriously constructed. In that sense, the Ghanaian nationalism of the CPP was the favoured stepchild of British imperialism', and independence became the 'highly acceptable price for a unified state and the co-operation of local politicians' (Darwin 1988: 179, 183). Released from jail after elections produced a clear majority for the CPP, Nkrumah became First Minister before steering the Gold Coast towards self-government in 1954 and full independence (as Ghana) on 6 March 1957. Beyond the Sudan, Ghana and Malaya, however, retrenchment remained the policy norm between 1951 and 1959. Indeed, far from promoting decolonisation, in November 1956 Anthony Eden appeared bent on reviving the whiff of British gunpowder as a strategy for imperial management.

The Suez crisis, 1956: the last blast of imperialism?

The Suez crisis of 1956 represented a catastrophic failure for British external policy and a major turning point with regard to its position in the Middle East and within the empire as a whole. As Map 3.1 illustrates, in 1945 Britain dominated this region, both militarily and politically. It was the ruling mandate holder in Palestine and Transjordan

Map 3.1 Britain's informal empire in the Middle East, 1945

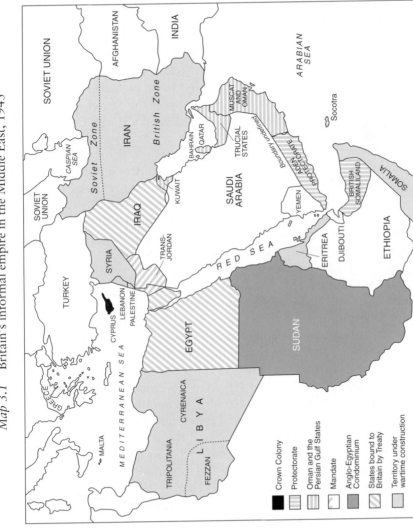

while Iraq and Egypt, the two leading independent states of the region, were both bound by treaties of alliance to Britain and these conferred substantial military rights upon the colonial power. The enormous importance of the Middle East to British foreign policymakers was based on a number of factors. The traditional strategic imperative of defending the Suez Canal as the lifeline to British India and the Far East was reinforced by the need for easy access to abundant supplies of oil from British-owned sources in Iraq and Iran that did not require the expenditure of scarce dollars. In addition, the Cold War obsession with the spectre of Soviet expansion into the Middle East and the fear of an eastern Mediterranean 'domino effect' added further significance to the area. Finally, the region was considered to be of special strategic value as a means of delivering an air attack upon the Soviet Union's industrial heartland in the Ukraine and its oil supply in the Caucasus – less than 500 miles from British bases in Iraq.

The Second World War reinforced Britain's perceived dependence upon its bases in Egypt, while simultaneously sensitising Egyptian nationalists to the affront which a colonial military presence posed to their national pride and sovereignty. When negotiations to end this military presence broke down in January 1947, Britain insisted on its right to station some 80,000 troops in the Suez Canal Zone until the 1936 Anglo-Egyptian Treaty expired in 1956, while Egypt unilaterally abrogated the Treaty in October 1951. After this, relations deteriorated rapidly. Britain's scuttle from Palestine, followed by Israeli military triumph over its Arab neighbours in 1948–9, fuelled anti-British sentiment in Egypt and left its bases in the Canal Zone subject to terrorist attacks, strikes and the complete withdrawal of local labour. To make matters worse, after a successful military coup to overthrow the conservative King Farouk in July 1952, Colonel Gamal Abdul Nasser assumed sole control of the Egyptian government in December 1954 with a radical agenda of land reform, economic modernisation and a desire to make Egypt the principal champion of pan-Arab nationalism.

Ironically, the British initially greeted the arrival of the Nasser regime as a possible opportunity to improve relations. To this end, in 1953 it was agreed to end British rule in Sudan within three years and, in the following year, Eden assured Nasser that British troops would be withdrawn from the Canal Zone by June 1956 with certain provisos about its use in an emergency. Unfortunately, Eden's hopes that imperial generosity would transform Egypt into an ally of the West were soon brutally dispelled. Indeed, far from improving relations, during 1955–6 Nasser adopted a highly provocative and confrontational strategy designed to undermine Western influence in the Middle East. First, he attempted to undermine the Hashemite kingdoms of Iraq and Jordan –

both close allies of Britain in promoting the Baghdad Pact as the Middle Eastern equivalent of NATO. According to Sir Anthony Nutting, the junior Foreign Office minister who resigned over the Suez affair, Nasser's responsibility for nationalist riots in the Jordanian capital, which forced King Hussein to dismiss General Glubb, his long-standing British military adviser, in March 1956, was arguably the starting point for Eden's highly personal and somewhat irrational obsession with Nasser which culminated in the Suez crisis eight months later (Nutting 1967: 34). Nasser then compounded the offence by attempting to play off both sides in the Cold War by entering into separate negotiations with Britain, the United States and the Soviet Union with a view to securing finance for the construction of the Aswan High Dam. Similarly, his efforts to modernise the Egyptian military by accepting a Czech offer of modern weapons was perceived in Washington and London as effectively a deal with the Soviets. Ultimately, it was Nasser's flirtation with Moscow and his socialist rhetoric which increasingly alienated Eden and led directly to the Suez crisis. On 19 July 1956, the Eisenhower administration announced that it was not prepared to finance the Aswan Dam and Britain immediately followed the same line. A week later, Nasser nationalised the Anglo-French Suez Canal Company as a means to fund the project himself and to consolidate his position as the champion of Arab nationalism against Western imperialism.

Eden was outraged by Nasser's action, which he interpreted as a violation of the spirit of the 1954 agreement he had negotiated personally as Churchill's Foreign Secretary. He also regarded it as a deliberately provocative threat when a quarter of British imports and a third of its shipping passed through the Canal. As he expostulated on hearing the news, 'the Egyptian has got his thumb on our windpipe' (Thomas 1970: 35). Although stress and ill-health undoubtedly played their part in the crisis, Eden's behaviour was primarily influenced by a well-developed Realist world view. All his experience as Foreign Secretary under both Neville Chamberlain (when he resigned in February 1938 in opposition to appeasement) and Churchill between 1940 and 1954, when dealing with the Soviets, convinced Eden that it was essential to confront aggressive dictators with force rather than diplomacy. This is significant because Eden mistakenly tended to regard Nasser as a 'pocket Hitler' or more accurately as a 'Moslem Mussolini' and he detected a direct parallel between Nasser's action and Mussolini's seizure of Abyssinia in 1935 and Hitler's remilitarisation of the Rhineland in 1936; events he regarded as decisive moments at which the dictators could have been stopped if only the Western powers had stood up to them. Coming so soon after the forced nationalisation of the Anglo-Iranian Oil Company and the loss of its profitable British-owned oilfields in 1951, Nasser's challenge over Suez thus prompted the conclusion that Britain must act decisively to warn other potential imitators that actions of this sort would be met by an overwhelming display of force.

In retaliation for Nasser's nationalisation, Eden's ministerial Egypt Committee spent the next three months plotting the restoration of Anglo-French control over the Canal and the removal of Nasser from power. The final plot was hatched at an extraordinarily secret conference in the Paris suburb of Sevres on 22–24 October 1956 – at which the British Foreign Secretary apparently arrived wearing a false moustache to disguise his identity! At these meetings, Britain cynically colluded with France and Israel to create a pretext for justifying military intervention. The agreed scenario was for Israel to attack Egypt on 29 October in such a way as to enable Britain and France to claim that the safety of the Suez Canal was at risk. They would then issue an 'appeal to the combatants' offering to intervene, supposedly to separate the two armies conveniently along the Canal Zone. Having landed their troops, the expectation was that Nasser would be overthrown by his own disgruntled people to be replaced by a leader far more acceptable to the West. In retrospect, it is difficult to believe that the participants in this plot seriously imagined that this pathetically transparent pretext would deceive anyone for a moment – but they did.

On 5 November, an Anglo-French force of paratroopers landed on the Suez Canal while British aircraft bombed Cairo. Within hours of the invasion, however, a ceasefire was ordered as a prelude to complete withdrawal. This dramatic turn of events is explained by the hostile response of the United States. Britain clearly anticipated that Washington would acquiesce in its action – particularly as Eisenhower was expected to be heavily involved with the final stages of his presidential re-election campaign fought on a peace platform. The President, however, had always opposed military action and news of the Anglo-French landings was greeted with fury. In retaliation, the United States forced through a UN resolution demanding an Anglo-French withdrawal while the US Treasury orchestrated a run on sterling on the international money markets which resulted in the loss of £100 million from gold reserves during the first week in November and an outflow of 15 per cent of Britain's total gold and dollar reserves during November as a whole. British appeals to the IMF to help combat this threat were then rejected until a ceasefire was agreed. As a direct result of these financial pressures, Harold Macmillan (as Chancellor of the Exchequer) deftly executed an immediate volte face as he switched from being the leading Cabinet 'hawk' to the principal advocate of withdrawal, leaving Eden completely isolated.

Eden's ill-conceived military action over Suez was intended to restore Britain's traditional dominance in Egypt but it ended in its most severe political and military reverse since the Second World War and the adverse consequences were vast and far-reaching. Eden was accused of engaging in the worst sort of 'gunboat diplomacy' a century too late. Britain's prestige plummeted in its Middle Eastern 'informal empire' with Iraq, suggesting that it should be expelled from the Baghdad Pact, while Jordan abrogated its 1953 defence treaty with Britain and both Syria and Saudi Arabia broke off diplomatic relations. The Commonwealth reaction was little better. Only Australia and New Zealand supported Britain while Canada, India and Pakistan were prominent in condemning it; the first depressing sign that the Commonwealth would not become a kind of substitute empire enhancing Britain's authority on the world stage. More problematical is an assessment of the influence of the Suez debacle upon the pace and scale of British decolonisation. Like many others, David Sanders argues that Suez did not create demands for independence but 'it certainly gave them a significant boost' (Sanders 1990: 103). While this may be true, John Darwin comes far closer to the truth when he asserts that 'the effects of the Suez crisis upon Britain's imperial role were ... certainly not obvious, simple, clear cut or immediate' (Darwin 1988: 231).

Withdrawal from Empire, phase 2: Harold Macmillan and the 'Wind of Change'

Harold Macmillan's succession to the premiership in January 1957 in the immediate aftermath of the Suez crisis represented far more of a major watershed in the process of British colonial withdrawal. On his Far East tour in February 1958, Macmillan declared he had 'no intention of presiding over the liquidation of the British Empire' but he brought with him into Downing Street a new political will to transform the remaining parts of the dependent Empire into members of the Commonwealth and one of his first acts as Prime Minister was to order the compilation of a 'profit and loss' account for each colony to understand precisely the costs and implications of granting independence (McIntyre 1998: 45–6). The results of the survey were inconclusive but between 1957 and 1966 Britain granted independence to 22 colonial territories on the basis of a pragmatic cost–benefit calculation tempered by the increasing realisation that nationalist sentiment was rapidly becoming more articulate and determined and that delay would risk violence and future antagonisms: lessons driven home by the bloodbath

Table 3.2   The rapid dissolution of the British Empire, 1960–97

1960	Macmillan's 'wind of change' speech in South Africa; British Somaliland, Cyprus and Nigeria gain independence; UN Resolution 1514 calling for rapid end of colonialism (December)
1961	South Africa withdraws from Commonwealth; Sierra Leone, Northern Cameroons (as part of Nigeria), Kuwait, Southern Cameroon (as part of Cameroon) and Tanganyika (Tanzania from 1964) gain independence
1962	West Indies Federation breaks up; Western Samoa, Jamaica, Trinidad and Tobago and Uganda gain independence; pro-Nasser revolt in Yemen forces British troops to quell riots in Aden (September); Britain suppresses rebellion in Brunei (December)
1963	Indonesian 'Confrontation' with Malaysia begins (April); Northern Borneo (Sabah), Sarawak, Singapore (as part of Malaysia), Zanzibar (as part of Tanzania in 1964) and Kenya all gain independence
1964	British troops suppress mutinies in former East African colonies (January); Commonwealth Secretariat established; Nyasaland (Malawi), Malta and Northern Rhodesia (Zambia) gain independence
1965	Southern Rhodesia issues Unilateral Declaration of Independence (November); The Gambia, Maldives, and Singapore gain independence
1966	British Guiana (Guyana), Bechuanaland (Botswana), Basutoland (Lesotho) and Barbados gain independence
1967	Aden (South Yemen) gains independence (November)
1968	Nauru, Mauritius and Swaziland gain independence

◼▶

in the immediate wake of Belgian withdrawal from the Congo in January 1959, the vicious civil war in Algeria which destroyed the French Fourth Republic and, closer to home, a supposed murder plot in Nyasaland, the Mau Mau uprising in Kenya, the Sharpeville massacre in the Transvaal in March 1960 and widespread rioting in Southern Rhodesia in July 1960. As Macmillan famously declared to the South African Parliament on 3 February 1960, 'The wind of change is blowing through this continent and, whether we like it or not, this growth of national consciousness is a political fact . . . our national policies must

Table 3.2   The rapid dissolution of the British Empire, 1960–97 – *continued*

1969	Northern Ireland 'Troubles' begin (August)
1970	Tonga and Fiji gain independence
1971	Bahrain, Qatar, United Arab Emirates and Bangladesh (seceded from Pakistan) gain independence
1973	Bahamas gains independence
1974	Grenada, Papua and New Guinea gain independence
1976	Seychelles gains independence
1978	Solomon Islands, Ellice Islands and Dominica gain independence
1979	St Lucia, Gilbert Islands, Saint Vincent and the Grenadines gain independence
1980	Lancaster House settlement over Southern Rhodesia (Zimbabwe); New Hebrides (Vanuatu) gains independence
1981	Belize, Antigua and Barbuda gain independence
1982	Falklands War (May-June); Maldives gain independence.
1983	St Kitts and Nevis gains independence
1984	Brunei gains independence; Sino-British agreement on Hong Kong
1985	Britain isolated over sanctions against South Africa
1987	Fiji leaves Commonwealth after military coup
1990	Independence of South-West Africa (Namibia) recognised
1994	After multi-racial elections, South Africa rejoins Commonwealth
1995	Bermuda votes to remain a colony; Nigeria suspended from Commonwealth
1997	Hong Kong returned to the People's Republic of China

take account of it' (Horne 1989, II: 195). Macmillan was ably assisted in this task by the Conservative radical Iain Macleod, who arrived at the Colonial Office declaring he wanted to be the last Colonial Secretary. Convinced that Britain needed to advance 'not as fast as the Congo and not as slow as Algiers', during a frenetic two years he shepherded five states to full independence and laid the foundations for majority rule in six more (Shepherd 1994: 161). Between 1960 and 1964, no fewer than 17 British colonies gained independence, many previously deemed unfit for decolonisation for several generations.

Map 3.2   Britain's imperial withdrawal from Africa, 1957–89

Suez Canal
Zone
(1956)

Libya
(1951)

Egypt
(1922)

Eritrea
(1952)

British
Somaliland
(1960)

Gambia
(1985)

Sudan
(1956)

Nigeria
(1960)

Sierra Leone
(1961)

Gold Coast
(1957)

Southern
Cameroons
(1960)

Uganda
(1962)

Kenya
(1963)

Somalia
(1960)

Zanzibar
(1963)

Tanganyika
(1961)

Nyasaland
(1964)

Northern
Rhodesia
(1964)

Rhodesia
(1980)

Bechuanaland
(1966)

Swaziland
(1968)

South-West Africa
(South African Mandate)
(1989)

South
Africa
(1910)

Basutoland
(1966)

By this stage, the process of decolonisation had acquired a momentum of its own. Harold Wilson's Labour government entered office in October 1964 confidently declaring that Britain's frontiers lay on the Himalayas but by the time he left office in 1970, 13 more colonies had gained independence and some of these withdrawals were extremely hasty affairs even by the standards of the recent past – so much so that in the wake of the devaluation crisis in November 1967 beleaguered British forces actually left their stores behind when they withdrew from Aden. After 1970, the last remnants of empire were finally swept away in the Pacific, the western hemisphere and the Persian Gulf. By the time Margaret Thatcher entered office in May 1979, all that remained of a once great empire were a few isolated islands scattered around the world and one or two seemingly intractable problems.

Forces driving the process of decolonisation

The relationship between cause and effect with regard to Britain's retreat from empire is complex, and historians are divided about the relative significance of metropolitan factors, the influence of the international environment and the power of local nationalism in determining its pace and extent (see McIntyre 1998; Darwin 1991). Nevertheless, while the search for a monocausal explanation is likely to prove unproductive, certain general conclusions seem reasonable. First, although financial cost was often a major factor in calculations, most notably the withdrawal from Palestine and 'East of Suez', in each case the decision was essentially a political choice rather than a financial imperative (see Chapter 6). Indeed, in its second phase, the retreat from colonial rule was often expected to add to Britain's economic burdens in the short term rather than reduce them. Fundamental structural changes in the pattern of British trade played a more important part in reducing the significance of the Empire in British thinking. In 1936, the Empire supplied nearly 40 per cent of imports and took nearly half of Britain's exports – a dependence increased further during the Second World War. Even in 1960, some 40.2 per cent of British exports went to Empire markets. But by 1970 this figure had fallen to 24.4 per cent and a decade later over half Britain's trade was with Europe while only 12 per cent was with the Commonwealth – and Britain's external policy inevitably followed its economic interests (Sanders 1990: 118–19; McIntyre 1998: 85). On the other hand, however, it is important not to attribute too much significance to economic factors. Ultimately, Macmillan's decision to accelerate decolonisation after the 1959 general election was made before the chronic economic problems of the 1960s became fully apparent, and was motivated chiefly by political and diplomatic calculations rather than financial necessity.

The impact of indigenous nationalism was also often of marginal significance, although the radicalising impact of the war, urbanisation, the humiliation of Suez and the contagion effect of British, French and Belgian decolonisation all provided a stimulant for colonial nationalism. Occasionally, this was reinforced by the machinations of the Soviet Union providing arms, anti-British propaganda and training for nationalist leaders. More importantly, indigenous nationalism was encouraged by the emergence of a new generation of black intellectuals like Franz Fanon in North Africa and C.L.R. James in the West Indies, while some very effective political leadership was provided by Kwame Nkrumah in the Gold Coast, Julius Nyerere in Tanganyika, Kenneth Kaunda in Northern Rhodesia and Dr Hastings Banda in Nyasaland. In most parts of the British Empire, however, decolonisation was not a direct or immediate response to the power of local nationalism.

On the other hand, international pressures unequivocally played a major role in accelerating the process of British decolonisation by transforming the environment in which European colonial empires continued to exist. First, US concerns about Britain's continued colonialism had been an important force since the Second World War and it became increasingly powerful when Washington found its own efforts to win the support of newly independent states were handicapped by Britain's continued colonialism. Secondly, the brutality witnessed in the Belgian Congo in 1960–1 brought home to British policymakers like Macmillan and Macleod the appalling risks of retaining any direct responsibility for government in Africa. A third factor concerned the attitudes of the international community and the UN towards the last vestiges of 'imperialism'. Tanganyika was a UN trusteeship held by Britain and, after a UN visit had called for an African majority legislature in 1955, colonial rule was increasingly subject to criticism from newly independent African members while the Soviet Union eagerly exploited this hostility to extend its influence in Africa. Britain's colonial management also became the subject of widespread international condemnation when it was revealed in June 1959 that 11 Mau Mau detainees had been beaten to death at the Hola Camp, while the Devlin Report on disturbances in Nyasaland talked ominously of 'a police state'. International censure was formalised in December 1960 when the UN General Assembly passed Resolution 1514 calling for the speedy end to colonialism. Finally, British decolonisation took place within the context of a more general parallel process of imperial withdrawal by other European powers. In particular, Britain found itself in a competitive struggle with France to acquire economic and diplomatic advantage in Africa at a time when de Gaulle had simultaneously granted independence to 13 French colonies.

Constraints upon Britain's imperial retreat

Although Macmillan's political will injected a new sense of urgency into the decolonisation process after 1959, there were also some substantial constraints upon British freedom of action in this sphere. White settler opposition certainly represented a major obstacle, particularly in Central and East Africa. Above all, in Kenya 30,000 wealthy white settlers were firmly entrenched in the Highlands and they were determined to maintain their highly privileged racial dominance. As a result, the first Africans were not nominated to the Kenyan Legislative Council until 1944, and the 1948 constitution accorded the white settlers the same total representation as the five million Africans and 120,000 Asians – an all too typical interpretation of the concept of 'balanced representation' in the region. The settler's position was further safeguarded by the imprisonment of Jomo Kenyatta, the veteran Kikuyu leader, and the ban upon his Kenyan African Union in 1950. Nevertheless, having defeated the Mau Mau insurgency, Iain Macleod had the political will to overcome white settler resistance. After swiftly ending the state of emergency, he pushed Kenya towards independence in December 1963. An even more intractable problem was created by white settler resistance in Southern Rhodesia. Unlike Kenya, the great majority of whites in Southern Rhodesia lived in towns and often worked in skilled or semi-skilled unionised jobs in industry – an economic position and livelihood they were determined to protect against black advance. Against the brutal backcloth of the Congo's collapse into anarchy, the Rhodesian Front's election victory in December 1962 was a prelude to its Unilateral Declaration of Independence (UDI) in November 1965. The problem lingered on to damage Anglo-Commonwealth relations until 1980 (see p. 63 below).

Strategic and military constraints represented another important brake upon the process of imperial withdrawal in some colonies. British refusal to quit Egypt in the early 1950s reflected the crucial strategic importance of the Suez Canal, while the retention of Palestine was partly influenced by the need to use it as an alternative Middle East base until Jewish terrorism made this option unviable. After the evacuation of the Suez Canal Zone in October 1954, Cyprus also acquired great strategic significance. In the following year, however, the National Organisation of Cypriot Fighters (EOKA) launched a terrorist independence campaign which British troops were unable to suppress; a recognition which in 1959 led to agreement that Cyprus should become a sovereign independent republic within the Commonwealth in return for Britain's retention of rights to sovereign bases at Akrotiri and Dhekelia.

Similar considerations applied in Malta, where pressure for independence led to direct British rule in 1959 on the grounds that it was far too strategically important to lose as a naval base. By 1962, however, the Defence White Paper signalled its declining significance for British strategy and two years later Malta was granted independence, although again Britain retained the right to station forces there for 10 years in return for grants and loans of £50 million. Aden was in a rather different category. Britain had acquired this barren wasteland in 1839 as a base guarding the entrance of the Red Sea and by the 1950s it was regarded as vital to the defence of Europe's oil supplies. As such, it was classified as one of the territories never to be granted independence by both the Macmillan and Wilson governments – particularly after it became the military headquarters for the Middle East in the early 1960s. In the event, however, external pressures and increasing unrest among Arab migrants to the colony after Nasser's victory in 1956 forced the British into a rapid withdrawal in November 1967.

Britain and the transition to black majority rule in southern Africa

Although Margaret Thatcher was relatively uninterested in the Commonwealth, under her leadership most of the remaining problems associated with the dismemberment of the British Empire were finally resolved. Having fought off Guatemala's repeated claims to territorial sovereignty over the former British Honduras, Belize finally achieved independence in September 1981. In 1984, an agreement was also reached with China to return Hong Kong at the end of its 99-year lease in July 1997 on unexpectedly favourable terms which safeguarded the colony's economic autonomy under China's 'one country, two systems' formula. The first and most pressing problem for the Thatcher government in May 1979, however, concerned the fate of Southern Rhodesia, which had been a continual irritant and embarrassment to successive British governments since Ian Smith's white minority government declared UDI in November 1965. Despite Wilson's talks with the Rhodesian Prime Minister aboard HMS *Tiger* in December 1966 and HMS *Fearless* in October 1968, there was no hope of a diplomatic solution even on the understanding that the black population would not command a political majority for 30 or 35 years. Confronted by this impasse, and in the absence of a viable alternative, the Wilson, Heath and Callaghan governments publicly supported the diplomatic isolation of Rhodesia, while half-heartedly orchestrating an ineffectual international campaign of economic sanctions which was widely violated (even by British companies) with South African connivance.

It is ironic that Margaret Thatcher's government should have presided over the end of white minority rule in both Rhodesia and South Africa. According to her loyal press secretary, Thatcher 'hated apartheid', but her private sympathies were instinctively aligned with the right of her party in support of white supremacist regimes in Southern Africa (Ingham 1991: 276). When she became Prime Minister, however, Lord Carrington, her first and much-respected Foreign Secretary, persuaded her to insist upon the inclusion of Robert Mugabe and Joshua Nkomo as representatives of the Patriotic Front in talks to find a final settlement to the guerrilla war gripping the country. The resulting Lancaster House Agreement on 21 December 1979 established a framework for Rhodesia's peaceful transition to full independence as Zimbabwe under black majority rule. Although the victory of Robert Mugabe's ZANU (PF) party at the ensuing election came as an unwelcome surprise to the Thatcher government, this effectively resolved the Rhodesia issue for two decades.

In the spring of 2000, Zimbabwe again rose to the top of the international agenda when Robert Mugabe gave his prime ministerial support to the illegal occupation of white-owned farms by so-called 'war veterans'. This development set what had previously been one of the richest countries in Africa on a path towards violence, rampant inflation, bankruptcy and economic collapse. In response to this illegal expropriation, the Blair government denounced Mugabe's ruinous leadership with increasing vigour, while applying financial and trade sanctions against the regime in order to isolate it from the international community – albeit that the extremely heavy moral pressure on the England cricket team to boycott a World Cup match to be held in Zimbabwe in January–February 2003 was not accompanied by any real attempt to prohibit over 300 British companies from trading with the regime (*Guardian*, 23 January 2003). Given the belief that Britain's colonial past excluded it from leadership on the issue, however, the Blair government accepted that the burden should fall on African shoulders. Despite concerted pressure from Whitehall after a rigged ballot and widespread intimidation during the 2008 elections, however, Thabo Mbeki, the South African president, and other African leaders refused to condemn one of the heroes of the African independence struggle. Impotent to do anything else, all Britain could do was to abandon the last vestiges of a softly-softly approach by accusing Mugabe of 'beating his own people to death' while stiffening its calls for an international boycott of the regime (*Guardian*, 22 April 2008).

While the Lancaster House Agreement marked the formal end of Britain's imperial role in Southern Africa, it still remained heavily engaged in the Republic of South Africa. South Africa left the Commonwealth in 1961, but a strong economic and familial relationship continued to exist with its 800,000 residents who claimed British citizenship. Labour governments during the 1970s did not sever these links but they were allowed to wither until Thatcher joined Reagan in emphasising the need for 'constructive engagement' with the South African regime. To this end, she was the first Prime Minister in 23 years to welcome a South African head of state to Britain in June 1984. Thatcher's discussions with P.W. Botha were reported to be 'firm and forthright', but the fact remains this meeting enhanced the international status of a pariah state and undermined international attempts to isolate it. She also consistently and vigorously opposed the imposition of sanctions against South Africa. In public this was justified by claims that South Africa was being unfairly singled out when other repressive regimes like Uganda were not subject to sanctions. Anyway, Thatcher argued, such measures would harm not only British companies but also the black population they were intended to help. But underlying this rhetoric was a strong Anglo-American conviction that South Africa was far too valuable an asset to risk falling under Soviet influence by allowing the emergence of an ANC (African National Congress) government which she considered to be not only 'a terrorist organisation' but also dangerously 'socialist' in inclination. Although her high-handed opposition to sanctions was characteristic of her disdain for gesture politics, it also reflected an inability to appreciate the need for symbolic action and it left Britain isolated within the Commonwealth, the EU and the international community as a whole (see p. 69 below).

Fighting for the Falklands

With Zimbabwe independent, by the beginning of the 1980s it appeared as if Britain had finally discharged the last of its imperial responsibilities. Such calculations reckoned without the Falklands crisis. In 1982, the Falklands archipelago consisted of over 100 windswept islands, barely 20 miles of paved roads, 1849 inhabitants and an abundance of the sheep which for decades had been the principal export. The island's economy, revenues and population were also in unremitting decline, largely because the conflicting Anglo-Argentine claims to sovereignty over the islands inhibited their full development (Little 1988: 144; Cmnd 8787 1983). In reality, neither country possessed an unassailable legal claim to the Falklands Islands but the overriding political reality was that the islanders (95 per cent of British descent) had an unshakable determination to remain a British territory and these preferences were vigorously supported by a well-organised cross-party parliamentary lobby (Freedman 1988: 17–20).

From the FCO perspective, the needs of a few islanders 8000 miles away never ranked very highly on its list of priorities and if the islands had been uninhabited in 1982 it is almost certain that Britain would have made no attempt to hold on to them in face of the strong national sentiment evoked by the 'Malvinas' issue in Argentina. Indeed, the idea of condominium or the transfer of sovereignty to Argentina with some sort of 'leaseback' to Britain had been under consideration since 1966 and it had been revived as recently as November 1980 by Nicholas Ridley, Thatcher's junior Foreign Office minister responsible for the issue. On each occasion, however, the proposal had been decisively thwarted by the adamantine opposition of the islanders and their supporters at Westminster who suspected the FCO of wishing to sell them out (see Freedman 1988: ch. 2; Dillon 1989: 1–8).

The threat of force always lurked behind Argentina's diplomatic negotiations. Yet when the Joint Intelligence Committee (JIC) warned in July 1981 that Argentine suspicions that Britain was no longer serious about the transfer of sovereignty might prompt 'more forcible measures . . . swiftly and without warning', Whitehall succumbed to a collective sense of denial in which it gave credence only to information which conformed with its own preference for a diplomatic solution while ignoring intelligence which conflicted with this position (Boyce 2005: 19). As a result, the Thatcher government only became convinced about the threat of invasion two days before it actually happened – by which time it was far too late to do anything to save a colony the naval task force would take at least three weeks to reach.

In most respects, the Falklands invasion was a crisis of the Thatcher government's own making. The low priority placed on the islands, and the contradictions within its own policy, prompted the Argentines to draw the misguided conclusion that Britain would not take firm action in the event of an invasion. Undoubtedly, the most important negative signal in this respect was the decision to scrap the ice patrol ship HMS *Endurance* as part of John Nott's Defence Review published in June 1981 – despite the fact that it had previously been kept on station in the South Atlantic as a symbolic statement of commitment designed to deter Argentine aggression (see Chapter 6). This misleading message was further reinforced by the British Nationality Act of 1981, which deprived the Falkland Islanders of full patrial status. Again, therefore, the message appeared to be that Britain did not regard the Falklands as a major interest for which it would fight.

This disastrous sequence of events and misapprehensions prompted the beleaguered Argentine military dictatorship under General Leopoldo Galtieri to invade South Georgia and then the Falklands in April 1982. Thatcher was clearly shaken by this sudden turn of events and the spectre of the Suez debacle haunted ministers, but for the Prime Minister the fundamental issue was unequivocal: 'We were defending our honour as a nation, and principles of fundamental importance to the whole world – above all, that aggressors, should never succeed and international law should prevail over the use of force' (Thatcher 1993: 173). A large makeshift naval task force of over 100 ships carrying 15 squadrons of naval aircraft and over 10,000 troops was rapidly dispatched to the South Atlantic. After six weeks of heavy fighting during which almost 1000 men died – 255 of them British – the Argentine garrison in Port Stanley surrendered on 15 June 1982. The margin between victory and failure was perilously narrow, with the task force operating at the extreme limit of its capability and with winter imminent in the South Atlantic. Nevertheless, soon after recapturing the Falklands, Thatcher declared triumphantly in her best Boudica style: 'We have ceased to be a nation in retreat. . . . Britain found herself again in the South Atlantic and will not look back from the victory she has won' (Thatcher 1993: 235).

Contrary to these confident assurances, military victory did not resolve the underlying diplomatic problem; it merely deferred and complicated the search for a mutually acceptable solution. As Walter Little concluded eight years after the conflict, the problem was that 'the British were prepared to discuss everything except the one thing that Argentina wanted. Argentina, for its part, was interested primarily in discussing the one thing that the British had declared they could not discuss' (Little 1988: 142). Worse still, the conflict created new problems of its own. Above all, Whitehall's previously weary indifference and desire for compromise was transformed overnight into an unshakeable commitment to defend 'Fortress Falklands' against future Argentine aggression at any cost. This once isolated vestige of empire was thus rapidly transformed into Britain's largest overseas garrison and, unlike Hong Kong and Brunei, none of the costs were met by the host country. The short-term cost of the military campaign and the replacement of lost vessels and equipment is now estimated at around £2 billion. Over the next five years, some £3.01 billion was spent and the official estimates of annual garrison costs from 1988 onwards amounted to around £100 million per year. Or, to put it another way, by 1990 the total cost had reached £3.5 billion – a figure which equates to an almost unbelievable £2 million per islander to preserve British control over what Denis Thatcher memorably declared to be 'miles and miles of bugger all' (J. Campbell 2008: 153).

Almost 30 years after the conflict, Argentina and Britain still remain at loggerheads over the future of the islands and this antagonism periodically boils towards a crisis. Britain has repeatedly sought to reduce the state of tension by proposing a formal end to hostilities and the normalisation of diplomatic relations, but these efforts have been driven as much by self-interest as by any desire for a settlement – not least because the need to maintain a high state of alert to fend off even minor Argentine sorties in the unforeseeable future is an extremely expensive burden on the defender. The territorial adjustments Britain has offered in the South Atlantic are also as much for its own benefit as they are concessions to Argentina. For example, the replacement of the 200-mile exclusion zone around the islands with a 150-mile protection zone reflected Britain's logistical need to reduce the size of the area to be patrolled. Similarly, Britain's offer to reduce the size of its garrison as a contribution to the demilitarisation of the region in return for Argentina's formal declaration of the end of hostilities was prompted by the same desire to reduce troop numbers and expenditure. The vulnerability of Britain's long-term position in the South Atlantic helps to explain Argentina's refusal to negotiate a formal ending of hostilities given the belief that the cost of defence alone will eventually force the British back to the negotiating table.

While future Argentine intentions are unclear, what is absolutely certain is that the issue will not simply disappear. On the contrary, the Falkland Island economy has boomed since the war, its population has almost doubled and its annual government revenue has jumped from under £5 million in 1982 to around £45 million today, largely as a result of the income from commercial fishing licences. This new prosperity has produced a per capita income higher than that of the UK while substantially reinforcing the intransigence of the islanders towards Argentina. Conversely, from the Argentine perspective, the future of the Malvinas remains a high salience issue in domestic politics; a fact demonstrated in March 2007 by the Argentine repudiation of its September 1995 joint declaration concerning cooperation on the exploitation of oil and mineral resources around the Falkland Islands on the grounds that this was 'an instrument the UK sought to use to justify its illegitimate and unilateral actions to explore for resources that belong to the Argentine citizens'. Although little had actually been achieved under this joint declaration, this symbolic gesture was rightly perceived by the Islanders as part of a concerted campaign of 'economic warfare' designed to wreck the local economy by refusing to cooperate over fisheries management or oil and gas extraction while damaging the cruise ship trade by severing the air link between the Falklands and Chile (*Guardian*, 29 March 2007; 15 June 2009). For this reason, when President Christina Kirchner reasserted Argentina's claim during her election campaign in March 2009, Gordon Brown was obliged to reaffirm the 'essential principle' that the 'needs and wishes of the islanders' remained paramount (*Guardian*, 28 March 2009).

Tensions with Argentina have been further aggravated by Britain's response to the UN Commission on the Limits of the Continental Shelf

(UNCLCS). This will permit the extension of rights to extract oil, gas and minerals up to 350 miles beyond a country's coastline if it can demonstrate that this is a 'prolongation' of an adjoining continental shelf. In September 2007, it became clear that Britain was preparing to lodge a territorial claim with the UNCLCS covering over one million square kilometres (396,000 square miles) of the Atlantic seabed around the Falklands, Ascension Island and Rockall in the hope of annexing their surrounding lucrative gas, mineral and oilfields. This curious scramble for territory angered the Danish, Irish and Icelandic governments with regard to British claims regarding Rockall around which minerals and hydrocarbons have been the subject of a diplomatic dispute since 2001. But far more important are the implications of Britain's claims in the South Atlantic, where its proposed exclusive economic zone would extend well into the Southern Ocean in defiance of the 1959 Antarctic Treaty designed to prevent territorial disputes in the area and in direct conflict with the claims of Argentina and Chile. While Britain invited 'technical and legal' discussions on the issue with these countries, Argentina subsequently lodged a hostile counterclaim to 660,000 square miles of the South Atlantic seabed to overturn what it called 'the illegitimate British occupation of the Southern archipelagos'. As the FCO then presented a rival submission, the outcome has been to prevent either country from exploring the seabed beyond its existing territorial waters. (*Guardian*, 19 October 2007; 28 August 2008; 24 April 2009). The intransigence on both sides has been reinforced by estimates that there are 18 billion barrels of oil in the waters around the Falklands.

Britain and the Commonwealth of Nations

A central objective of British policy throughout the process of decolonisation was the desire to convert former colonies into prosperous self-sufficient members of a British Commonwealth capable of enhancing 'the Mother Country's' diplomatic weight on the world stage. In order to achieve this goal, it was prepared to make considerable concessions to enable the organisation to adapt itself to changing needs and circumstances. In the late 1940s, India's decision to become a member of the Commonwealth as a republic set a precedent and today a majority of its members are republics. In the late 1950s, the debate over the Gold Coast's demand for Dominion status forced a recognition that if its application was denied there would be little chance of attracting the rest of Africa into the Commonwealth, while discussions about membership for Cyprus in 1960–1 ended with agreement on the admission of smaller states, and these now also account for over half the total membership. London's rejection of a two-tier Commonwealth of 'old' (mainly white) and 'new' (mainly Asian or African) members was based on a similar desire to make Commonwealth membership easy and attractive in order to bolster the influence of this supposed surrogate empire (McIntyre 1998: chs 12–13).

By transforming the dependent empire into independent members of the Commonwealth, Britain also hoped to retain great influence over the post-colonial states they had helped to construct. The final phases of British rule were thus often geared towards ensuring the emerging states would be useful and stable partners who would naturally turn to Britain for trade, capital, technical assistance, defence, aid and diplomatic leadership. Such hopes were soon brutally disappointed – in part because increasing economic difficulties at home meant that Britain had less to offer in economic aid than its rivals. But there was also an increasingly obvious divergence of interest and view between Britain and its former colonies which made closer relations a source of mutual embarrassment (Darwin 1988: 302). The Suez crisis in 1956 shook the Commonwealth to its foundations and exposed a profound lack of deference towards the 'Mother Country' that culminated in 1962 with the formation of the Non-Aligned Movement led by Nkrumah and Nehru, to which half of the Commonwealth now belongs. After this, it became increasingly evident that this almost meaningless consultative association existed only to provide a forum for former colonies to express their intense disapproval of Britain's foreign policy while at the same time importuning special concessions from its overseas aid budget.

This gulf was increased by continued conflict over British policy and investments in South Africa after the introduction of apartheid in 1948, the half-hearted response to the Rhodesia problem after UDI in 1965, the introduction of two Commonwealth Immigration Acts in 1965 and 1968, which severely restricted the entry of 'new Commonwealth' citizens to Britain, and the decline of the Overseas Sterling Area as an international monetary arrangement. In this respect, Margaret Thatcher's premiership signalled a new nadir in Britain's relationship with the Commonwealth. Initially, Thatcher won favour at the Lusaka summit in 1979 by somewhat surprisingly recognising the legitimacy of the Patriotic Front's claim to be represented at the Rhodesian peace settlement. After the removal of Lord Carrington's moderating influence in April 1982, however, she appeared increasingly unsympathetic to, and detached from, an organisation she regarded 'with a mixture of puzzlement and contempt' (Porter 1996: 364). Above all, her vigorous opposition to the imposition of sanctions against South Africa after 1985 left Britain completely isolated within the international community and, as Sir Percy Cradock recalled, having been cast as the villain of the piece it was 'a part she played, or overplayed, with relish' (Cradock 1997 153). Relations reached their lowest ebb at the mini-summit on sanctions in 1986, where she broke decisively with the consensus and remained intractable throughout the rest of her premiership, declaring in Kuala Lumpur in 1989: 'If it is forty-eight against one, I'm sorry for the forty-eight.' The new atmosphere created by the fall of Thatcher and the collapse of apartheid in South Africa has arguably led to 'a rediscovery of the Commonwealth in Britain' in a 'post-Britannic' form (McIntyre 1999: 693, 700). But it is equally plausible to suggest that the significance of the Commonwealth today can be characterised as purely sentimental – and of more relevance to the departmental affairs of the Minister of Culture, Media and Sport than those of the Foreign Secretary.

Britain and European decolonisation: a comparative perspective

Within a period of only 30 years, the once vast British Empire was reduced from a population of 700 million in 1945 to less than five million – and over four million of those were in Hong Kong. By the late 1970s, all that remained were just a few island 'limpet colonies' like Pitcairn Island, Tristan da Cunha, St Helena and Ascension Island possessing tiny populations and even less political and economic significance (see Map 3.3). The pattern of British decolonisation does not represent a seamless incremental process of gradual transition from Empire to Commonwealth which began with India in 1947 and ended with the return of Hong Kong to China exactly 50 years later. Rather, the retreat from empire is best considered in terms of 'two great convulsive movements, one centred in Asia in 1945–48, the other in Africa between 1960 and 1964' (Darwin 1988: 334). Equally clearly, the motivations and forces varied considerably from one phase to another and from one colony to another. In the case of India and Palestine, Britain had very little choice in the matter of timing and the Attlee government's solution to the Indian problem was essentially 'the art of the possible writ large' (Owen 1991: 168). When the Macmillan government decided that decolonisation was the best course, however, the process was consciously planned and astonishingly rapid. Twenty colonies achieved independence between January 1957 and the Conservative election defeat in October 1964. After this, British withdrawal became an avalanche as another 35 states acquired independence from a Britain anxious to free itself from the imperial legacy –

Map 3.3 Remnants of the British Empire, 1997

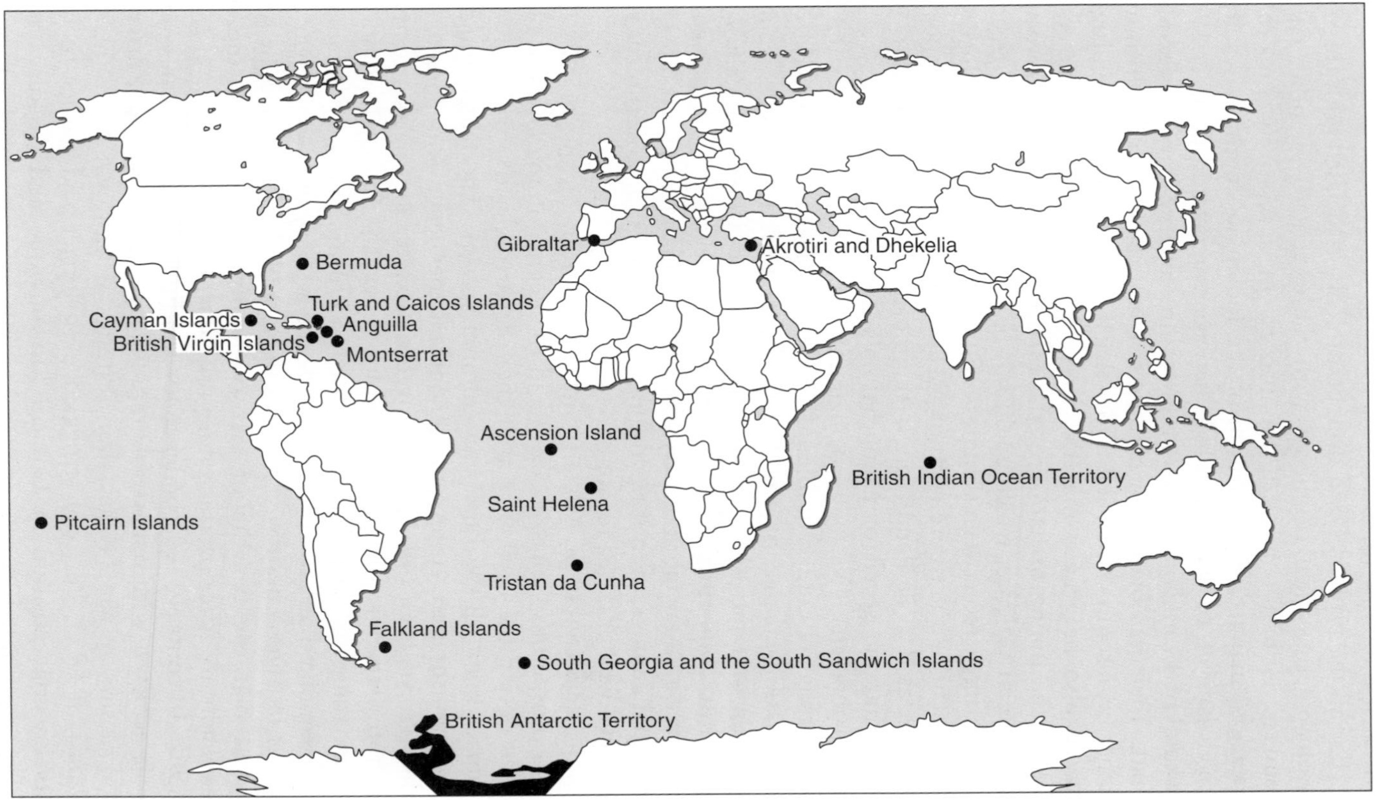

even if this meant creating new states dependent on British overseas aid for their economic survival.

For all the problems and disappointments associated with the retreat from empire, when compared with the experience of other colonial powers, Britain conducted the process in a relatively smooth and peaceful manner. The partition of the Indian subcontinent resulted in the loss of at least a million lives between August and October 1947 as a total of 13 million Hindus and Muslims engaged in a mass exodus to make their way back to their respective homelands – and British scuttle must bear some responsibility for that tragedy. But, with hindsight, it could also be argued that the colonial power had little choice over either the timing or nature of the final outcome given the ferocity of communal violence, which could not be controlled, and the irreconcilable differences between Congress and the Muslim League, which made agreement on the future form of government and statehood impossible. Indeed, as Rob Holland argues, 'the most balanced judgement is probably that the speed of Mountbatten's decolonisation exercise saved, rather than cost, lives by recognizing the partition momentum and foreshortening its course' (Holland 1985: 84). Despite the brutality and devastation created by the Nigerian civil war, Idi Amin's regime in Uganda and the more recent catastrophe of Robert Mugabe's later years in Zimbabwe, the fact remains the transfer of power was achieved in a far more orderly and peaceful manner than in most other colonial empires, even if the trappings of democratic government rarely worked well or lasted for long.

The suddenness of Belgian withdrawal from the previously stable and prosperous Congo in 1959 and the degree of anarchy and bloodshed during the Civil War after their departure had a truly traumatic impact upon all the European colonial powers. The Dutch fought to re-establish their Asian empire but independence was forced upon them in August 1949. France proved more tenacious in its attempts to restore imperial control but, despite heavy US financial support, its bitter campaign in Indo-China ended in crushing military humiliation at Dien Bien Phu in May 1954, while the ferocity of its eight-year campaign in Algeria destroyed the Fourth Republic before de Gaulle recognised that the benefits of victory simply did not merit the huge expenditure. After protracted negotiations, France withdrew in March 1962. In contrast, independence for the French West African colonies was achieved with remarkable rapidity by the end of 1960, driven by the desire to win favour after Britain's withdrawal from the Gold Coast in 1957. Portugal struggled even longer and harder to retain its imperial position in Guinea, Mozambique and Angola but the effort devastated its economy and eventually precipitated a successful military coup which destroyed the dictatorship of President Salazar in April 1974.

Britain avoided these catastrophic consequences. Yet, as John Darwin rightly points out, had more of its colonies been in the position of Gibraltar or the Falklands, threatened by greedy annexationist neighbours, the entire history of Britain's retreat from empire 'might have been very different – more painful, and much more controversial' (Darwin 1988: 314). Even in the relatively favourable circumstances in which it found itself, there can be little doubt that Britain often clung to imperial responsibilities long after the diplomatic, military and material resources to maintain them had been undermined. Nevertheless, the final steps in the retreat from empire opened the way for Britain to pursue its destiny and security within a European context for the first time in centuries. When it did so, as Chapter 5 demonstrates, the sentimental bonds of Commonwealth and a shared kinship and heritage did little to shield former Dominions and colonies from the loss of once-guaranteed British markets.

Chapter 4

Britain, the Atlantic Alliance and the 'Special Relationship'

In his famous 'Iron Curtain' speech at Fulton, Missouri, on 5 March 1946, Churchill conjured up the captivating vision of a 'special relationship' between the British Commonwealth and the United States founded upon the 'fraternal association of the English-speaking peoples'. Ever since, this beguiling idea has been the subject of such fierce controversy that many argue it can now 'hardly appear in public unless wrapped in inverted commas and accompanied by a question mark' (Ashton 2002a: 6). It has survived in spite of much research, which suggests that even at its wartime zenith this was an 'ambiguous partnership' (Hathaway 1981) between 'allies of a kind' (Thorne 1978) and even greater evidence that in recent years it is 'special no more' (Dickie 1994). Yet, notwithstanding the frequency with which the 'special relationship' has been consigned to the dustbin of history, the concept continues to display what one recent analysis has described as 'something of a Lazarus quality'(Marsh and Baylis 2006: 174). We are left, therefore, with an enigmatic concept which has rightly been characterised as 'natural, and easy, ambiguous, ambivalent, sweet and sour' (Edmonds 1986: 6).

Wartime cooperation and conflict

Although Anglo-American relations oscillated violently between the wars, Churchill's emergence as Prime Minister in May 1940 inaugurated a period during which there was 'a much higher degree of co-operation and unforced fusion than had ever before existed between two sovereign states' (Nicholas 1975: 101). Indeed, the entire notion of an Anglo-American 'special relationship' supposedly reached its apogee in the close personal relationship between Churchill and Roosevelt during 1940 to 1945, and the publication of Churchill's carefully sanitised war memoirs between 1948 and 1954 translated this rather rosy version of history into a powerful unifying myth just as the Cold War reached its peak. For Churchill, this relationship was a real living entity rooted in a shared kinship, history, culture and commitment to democratic institutions. As he put it on Christmas Eve 1941 from the balcony of the White House, Britain and America were united by 'the common cause of great people who speak the same language, who kneel at the same altars, and, to a very large extent, pursue the same ideals' (Stoler 2007: 55). The two peoples must stand together, he told a Harvard audience in September 1943, because they were 'united by other ties besides those of State policy and public need. To a large extent, they are the ties of blood and history' (Meacham 2003: 238–9).

Churchill had every reason to be grateful for Roosevelt's crucial assistance long before America formally entered the war in December 1941. The amendment of the Neutrality Act to a 'cash and carry' basis in November 1939 favoured Britain and France with their larger foreign reserves and merchant fleets. After the German invasion of France, Roosevelt urged Congress not to hamper aircraft deliveries to the Allies. In September 1940 he agreed to train British aircrew in the United States and secret staff talks in Washington early in 1941 laid the foundations for a close and enduring intelligence relationship. In response to Churchill's warning in December 1940 that Britain was bankrupt and unable to continue the war long into 1941, Roosevelt forced the Lend-Lease Act through Congress in March 1941, which enabled the President to provide whatever assistance he felt necessary to assist the fight against Germany. By July 1941, the 'destroyers for bases' deal gave Washington 99-year leases on eight Western Hemisphere bases in exchange for some First World War destroyers which though of little practical value were of massive symbolic significance. Finally, Roosevelt skilfully exploited the carefully contrived German U-boat attack on the USS *Greer* in September 1941 as a pretext to engage the US Navy in the protection of British convoys well into the mid-Atlantic. As a result, therefore, the United States was effectively engaged in an undeclared naval conflict on the North Atlantic some months before it formally entered the war in December 1941.

Evidence of Anglo-American wartime cooperation should not obscure the fact that Britain paid a high price for this aid. The 'destroyers for bases' deal was accompanied by such hard bargaining that former Prime Minister Lloyd George denounced the Americans as 'gangsters'. According to Churchill, Lend-Lease was America's 'most unsordid act' but it was accompanied by a range of severe restrictions on British trade, finance and commerce which conferred a massive competitive advantage on the United States. Moreover, even at its apogee, this relationship was marked by some bitter disputes over policy. At the Atlantic conference in August 1941, sharp differences emerged between

Churchill and Roosevelt over post-war territorial arrangements, the future of Britain's imperial preference system and its colonial empire. These disagreements became even greater after America's entry into the war – particularly with regard to the remorseless US pursuit of advantage in Latin American trade, Middle Eastern oil and the shape of the post-war financial order enshrined in the Bretton Woods Accords in 1944; an agreement whose non-preferential multilateralism to the benefit of the United States was regarded by British negotiators as hypocritically self-interested and profoundly damaging to an economically exhausted ally in need of protected markets to avoid economic ruin. There were equally sharp disputes over military strategy regarding the priority to be accorded to Japan, conduct of the Italian campaign, strategic bombing, the Second Front and what became Operation OVERLORD for the invasion of Europe in the spring of 1944. Indeed, so bitter were these disputes that after the Casablanca conference in January 1943, Eisenhower angrily observed: 'one of the constant sources of danger in this war is the temptation to regard as our first enemy the partner that we must work with in defeating the real enemy' (Stoler 2007: 21, 91, 168). As Christopher Thorne warns, 'the fact that the relationship between the UK and America . . . was at times a remarkably close one can be established without the need to wander off however well-meaningly into mythology' (Thorne 1978: 725).

Among the fiercest Anglo-American disagreements were those engendered by conflicting views of Stalin and Soviet ambitions in Eastern Europe. Even after the Yalta conference in April 1945, Roosevelt seriously misjudged the threat from Soviet expansionism in his desire to establish good relations with the rising superpower. To conciliate Stalin, both Roosevelt and Truman were prepared to alienate and ignore Churchill and the declining imperial power he represented. In May 1943, Roosevelt deliberately deceived Churchill about his secret plans to meet Stalin without him. Churchill was aware of the deception and resented being sidelined. It rankled even more when the 'Big Three' met at Tehran in November 1943 and Churchill found himself being marginalised over policy, while he fumed angrily when Roosevelt joined Stalin in taunting him over his resistance to Operation OVERLORD to convince 'Uncle Joe' that no Anglo-American front existed in opposition to the Soviets (Meacham 2003: 226). This was all the more frustrating because by now Churchill identified Soviet expansionism as the real threat for the future, and he simply could not understand why the President did not recognise either the nature of that threat or the need for concerted Anglo-American strategy to counter it. 'I realised at Tehran for the first time what a small nation we are', he noted dismally. 'There I sat with the great Russian bear on one side of me, with paws outstretched, and on the other side the great American Buffalo, and between the two sat the poor little English donkey who was the only one . . . who knew the right way home' (Stoler 2007: 142). To avoid the appearance of 'ganging up' on Stalin, there was no preliminary coordination of Anglo-American policy at the Yalta conference in February 1945 or with President Truman at the final meeting of the 'Big Three' at Potsdam in July 1945.

Ernest Bevin and the policy of containment

When Ernest Bevin became Foreign Secretary in July 1945, Anglo-American relations were already cooling rapidly. Truman's cancellation of Lend-Lease only six days after the Japanese surrender was a bitter blow for an already economically devastated Britain. Equally disillusioning were the three months of tough bargaining in Washington during the last months of 1945 to obtain an American loan to fund Britain's post-war reconstruction. Lord Keynes, the British negotiator, rather naively expected to be offered $5,000 million in the form of a grant-in-aid or an interest-free loan in recognition of America's moral obligation to a country which had fought on alone for two years. Instead, Keynes's 'Justice gambit' provoked much acrimonious dispute before he settled on $3,750 million (£930 million) at an annual rate of 2 per cent; terms sufficiently onerous for several angry ministers to propose rejection until warned of the potentially disastrous consequences for Anglo-American relations. To make matters worse, the loan agreement signed in Washington on 6 December committed Britain to fundamental changes to its foreign economic policies to the benefit of United States – not least by making an overvalued sterling freely convertible with other currencies within a year; to eliminate imperial preference because it discriminated against US trade; and to abolish the Overseas Sterling Area. These draconian terms represented a major triumph for US self-interest wholly disadvantageous to an ally that it still perceived to be a dangerous competitor in the post-war world (Dobson 1988: 87). Equally disappointing, the McMahon Act in August 1946 unilaterally renounced the US pledge to share its atomic secrets despite assurances of post-war collaboration from both Roosevelt and Truman (see Chapter 7). As Bevin noted bitterly in March 1947, Washington had 'given us a pretty raw deal' (Pelling 1984: 124).

These alarming indications of a return to US isolationism were soon abruptly overtaken by the onset of the Cold War. Stalin's apparent duplicity and obstructionism during the Soviet–US meetings in Moscow in December 1945 finally convinced Truman that it was time to stop

Table 4.1   Outline chronology – Anglo-American relations
since 1945

August 1945	Japan surrenders; Truman administration ends Lend-Lease
December 1945	Britain secures US loan of $3750 million
August 1946	McMahon Act prohibits disclosure of nuclear secrets to any foreign power
September 1946	Montgomery and US Joint Chiefs of Staff lay foundations of military agreement
February–March 1947	British warning of withdrawal from eastern Mediterranean prompts declaration of the 'Truman Doctrine'
June 1947	Marshall Plan for European recovery announced
March 1948	Brussels Treaty signed
June 1948	Soviets begin Berlin Blockade
July 1948	US B-29 bombers return to Britain
April 1949	North Atlantic Treaty signed in Washington
July 1950	British brigade deployed in Korea under US command
April 1952	NATO formed
Oct-Nov 1956	Anglo-French invasion of Suez Canal
March 1957	Macmillan meets Eisenhower at Bermuda to restore relations after Suez
October 1957	Soviet launch of Sputnik prompts Eisenhower to reaffirm mutual interdependence and indicates amendment of McMahon
July 1958	Anglo-American invasion of Jordan and Lebanon
March 1960	Macmillan negotiates purchase of Skybolt
November 1962	Skybolt cancelled by the US Defense Department
December 1962	Macmillan's Nassau meeting with Kennedy obtains Polaris as replacement for Skybolt

Table 4.1   Outline chronology – Anglo-American relations
since 1945 – *continued*

March– Sept 1965	Wilson and Callaghan negotiate deal with Johnson administration for US support for Sterling in return for a continued British presence 'East of Suez'
July 1967	Britain announces withdrawal from 'East of Suez' by mid-1970s
January 1968	Timetable for withdrawal from East of Suez advanced to the end of 1971
January 1979	US indicates Britain can purchase Trident
July 1980	Thatcher agrees to purchase Trident I (C4)
March 1982	Thatcher agrees to purchase Trident II (D5)
Apr–June 1982	Falklands War; US supplies British task force with crucial intelligence and military equipment
June 1982	Reagan imposes sanctions on European companies supplying the Siberian gas pipeline project
October 1983	US invades Grenada
January 1984	Cruise missiles deployed in UK
February 1984	Thatcher's visit to Moscow opens new phase in East-West relations
April 1986	US planes attack Libya from British bases
Jan–Feb. 1991	Gulf War to liberate Kuwait after Iraqi invasion in August 1990
December 1998	Britain supports air bombardment of Iraqi installations in Baghdad
September 2001	9/11 Al Qaida attacks on the US; Blair leads European declarations of support
Oct–Nov 2001	War in Afghanistan deposes the Taliban government
March 2003	War begins in Iraq to depose Saddam Hussein
February 2007	Britain joins US anti-ballistic defence system in Europe
December 2007	British troops hand over to Iraqi forces in Basra

'babying the Soviets'. But equally important, American attitudes were transformed by Bevin's diplomatic prowess. In March 1944 a Foreign Office memorandum on 'The Essentials of an American Policy' had unashamedly espoused the need for Britain to employ what were perceived to be its superior diplomatic skills to 'make use of American power for purposes which we regard as good' (Edmonds 1986: 21). This logic was central to Bevin's foreign policy from the outset as he sought to entangle the United States permanently in European defence against the Soviet threat.

Like Churchill, Bevin regarded the Atlantic alliance as by far the most important of Britain's external relationships. But for him, this conviction was based upon a hard-headed realpolitik recognition of the broad congruence of view between two democratic countries with similar foreign policy interests – not least, the 'containment' of Soviet influence through a combination of military strength and the restoration of European economic prosperity. To this end, Bevin set out to 'educate Washington' to what he saw as the reality of the Soviet threat and Europe's inability to contain it without active US support. By 1949, he had achieved both of these objectives with consummate skill and effectively closed the door on the very real possibility of Soviet expansion in Western Europe. As such, Ernest Bevin must be regarded as the real architect of the Western alliance and the US commitment to a policy of 'containment'.

In the midst of the severe economic crisis in February 1947, the Cabinet decided that Britain must withdraw from its commitments in the eastern Mediterranean by the end of March. As Greece was in the grips of a civil war with local communists, and Turkey and Iran were threatened by Soviet subversion, Britain's withdrawal represented a critical threat at a time when many believed in a 'domino theory' of communist expansion via Turkey and Iran into much of the Near and Middle East and potentially capable of infecting even France and Italy. Some debate remains as to whether the Foreign Office note on 21 February 1947 informing Washington of this decision was an inspired diplomatic gambit, cunningly designed to force the Americans to accept an expensive new responsibility in the eastern Mediterranean, or whether it was the product of a desperate domestic need to cut public expenditure, but the fact remains that this action compelled the US to jettison its isolationist tendencies and accept an active role in the defence of Western Europe; a recognition enshrined publicly on 12 March 1947 in the 'Truman doctrine', which declared that the United States was prepared to support all free peoples seeking to resist communism whether from external pressure or internal subversion.

But there was far more to Bevin's strategy than simply abdicating Britain's existing overseas responsibilities. He also pursued a two-pronged strategy to convince Washington that Europe was cooperating in its own defence – but was still manifestly unequal to the Soviet threat without direct US involvement. In diplomatic terms this led, via the Anglo-French Treaty of Dunkirk in March 1947 (an explicitly anti-German mutual assistance pact), to the Brussels Treaty in March 1948 in which the Benelux countries joined Britain and France to form an overtly anti-Soviet pact that evolved into the Western European Union in 1954 (Baylis 1982; S. Greenwood 1983). Having created this edifice, Bevin skilfully exploited increasing evidence of the Soviet menace to complete his strategy. In particular, the Soviet blockade of the Western sectors in Berlin between June 1948 and May 1949 and the ensuing Anglo-American airlift of over 200,000 flights carrying 1.5 million tons of supplies into the besieged city did much to restore the wartime intimacy of the alliance by reinforcing Britain's status as Washington's staunchest and most valuable ally. A month after the blockade ended, the first USAF B-29 Super-Fortress bombers returned to Britain – armed with a nuclear capability from 1949. These developments all added weight to Bevin's pressure on Washington regarding the need for a broader Atlantic security system; proposals which culminated in the North Atlantic Treaty in April 1949 and the formation of NATO in which the US joined Britain and 10 other states in the first peacetime military alliance in its history (Baylis 1984: 60–1).

The second prong of Bevin's strategy for embroiling the United States in European affairs was economic in nature. Already confronted with what Keynes described as a 'financial Dunkirk', the winter of 1946–47 was the worst since 1880–81 and it brought Britain and much of Western Europe to a complete standstill. Forced to recognise that Europe was so economically devastated that it could not provide an effective bulwark against communist expansion, the crisis prompted the US offer of Marshall Aid on 5 June 1947 to help finance the continent's economic recovery. As General Lucius Clay, the US commander in Germany, encapsulated the underlying logic, 'there is no choice between becoming a Communist on 1500 calories and a believer in democracy on 1000 calories a day' (Reynolds 1991: 174). The day after Marshall's speech, Bevin took the lead in the creation of what became the Organisation for European Economic Co-operation (OEEC) established to administer the $14 billion Marshall Aid programme donated by the US between 1947 and 1951, of which Britain obtained the largest share with $2.7 billion. In many respects, this was Bevin's 'finest hour' (Morgan 1984: 270).

These achievements were not without their complications for post-war Britain. The FO paper on 'The Essentials of an American Policy' in March 1944 had talked confidently of harnessing US power to serve

British ends: 'If we go about our business in the right way we can help steer the great unwieldy barge, the United States of America, into the right harbour. If we don't it is likely to continue to wallow in the ocean, an isolated menace to navigation' (Marsh and Baylis 2006: 177). This commitment to what David Reynolds calls 'the policy of power by proxy' became a central article of faith in British official circles after 1945 (Reynolds 1991: 178). But, as Bevin recognised in September 1947, to exercise real influence 'we must free ourselves of financial dependence on the United States of America as soon as possible. We shall never be able to pull our weight in foreign affairs until we do so' (Greenwood 2002: 212). The Permanent Under-Secretary's Committee (PUSC) arrived at similar conclusions in its 1949 report on the basis of British foreign policy, and when endorsing its report the Cabinet also noted that while '[t]he interests of the United Kingdom ... demand that the present policy of close Anglo-American cooperation in world affairs should continue such co-operation will involve our sustained political, military and economic effort' (Ovendale 1990: 222–4). Significantly, all three of the major external policy reviews of the 1950s echoed these sentiments and accepted the concomitant military and financial burden it implied. As the Macmillan government's paper on 'The Position of the United Kingdom in World Affairs' noted candidly in June 1958, in the long term Anglo-American 'interdependence' should save resources through 'the sharing of burdens which we could not carry alone', but 'if ... we are to retain our influence in the Alliance, we shall have to make our contribution towards the execution of agreed policies' (Ruane and Ellison 2007: 160).

The Labour government of 1945–51 recognised that mutual need did not preclude the possibility of serious tensions with Washington any more than it did during wartime. Washington treated Britain's *de facto* recognition of the People's Republic of China in October 1949 as a gross betrayal at a time when it regarded communism as a monolithic ideology to be resisted everywhere. Conversely, Whitehall contemptuously dismissed American naiveté about communist China on the grounds that diplomatic recognition would help both to separate Peking from Moscow while simultaneously safeguarding Britain's Hong Kong colony and business interests in China (Edmonds 1986: 147). There were even more important differences over the Middle East. Attlee and Bevin never forgave Truman for pursuing a policy in Palestine designed primarily to secure his own re-election while British troops were being murdered with weapons bought with tax-deductible Jewish-American subscriptions (Ovendale 1998: 97). There were also acute differences over Israel's war against Egypt in 1948–49 when the US supported the former while Britain almost intervened to limit Israeli territorial gains

under the terms of the 1936 Anglo-Egyptian Treaty. After warnings
from London, Washington pressed the Israelis into withdrawing their
troops from some areas, although, as Bevin angrily declared in 1949, US
policy was essentially to 'let there be an Israel and to hell with the consequences' (Hahn 2000: 282). Rivalry over the control of Middle Eastern
oil also briefly jeopardised both the Anglo-American loan agreement in
1946 and the distribution of Marshall Aid in 1949. Other sources of
tension included conduct of the Korean War and fundamental differences over the 'Uniting for Peace' resolution in 1950, when US plans to
turn the UN into a coercive instrument of collective security met with
unconcealed British scepticism (Bourantonis and Magliveras 2002). By
this juncture, however, Bevin was a confirmed member of what his
junior minister described as the '"don't be rude to the Americans"
school', which meant that the government baulked at anything
approaching an open breach (Greenwood 2002: 213).

Fluctuating fortunes: Churchill, Eden and Macmillan, 1951–63

The Conservative governments between 1951 and 1964 wholeheartedly
endorsed and consolidated Bevin's view that the Anglo-American
alliance should be the cornerstone of British foreign policy. Alarmed by
the growing disparity in power between the two states, Churchill's premiership (1951–55) was characterised by a desire to strengthen the
transatlantic partnership through both overt structures of cooperation
and regular informal contact with the President (Marsh and Baylis
2006: 182). Despite the triumphal tone of his visit to Washington in
January 1952, however, he soon found there was little meeting of
minds, even less desire for regular personal meetings and no wish what-
soever to be patronised by British assumptions about their superior
diplomatic finesse. On the contrary, as Eden gloomily reported to the
Cabinet: 'They are polite; listen to what we have to say, but make (on
most issues) their own decisions. Till we can recover financial and economic independence, this is bound to continue' (Horne 1989, I: 347).
Unfortunately, contrary to Churchill's hopes, the election of a
Republican administration in 1953 did little to improve relations given
the determination of Eisenhower and Secretary of State Dulles to rele-
gate Britain from its position as *the* 'special' relation to merely one of
several possible allies. As a result, after some extremely awkward con-
versations during the Bermuda conference in December 1953,
Eisenhower rebuffed Churchill's offer of further talks with the stinging
observation that 'the United States and Britain seem to reach drastically

different answers to problems involving the same set of basic facts'
(Hennessy 2007: 336).

This cooling of relations during the 1950s was fuelled by severe disagreements over a wide variety of issues. In the economic sphere, these
included Britain's continued reluctance to give a lead to European integration, sterling convertibility, imperial preference and a clash of commercial interests over oil following the nationalisation of the
British-owned Anglo-Iranian Oil Company with the loss of the world's
largest oil refinery at Abadan. Conflict also arose over the Korean War
and US resentment over Eden's success at the Geneva summit in 1954
when forcing the partition of Indochina as a means to deny
Washington any pretext for further military intervention likely to provoke a global conflagration (Ruane 1996: 142–3). Britain's exclusion
from the ANZUS security treaty between the US, Australia and New
Zealand in September 1951 and America's refusal to join the Baghdad
Pact in February 1955 were also interpreted as efforts to displace
Britain in traditional spheres of influence. Underlying these specific
conflicts lay a far more fundamental divergence over the conduct of the
Cold War itself, in that the US priority on defeating communism everywhere appeared to conflict with the British desire to contain East–West
tensions – particularly after the death of Stalin in 1953 (Seldon 1981:
chapter 1; Bartlett 1992: 6).

Undoubtedly the most public rift came in November 1956, when
Anglo-French military action to reoccupy the Suez Canal Zone ended in
a humiliating withdrawal after US financial pressure was applied to
Britain (see Chapter 3). Despite the severity of this crisis, however, the
breach was astonishingly short-lived. Within weeks of the military
withdrawal, Macmillan entered Downing Street convinced 'the most
urgent, and ... the most delicate, task which confronted me on
becoming Prime Minister was to repair and eventually to restore our
old relationships with Washington' (Macmillan 1971: 240). While
Britain should continue to pursue a policy of power by proxy, he also
believed it 'should not pursue her independent ambitions to the point
where they brought her into an open confrontation with America'
(Ruane and Ellison 2007: 155). Macmillan's emollient personal style,
his close wartime contact with Eisenhower in North Africa and his
actions during the later stages of the Suez crisis all played a part in
repairing the breach. At an extremely friendly meeting with Eisenhower
in Bermuda in March 1957, Macmillan thus agreed to station 60 US
Thor intermediate-range ballistic missiles (IRBMs) in East Anglia, in
return for a presidential pledge to repeal the McMahon Act and replace
it with a new agreement giving Britain preferential access to US nuclear
technology (Clark 1994: 38–76).

The near panic in Washington engendered by the launch of the Soviet Sputnik satellite in October 1957 (so soon after the Soviets were the first to test an ICBM) further consolidated a relationship that Macmillan now described as 'interdependence'. In the ensuing exchange, America assisted the development of Britain's medium-range Blue Streak missile and after its failure in March 1960 they supplied the Skybolt missile system as a replacement (see Chapter 7). In return, US nuclear submarines were given access to a base at the Holy Loch in Scotland (Clark 1994: 157–89). The agreement to establish a number of secret joint Working Groups on matters of shared interest in October 1957 was also warmly welcomed in London as an opportunity to institutionalise transatlantic consultation but these hopes rapidly came to nothing (Jones 2003). Nevertheless, this new era of 'complete understanding and splendid co-operation', as Macmillan described it, was further confirmed in July 1958 when Anglo-American forces were dispatched to assist King Hussein of Jordan and the Lebanese president in suppressing Soviet-backed civil disturbances in a Western sphere of influence (Macmillan 1971: 534).

The even more extraordinary personal rapport which developed between Kennedy and Macmillan is often portrayed as the golden age of the 'special relationship', possibly even closer than that between Churchill and Roosevelt. Despite the generation gap, the two leaders simply got on well together (Horne 1989, II: 287–90). During this period Kennedy regularly elicited Macmillan's opinions and reactions, if not his actual advice. There was also successful joint action over the Sino-Indian border dispute in 1962, while the extremely close collaboration over the Partial Nuclear Test Ban Treaty in August 1963 suggested an astonishing level of British influence over US policy (Dickie 1994: 125–9). Undoubtedly the most remarkable demonstration of this newly restored special relationship, however, was provided by the Nassau conference in mid-December 1962, when Macmillan's angry protests at the sudden US scrapping of Skybolt enabled him to return home with Kennedy's pledge to provide Britain with the new Polaris missile system at a knock-down price (see Chapter 6). Yet for all his success in resurrecting the 'special relationship', Macmillan's own review of foreign relations in December 1960 recorded anxiously 'the uncertainty of American policies towards us – treated now as just another country not as an ally in a special and unique category' (Ruane and Ellison 2007: 163).

The Atlantic alliance in decline, 1964–79

Macmillan's concerns about the future of the Anglo-American alliance were vindicated soon after his sudden withdrawal from the premiership in October 1963 and Kennedy's assassination a month later. As Foreign Secretary between 1961 and 1963, Sir Alec Douglas-Home had been even more pro-American than Macmillan, but his brief premiership (1963–64) was characterised by considerable transatlantic antagonism over the sale of British buses to Cuba and Britain's lukewarm response to US proposals for a NATO Multilateral Force (MLF) on the grounds that it threatened the independence of its own nuclear deterrent. (Holt 2005). After Labour's election victory in October 1964, prospects appeared to improve, but these hopes also soon foundered. Harold Wilson was certainly sincere when he declared in Washington in December 1964 that he regarded Britain's relationship with America 'not as a special relationship but as a close relationship, governed by the only things that matter, unity of purpose and unity in our objectives'. More to the point, he was prepared to accept global overextension in order to sustain that 'close relationship' with Washington (Wilson 1971: 50). Unfortunately for Harold Wilson, two key problems conspired to frustrate his hopes.

The first obstacle concerned the Labour government's inability to comply with President Johnson's repeated demand for some British support in Vietnam, 'even if only on a limited – even a token – basis' (Wilson 1971: 79). Despite the clandestine assistance of British Special Forces, Wilson always recognised that an overt military commitment would be impossible given hostile party and public reactions to the war, but the refusal created outrage in Washington. 'A platoon of bagpipers would be sufficient', an angry Johnson told Wilson as the war escalated in July 1966: 'it was the British flag that was wanted' (Wilson 1971: 341). Wilson's second problem stemmed from Britain's chronic sterling crisis. In order to sustain the illusion of Britain's great power status, while averting the disaster of devaluation, Wilson and James Callaghan, the Chancellor of the Exchequer, made a secret deal with Lyndon Johnson in mid-1965. Washington would support sterling on the international money markets to avoid a forced devaluation and, in return, Britain would maintain both its military presence 'East of Suez' and its US arms contracts, while also offering tacit support for US intervention in Vietnam. (Ponting 1989: chs 3, 13; Dobson 1995: 131–5). In the event, this understanding collapsed when severe financial weakness finally compelled the Labour government to announce major defence cuts in July 1967, including a massive reduction in its commitments 'East of Suez' and the cancellation of an order for American F-111 aircraft (see Chapter 6). Devaluation in November 1967 finally destroyed the last vestiges of Anglo-American accord when it was announced that withdrawal would be completed by the end of 1971. After this, the once 'special relationship' became anything but special, for the simple reason that there was no advantage for either side in paying the price to maintain it (Ponting 1989: 103–6, 288, 306–9). As the US Ambassador in London noted contemptuously, the phrase was now little more than 'sentimental terminology' (Bartlett 1992: 118).

During the early 1970s, transatlantic relations deteriorated even further. In part, this was because entry to the European Community meant more to Edward Heath than what he ambiguously described as Britain's 'natural' relationship with the United States, and he feared a third veto if it appeared to be 'America's Trojan horse in Europe' (Kissinger 1982a: 191). Tensions also erupted over Heath's pro-Arab stance during the October 1973 Arab–Israeli war, when Britain refused either to supply spare parts for Israeli Centurion tanks or to assist the US airlift of arms supplies to Israel. In stark contrast, the Labour governments of 1974–79 made strenuous efforts to restore relations and, like Wilson, James Callaghan as Foreign Secretary (1974–76) and then Prime Minister (1976–79) was a staunch Atlanticist who enjoyed a warmly cordial relationship with Presidents Ford and Carter. By this juncture, however, Washington was far more interested in superpower dialogue on strategic arms limitation – and there was no place at the 'top table' for Britain as there had been in the past. Despite Callaghan's efforts, therefore, by the late 1970s the so-called 'special relationship' had been superseded by a significantly less privileged state of 'complex interdependence' (Smith 1988: 9).

'Special' once more? Thatcher, Major, Reagan and Bush, 1979–97

Margaret Thatcher first visited the United States in 1967 while Shadow Treasury spokesman as part of the US State Department's International Visitor Program, and the experience left an indelible impression upon her world view (Scott-Smith 2003). For Thatcher, the Anglo-American relationship was not only 'natural' but also 'extraordinary' and 'very, very special', described by her in 1991 as 'the greatest alliance in defence of liberty and justice the world had ever known' (Dumbrell 2001: 89). As she declared at a dinner to celebrate two centuries of diplomatic relations between the two countries in 1985: 'There is a union of mind and purpose between our peoples which is remarkable and which makes our relationship truly a remarkable one. It is special.

It just is, and that's that' (Ovendale 1998: 154). As a result, it was inevitable that the Anglo-American alliance remained the cornerstone of Britain's foreign policy.

Thatcher's efforts to repair transatlantic relations began within a few months of her election in May 1979. By January 1980, the announced deployment of 160 US Cruise missiles was interpreted as an affirmation of London's confidence in Washington at a time when most European opinion was increasingly hostile. Six months later, London purchased Trident I from the US (to replace the outdated Polaris system) at a bargain price. Yet, what is often forgotten about these important developments is that they all occurred before Ronald Reagan became President in January 1981, and were driven not by ideological sympathy or personal rapport with Jimmy Carter, but rather the powerful Atlanticist inclinations of a Prime Minister whose world outlook had been strongly influenced by her direct personal experience of the Cold War, and who wanted to become America's partner, rather than its poodle, in defence of Western interests and security.

Thatcher's relationship with Reagan is legendary, but it was also complex and multifaceted. They first met in April 1975 and there was an instant rapport – both personal and ideological. Some observers have thus tended to emphasise the particular importance of personal, even 'sexual chemistry' (J. Campbell 2008: 261; Smith 1990: 1). According to this version, the strength of the relationship was ultimately rooted in 'a mutual male–female empathy of utmost innocence but considerable power' which quickly flourished into what Sir Anthony Parsons, the British Ambassador to Washington, later described as a 'political love affair' (Young 1989: 561; Parsons 1991: 161). Furthermore, the warmth of this personal relationship gained much from a genuine empathy based on a shared ideological vision in which Thatcher's strident brand of free market 'conviction politics' coincided conveniently with Reagan's attachment to monetarist neoliberal economics. There was also a meeting of minds on the Cold War against what Reagan described in March 1983 as the 'Evil Empire'. Thus, while they had very different personalities (and despite her occasionally caustic remarks about Reagan's intellectual limitations), it was clear from the outset that she was determined to become the best friend of Reagan's America, even if this meant abandoning the traditional Whitehall conceit of posing as the mature mentor to their simpleminded American cousins. As Paul Sharp puts it, 'instead of the diplomacy of the influence . . . Margaret Thatcher built her US policy on the diplomacy of support, that is, encouraging the American administration to do what it wanted to do anyway' – and usually what she thought was right (Sharp 2002: 267).

Other commentators have argued that this was an essentially political relationship rooted in tangible geostrategic and economic interests, and founded upon a strong sense of reciprocity and mutual benefit. Thatcher was the first official visitor to the Reagan White House in February 1981, and she assured the President that 'we in Britain stand with you ... Your problems will be our problems and when you look for friends we will be there'. In this she was as good as her word, by providing strong support for Reagan throughout his presidency. Indeed, John Dumbrell accuses the Thatcher government of carrying loyalty to the point of being 'little more than an enthusiastic anti-communist client of the US'. This was certainly true of Thatcher's unwavering support for US policy in Nicaragua, when defending Reagan during the Iran-Contra scandal and in July 1986 she ensured the UK abstained in a Security Council vote on the International Court of Justice ruling against US policy in that country (Dumbrell 2001: 90). At American behest, the Thatcher government played a covert role in arming Saddam Hussein's regime in Iraq during the Iraq–Iran war in the 1980s and used the SAS secretly to train Afghan guerrillas in the Scottish Borders (Hodder-Williams 2000: 242). The Thatcher government also felt obliged to join the US in a multinational force to assist the extremely delicate Israeli withdrawal from Lebanon in March 1984. Thatcher's most crucial assistance to Reagan came in the form of her agreement to allow the US to use British air bases to bomb Libya on the night of 14/15 April 1986 in retaliation for a terrorist attack on US servicemen at a Berlin nightclub. This decision posed embarrassing problems for Thatcher, not just because she had previously declared that retaliatory strikes were difficult to justify under international law, but also because France and Spain refused to participate, the Cabinet opposed involvement, the FCO feared it would provoke retaliatory attacks on British interests abroad and opinion polls showed 70 per cent of the electorate were hostile to the action (Bartlett 1992: 158). Nevertheless, Thatcher and her Foreign Secretary, Sir Geoffrey Howe, recognised that long-term British interests demanded support for Washington. As she told one of her ministers, 'this is the right decision in the long-term interests of Britain' (Baker 1993: 121).

In return for her loyalty, the Reagan administration did much to strengthen the position of a like-minded ally and staunch supporter. In October 1981, it offered Trident II (D5) to Britain as a replacement for Trident I on extremely favourable and preferential terms (Ovendale 1994: 131, 158–61). Perhaps most importantly, in April 1982 Britain received crucial US diplomatic, military and intelligence assistance during the Falklands War (see Chapter 3). After Thatcher 'personally and urgently' appealed to Reagan, he also reluctantly took the unprecedented step of cancelling the grand jury's antitrust investigation into British Airway's price-fixing arrangements with major US airlines in November 1984, and four months later her 'sheer persistence' prodded him into persuading US creditors to abandon the accompanying civil action to clear the way for BA's privatisation. As explicit payback for the risks she had taken over the Libyan bombing, he also intervened personally during the summer of 1986 to secure Senate ratification for a new extradition treaty easing the deportation of IRA terrorists in Britain (J. Campbell 2008: 270; Renwick 1996: 361).

Thatcher's good relations with the Reagan administration did not prevent the President from simply ignoring Britain's opinions when US national interests demanded it. This was vividly illustrated by the US invasion of the Commonwealth state of Grenada to depose a Marxist dictator in October 1983; an operation launched without any fore-warning to the Thatcher government, which had already denied pub-licly that any invasion was likely (Williams 1997). As Geoffrey Howe later conceded, 'the government had been humiliated by having its views as plainly disregarded in Washington' and its discomfiture was intensified when Labour's Denis Healey exploited the opportunity to describe Thatcher as 'Mr Reagan's poodle' (Dumbrell 2001: 100). Thatcher was incandescent with fury at both the action and the lack of consultation. Nevertheless, beyond a sharply worded private telephone protest to the Oval Office, Thatcher was powerless to do anything other than acquiesce in the rebuff, although, in conjunction with a US leak about British efforts to conceal the discovery of a Soviet spy ring at GCHQ in October 1982, some commentators argue that Anglo-American relations reached a lower point than at any time since Suez (Baylis 1984: 193).

Like its predecessors, the Thatcher government combined a largely uncritical support for US initiatives, with the recognition that overtly slavish obedience was not the most credible method of exerting influ-ence on the world stage. As a result, Britain's position as a loyal subor-dinate did not preclude criticism or independent action where British interests conflicted with US policy. For example, in 1980 she sided with the EC in advocating a greater role for the Palestine Liberation Organisation in the Arab–Israeli peace negotiations (Hathaway 1981: 116–17). During the Falklands crisis, a presidential aide also recalled that 'she practically bit Reagan's head off' when he proposed further negotiations, and she later rebuffed his efforts to call a halt to the fighting short of Argentina's total surrender as an effort to 'snatch diplomatic defeat from the jaws of military victory' (J. Campbell 2008: 148; Thatcher 1993: 230). Similarly, while Britain was alone in assisting the US bombing raid on Tripoli in April 1986, the Thatcher government pointedly emphasised its reluctant acquiescence and warned that it was unlikely to happen again. As a result, while it participated in the US-led Armilla Patrol escorting shipping between Bahrain and the mouth of the Gulf, when Iran mined the main shipping channels in August 1987, Thatcher flatly rejected a US request to deploy British minesweepers, for fear of becoming embroiled further in the conflict, until Iranian mining operations threatened the principle of free passage (and thus British commercial interests), after which six Navy minesweepers were deployed in the area. As a presidential adviser later recalled, she never adopted 'a position of supplication or inferiority. Quite the contrary' (J. Campbell 2008: 267).

Thatcher's unqualified support for Reagan's confrontational anti-communism should not be overstated either. Thatcher undoubtedly relished her reputation as 'the Iron Lady' and she enthusiastically supported firm retaliatory action after the Soviet invasion of Afghanistan in 1979 (Smith 1988: 15). But she also helped soften Reagan's stridently anti-Soviet tone in 1981–82, by playing on his anxiety about the increasing influence of the European disarmament movement. More importantly, after a Chequers foreign policy seminar in September 1983, Thatcher swiftly abandoned her self-styled 'megaphone diplomacy', while the Foreign Secretary embarked on a series of official visits to Warsaw Pact capitals to stress the need for constructive engagement with the new generation of more moderate Soviet leaders. Thatcher's own visit to the Soviet Union in February 1984 marked the beginning of a far more balanced approach to Anglo-Soviet relations, and after it she led the way in establishing a rapprochement with the new Soviet leadership. As she told the US Congress in 1985, 'despite our differences with the Soviet Union we have to talk to them'. The arrival of Mikhail Gorbachev as Soviet leader in 1985 cemented this new Anglo-Soviet relationship because she believed he was a leader the West could 'do business with', and her vocal support enabled Reagan to reassure the American public that he was not 'going soft' on the Soviets (Young 1989: 393).

The process of East–West detente illustrated clearly the parameters of Thatcher's influence over US policy under Reagan. On one hand, her hopes of positioning herself as a vital intermediary between Reagan and Gorbachev were brutally dispelled by Britain's exclusion from the superpower summits in Geneva in November 1985 and Reykjavik in October 1986. On the other hand, when superpower talks in Reykjavik led to possible agreement on the so-called 'zero-zero option' (removing all IRBMs from Europe to the detriment of Britain's independent deterrent and the security of Europe generally), Thatcher very effectively reasserted her influence by dispelling a few of Reagan's more unrealistic ideas about arms control, while extracting a pledge to exclude Anglo-French weapons from any future agreement. Consulted by both sides as to how to make further progress, her visit to Moscow in March 1987 helped pave the way for agreement on intermediate nuclear forces and the negotiated end to the Cold War.

The Conservative government's desire to strike a credible balance between loyalty and the right to independent counsel was equally conspicuous in Thatcher's efforts to present herself as an honest broker between US and European interests. As she recalled in her memoirs, throughout her premiership she 'saw it as Britain's task to put the American case in Europe' (Thatcher 1993: 171). But this did not preclude tough action, as in June 1982, when she responded in robustly confrontational style to the US extension of trade sanctions to European companies supplying the Siberian pipeline carrying Soviet natural gas to Germany. Although imposed upon American companies in retaliation for the introduction of martial law in Poland, she resented this high-handed US action, denounced it publicly and then passed the Protection of Trading Interests Act effectively compelling British firms to honour their contractual obligations in direct defiance of American policy. She adopted a similar approach to Reagan's 'Star Wars' SDI initiative for laser-based anti-missile defence announced in March 1983, when she articulated European fears that this might encourage Washington to withdraw under its own defensive umbrella at arm's length from the main potential battleground in Europe (Smith 1990: 146–59; Dumbrell 2001: 96–7). There were also recurrent economic disagreements over trade questions and competition in financial services. By the late 1980s, therefore, although the Thatcher government was not an automatic supporter of every American policy, it undoubtedly shared the Reagan administration's vision of the gravity of the global threat to Western interests and this engendered a high level of rapport throughout Thatcher's premiership. As David Sanders notes, 'Thatcher might not have restored *the* special relationship . . . but she had without doubt re-established *a* special relationship with Ronald Reagan's America' (Sanders 1990: 186).

The presidential style of George Bush between 1989 and 1993 was very different from Ronald Reagan's – and so was his relationship with Margaret Thatcher. As she recorded in her memoirs, he 'felt the need to distance himself from his predecessor' and this involved 'turning his back fairly publicly on the special position I had enjoyed in the Reagan Administration' (Thatcher 1993: 783). This demotion was possible because the international environment had been fundamentally transformed by the collapse of the Warsaw Pact and the disintegration of the Soviet Union; events which threatened to undermine the entire basis of a 'special relationship' founded on the past existence of a direct threat from a clearly identifiable enemy. These tensions were further intensified by a fundamental conflict over German reunification, largely due to Thatcher's 'Alf Garnett version of history' rooted in a virulently atavistic hostility towards the wartime enemy (Urban 1996: 100–40). According to Percy Cradock, her unbending opposition on this issue was 'the single most spectacular miscalculation' of her entire foreign policy and it seriously damaged relations with Europe, and even more with the Bush administration, which increasingly regarded her as a relic of a bygone age (Cradock 1997: 111). This steady decline in Britain's influence might have continued indefinitely had it not been for the Iraqi invasion of Kuwait in August 1990. Thatcher was in Washington when the invasion occurred, and she vigorously exploited this golden opportunity to reassert her former position by both stiffening the president's resolve and providing a substantial military contribution to the American-led coalition that expelled the Iraqi invaders in January–February 1991. Before this resurrection came about, however, Thatcher had been deposed as Prime Minister in November 1990, leaving John Major to reap the diplomatic rewards of the Gulf War.

Like Thatcher, Major was convinced that by lending military support, Britain would demonstrate its continuing value to Washington. 'Although the term "special relationship" is often misused', he later recorded in his memoirs, 'there is a unique rapport between Britain and the United States. British politicians and the military do not have the reserve in dealing with their American counterparts that they show elsewhere, and confidences are shared as a matter of course.' This was certainly his experience when he met Bush in December 1990 to discuss the crisis (Major 1999: 225, 496). Yet for all that, the decision to terminate the military campaign short of Baghdad without regime change was taken in Washington without any consultation with London, as were US decisions to press ahead with an agreement between Israel and the PLO in September 1993 and the imposition of an oil embargo against Libya. On the other hand, the Major government acted equally unilaterally at the European summit in Luxembourg on 8 April when proposing 'safe havens' to protect Kurdish refugees in northern Iraq without consulting Washington; an idea initially received coolly by the Bush administration before it decided to issue warnings to Baghdad to cease military action where this threatened relief operations.

Convinced that Britain 'straddled the divide between United States and Europe', Major also attempted to reassert Britain's traditional role as the interlocutor between the EU and the US (Major 1999: 578). Like his predecessors, however, in this capacity Major earned more respect and gratitude in Washington than Brussels given his resistance to both

the EC's more protectionist tendencies and its efforts to create a separate foreign and defence identity that might weaken NATO. In this
respect, his emphasis remained primarily Atlanticist rather than
'European'. As Douglas Hurd, the Foreign Secretary, warned in Berlin
in December 1990, 'European security without the United States simply
does not make sense. If we were ever foolish enough to try it, we
should soon realise what nonsense it was' (Bartlett 1992: 176). For all
that, however, the Major government still confronted significant difficulties with Washington over issues like short-range tactical nuclear
forces, while differences in approach to ethnic warfare in Yugoslavia
strained relations almost to breaking point.

Any problems the Major government had with the Bush administration paled into insignificance when compared with those which
afflicted relations during the Clinton presidency. Clinton bitterly
resented the Major government's efforts to assist the Bush election campaign in 1992 by exposing him as a potential draft-dodger, and in
revenge, Major suffered the humiliating indignity when visiting
Washington soon after Clinton's election of having to content himself
with a brief telephone call to the President-elect after being refused a
personal meeting. The relationship did recover marginally from this
inauspicious beginning, but the rapprochement was always limited by
the Clinton administration's tendency to accompany ostensibly friendly
words with policies perceived in Whitehall to be distinctly anti-British.
This was true of the US proposal to make Germany and Japan permanent members of an enlarged UN Security Council in June 1993,
Clinton's unwanted interference in the Northern Ireland problem and
the decision to terminate Britain's favoured access to nuclear testing
facilities in the Nevada desert. The relationship also witnessed significant tensions over the settlement of refugee Vietnamese 'boat people' in
Hong Kong, the unilateral US air attack on Iraq on 27 June 1993
without prior consultation with London, and its tactics towards nuclear
development in North Korea.

New Labour, Clinton and George W. Bush

It has been argued that Blair's first government between 1997 and 2001
did not seek 'any exclusive, major relationship; it does not wish to
choose between its many potential partners. Rather, New Labour has
sought to be friends with everyone. They built a new relationship with
the EU, while staying close to the Clinton White House' (Hill 2001:
347–8). It is certainly true that both Blair and Robin Cook, his first
Foreign Secretary, regularly talked of Britain as 'a natural bridge

between our partners in Europe and friends in North America', and Blair repeatedly argued that the British had been 'deluding [them]selves for too long with the false choice between the US and Europe' because the stronger it was with one, the stronger it was with the other (Coates and Krieger 2004: 13). But, in retrospect, it is the overwhelming ascendancy of the transatlantic connection and Blair's unstinting propensity to appease and conciliate two polar-opposite American presidents that most poignantly characterised British foreign policy during his premiership.

According to Blair's biographer, 'the all-governing mantra that Blair stuck to with the White House was "total support in public, total candour in private". His influence, he believed, was best exercised behind the scenes.' The nature of the relationship was eloquently expressed by Blair's chief of staff when briefing Sir Christopher Meyer, Britain's new Ambassador to Washington: 'Your job is to get up the arse of the White House and stay there' (Seldon 2005: 370, 511). Blair was equally candid in March 2001 when he confessed, 'I have been as pro-American a Prime Minister as it is possible to have. There is not a single issue I can think of in which we haven't stood four-square with America' (Coates and Krieger 2004: 90.) In every sense, Tony Blair was 'the accidental American' and his reputation will probably never recover from the foreign policy implications of that uncritical orientation (Naughtie 2004).

Blair's relationship with Clinton was extraordinarily close from the outset, and during the President's celebratory visit to London soon after Blair's victory in May 1997 he spoke publicly about re-forging the 'special relationship' (Hodder-Williams 2000: 248–9). In part, this marked improvement in relations reflected the emergence of a group of British politicians, led by Tony Blair and Gordon Brown, who admired Clinton and his 'New Democrats' and who drew heavily upon their modernising ideas for both electoral strategy and government policy. The bond was reinforced by a common generational and ideological identity and a shared earnestness about their political mission to tread a new 'Third Way'. The Blair–Clinton outlook on major policy issues, such as EU development and Northern Ireland, was also more coordinated and harmonious than that between Clinton and Major. But, ultimately, underlying the personal rapport and close policy alignment, the strength of the relationship was to a considerable extent reinforced by Blair's willingness to pay whatever price was necessary to maintain some degree of 'special' influence and access. Worse still, to the intense frustration of the FCO and the embassy in Washington, this tendency was accompanied by an instinctive reluctance to demand adequate compensation from the 'gratitude dividend' – a problem which would become far more damaging during the Bush years (Seldon 2005: 375).

In practice, Blair's support for Clinton's policy of armed intervention had mixed results at best. Although an embarrassment for his government, Blair offered tacit support for Clinton's 1998 anti-terrorist strikes on Sudan and Afghanistan. Already personally convinced that Saddam Hussein represented a major threat to regional stability, Britain's lone support for the air bombardment of Iraqi installations in Baghdad in December 1998 isolated it from its European allies between 1999 and 2001, as did Blair's subsequent support for the more prolonged campaign of air-strikes over the Iraqi 'no-fly zone' (Coates and Krieger 2004: 14). Conversely, military action in Kosovo created far greater tensions in Anglo-American relations. Initially, Britain stood firmly behind the US view that NATO should be the dominant force in resolving the conflict, in stark opposition to EU efforts to promote a European solution, and this loyalty inevitably revived allegations that Blair was 'Clinton's poodle'. Yet the Anglo-American consensus on the use of air attacks to prevent further Serbian 'ethnic cleansing' in Kosovo in March 1999, soon gave way to bitter recrimination when Blair demanded the deployment of ground troops and the transformation of NATO into an offensive peace-imposing organisation; an option the beleaguered Clinton vigorously opposed on the grounds that Blair's apparent toughness only highlighted Clinton's domestic weakness as President (A. Campbell 2008: 254). For all the short-term differences, however, relations were soon restored to the generally harmonious tone which characterised the Blair–Clinton years, although, as Anthony Seldon argues, they 'never recovered the extraordinary euphoria and mutual adulation of 1996–98'. The principal legacy of the Clinton presidency, however, was that it 'helped school Blair into thinking that he could help shape US policy and its relationship with Britain and the rest of the world; a realisation that was to flower fully with Blair's far more historically important relationship with ... George W. Bush' (Seldon 2005: 377, 382).

The election of a Republican administration in 2000, filled with conservative old-style Cold Warriors like Vice-President Dick Cheney and Secretary of Defense Donald Rumsfeld, inevitably aroused apprehension in London – particularly as these so-called 'Vulcans' believed that America had both the right and duty to act unilaterally to seek out enemies before these could attack the United States (Seldon 2005: 568). Undaunted by these unsettling indications, immediately after the presidential election Blair made it abundantly clear that he wanted to become George W. Bush's most valued counsellor. His congratulatory message after Bush's victory thus stressed the 'special friendship between Britain and the United States', and significantly he was the first European leader to visit Camp David in February 2001. Moreover, to demonstrate his goodwill, Blair ensured that any lingering policy disagreements were safely mothballed. It is even suggested that Robin Cook was removed from the Foreign Office in June 2001 partly because he appeared insufficiently pro-American in outlook (Hill 2001: 388). Unfortunately for Blair, at their first meeting at Camp David there was some personal rapport between the two leaders, but it became painfully apparent that beyond a shared preference for Colgate toothpaste there was relatively little political chemistry (Seldon 2008: 48).

In much the same way as the Iraqi invasion of Kuwait provided Major with an opportunity to resurrect the 'special relationship', Blair's moment arrived on 11 September 2001 with the Al Qaida attacks upon the United States. In the immediate aftermath of 9/11, Blair seized his opportunity to present himself as Europe's self-appointed spokesman, determined to cement Britain's privileged relationship with Bush by adopting the crisis as his own and by universalising its significance. On the day of the attack, Blair declared that Britain stood 'shoulder to shoulder' with the United States in its 'global war on terror'. 'Your loss is our loss', he declared on his arrival in New York and the President conceded that 'America has no truer friend than Great Britain' in his speech to Congress with Blair in the audience. This remained the central theme of Blair's external policy for the remainder of his premiership. Addressing the US Congress in July 2003 (only the fourth British Prime Minister to do so), he repeated the same message. America's destiny was to 'bequeath to this anxious world . . . the light of liberty . . . and our job . . . is to be there with you. You are not going to be alone. We'll be with you in this fight for liberty' (Coates and Krieger 2004: 9, 43). Convinced that only by actively supporting Bush in his chosen course would it be possible to prevent a disastrous US overreaction, Blair accepted that cooperation could be only on Washington's terms. On this basis, the alliance blossomed into 'the unlikeliest of our age, and one of the most potent' (Naughtie 2004: xi).

There was a heavy price to be paid for the maintenance of some semblance of 'specialness' in the absence of much ideological or personal affinity, and Blair was forced to purchase Bush's goodwill in a variety of currencies. The most obvious price has taken the form of British participation in two extremely costly conflicts since October 2001. Blair clearly believed that he exerted some real influence in deflecting Bush from an immediate attack on Saddam Hussein in order to prepare a measured response commanding international support while dealing with the hosting by the Taliban regime in Afghanistan of the Al Qaida terrorists held responsible for 9/11 (Seldon 2008: 50–1). In reality, however, Blair's was just one voice in an almost unanimous chorus urging Bush to adopt this course, and he had even less influence over planning for the war against Iraq (Seldon 2004: 494). On the other hand, Afghanistan did demonstrate unambiguously the fundamental truth of the proposition that the Bush administration wanted support – but only on its own terms, and that the role of Britain and its European allies was essentially to confer legitimacy upon US operations without much hope of consultation in return.

Military action against Saddam Hussein's Iraqi regime in March 2003 still more poignantly illustrated Blair's propensity to offer almost unconditional support for US policy. His personal pledge, in Texas on 5 April 2002, to stand beside the United States in the event of a war in Iraq unquestionably reflected his long-standing personal hostility to Saddam Hussein (Seldon 2008: 85). But, as Robin Cook later recalled, 'I am certain that the real reason we went to war was that he found it easier to resist the public opinion of Britain than he did the request of the President of the United States' (Coates and Krieger 2004: 127). For Blair, Britain's commitment to war with Iraq was a price worth paying for US friendship. Yet, far from enabling him to exercise real influence over decisions in Washington by acting as a loyal partner in the enterprise as he hoped and expected, Blair's pledge effectively manacled British foreign policy to the coat-tails of the Bush administration; a situation which prompted many to echo former US President Jimmy Carter's indictment that Blair's undeviating support had been 'a major tragedy for the world' which showed him to be 'loyal, blind [and] apparently subservient' (*Guardian*, 21 May 2007).

The cost of American goodwill during the Bush years was not confined simply to electorally unpopular military entanglements. In the vague hope of exerting influence through participation in Bush's overseas adventures, Blair was forced to defend the US detention without trial of alleged terrorist suspects at Guantanamo Bay, despite posing previously as a defender of international morality and in face of repeated international censure. In December 2005, it was also revealed that the government had turned a blind eye to 'extraordinary rendition' stopovers at UK airports by CIA planes transporting abducted terrorist suspects to secret interrogation centres to be tortured; a breach of international law widely condemned by human rights organisations, while Lord Steyn, a recently retired Law Lord, suggested that 'our Prime Minister and the present Cabinet have allowed our country to become the lapdog of the Bush administration'. For similar reasons, Blair appeared to support Bush's crude lumping together of Iraq, Iran and North Korea into an 'Axis of Evil' in his January 2002 State of the Union address, despite coordinated European efforts to reach a policy of constructive engagement with the two latter states (*Guardian*, 5 December 2005; 7 June, 18 October and 29 November 2006).

Beyond Iraq, Afghanistan and Bush's 'Global War on Terror', Blair's Britain acquiesced in US efforts to undermine the War Crimes Tribunal and International Criminal Court in 2004 because of its reluctance to allow American troops to be tried for war crimes (*Guardian*, 11 February and 2 March 2004). It also unsuccessfully attempted to overturn the EU ban on GMO crops by warning that this could lead to a transatlantic trade war in June 2005, and it permitted the CIA secretly to trawl UK bank details despite the fact that this was probably illegal under British and EU law (*Guardian*, 25 June 2005, 21 August 2006). At an entirely different level, the *Economist* revealed in February 2007 that the Blair government had invited the United States to incorporate British bases into Bush's 'son of Star Wars' anti-ballistic missile defence architecture without any Parliamentary consultation (*Economist*, 24 February 2007). Despite an initially tepid US response, it was later revealed that the Fylingdales and Menwith Hill early warning bases had been upgraded to receive satellite warnings of potentially hostile missiles (see Chapter 7; and *Guardian*, 2 July 2007).

Most of these developments placed a heavy strain on Britain's relations with its European partners, but it was even more painful for the Blair government that Bush offered no quid pro quo for his loyal public support over Afghanistan, Iraq and the 'war on terror'. On the contrary, far from winning the active assistance of a grateful White House for his plans for a broader Middle East settlement, Kendall Myers, a senior State Department adviser, recalled that 'there was . . . no payback, no sense of reciprocity in the relationship' (Lunn, Miller and Swift 2008: 56). This was a grievous blow because as early as April 2002 the Blair government had pressed the Bush administration to adopt the UN's twin-track approach, in which pressure on Iraq would be accompanied by a corresponding effort to compel Israel to negotiate a viable peace settlement with the Palestinians to help build Arab support for the 'war on terrorism'. Instead, Bush's refusal to act against the intransigence of the Sharon regime in Tel Aviv fuelled Anglo-American tensions – particularly after April 2004, when Bush declared his support for Israel's abandonment of the so-called 'Middle East road map' without any consultation with the Blair government. Worse still for Blair's leadership and reputation, during the Israeli attack on the Lebanon (in retaliation for the seizure of two Israeli soldiers) in July 2006, Blair unequivocally backed Bush's efforts to block intense international pressure for an immediate cease-fire to allow the Israelis another week to inflict maximum damage on Hezbollah (and the civilian population of Lebanon). Confronted by fierce condemnation from his Parliamentary Party, in his annual Guildhall foreign policy speech in November 2006, Blair prudently returned to his original theme, arguing that the Palestinian–Israeli conflict lay at the core of wider Middle East problems and that Syria and Iran should be integrated into the peace process (*Guardian*, 13 November 2006).

Blair's timid response to this betrayal astonished and infuriated many of those around him. Not only had he failed to lay out explicitly the price of his support, but he also failed to press with sufficient vigour to obtain an appropriate 'payback' after victory had been achieved. Appalled by this negligence, in April 2004 no fewer than 52 senior British diplomats publicly condemned Blair's ineffectual diplomacy (*Guardian*, 28 April 2004). Yet, throughout the rest of his premiership Blair stuck doggedly to the line that he had expounded in Cabinet in early March 2003. 'I tell you that we must stand close to America', he told sceptical colleagues. 'If we don't we will lose our influence to shape what they do' (Cook 2003: 135). It is an argument which sounded progressively less credible as time went on and he received no meaningful quid pro quo for his support. More than ever before, perhaps, the special relationship had become a one-way street in which Britain did all the giving while Washington felt under no obligation to reciprocate.

This is not to suggest that New Labour offered its completely uncritical support for the Bush administration on every issue. Blair declared his public frustration at the US rejection of the Kyoto Protocol on carbon emissions, the imposition of 'safeguard' tariffs of up to 30 per cent on steel imports in March 2002 and Washington's opposition to the comprehensive test ban treaty, the Ottawa Convention on land-mines and the November 2008 agreement banning cluster bombs. But, when viewed as a whole, Anglo-American relations during the second half of the Blair premiership are rightly characterised by Tim Garton Ash as part of 'the Jeeves school of diplomacy', in which Britain plays the faithful manservant to a bumbling US Bertie Wooster and demonstrates impeccable loyalty to his master in public while privately whispering 'Is that wise, sir?' (Garton Ash 2007: 635). Unfortunately, Afghanistan and Iraq brutally revealed the utter futility of the underlying assumption that participation in American adventures automatically enhanced Britain's influence over US policy. With characteristic hubris, Blair remained unrepentant to the end. In a classical exposition of the traditional strategy, he told a meeting of ambassadors in London in January 2003 that Britain 'should remain the closest ally of the US, and as allies influence them to continue broadening their agenda. . . . The price of British influence is not, as some would have it, that we have obediently to do what the US asks. . . . The price of influence is that we do not leave the US to face the tricky issues alone . . . international terrorism is one such issue. Weapons of mass destruction are another' (Coates and Krieger 2004: 52). Unfortunately, in the absence

of a receptive President, this logic easily degenerated into slavish support for American positions at heavy cost to Britain's diplomatic effectiveness. As the outgoing chairman of Chatham House, the influential
international relations think-tank, noted scornfully in December 2006,
'Tony Blair has learned the hard way that loyalty in international politics counts for very little' (*Guardian*, 19 December 2006).

Gordon Brown and 'our most important bilateral relationship'

When Gordon Brown succeeded Tony Blair as Prime Minister in June
2007, his affection for the United States was well attested, but initial
indications suggested that he intended to distance Britain from the
excessively close association established by his predecessor. The tone
was set immediately by Douglas Alexander, one of Brown's closest
Cabinet allies, who told the Council of Foreign Relations in
Washington:

> In the 20th century a country's might was too often measured in
> what they could destroy. In the 21st century it should be measured
> by what they can build together. And so we must form new
> alliances, based on common values, ones not just to protect us from
> the world, but ones we should reach out to the world . . . we need
> to demonstrate by deeds, words and our actions that we are inter-
> nationalist not isolationists, multilateralists not unilateralists, active
> and not passive, and driven by core values, consistently applied, not
> special interests. (*Guardian*, 13 July 2007)

This message clearly worried US Neo-Cons, partly because it explicitly
challenged the US 'to recognize the importance of a rules-based international system' and partly because it coincided with the appointment to
the FCO of Lord Malloch Brown, the former UN Deputy Secretary and
an outspoken critic of the Bush–Blair foreign policy. On this basis,
commentators concluded that relations would be different under
Brown. As one Whitehall spokesman put it, 'It will be more busi-
nesslike now, with less emphasis on the meeting of personal visions you
had with Bush and Blair' (*Guardian* 13 July 2007). Immediately after
his appointment, Brown dutifully followed in the footsteps of his predecessors and arrived in Washington declaring that because of 'the values
we share, the relationship with the United States is not only strong, but
can become stronger in the years ahead'. But beneath the official
rhetoric the reports of his 'full and frank' talks with Bush suggested a

new determination to counter the allegation that Britain was a 'US poodle'. In particular, while the Prime Minister asserted the right to withdraw British troops from Iraq far more rapidly than Bush wanted, Malloch Brown simultaneously announced that, henceforth, the two countries would not be 'joined at the hip' as they had been under Blair (*Guardian*, 30–31 July 2007).

These early indications of a new approach rapidly proved deceptive. In the same month that Brown staked out his new position, David Miliband, the Foreign Secretary, declared there would be 'no change' in the relationship with Washington. Britain wanted to be one of the 'serious players' in the world, he argued, and 'you do that with United States, not against [it]' (*Guardian*, 15–16 July 2007); a message he pointedly echoed in his first speech at Chatham House a few days later. With world power more dispersed than at any time since the nineteenth century, Miliband concluded that 'this makes our most important bilateral relationship – with the US – more not less important' (*Guardian*, 20 July 2007). After this, the Prime Minister appeared to execute a complete volte face in his annual Mansion House foreign policy speech in November, when he underscored his determination to cooperate with Washington, in language identical to that of his Foreign Secretary. 'It is no secret that I am a life-long admirer of America. I have no truck with anti-Americanism in Britain or elsewhere in Europe and I believe that our ties with America founded on values we share constitute our most important bilateral relationship' (*Guardian*, 12 November 2007).

Having executed this rapid reversal of direction, Brown reverted to all the now-familiar themes. In a CBS interview in April 2008, he cast himself as the leader best able to bring Europe and United States together after the bitter divisions over Iraq – although he conspicuously avoided the 'bridge' analogy much favoured by Thatcher, Major and Blair. In a speech at the JFK Memorial Library in Boston three days later, he returned to the theme by warning that the EU and the US would face 'terrific risks' if they failed to unite to fight global terrorism, poverty and disease, and he hoped for 'a new dawn of collaborative action between America and Europe' under a new President prepared to operate in a more consensual manner (*Guardian* 16–19 April 2008). In return, during his last official visit to London on 16 June, Bush praised Brown for being 'tough on terror' and a 'good partner'; suitable epithets, given the simultaneous announcement that Britain would intensify sanctions against Iran's largest bank while deploying more troops in southern Iraq (*Guardian*, 17 June 2008). Another familiar theme was Brown's repeated emphasis upon the primacy of NATO over any EU defence structure to allay Washington's fears about the development of an EU Rapid Reaction Force and its military planning cell (*Guardian*, 27 July 2008).

The election of President Barak Obama in November 2008 returned a more ideological congenial administration to power, particularly as US Secretary of State Hillary Clinton had known her British counterpart since the mid-1990s when close ties developed between Clinton's New Democrats and New Labour seeking to emulate their 'Third Way' success. The fact that Gordon Brown was the first European leader to speak to the President-elect after his election and the first to visit him after his inauguration was considered to be indicative of this closer relationship – particularly after Obama's assurance that 'he looked forward to continuing and strengthening the special relationship between our two countries' (*Guardian*, 24 January 2009). Hillary Clinton was even more fulsome after her meeting with her British counterpart:

> It is often said that the United States and Britain have enjoyed a special relationship. It is certainly special in my mind and one that has proved very productive. Whoever is in the White House, whichever party in our country, this relationship really stands the test of time and I look forward to working with the Foreign Secretary.

and she subsequently went on to replace the politely evasive '*a* special relationship' with the far more definite reference to '*the* special relationship'.

Beneath the friendly rhetoric, policy differences engendered by conflicting national interests inevitably remained. Miliband was thus pressed to commit more British troops to Afghanistan soon after the inauguration, while Whitehall protested at the Obama administration's intention to safeguard US jobs by enshrining a protectionist 'Buy American' clause in its multi-billion dollar economic stimulus package in contravention of WTO rules on government procurement. Nevertheless, the commonality of policy and perspective was evident from the outset, as Brown and Obama spearheaded calls for a massive international fiscal stimulus to lift the world out of recession at the G20 meeting in London in April 2009 in face of determined opposition from France and Germany. They were rather more successful in March when coordinating action to force international tax havens to accept the OECD protocol, compelling them to reveal information on suspected tax evaders, and a similar level of cooperation was achieved in April–May 2009 with regard to the reorientation of policy towards Afghanistan.

The nature of the 'Special Relationship'

The extent to which the Anglo-American relationship has ever been truly 'special' has been the subject of much controversy. One school of thought contends that the idea of a 'special relationship' was never more than an agreeable myth designed to help cushion the shock of national decline and shroud it in the reassuring sentimental language of the Anglo-Saxon family. For David Reynolds, 'the wartime alliance was neither natural nor inevitable, but the consequence of the unexpected global emergency of 1940–41'. It was simply 'a marriage of necessity, uniting two major states whose recent history has been one of peaceful rivalry' (Reynolds 1986: 38). From a similar perspective, Max Beloff lamented the need to 'dress up in this way a perfectly honourable relationship as though national self-interest were something which should play no part in this branch of international politics' (Beloff 1966: 170). Much evidence exists to support this conceptualisation. As a US State Department assessment noted on 1 April 1946, if Soviet Russia was to be denied the hegemony of Europe, 'the United Kingdom must continue in existence as the principal power in Western Europe economically and militarily' and the US should provide it with 'all feasible political, economic, and if necessary military support' in 'areas and interests which are in the opinion of the US vital to the maintenance of the United Kingdom . . . as a great power' (Bartlett 1992: 25). Twenty years later, McGeorge Bundy, a National Security Council adviser, conceded that in 'the very nature of things, British interests and ours intersect in every continent, and usually in rather complicated ways . . . [but] . . . our real interests will nearly always turn out to be very close to each other indeed' (Hathaway 1981: 86–7). From this perspective, then, the phrase 'special relationship' is simply a shorthand term for the congruence of Anglo-American interests and policy objectives – particularly when confronted by a clearly defined threat, whether from Nazi aggression, communist expansionism during the Cold War era or from an amorphous Al Qaida terrorist threat in the twenty-first century.

An alternative school follows Churchill in emphasising the bond created by a shared language, history, culture, kinship and value system; ties which have strengthened and deepened the intimacy of a relationship between states pursuing similar goals. As H. G. Nicholas observed, although conflict and competition are inevitable between states, 'beneath these clashes of personality and national moods lay deeper long-range similarities of outlook and interests' (Nicholas 1975: 68). Britain and the United States have thus become linked through an enduring 'double bond' because 'cultural values have pulled in the same direction as national interest' (Dimbleby and Reynolds 1988: 355). Beyond the powerful personal bond between Churchill and Roosevelt, many of the postwar foreign and defence policy elite on both sides of the Atlantic also developed close ties with their counterparts during the Second World War and the ensuing Cold War. As a result, it is often argued that the post-war relationship began to defy conventional theories about alliances as the British engaged in a long-term act of faith which was 'difficult to understand in traditional power terms . . . History, tradition, affinity were crucial to the alliance' (Dawson and Rosecrance 1966).

John Dumbrell is right to warn against the dangers of placing too much importance upon personal relationships, on the grounds that it confuses form and substance (Dumbrell 2001: 49). After all, Eisenhower recalled his meeting with Churchill as 'a sort of home-coming, a renewal of an old and close relationship', but this did not prevent him demoting Britain from its position as *the* special relation to being merely one of several potential allies (Eisenhower 1963: 249). Yet, while foreign policy is not formulated on this basis of personalities alone, the significance of elite interaction should not be dismissed alto-gether. At times, personal friendships have played a crucial part in oiling the wheels of Anglo-American interaction, while periods of strained relations have often coincided with poor personal relation-ships. Bevin's friendly relations with Secretary of State George Marshall and his successor Dean Acheson did much to revive Anglo-American alliance. Macmillan rapidly established close personal relations with Eisenhower, on the basis of their shared wartime experiences in North Africa. As Eisenhower later recorded, 'Macmillan is . . . one of my inti-mate wartime friends so it is very easy to talk to him on a very frank, even blunt, basis' (Hahn 2000: 283). Personal factors were so impor-tant to Macmillan's dealings with Kennedy that he later compared the relationship to that between father and son (Horne 1989, II: 300–5). They were equally crucial to the Thatcher–Reagan and Blair–Clinton connections. But, whatever the basis of the Anglo-American relation-ship, it has proved remarkably resilient. Despite many transatlantic dis-agreements since 1945, as Henry Kissinger recalled of his own experience as US Secretary of State during the 1970s, the very essence of this 'extraordinary partnership' lay in its unique ability 'to overcome the occasional squabbles that form the headlines of the day and, even more important, meet the objective new challenges [of tomorrow]' (Kissinger 1982b: 572–3).

'Special relationships': a sectoral perspective

The debate about the 'special relationship' is further confused by the tendency to treat it as a single monolithic association across all areas of interaction. Yet, in reality, this offers a misleading benchmark against which to measure the fluctuating fortunes of Anglo-American coopera-tion. If there is anything 'special' about the Anglo-American alliance, it may be better conceptualised in terms of a complex multidimensional series of parallel relationships ranging across all sectors of policy. When viewed from this perspective, relations have undoubtedly been closest and most comprehensive over intelligence, surveillance, and defence issues (see Chapters 6–7). In these areas, the habit of privileged collaboration became so deeply rooted, instinctive and institutionalised at all levels during the Second World War, that it continued underground into peacetime despite the marked cooling of Anglo-American relations in the immediate aftermath of victory. Cooperation was then substantially reinforced during the Cold War – to such an extent that since the early 1950s US intelligence officials attend at least part of the weekly meetings of the Cabinet's Joint Intelligence Committee (see Chapter 9). As the US ambassador to London noted in the early 1990s: 'The integration of operations and personnel between the respective military services is legendary. We exchange sensitive intelligence with each other by the bucketful' (Seitz 1998: 337). Moreover, British expertise in codebreaking, signals intelligence and intelligence-gathering has created a far more balanced relationship between comparative equals than in other spheres of interaction (Aldrich 1994). A correspondingly close relationship has also recently emerged in the fight against transnational criminals and terrorists, which culminated in 2008 in the launch of an International Information Consortium supported by a 'Server in the Sky' allowing Britain, America, Australia, New Zealand and Canada to share not just policing strategy but also biometric measurements, iris and palm prints (*Guardian*, 15 January 2008).

At the diplomatic level, a special relationship of sorts has also traditionally existed in terms of preferential consultation and collaboration. In the early 1970s, Henry Kissinger claimed that he routinely kept Whitehall better informed than he did his own State Department (Renwick 1996: 272–5). There was certainly 'no other government which we would have dealt with so openly, exchanged ideas with so freely, or in effect permitted to participate in our deliberations' (Kissinger 1982a: 281–2). As he later recalled, this pattern of Anglo-American consultation developed 'so matter-of-factly intimate that it became psychologically impossible to ignore British views ... [and] meetings so regular that autonomous American action somehow came to seem to violate club rules' (Kissinger 1979: 90–1). Twenty years later, Raymond Seitz's experience as US ambassador in London suggested that little had fundamentally changed. 'For almost any diplomatic initiative in Europe, London is customarily the first port of call and it is a rare British initiative that isn't first aired in Washington.' As such, he believed 'the collaboration between London and Washington does put the relationship in a league by itself' (Seitz 1998: 101, 337).

This view is confirmed by Douglas Hurd, a former Foreign Office official and later Foreign Secretary (1989–95), who observed that what the 'special relationship' 'actually means in practice is that we are involved in [US] thinking at an earlier stage than most people, and that is crucial' (Baylis 1997: 226). By standing resolutely 'shoulder to shoulder' with the US, Britain has earned the right at least to be consulted much of the time and always before any other ally. Margaret Thatcher believed it also gave her the right of plain speaking. 'I regard the *quid pro quo* for my strong public support of the President as being the right to be direct with him and members of the administration in private', she recalled in memoirs. Richard Perle, a senior Reagan adviser, put it more strongly: 'She not only had her say, but was frequently the dominant influence in policy-making' (J. Campbell 2008: 266). Blair also believed that public support authorised private influence. 'I tell you that we must stand close to America', Robin Cook recalled him saying (and quoted earlier). 'If we don't, we will lose our influence to shape what they do' (Cook 2003: 135). In this case, however, such expectations of the Bush administration were largely unfulfilled.

On the other hand, over questions of trade, multilateralism and markets the relationship has always been characterised by a fierce 'competitive co-operation'. (Reynolds 1981). Washington successfully exploited the terms of the original Lend-Lease agreement to extract advantage in the competition for markets and access to crucial commodities like Middle Eastern oil. At the Bretton Woods and Dumbarton Oaks conferences, they were equally adroit at imposing their views on multilateralism, the post-war financial order and the dismantling of Britain's system of imperial preference that had always been anathema to US official thinking. This battle continued with renewed vigour throughout the post-war years, and even the neoliberal meeting of minds between Thatcher and Reagan was accompanied by serious tensions over trade balances, covert protectionism and competition in the financial services sector (Dobson 1988: 98–102). Against this background of variable fortunes, therefore, it is perhaps useful to think less in terms of *the* 'special relationship' and rather more of a parallel series of transatlantic relationships in different policy sectors – some of which are more 'special' than others.

Anglo-American relations since 1945: a cost–benefit analysis

The continued lip-service paid to the Anglo-American partnership suggests that policymakers on both sides of the Atlantic have regarded it as mutually beneficial. For Britain, the benefits of basking in the reflected power and influence of a global superpower are relatively self-evident – particularly given its determination to remain a global actor 'punching above its weight' in international affairs at a time when the economic resources to support that position were progressively diminishing. For many years, the logic behind the strategy of great power status by proxy captivated policymakers with the hope that Britain's superior diplomatic experience and finesse would enable it to steer US policy while Washington gladly deferred to the greater wisdom of the 'old country'. In this respect, post-war attitudes reflected a high level of continuity with the effortless superiority displayed by Whitehall in the interwar era towards the diplomatic efforts of their brash and naive country cousins across the Atlantic. An anonymous verse penned during Lord Keynes's mission to Washington in 1945 encapsulating the prevailing view:

> In Washington Lord Halifax
> Once whispered to Lord Keynes
> It's true *they* have the money bags
> But *we* have all the brains. (Self 2007: 299–300)

It was on precisely this basis, Attlee noted in December 1950, that Britain and America were 'partners unequal no doubt in power but still equal in counsel' (Danchev 2000: 596).

Although this conceit persisted into the later years of the century, post-war relations proved rather more difficult than Attlee anticipated. Nevertheless, in diplomatic terms, the reward for Britain has been access to unparalleled levels of consultation and integration into US deliberations. It has also enabled it to acquire a high technology nuclear arsenal it could not otherwise have afforded.

Sympathetic observers rightly describe the underlying objective of British policy since 1945 as 'being close to, but independent of, the US' (Marsh and Baylis 2006: 201). Unfortunately, the line separating independent 'support' from slavish 'subservience' has often appeared perilously narrow, but, as former British Ambassador to the US, Sir Robin Renwick, explained: 'The price of consultation has always been presence and participation' (Renwick 1996: 394). This requirement has been particularly notable in terms of Britain's military 'presence and participation' ever since the Attlee Cabinet overruled the Chiefs of Staff and deployed a Commonwealth brigade in Korea simply because the exigencies of Anglo-American solidarity outweighed the military disadvantages (Ovendale 1998: 93). Similar logic has been applied variously to British military engagement in Jordan in 1958, Lebanon in 1982, the first Gulf War in 19910, Operation Desert Fox in 1998, the Balkans, Afghanistan and later Iraq. As Blair declared in the aftermath of 9/11: 'When America is fighting for those [shared] values, then, however tough, we will fight with her. No grandstanding, no offering implausible but impractical advice from the comfort of the touchline, no wishing away the hard choices on terrorism and WMD, or making peace in the Middle East, but working together side-by-side' (www. fco.gov.uk). Conversely, when the expected military support has not been forthcoming, relations have rapidly soured – as Wilson found to his cost over Vietnam. Some argue a further high price has been paid for this privileged status by turning Britain into 'airstrip one' or America's 'unsinkable aircraft carrier', which (according to Defence Chiefs in October 1953) made it the principal Soviet first-strike target for a nuclear attack against the West (Bartlett 1992: 52; Duke 1987: 31–56, 106). But, as a Foreign Office memorandum noted sanguinely in January 1950, 'We must face the fact that this island is strategically well-placed as an advanced airbase and that we must accept this role' (Reynolds 1991: 180–1).

A significant diplomatic price has also been paid to maintain this relationship. In particular, British policy has often been compelled to conform with US positions and actions on the world stage – whether it agreed with those positions or not and whatever the cost to Britain's relations with other significant powers. At times, this has included defending the almost indefensible. Margaret Thatcher stood by Reagan over Iraq, Iran and Contragate; she supported the deployment of Cruise missiles in Europe when opposed by most European leaders, and assisted US retaliation against Libya despite widespread opposition because 'the cost to Britain of not backing American action was unthinkable' (Thatcher 1993: 443–4). Blair offered equally dogged support for Clinton against the efforts of European colleagues to limit the first wave of NATO enlargement, he endorsed the unilateral US bombing of Afghanistan and Sudan, and subsequently supported Bush in military intervention against Afghanistan and Iraq while condoning detention at Guantanamo Bay, extraordinary rendition and torture. This might be the price of sustaining Britain's position in the world, but for the critics, it is a heavy cost to bear for the privilege of becoming an American 'poodle' – if not an outright 'apologist for atrocities' (Curtis 1995: 146).

In assessing the costs and benefits of this increasingly unequal and asymmetrical relationship, it would be wrong to underestimate Britain's value to the United States throughout the post-war period. Once the US strategy of 'containment' expanded to a global basis, it desperately needed allies to guard the perimeter of the free world and none was more important than Britain. Various State Department and CIA assessments in the early post-war period, portrayed Britain as a nation willing to bear a heavy international burden, high levels of scientific expertise, armed forces comparable with those of the United States and far more pro-American in its attitude than any other significant European power. On these grounds, it was concluded: 'The United Kingdom is, by a vast margin, the most valuable and dependable' of America's allies (Bartlett 1992: 39). Almost two decades later, even after the withdrawal from 'East of Suez', the State Department's evaluation of the 'special relationship' still noted that despite its current economic difficulties, Britain would remain of unparalleled importance to the United States and that the US should be prepared to pay a high price to support its 'only powerful ally' (Coleman 2008). If anything, this reasoning has become more important since the end of the Cold War, given the US preference for operating through 'coalitions of the willing' to defend its interests around the world.

One crucial aspect of Britain's value to the US, until at least the early 1970s, was its possession of a global empire encompassing a network of strategic bases capable of striking at 80 per cent of Soviet industry and its Caucasus oilfields, while the ability to deploy forces in the Persian Gulf, Aden, Singapore and the Indian Ocean was of crucial concern when the US was deeply engaged in Vietnam. As Denis Healey, the Defence Secretary, reported to the Wilson Cabinet after his visit to Washington in December 1964, the Americans wanted Britain to keep a foothold in Hong Kong, Malaya and the Gulf region because this would 'enable us to do things for the alliance which they can't do. They think our forces are much more useful to the alliance outside Europe than in Germany' (Crossman 1976: 95). In addition, the US variously used Britain's overseas territories, such as Christmas Island, for high-altitude hydrogen tests in the early 1960s, Diego Garcia as a communications base from the mid-1960s onwards and the Chagos Islands in the Indian Ocean as a US military base and suspected CIA torture centre. Beyond access to strategically vital bases, Britain's value has traditionally been enhanced by its ability to exercise far more political influence in Western Europe, the Near East and South East Asia than the United States could, while for many years it also retained an influential position at the centre of the Commonwealth and the Overseas Sterling Area. As a recent British ambassador to Washington put it, the maintenance of these overseas commitments was, at least in part, based on the assumption that 'Britain has influence on American policy to the extent that it still has some power and influence itself in various parts of the world' (Renwick 1996: 394).

Another key factor in enhancing Britain's value as a useful partner has been its ability to sustain a disproportionately high level of defence expenditure (see Table 6.6) and its possession of a nuclear arsenal and well-established scientific defence infrastructure which has pioneered a variety of major innovations, such as vertical takeoff and landing (VTOL) technology and Chobham armour. US policymakers developed an even higher respect for Britain's Atomic Weapons Establishments (AWE) and their ability (through financial stringency) to devise cheap but ingenious solutions to shared problems which they often adopted for their own use (Freedman 1980: 41; Baylis 1984: 97, 171, 215). Indeed, in February 2009 it was revealed that the US had secretly amended the Mutual Defence Agreement to permit it to conduct research at AWE Aldermaston on a new generation of Reliable Replacement Warheads; a possible breach of the nuclear Non-Proliferation Treaty (NPT) defended by the Policy and Planning Director of the US Nuclear Security Administration on the grounds that there 'are some capabilities that the UK has that we don't have and that we borrow' (*Guardian*, 9 February 2009). The high professional reputation of Britain's armed forces has also proved an asset.

In view of such interrelationships, the Anglo-American alliance since 1945 cannot be depicted entirely as a one-way street in which an importunate Britain slavishly follows the lead of its US patron in return for the scraps so benevolently thrown down from its richer relation's table. During the last 60 years, the wartime alliance of near equals has undoubtedly been superseded by something approaching a patron–client relationship, but even today there is still something genuinely reciprocal about at least parts of Britain's complex relationship with the United States. In part, this 'special' position is derived from the unique combination of the 'hard' and 'soft' power assets Britain commands as an ally in its own right. But, notwithstanding these positive assets, the relationship is also founded in large part upon the willingness of successive British governments to pay almost any price to maintain Britain's privileged position in Washington, in the belief that this is the necessary precondition for its ability to exercise a significant influence on the international stage.

Chapter 5

Britain and Europe

Paying the 'Price of Victory'

Until the late 1950s, Britain's globalist priorities ensured that Europe was by far the least important of Churchill's three 'interlocking circles'. 'Our policy should be to assist Europe to recover as far as we can', an interdepartmental committee concluded in January 1949. 'But the concept must be one of limited liability. In no circumstances must we assist them beyond the point at which the assistance leaves us too weak to be a worthwhile ally for [the] USA if Europe collapses' (Reynolds 1991: 193). As a combination of chronic strategic overextension and long-term economic difficulties made it progressively more difficult to maintain Britain's influence in all three circles, however, foreign policy-makers belatedly shifted their attention towards Europe as a means of retaining a significant voice in world affairs. Yet such a reorientation of policy was always belated, hesitant and never wholehearted – with the inevitable consequence that Britain rapidly acquired a reputation for being the 'reluctant European' and an 'awkward partner' (George 1998: 1).

The reasons for Britain's painful transition, from condescending aloofness in 1945 to its first attempt to enter the European Community less than two decades later, are many and varied, but the reluctance of British policymakers to embrace a European future in 1945 can be attributed to the vast qualitative and quantitative gulf perceived to exist between the position of Britain and the rest of mainland Europe in the aftermath of a devastating world war. France, the Benelux countries, Italy and Germany had been economically devastated by defeat, war, occupation, near-starvation and financial collapse. Equally important, their political systems had also been uprooted and destroyed by Nazi domination. As such, it seemed unsurprising that they were prepared to surrender some degree of sovereignty in order to guarantee the effective reconstruction and future peace of the continent. In stark contrast, Britain emerged from the war with a sense of national pride and achievement at what it regarded as a truly national victory – with the result that there was no crisis of national identity and absolutely no emotional support for either integration or any surrender of national sovereignty. As Miriam Camps puts it, for disorientated new governments on the continent, 'Europe' was a political aspiration but for British policymakers, it was little more than a geographical expression (Camps 1964: 1).

In view of this European weakness in the immediate aftermath of the war, some critics of post-war policy argue that this was Britain's great 'missed opportunity' (Adamthwaite 1985; Denman 1997). Dean Acheson characterised Britain's failure to join the Schuman Plan in 1950 as its 'great mistake of the post-war period'. (Hennessy 1993 364). With British prestige and influence at their zenith, it could have 'had the leadership of Europe for a song' and shaped it precisely how it wished (Denman 1997: 1). Instead, as Hugo Young argues, the history of Anglo-Community relations demonstrates that Britain's interests have repeatedly suffered because it failed to be at the heart of Europe; an argument which strongly influenced Tony Blair's premiership (Young 1998). 'The history of our engagement with Europe is one of opportunities missed in the name of illusions and Britain is suffering as a result', Blair declared in Birmingham in November 2001. 'It is time for us to adjust to the facts. Britain's future is in Europe' (Seldon 2008: 122).

While this is a beguiling vision, as Sir John Coles, a former Permanent Under-Secretary at the FCO (1994–97), points out, it is far easier to separate reality from illusion in retrospect than it was at the time. In part, this is because Britain declined in influence far more rapidly than almost anyone anticipated after 1945. But advocates of the 'missed opportunity' thesis are also guilty of underestimating the importance of Britain's traditional self-image as a great nation rooted in its past imperial glories; a self-image powerfully reinforced by a wartime legacy of being one of the 'Big Three' victorious powers who had won the war and who were expected to go on to dominate the peace. According to critics like Michael Charlton, this inflated self-image was 'the price of victory' (Charlton 1989). Or as Jean Monnet, one of the fathers of European integration, put it, early post-war Britain was bedazzled by the 'illusion of victory' and this encouraged it to maintain a global role while ignoring Europe as a sphere for active involvement (Hennessy 1993: 364). But, while there may be something in this view, it is also distorted by retrospective wisdom. After all, as Coles argues, 'the reduction of the British role to a purely European one was not a realistic policy option during the Cold War when the containment of communism and Soviet ambition was a clear national interest and Britain had the capacity to make a contribution to that end' (Coles 2000, 40–4).

Table 5.1 Outline chronology: Britain and European integration

March 1947	Anglo-French Treaty of Dunkirk
June 1947	Marshall Aid for European recovery
March 1948	Brussels Treaty; Britain, France and the Benelux countries agree a mutual security and economic cooperation pact
May 1950	Schuman Plan proposes European Coal and Steel Community
October 1950	Pleven Plan proposes European Defence Community – to include a German contingent within a European army
April 1951	Treaty of Paris establishes ECSC
May 1952	Treaty of Paris; the Six establish the EDC; Britain signs 'Treaty of Association' with the EDC
August 1952	French National Assembly refuses to ratify EDC
October 1954	The Brussels Treaty Organisation expanded and renamed Western European Union
June 1955	Messina Conference: ECSC members establish the Spaak Committee to consider progress towards a European 'Common Market'; Britain invited to attend
March 1957	The Treaties of Rome establish the EEC and Euratom
May 1960	European Free Trade Association launched
August 1961	Britain makes its first application to enter the EEC
January 1963	President de Gaulle vetoes British application
July 1966	Second British application for EC membership
July 1967	Merger of the three Communities into a common institutional structure
December 1967 1970	Second veto by President de Gaulle Britain, Denmark, Iceland and Norway apply to join the EC
January 1973	Britain, Ireland and Denmark formally enter the Community
1974– March 1975	Britain's renegotiation of terms of membership concludes at the first European Council meeting in Dublin in March 1975 ⅢⅢ➡

Table 5.1 Outline chronology: Britain and European integration – *continued*

June 1975	British referendum votes 57 per cent in favour of continued EC membership
November 1979	Dublin European Council; Thatcher demands rebate from European budget.
March 1980	Thatcher threatens to withhold Britain's VAT contributions to EC budget
June 1983	Stuttgart European Council produces federalist moves towards European union; Thatcher ridicules the proposals and fellow leaders
June 1984	Fontainebleau European Council finally agrees a compromise on Britain's budget contribution; Britain submits paper, ' Europe – the Future' envisaging closer cooperation on technology, pollution, industry, etc.
April 1986	Single European Act pushed through Commons in six days
May 1986	UK presidency used to promote Thatcher's economic liberal agenda
March 1988	Lawson and Howe clash with Thatcher over exchange-rate policy and ERM
September 1988	Thatcher's Bruges speech fiercely critical of EC efforts to assert greater control over national policy
June 1989	Madrid European Council presses ahead with integration; Thatcher 'ambushed' by Lawson and Howe over ERM
October 1989	Lawson resigns after clash with No. 10 over European policy and his efforts to shadow the Deutschemark
October 1990	Major persuades Thatcher to join the ERM; Rome European Council shows Thatcher to be isolated on monetary and political union
November 1990	Thatcher's anti–EC speech provokes Howe resignation; Thatcher resigns
December 1991	Maastricht Treaty establishes European Union with a timetable for EMU. Britain negotiates 'opt out' on the Social Chapter and EMU
September 1992	'Black Wednesday': Britain forced out of the ERM

Table 5.1   Outline chronology: Britain and European integration – *continued*

December 1995	Madrid European Council agrees introduction of single currency in January 1999.
April 1996	Major Cabinet agree on a referendum on EMU before any decision on entry to the single currency
November 1996	Cabinet reaffirms the 'negotiate and decide' strategy
December 1996	Draft European treaty discussions at Dublin Council shows Britain to be isolated on future EU development
January 1997	Major Cabinet agrees EMU entry unlikely in 1999.
June 1997	Amsterdam summit; Blair makes concessions on extended use of QMV, open frontiers and merger of WEU and EU
October 1997	Blair government agrees not to join the Euro-zone; Amsterdam Treaty signed
December 1998	Anglo–French St Malo agreement on European defence cooperation
January 1999	Start of the changeover to the Euro (introduced in 2002)
March 2000	Lisbon Agenda to make the EU the most competitive knowledge-based economy in the world by 2010
December 2000	Nice summit establishes committee to consider a new EU constitution; Blair opposes European Charter of Fundamental Rights
October 2002	Brussels Council attack on Britain's budget rebate
June 2003	Treasury assessment of the 'five economic tests' concludes Britain should not join the Euro-zone immediately
May–June 2005	French and Dutch voters reject the constitutional treaty
December 2005	Blair settles budget issue by linking it to fundamental review of EU expenditure by 2009
December 2007	EU 'reform' treaty signed in Lisbon; Brown arrives too late for ceremony
March 2008	Brown and Sarkozy forge an 'entente formidable' in London
June 2008	EU (Amendment) Act passed enacting the 'reform' treaty

Britain and the limits of cooperation, 1945–55

It is often argued that the Attlee governments never seriously considered the opportunities offered by Western Europe because of a failure of imagination and political will at the highest level. Yet, as Geoffrey Warner demonstrates, 'this fundamentally negative view of the Labour government's European policy is inaccurate and unfair' (Warner 1984: 62). In part, this is because Bevin played a leading role in the rehabilitation of the German economy, the restoration of France as one of the Western 'Big Four' and in the formation of the OEEC, the Brussels Treaty organisation and NATO (Roberts 1984: 34). But, at a more fundamental level, criticisms of Bevin's indifference towards Europe also often ignore his early enthusiasm for the idea of a 'Western Union'. Only a month after coming into office, the Foreign Office considered proposals to link Western Europe, the African colonies and the British-dominated Middle East into an economic and political bloc possessing manpower and economic resources comparable to those of the two superpowers. By creating this powerful 'Third Force', Britain would be able to reassert its former position by emerging as the principal spokesman and *de facto* leader of a new superpower. As Orme Sargent, soon to become Permanent Under-Secretary at the FO, noted in July 1945, Britain must assume the leadership of Western Europe and the Commonwealth 'to compel our two big partners to treat us as an equal' (Young 1993: 7–8). In the event, the proposal was undermined by the opposition of the Treasury and Board of Trade and by fears about hostile reactions in France, the Soviet Union and the US but it remained a central objective of Bevin's Foreign Office until February 1949, and even then it was abandoned only with great reluctance.

Although Bevin understood that 'Britain cannot stand outside Europe and regard her problems as quite separate from those of her European neighbours', there were always clearly defined limits to his willingness to engage with Europe (Northedge 1974: 51) Above all, Bevin remained a vehement opponent of European federalism. As he put it in one of his famous mixed metaphors: 'I don't like it . . . When you open that Pandora's Box you will find it full of Trojan horses' (Strang 1956: 290). Like many of his contemporaries, for Bevin the idea of Western European cooperation on an intergovernmental basis was one thing, but federalism and integration with common institutions under supra-national control was quite another. This distinction is crucial to any understanding of post-war policy towards cooperation with Europe. Bevin had absolutely no objection to taking the lead with regard to intergovernmental cooperation, whether to distribute Marshall Aid through the OEEC or in the defence of Western Europe via NATO (see

Chapter 2). From the outset, however, policymakers demonstrated an intense aversion to any proposal which reduced Britain's freedom of manoeuvre in either of the two more important circles of influence or which required some surrender of sovereignty to a supranational 'high authority' able to dictate to national governments.

This hostility manifested itself in Bevin's opposition to demands from the Hague Congress in May 1948 for a European Parliament with powers over a political union, and he continued to resist such ideas from the newly created Council of Europe in May 1949. Bevin was equally reluctant to bow to US pressure for Britain to assume the leadership of a united Europe and during 1947–49 he engaged in a spirited and ultimately successful battle with the Americans, who wanted the OEEC to become more of a supranational body promoting European integration. Above all, this antipathy towards supranational organisation prompted the rejection of a plan presented by Robert Schuman, the French Foreign Minister, in May 1950, proposing the pooling of French and West German coal and steel supplies and inviting the participation of other European states in a community which would delegate a large measure of decision-making power to a supranational 'high authority' able to act without the unanimous consent of member governments (Pelling 1984: 137–8). This plan had been devised by Jean Monnet and his associates in the French economic planning commission who had learned from the failure of their plans for a European customs union in 1947 that complete integration in a single step was too much to expect and that they should tackle integration on an incremental and functional basis. While beginning with coal and steel as two of the most important sectors of the modern industrial economy, Monnet was confident that this would eventually lead to full European economic union through the back door.

Britain immediately rebuffed the Schuman Plan for a variety of reasons. Bevin was annoyed at receiving no advance warning of the announcement and even more irritated to learn that the US State Department had been informed; a fact he interpreted as proof that this was a Franco-American plot to undermine Britain's leadership in the reconstruction of Western Europe. The Foreign Office was even more infuriated by French insistence upon prior acceptance of the principle of supranational control over these industries without any adequate definition of precisely what this meant – particularly when allowed only 24 hours to decide whether to attend the inaugural conference. These concerns were further fuelled by suspicions that the scheme's neutralist implications would impinge upon Britain's relationship with the United States and the Commonwealth, while the economic ministries vigorously opposed membership on the grounds that it would damage the British coal and steel industry at precisely the moment they had been taken into public ownership. In these circumstances, the Labour government argued that it was hardly likely to have nationalised these 'commanding heights of the British economy' only to pass control over to a supranational 'high authority' dominated by envious foreigners (Young 1991: chs 15–16). On this basis, the 'Inner Six', consisting of France, West Germany, Italy and the Benelux countries, formed the European Coal and Steel Community (ECSC) in April 1952 without British participation.

The Conservative government, which entered office in 1951, adopted broadly the same approach to European integration. On the face of it, this is curious given Churchill's established reputation as a supposed champion of European federation. In June 1940, Churchill had floated Monnet's plan for an Anglo-French 'indissoluble union' with shared sovereignty, a single cabinet, parliament and common citizenship, and in 1943 he reinforced this reputation in a broadcast calling for a 'Council of Europe' supported by structures for economic and military cooperation. Most importantly, at Zurich in September 1946, Churchill talked about the possibility of building 'a kind of United States of Europe' to which Britain would act as the 'friend and sponsor': an aspiration he repeated at The Hague in May 1948. Yet, beneath the portentous language, Churchill's commitment was always strictly qualified and more rhetorical than real. His proposals in June 1940 were designed simply to prevent France from surrendering until the last possible moment, and his much-quoted post-war speeches, on closer examination, were actually extremely ambiguous – particularly about the degree of British participation in any scheme for a United States of Europe. Moreover, when he did clarify his position (as in May 1953) it was usually to suggest that Britain was 'with them, not of them'; a role he conceptualised in terms of a benevolent sponsor and encouraging supporter rather than a direct participant in an integrated Europe (Charlton 1989: 137). Furthermore, as Churchill's Foreign Secretary, Anthony Eden shared much of Bevin's mistrust of abstract federal schemes while placing his principal emphasis firmly upon the Atlantic alliance.

Any doubts about the real position of Churchill's government were dispelled by its chilly response to proposals from the French Prime Minister, René Pleven, in October 1950 for a European Defence Community (EDC). Like the ECSC, this was designed to pool the military resources of the member states along supranational lines with a single defence minister directing a European Army. British refusal to participate in this ill-conceived response to US demands for a larger European contribution to its own defence (by deploying German troops in a cross-national force without the need to create a new German army) was a significant factor in the French Assembly's rejection of the scheme in September 1954. Unfortunately, the lesson learned in Whitehall from the failure of the EDC (and the subsequent success of Eden's counter-proposal for West Germany simply to be admitted to NATO) was that they had been correct all along in believing that it was possible to achieve European reconstruction through limited intergovernmental cooperation, without the need for supranational integration. In complete contrast, in other Western European capitals the success of the ECSC and the very failure of the EDC both served to increase the determination to ensure that next time their plans for economic union came to fruition.

'Missing the boat': Britain's first two applications, 1955–69

A variety of factors help to explain British myopia about the developing European project in the mid-1950s. The preoccupation with re-establishing Britain's world role simply diverted attention from the less important European circle at a time of increasing difficulties with the US and the Commonwealth. Growing anxiety about British economic performance, after the appearance of the first signs of the 'stop-go' cycle in the mid-1950s, was equally distracting. Similarly, the failure of the EDC encouraged the fatal belief, in Whitehall, that any future efforts at European integration were equally doomed to failure (George 1998: 26–7). Whatever the reasons, critics often suggest that British policymakers never fully comprehended the significance of the negotiations which led from the Messina conference in June 1955, via the detailed deliberations of the Spaak Committee, to the Treaty of Rome in March 1957 and the foundations for the European Economic Community (EEC) and the European Atomic Community (Euratom) in January 1958. In reality, however, the evidence indicates that they understood only too well the significance of these negotiations – and wanted no part of them. As Anthony Eden predicted, 'the experiment of the six cannot succeed without federation . . . in the sense of one Parliament, one foreign policy, one currency, etc. . . . I do not want to become part of such a federation' (Turner 2000: 50).

Britain was represented on the Spaak Committee for the first five months of its deliberations, but, from the outset, fundamental differences in approach were always evident, given the British delegation's insistence on the creation of a free-trade area rather than a high tariff customs union, its enthusiasm for intergovernmental cooperation and institutions rather than supranationalism, and its tendency to treat European integration as an essentially commercial matter rather than as the harbinger of closer political integration (Camps 1964: 28–30; Kitzinger 1973: 40). Given the extent of these differences, it is scarcely surprising that Britain withdrew from the negotiations in November 1955 after a long period of uneasy disagreement. Undeterred by the British retreat, the 'Inner Six' pressed on to sign the Treaty of Rome 16 months later, with the intention not only of creating a single 'Common Market' for labour, services and capital, but also laying the foundations of 'an ever closer union among the peoples of Europe'.

In October 1955, a British working party on the Common Market had concluded that the establishment of such an organisation 'would be bad for the United Kingdom and if possible should be frustrated' (Hennessy 2007: 395). To this end, Britain's response to these surprise developments was to launch the idea of a European Free Trade Area (EFTA) at Stockholm in November 1959, largely as a spoiling tactic cynically designed to undermine the cohesion of the 'Inner Six' (see Map 5.1). The appeal of this idea for Whitehall was that the looser structure of a free-trade area confined only to industrial goods would be more attractive to Germany and the Benelux countries than the high tariff barrier around the EEC's customs union. In addition, it would not threaten either Commonwealth trade in food products or the British system of agricultural subsidy – although, as Miriam Camps argues, if Britain had accepted the idea of a customs union it was in a strong position to negotiate sweeping exemptions for agriculture and the Commonwealth (as France did) in a manner which would later prove impossible to achieve. Unfortunately for Macmillan, hopes of sabotaging the new organisation were soon dispelled and within months his government had begun the process of bridge-building with the EEC (Camps 1964: 169, ch. 5).

According to Uwe Kitzinger, there were 'five milestones' on the road to the British application to join the EEC in 1961 (Kitzinger 1973: 27–34). Firstly, the Suez crisis supposedly represented a major blow to post-war confidence by raising fundamental doubts about Britain's great power status. Secondly, the abandonment of the Blue Streak missile on technical and financial grounds in 1960 and the purchase of Skybolt from the US as a replacement was yet another painful example of Britain's increasing dependence upon Washington at a time when the Kennedy administration saw it as 'the grand opportunity to terminate the special relationship and force Britain into Europe' (Kitzinger 1973: 34). Thirdly, the dismal failure of the Paris summit in 1960 represented Britain's last major diplomatic initiative on the world stage and some contemporary observers suggest Macmillan's conversion to Europe was

Map 5.1   The 'Inner Six' and the 'Outer Seven': the EEC and EFTA

a direct consequence of his 'failure to gain a niche in history by acting as a bridge between the American and Russian superpowers' (Pliatzky 1982: 45; Macmillan 1972: 310–13). Fourthly, the major sterling crisis during the summer of 1961, and the unpopular remedial measures that followed it, delivered another unwelcome jolt to post-war optimism. Kitzinger's final milestone relates to more general doubts about the illusory strength of the British economy. While annual growth rates during the 1950s were relatively impressive by British standards (justifying Macmillan's 1959 election claim that most Britons had 'never had it so good'), in comparison with the six members of the EEC they appeared relatively sluggish, prompting the (erroneous) inference that EEC membership had itself promoted faster economic growth. In addition, others claim that perhaps the most important factor in the sudden conversion to a European future in 1960–61 was Britain's changing pattern of overseas trade, which from the late 1950s onwards shifted dramatically away from the Empire circle towards Europe and the US (Sanders 1990: 119, 144–5).

These arguments are not equally persuasive. Despite Kitzinger's emphasis upon 'time lags in political psychology', the supposed impact of Suez probably exaggerates its direct importance, while arguments about economic decline and trade patterns are ostensibly convincing until we recall that an interdepartmental committee of senior officials concluded in 1960 that 'on political grounds – that is, to ensure a politically stable and cohesive Western Europe – there was a strong argument for joining the Common Market', but the economic case was far less compelling (George 1998: 29). At a general level, however, Kitzinger is correct to suggest that collectively these five 'milestones' precipitated a general crisis of confidence within Whitehall about the country's standing in the world and its ability to maintain that position. As the Foreign Office warned in October 1959, the EEC might soon 'completely out-class the UK in terms of military and economic importance' (Ruane and Ellison 2007: 162). Indeed, if anything, Kitzinger understates the degree to which this period witnessed even more fundamental doubts about the whole basis of British post-war foreign policy given the recognition that the Commonwealth was more of a diplomatic and economic constraint than an asset. More important, US reactions were crucial to Harold Macmillan's change of direction.

The United States had been pushing Britain towards European cooperation since 1947 through conventional diplomatic channels, while the CIA was covertly funding the European Movement, in the hope of promoting entry and undermining Labour resistance to it (Aldrich 1997). This was a factor which British governments could not easily ignore, even though they suspected that Washington was living in 'a fool's paradise about Messina' (Hennessy 2007: 398). As the Cabinet noted in 1957: 'Our special relationship with the United States would be endangered if the United States believes that our influence was less than that of the European Community' (Reynolds 1991: 217). On this basis, Miriam Camps concludes, the conviction that 'the shortest, and perhaps the only, way to real Atlantic partnership lay through Britain's joining the Common Market seems to have been a very important – perhaps the controlling – element in Mr Macmillan's own decision that the right course for the United Kingdom was to apply for membership' (Camps 1964: 336; see also Kaiser 1996: 108). Conversely, others

Table 5.2   Average percentage annual growth of GDP, 1950–80

	1950–60	1960–70	1970–80
Average ECSC/EEC	4.08	4.2	2.6
UK	2.3	2.3	2.0

Source: adapted from Sanders (1990: 145).

argue the decision was not a means to strengthen the Anglo-American alliance but rather a hedge against the unreliability of Washington (Ashton 2002a: 246). Either way, Macmillan's decision betokened a crisis in British foreign policy prompted by the rapid realisation that 'the British government had lost the initiative and was reacting to European situations created by others; it was not itself setting the pace' (Camps 1964: 505). When viewed from this perspective, Britain's application in 1961 can thus be portrayed as a belated attempt to regain the initiative – or at least to prevent Britain being left behind at a time when Macmillan confessed that he 'did not like the prospect of a world divided into the Russian sphere, the American sphere and a united Europe of which we were not a member' (Macmillan 1972: 74).

Britain launched its first application for membership in July 1961 and negotiations made reasonable progress until 14 January 1963. As the British government had consistently underestimated the cohesiveness of the 'Inner Six', while significantly overestimating its own bargaining power, it came as a devastating surprise when the negotiations were brought to a dramatic halt by President de Gaulle's sudden French veto; a remarkably high-handed unilateral action justified by doubts about Britain's dedication to its European vocation – particularly given evidence of its potentially disruptive attachment to the United States symbolised by Kennedy's offer of Polaris missiles to Macmillan at Nassau in December 1962 (see Chapter 7). 'England ... is insular, maritime, bound by her trade, her markets, her supplies, to countries that are very diverse and often very far away', the French president declared. 'How can England, as she lives, as she produces, as she trades, be incorporated in the Common Market?' (George 1998: 34). In reality, this was never more than a convenient pretext to conceal de Gaulle's nationalistic determination to exclude a significant threat to continued French ascendancy within the EEC, but it very effectively achieved its objective.

When Labour entered office in October 1964, it had little enthusiasm for the idea of joining the EEC. This was partly because Labour's public attachment to the Commonwealth and the 'special relationship' was even stronger than that of the Conservatives, but the party was also instinctively opposed to what the Labour left condemned as a conservative, Catholic and capitalist club which Wilson had denounced in 1962 as 'anti-planning' (Kitzinger 1968: 4). Most important, however, Labour's hostility towards the EEC stemmed from the conviction that Britain's mounting economic difficulties could be solved by national indicative economic planning and purposive public ownership, and that past failures were attributable not to defective economic theories or policy instruments but rather the manner in which their Conservative predecessors had employed them. The creation of the Department of Economic Affairs (DEA) in 1964, with George Brown at its head, thus represented a radical attempt to apply this prescription by separating macro-economic planning from the day-to-day activities of the Treasury in the hope of reinvigorating the British economy.

Against this background, the real turning point in Labour thinking towards Europe was prompted by the recognition that indicative economic planning could not achieve its objective at a national level. This transition in policy focus from a 'national' to a 'European' solution to Britain's problems was signalled by George Brown's movement from the DEA to the Foreign Office in July 1966 (Kitzinger 1968: 13). Just as Blue Streak, Suez, the Paris summit and sluggish economic performance represented milestones on Macmillan's Damascene road towards Britain's first application, the equivalent forces driving the second application in 1966–67 were the failure of the DEA's 'National Plan', increasing anxiety about Britain's adverse balance of payments and nagging doubts about the entire basis of external strategy, given concerns about the value of the Commonwealth (after angry disputes over Rhodesia), and the rapid deterioration of Anglo-American relations (following the decision to withdraw from 'East of Suez' in July 1966) (Kitzinger 1968: 11-12). As John Young argues, by the mid-1960s entry to the EC 'did not mean the abandonment of traditional policies, it was a reaction to their collapse' (Young 1993: 174). Sir Con O'Neill, head of the UK delegation to the European Communities, encapsulated the broader underlying logic when he told ministers in October 1966:

> For the last 20 years this country has been adrift . . . we do not know where we are going and have begun to lose confidence in ourselves. Perhaps the point has now been reached when the acceptance of a new goal and a new commitment could give the country as a whole a focus around which to crystallise its hopes and energies. Entry into Europe might provide the stimulus and target we require. (Young 1998: 190)

Despite Wilson's announcement in November 1966 that 'we mean business', British diplomacy served only to alienate many potential European allies before de Gaulle issued a second French veto in December 1967 – this time justified by the weakness of the British economy after sterling's recent devaluation. Again, however, the public justification masked the same desire to maintain French dominance, combined with the not unreasonable suspicion that Britain was still guilty of what Wilson described as 'the mortal sin of Atlanticism' (Wilson 1971: 407–18, 523).

Edward Heath's European crusade and Labour's referendum, 1970–79

When Edward Heath's Conservative government entered office in June 1970, it was led by one of the few senior political figures in British politics at the time who sincerely believed in European integration. Europe had been the central defining theme of Heath's entire political career since his maiden speech in 1950 on the need to join the ECSC. He was a member of Jean Monnet's Action Committee for the United States of Europe and in 1961, as Lord Privy Seal and Foreign Office Minister with special responsibility for European Affairs, he had been Macmillan's chief negotiator for membership. Within two weeks of becoming Prime Minister, accession negotiations began in Luxembourg. In some respects, the circumstances were unpropitious. Public opinion had swung markedly against British membership since the failure of the 1966–67 application, with a Gallup poll showing 70 per cent of the electorate opposed to entry by March 1971. He also faced a number of difficult negotiating problems with regard to the international position of sterling, the substantial differences between the Common Agricultural Policy (CAP) and Britain's guaranteed price regime, and the scale of Britain's contribution to the Community budget, given that its heavy dependence on imports from outside the Community would force it to contribute significantly more to the EC budget than was justified by its relative share of GNP.

On the other hand, changing patterns of British trade meant that the Commonwealth represented much less of a problem than in 1961. The German decision to float the Deutschmark in May 1971 torpedoed French plans for rapid progress towards Economic and Monetary Union (EMU) and this removed the sterling problem altogether. More important, de Gaulle's resignation in April 1969 opened the way for Heath to develop a good working relationship with the far more pragmatic Georges Pompidou – particularly as he immediately assured the

French President 'that there could be no special partnership between Britain and the United States even if Britain wanted it' (Heath 1998: 364). Above all, Heath was extremely fortunate that the deadlock in entry negotiations was broken by the nationalisation of French oil interests in Algeria early in 1971; a presidential setback which encouraged Pompidou to seek a compensating foreign policy victory at the Paris summit with Heath in May 1971. After this, it took only a month to resolve all of the outstanding issues and in late June the agreements were signed paving the way for Britain's formal entry to the European Communities on 1 January 1973.

At this juncture, there was little reason to anticipate that Britain would prove to be a particularly 'awkward partner' in the European project. On the contrary, Heath was a true believer who interpreted British national interests to coincide precisely with those of the Community in its advance towards closer economic, monetary and diplomatic unity (Heath 1988: 203). But while a life-long advocate of the European project, even Heath soon encountered difficulties over the question of CAP reform, the European Regional Development Fund, negotiations with African, Caribbean and Pacific States, EMU and energy policy. As a result, even during its first year of membership, Britain had already acquired a reputation for being a reluctant, discordant force within the EC (George 1998: 56–70). After Heath's defeat in February 1974, this reputation was substantially reinforced by the apparent scepticism of the incoming Labour government and an extremely hostile public opinion.

The Labour party was bitterly divided over the European question. On one side, there was a dedicated group of largely centre-right pro-Europeans led by Roy Jenkins, then deputy leader of the party, and supported by David Owen, the Foreign Secretary, Shirley Williams and others who would later defect to form the nucleus of the Social Democratic Party. Ranged against them were the bulk of the Parliamentary Labour Party (PLP), constituency activists and the trade unions. In order to break this impasse without provoking a damaging schism, Wilson exploited Heath's pledge that membership would only occur with the 'full-hearted consent of the British people' to announce in Opposition that a future Labour government would 'renegotiate' the terms of entry before putting the question of membership to Britain's first national referendum. From a leadership perspective, this offered the perfect solution in that both sides in the debate could recognise the legitimacy of a decision ultimately made by the electorate. For the Labour anti-Europeans, the appeal of a referendum was also massively enhanced by the fact that the electorate appeared to be strongly opposed to membership. In reality, however, while voters had been generally anti-European since 1967, public opinion had been subject to sharp short-term fluctuations because most voters knew little and cared less about the entire European question. More important, it was clear that those who knew least about Europe were also those most hostile to it – and these tended to be working-class Labour voters (King 1977: 24).

Labour's commitment to 'renegotiation' was a fraudulent charade. The Wilson government always recognised that the founder members had no intention of renegotiating anything fundamental in the structure or policy framework of the EC, and most of the Labour Cabinet wanted to remain in Europe whatever the negotiations produced. Nevertheless, Wilson needed a suitable form of words to justify continued membership, and 'renegotiation' provided the necessary cloak of respectability. The process of renegotiation was concluded at the Dublin summit in March 1975. The government then announced that it was satisfied with the new terms and almost overnight public opinion swung dramatically towards remaining in the EC. As scarcely anyone actually knew what had been renegotiated, this dramatic shift in public opinion can be explained in two ways. Firstly, the softness of opinion meant that any powerful new stimulus would lead to change and in this context 'renegotiated' terms simply had to mean 'better' terms than those obtained by the Conservatives. Secondly, opinion was softest and most volatile among working-class Labour voters who, in the absence of either interest or hard information, tended to followed the leaders they knew, liked and trusted most and these were predominantly pro-Europeans like the Prime Minister and most of the Cabinet. As a result, public opinion swung immediately after Dublin in favour of continued membership by a ratio of 2:1 and it remained there during the next eleven weeks of the campaign.

The referendum on 5 June 1975 superficially appeared to be a ringing endorsement for membership, with 67.2 per cent in favour of continued membership to 32.8 per cent against on a turnout of 64.5 per cent; a margin of nearly nine million votes. Moreover, it was a truly national victory in that England, Wales, Scotland and Northern Ireland all voted 'yes' and it has been calculated that if the poll had been conducted on a constituency basis, only four or five of the country's 635 parliamentary constituencies would have voted 'no' (King 1977: 130; Butler and Kitzinger 1976: 263–73). Whatever the reason for this momentous victory, Harold Wilson declared in the immediate aftermath of the result: 'The verdict has been given by a vote and a majority bigger than that achieved by any government in a general election in the history of our democracy . . . it means that fourteen years of national argument are over' (Wilson 1979: 108). After this, however, the Callaghan government renewed its emphasis upon Anglo-American relations at the direct expense of Europe – not least by being the only member state not to join the Exchange Rate Mechanism (ERM) in March 1979.

Margaret Thatcher and the EU budget, 1979–84

Although Margaret Thatcher is famed for her Euro-scepticism while Prime Minister, as a relatively junior member of Macmillan's government in 1961 she supported Britain's application to join the EC 'in terms that seemed to indicate enthusiastic endorsement rather than obligations of ministerial loyalty'. She did much the same during Edward Heath's application and even as party leader in Opposition after 1975 she repeatedly described the Conservatives as 'the party of Europe' – albeit largely as a tactical measure to enable the Conservatives to attack the Callaghan government's lack of enthusiasm towards the EMS (Green 2006: 172–3). Once in office after May 1979, however, it rapidly became clear that she had none of Heath's instinctive sympathy for the European ideal and did not even appear to share his view that Britain's future lay in closer contact with the European Community. On the contrary, her personal foreign policy adviser recalled that her attitude to Europe 'ranged from suspicion to undisguised hostility' (Cradock 1997: 125). She believed her European counterparts had a grandiose but muddled vision of Europe, which was interventionist, protectionist, ultimately federalist and profoundly anti-British in its effects. Moreover, she suspected the entire project was inimical to freedom because it was equated in her mind with bureaucratic state control, creeping socialism, unnecessary regulation, lost sovereignty and a diluted sense of national identity. 'We believe in a free Europe, not a standardised Europe', she declared during the first European elections in 1979:

> We insist that the institutions of the European Community are managed so that they increase the liberty of the individual throughout the continent. These institutions must not be permitted to dwindle into bureaucracy. Whenever they fail to enlarge freedom, institutions should be criticised and the balance restored. (Thatcher 1993: 60–1)

This would soon become a central theme of her speeches as Prime Minister, when she reincarnated herself as Britannia defending national interests from envious and avaricious foreigners trying to profit at

Britain's expense. According to her Chancellor, these ideological considerations were privately reinforced by a form of 'saloon-bar xenophobia' which manifested itself in a 'pathological hostility to Germany and the Germans which in the end came to dominate her view of the European Community' (Lawson 1992: 274). Such attitudes undoubtedly played a major role in her vociferous opposition to German reunification. Little wonder that her biographer considered Europe to be her 'greatest blind spot' (J. Campbell 2008: 599).

Given this combative approach, Thatcher's governments inevitably found themselves embroiled in a series of major disputes with the European Community during her 11-year premiership. The size of Britain's contribution to the EC budget dominated the first years of Thatcher's leadership. Heath's acceptance of highly unfavourable budgetary terms meant that by 1979 Britain contributed 20 per cent of EC income in return for only 8.7 per cent of EC expenditure, making it the second highest net contributor after Germany, despite being only the seventh wealthiest member in terms of GDP per head; a problem which stemmed from Britain's heavy dependence on food and manufactured imports from outside the EU, upon which basis the budget contribution was largely calculated. At Thatcher's first European Council meeting in Strasbourg in June 1979, she put the case very reasonably when declaring that she could not 'play Sister Bountiful to the Community while my own electorate are being asked to forego improvements in the fields of health, education, welfare and the rest' (Cosgrave 1985b: 86). At her second European Council in Dublin five months later, however, her mood and tone had perceptibly stiffened and this led to an ugly squabble with her German and French counterparts. After this, her rhetoric became increasingly strident, to the extent that Lord Carrington, the Foreign Secretary, lamented that her 'firmness and intransigence' made her 'exceptionally unpopular' when she bluntly declared: 'I want my money back'. As he later ruefully recorded, 'I cannot pretend that the resultant atmosphere made all our foreign relations easier to conduct' (Carrington 1998: 319).

A number of factors contributed to the unpleasantness of the complex budgetary dispute which dominated Anglo-EC relations until 1984. There was unquestionably much ritualised posturing on both sides and this made compromise extremely difficult. Attempts to resolve the problem, by increasing the overall size of the EC budget to allow more to be spent on Britain, were unacceptable to a Conservative government committed to reducing overall public expenditure. On the other hand, any solution that reduced the benefits to other member states was equally unacceptable to them. As a result, the dispute revolved around the possible payment of a budgetary rebate to Britain. The dispute was undoubtedly further aggravated by Thatcher's shrill and hectoring manner when lecturing other heads of government. While her natural talent as a blunt and fiery debater was well adapted to the adversarial style of British politics, it was alien to the European tradition of coalition governments and negotiated concessions, and her conduct was widely condemned for violating the norms of accepted diplomatic behaviour – particularly given the widespread recognition that the crudely nationalistic populism of her Euro-scepticism was being exploited for party management purposes to consolidate both her backbench support and her public image as the 'Iron Lady' who was 'not for turning'.

Having virtually invented the figures to justify her demand for a £1 billion rebate, Thatcher remained intransigent throughout. To the fury of her European counterparts, she rejected a £350 million rebate at Dublin in November 1979 and £760 million at Luxembourg in April 1980 before the threat of mass Cabinet resignation forced her to accept a slightly more favourable compromise offered at Brussels in May 1980 (Young 1991: 190). Another interim rebate of £850 million was agreed in 1982, but these bruising budget battles continued unabated until the Fontainebleau summit in June 1984, when Britain received £1.1 billion as a single compensation payment along with agreement that the future British contribution should be reduced to a level broadly in line with its GNP. It was a substantial and enduring victory for her abrasive negotiating style against now less experienced and less well-briefed French and German leaders, but it seriously damaged Britain's standing within the EC, as did her refusal to accept a reasonable offer when the issue was revived in 1987–88 (George 1998: 189–90).

After this personal triumph over the British budget rebate, Thatcher turned to the related question of CAP reform during the middle years of the premiership. Although highly contentious, this battle aroused less animosity than the budget dispute. Nevertheless, Thatcher vigorously denounced the CAP as 'Mad-Hatter economics' on the grounds that its guaranteed price regime absorbed over two-thirds of the EC budget to subsidise inefficient farmers producing 'butter mountains' and 'wine lakes', which were then often dumped at rock-bottom prices in communist Eastern Europe. Although Thatcher wanted to dispense with the policy altogether, this was never practical politics. At the Brussels Council in February 1988, however, a package of reforms was agreed which included automatic price cuts beyond certain production levels to reduce agricultural surpluses. It was a limited victory for Thatcher's persistence, but once again it was achieved at a high price in terms of Anglo-EC relations.

The Single European Act, the Delors Report and monetary union, 1984–90

After the resolution of the budgetary issue, Britain's relations with the EC briefly entered a more constructive period of greater harmony – largely because the Community agenda conformed well with Thatcher's free-market orientations and minimalist view of the EC. As she records in her memoirs, 'I had one overriding positive goal . . . to create a single common market' (Thatcher 1993: 553). In June 1985, Britain's paper entitled *Europe – the Future* wholeheartedly endorsed the value of European Political Cooperation (EPC) and the desire to remove the remaining obstacles to the single European market by the end of 1992 – albeit without further governmental integration in the form of a 'European Union'. In 1986, Thatcher thus initially embraced the Single European Act in the belief that the promise of a neoliberal Thatcherite economic agenda being institutionalised across the entire EC within a genuinely single market by the end of 1992 was sufficiently attractive to justify compromise on institutional reform. In retrospect, however, Nigel Lawson, her Chancellor at the time, was absolutely correct when he later recalled that it is 'positively mind-boggling' that Thatcher should have signed the SEA, which extended the use of Qualified Majority Voting (QMV), and spoke of 'concrete progress towards European unity' and monetary union without comprehending that this implied an advance towards a single currency, the harmonisation of tax and social policy, and a major reduction in the power of the national veto (Lawson 1992: 904). Nevertheless, she did sign the SEA, largely because Geoffrey Howe and David Williamson, Thatcher's EC policy adviser, persuaded her that unless she supported the extension of QMV to implement single market directives, the Greek government would veto the entire proposal. When signing the SEA, however, she still assumed the Commission's powers would recede as the single market gained ground (George 1998: 180–89). When it became clear that the reverse was true, she rapidly emerged as a vitriolic critic of QMV as a sinister vehicle for the federalist and interventionist policies of Jacques Delors and his colleagues in the European Commission.

Franco-German momentum behind European Monetary Union (EMU) began to make itself felt in June 1988 with the German presidency of the Council of Ministers, and it gained further impetus from the second term of the European Commission President, Jacques Delors. His speech to the British TUC in July 1988 argued the case for a 'social Europe', while he declared in the European Parliament in the same month that within 10 years 80 per cent of economic legislation, and perhaps tax and social legislation, would be directed from the

European Community (George 1998: 192–3). Equally alarming for Thatcher was the acceptance by the Madrid summit in June 1989 of the Commission's draft European 'Social Charter' designed to introduce a social dimension into the internal market; a proposal she found particularly repugnant after all her efforts to deregulate the British labour market, roll back the frontiers of the state and destroy the necessary legal immunities of trade unions.

Outraged and alarmed by these developments, Thatcher struck back in her now infamous Bruges speech on 20 September 1988. This outspoken intervention was intended to apply the brake to any headlong rush towards Euro-federalism and monetary union but it ended by leaving her isolated within the Community. After a recitation of well-established British themes, Thatcher declared 'willing and active co-operation between independent sovereign states' was 'the best way to build a successful European Community'. She then added a thunderbolt: 'We have not successfully rolled back the frontiers of the state in Britain only to see them re-imposed at the European level, with a European super-state exercising a new dominance from Brussels' (Thatcher 1993: 744–5). Despite the fury it provoked in Europe, and the despair of the FCO, the speech indicated unambiguously that Thatcher would adopt an uncompromising stand on the next stage of European integration.

Having thrown down the gauntlet, the final phase of Thatcher's premiership was marred by disputes with both her European counterparts and leading members of her own Cabinet over the Exchange Rate Mechanism (ERM). The Delors report, published in April 1989, outlined a three-stage advance to full EMU, in which the first stage would ensure that all member states joined the ERM before the establishment of a European Central Bank and a single currency in later phases. As Chancellor, Nigel Lawson shared Thatcher's opposition to full EMU and the single currency, but both he and Howe had supported Britain's entry to the ERM since the late 1970s and they had been appalled by the hostile invective contained in Thatcher's Bruges speech (Howe 1995: 537–50; Lawson 1992: 784-90). The principal tactical objective for this powerful axis of Treasury and FCO was to accept the ERM in order to detach it from the unacceptable Stage II and III progress towards a common currency and they threatened concerted resignation in order to 'blackmail' her into action. Conversely, Thatcher adamantly opposed both the principle of membership and the diplomatic pragmatism of her senior ministers, but she was effectively forced to accede to their joint demands at the Madrid Council in June 1989. In its aftermath, however, Howe was humiliatingly reshuffled to the nominal position of 'Deputy Prime Minister' in July 1989, while Lawson was subsequently manoeuvred into resignation, after a dispute with Walters over the Treasury's policy of shadowing the Deutschmark in preparation for Stage I (Thatcher 1993: 711–14).

Despite the destruction of the Lawson/Howe axis, in October 1990, only six weeks before she was forced from office, John Major, the Chancellor and Douglas Hurd, the Foreign Secretary, finally compelled Thatcher to accept membership of the ERM against her wishes and better judgement: 'I had too few allies to continue to resist and win the day', she later lamented (Thatcher 1993: 722). But Thatcher was not called the 'Iron Lady' for nothing. At the Rome IGC in October 1990, she denounced her 11 partners for 'living in cloud cuckoo land' when they set the timetable for Stage II. Worse still, departing dramatically from the FCO script in her Commons statement on the Rome meeting, her defiant assertion that she would not 'hand over Sterling and the powers of this House to Europe' provoked Howe's angry resignation on the grounds that her uncompromising attitude jeopardised any British influence over Community development; an act which was the proximate cause of Thatcher's downfall from the premiership. As her biographer puts it, 'Thatcher's European policy was no policy at all' and it represented her 'greatest failure' because of 'her own confrontational, xenophobic and narrow-minded personality' (J. Campbell 2008: 622). In retirement, however, she remained unrepentant, declaring in her reflections on *Statecraft* that her efforts with Europe had been to no avail because the EU was 'fundamentally unreformable' (Thatcher 2002: 321).

John Major: a change of tone but not substance

Europe has rightly been described as 'the defining issue' for John Major's premiership and for the Conservative party he led (Wallace 1994: 294). From the outset, Major sought to project himself as the conscious antithesis of everything negative his predecessor had come to represent in the public mind after 11 years in office. Above all, during his 'charm offensive' in European capitals, he abandoned Thatcher's confrontational rhetoric in favour of conciliatory declarations about his desire to place Britain 'at the very heart of the Europe'. This new rhetoric was warmly welcomed in EC capitals as an indication of a more positive negotiating position, and the goodwill it created proved helpful at the Maastricht summit in December 1991 in enabling Major to thwart the federalist proposals of the Dutch presidency. More importantly, at Maastricht, Major successfully achieved a dual 'opt out' from two of the treaty's key provisions, allowing Britain to defer a decision on both full monetary union and the implementation of the Social Chapter. He was equally successful in frustrating Franco-German calls to extend QMV to other foreign policy matters, on the grounds that it conflicted with Britain's Atlanticist orientation and because of doubts about the ability of such a diverse conglomeration ever to be able to agree on a concerted course of action. On the other hand, Major accepted the view that European Foreign and Security Policy (CFSP) should ultimately encompass 'the security of the Union, including the eventual framing of a common defence policy, which might in time lead to a common defence' (Blair 1998).

Major's diplomatic triumph at Maastricht was soon negated by the living nightmare he endured at the hands of his own Euro-sceptic back-benchers during the passage of the necessary legislation through Parliament. To make matters worse, these problems were dramatically intensified by Britain's ignominious expulsion from the ERM on 'Black Wednesday' in September 1992. Having staked his domestic economic credibility on ERM membership, Britain's withdrawal at an estimated cost of £20 billion severely tarnished the image of the Major government while making Euro-scepticism a respectable intellectual position for hostile Conservatives (Turner 2000: 160). These problems of party management dogged the process of Maastricht ratification in 1992–93 and almost every other subsequent debate on the European question during the Major government, forcing Hurd and Major increasingly to talk about the 'variable geometry' of a 'multi-speed Europe' in order to soften the austerely simplistic differentiation between Britain languishing in obscure isolation while its continental allies surged ahead towards integration (King 1998: 79–93).

When considered as a whole, the European record of the Major governments is mixed. Stephen George and Matthew Sowemimo argue that his greatest achievement was simply to ensure 'the debate was no longer about whether there would be closer economic cooperation in the future. It was now about what sort of EU would emerge from that closer cooperation' (George and Sowemimo 1996: 263). This is a rather charitable interpretation, given that Major's staunch defence of his 'opt outs' at Maastricht and his rhetoric of selective Europeanism differed from Thatcher's in tone rather than in substance. As a result, rather more commentators would endorse William Wallace's criticism of Major's lack of direction as his government followed the now conventional trajectory from initially supportive rhetoric through tension to outright hostility while he attempted to reconcile a viable EU policy with an ill-informed and prejudiced domestic opinion (Wallace 1994: 299). Such was the degree of frustration with the Major government's obstructionism, that the EU intergovernmental conference on treaty reform virtually ceased its deliberations in the lead up to the 1997 general election in the hope that a more constructive government would be elected. Little wonder that the 'New Labour' victory in 1997 was greeted with such relief and acclaim on the continent.

Tony Blair and the 'Europeanisation' of New Labour

Under Neil Kinnock's leadership, the Labour Party reluctantly jettisoned its traditional hostility towards the EU so that by the time Tony Blair became leader in 1994, Labour's 1983 manifesto commitment to withdraw from the EC altogether had been consigned to the dustbin of history (see Table 5.2). 'New Labour' leaders were now thoroughly reconstructed as pro-European supporters of integration, even if domestic political failure and exclusion from power had played a major role in converting many within the party (Geddes 1994). Labour's manifesto in 1997 pledged to 'give Britain leadership in Europe' and talked of Europe as 'our destiny', while Robin Cook, as Foreign Secretary, announced that he intended 'a fresh start in Europe for Britain, working with Member States as a partner, not an opponent' (www.fco.gov.uk; Turner 2000: 228). In a speech in Cardiff on 29 November 2002, Blair declared:

> For Britain, there is a simple choice to be made. Are we fully partners in Europe, at the centre of its decision-making, influencing and shaping its direction; or are we at the back of the file, following warily a path beaten by others? For 50 years, that has been our choice. For 50 years we have chosen to follow, first in joining; then in each new departure Europe has made. (Riddell 2005: 362)

Within a few weeks of entering office, New Labour gave substance to the promise of a new approach and 'constructive engagement' by abandoning Major's 'opt out' from the Social Chapter and signing the Amsterdam Treaty, which included an employment chapter and powers to strengthen the European Parliament – all issues on which the Conservatives had been obstructionist and rightly regarded as an 'important symbol of positive intent' (Bache and Jordan 2006: 8).

On the other hand, to avoid alienating the Euro-sceptic press and public opinion, supportive language was qualified with suitably nationalistic rhetoric. In a classic example of Third Way 'triangulation', it was argued that a Labour government would be pro-European but also determined in its defence of British national interests. 'We will stand up for British interests in Europe ... but more than that, we will lead a campaign for reform in Europe'. Yet, as the manifesto went on to argue, 'But to lead means to be involved, to be constructive, to be capable of getting our own way' (Labour Party 1997). To reinforce the message, Blair declared on the eve of the Amsterdam summit in May 1997 (in language reminiscent of Thatcher) that 'British national interests must be properly safeguarded and Europe itself has got to refocus its horizons . . . on the things that really matter to the people' (Bulmer 2000: 243). In defending this position, Blair characteristically employed a rhetorical device which suggested that British and European interests were not opposed but likely to be enhanced through future collabora-

Table 5.3   Labour's manifesto commitments on Europe, 1979–97

1979 manifesto	1983 manifesto	1987 manifesto	1992 manifesto	1997 manifesto
Strengthen democratic institutions against multinational capital	Withdrawal from the EEC	'Work constructively with our EC partners to promote prosperity and combat unemployment'	Use the EU presidency to improve the UK's standing in Europe	Lead Europe towards rapid completion of the single market
Reform the CAP		Reform the CAP	Reform the CAP	Reform the CAP
Oppose moves towards a federal Europe		Resist EC interference in national policy for recovery		Sign up to the Social Chapter
			Support wider membership of the EC	Provide leadership for EC enlargement
Remain outside any European monetary union			Strengthen political control of European monetary institutions	Hold referendum on the single currency

tion; a stark contrast with Thatcher's emphasis upon a permanent zero-sum game. 'To be pro-British you do not have to be anti-European', Blair declared in May 1999. 'But in creating the European Union we have the chance not to suppress our national interest, but to advance it in a new way for a new world by working together' (www.number10.gov.uk). While the EU was not inevitably inimical to national interests in Blair's domestic discourse, however, he made it equally clear from the outset that his government opposed 'a European federal super-state'. Like his Conservative predecessor, Blair thus consistently expounded a vision of Europe as 'an alliance of independent nations choosing to co-operate to achieve the goals that they cannot achieve alone'. As he told a Warsaw audience in October 2000, his vision of the future was of an EU which would become 'a superpower without developing into a super-state' – particularly not one which required a single legally binding constitution (www.pm.gov/uk).

New Labour was initially able to have it both ways, because Blair entered office at a time when the EU appeared directionless and becalmed in the doldrums as the federalist tide had receded since Maastricht and it lacked effective leadership after the departure of Jacques Delors. It had also been debilitated during the late 1990s by various crises over corruption, the negative results of Maastricht referendums in France and Denmark, rising unemployment, frustrated progress towards EMU and its humiliating impotence in dealing with the conflict in the Balkans. In these circumstances, the Blair governments were able to provide leadership over a variety of EU innovations without jeopardising their domestic standing. Moreover, on the European stage, Blair's practice of 'promiscuous bilateralism' enabled him to form alliances with individual leaders of the member states over different issues to promote British goals – as, for example, his close cooperation with Chirac over EU defence policy, José María Aznar of Spain over the Lisbon Agenda and the leaders of Spain, Italy and the Eastern European states over Iraq (Smith 2005).

One major aspect of British leadership concerned EU enlargement, which Blair and Cook actively promoted as a moral duty as well as a political and economic necessity during Britain's first presidency in 1998. Ten new members officially joined the EU on 1 May 2004. In Helsinki in December 1999, Britain pressed for the accession of Bulgaria and Romania against widespread opposition and they also joined on 1 January 2007, increasing the EU from 25 to 27 (see Map 5.2). Blair's last push on enlargement concerned the possible admission of Muslim Turkey in December 2005. Ultimately, it can be argued that enlargement represented 'one of Blair's principal achievements in Europe, for which he received little recognition during his premiership' (Seldon

Map 5.2 Expansion of the European Community and Union

2008: 408). During this period the EU became larger without becoming significantly stronger – but given Blair's objectives this was also a triumph. Certainly one of the benefits of enlargement for Britain was that the new accession states were significantly more pro-American than France and Germany, and this proved particularly helpful prior to the Iraq war when the 'new Europe' vigorously defended the Anglo-American position against the criticism from the 'old Europe'.

Blair and Brown also led from the front in pressing for a dynamic liberal market model for EU development instead of the *dirigisme* of Delors's statist agenda. This was necessary because the single market, theoretically completed in 1992, was still filled with all sorts of obstacles to the free movement of labour and trade in services and public procurement. In practice, European leaders rapidly wearied of condescending lectures from Blair and his Chancellor, Gordon Brown, boasting about their flexible labour market and superior economic performance, but in pursuit of its goals Britain played a major role in sponsoring the Lisbon Agenda after March 2000. This embodied a series of ambitious economic reforms designed to transform the EU into 'the most competitive and dynamic knowledge-based economy in the world' by 2010 through improved education, research and the encouragement of entrepreneurship within an increasingly deregulated environment (Deighton 2001: 317). This agreement contained a classic New Labour mix of innovation, market liberalisation, enterprise, new technology, reduced state regulation and subsidies, flexible labour markets, social inclusion and sustainable development, and Blair hailed it as a 'sea-change in EU economic thinking' (Driver and Martell 2006: 176). Although results have not been impressive, Blair and Brown were undeterred and pressed ahead with a series of bilateral initiatives intended to complete the single market in energy, telecommunications and financial services, reduce business regulation and create more flexible labour, capital and product markets while at the same time vigorously opposing the works council directive for smaller enterprises and the inclusion of economic and social rights in the European Charter of Fundamental Rights negotiated in Nice in December 2000 (Riddell 2005: 377).

Perhaps the most important area in which the Blair governments provided leadership in the face of EU inertia concerned the development of the Common Foreign and Security Policy (CFSP). The Blair government initially endorsed Britain's traditional position that the EU should not challenge NATO's role, and at the Amsterdam summit in June 1997 it successfully prevented both the integration of the WEU into the EU and the greater use of QMV on issues where fundamental national interests were at stake. It thus came as something of a surprise when Blair and President Chirac signed an Anglo-French defence agreement at the St Malo summit in December 1998 designed to enable Europe 'to play its full role on the international stage'; a proposal which necessitated a credible military force and the means to deploy it in response to international crises (www.fco.gov.uk). Beneath the portentous rhetoric of St Malo, a senior official complained: 'it was typical Blair, dazzled by the bright lights but short on detail, and planning ahead and on substance' (Seldon 2005: 329). As a result, Whitehall was obliged to assuage the ensuing storm of protest from Washington with repeated assurances that NATO remained the West's principal defence structure and that Europe would conduct out-of-area operations only where the US did not wish to be involved.

For all its defects in planning and detail, in 1999 this remarkable development opened the way for the Cologne and Helsinki EU summits to establish an EU Rapid Reaction Force (or Military 'Security Pool') of up to 60,000 personnel capable of deployment within 60 days for humanitarian rescue tasks, peacekeeping and crisis management; a force which came to fruition in February 2004 and which enabled the EU to absorb all but the mutual defence obligations of the WEU. In November 2003, Britain also backed the creation of the European Defence Agency to improve common procurement procedures and, in an attempt to head off efforts to create a completely independent EU structure, it played a leading role in the development of an EU military 'planning cell', but only after US protests were silenced with still more assurances that this would be complementary to NATO and firmly located within its organisational framework (*Guardian*, 3 February, 2 and 12 December 2003; Menon 2004: 648). Although progress in operationalising European defence policy has been slower than anticipated, the EU did relieve NATO of its peacekeeping functions in Macedonia in 2003 and in Bosnia and Herzegovina in 2004.

The Blair government's enthusiasm for an EU security identity was prompted by a variety of motives. Firstly, there was a desire to be seen as a leading actor in international relations in a sphere in which Britain has traditionally exerted authority. Secondly, this initiative conformed with Blair's preoccupation with humanitarian intervention after the bitter experience of Kosovo in 1999 and his frustration at the inability of NATO to act in areas where the US had no direct interest. Thirdly, British leadership on this high-profile issue provided a counterbalance to its self-exclusion from EMU in a sphere in which it might possibly divide the Franco-German axis. Finally, the conclusion of an internal party review suggesting that it would take Britain 10 years to establish itself at the 'heart of Europe' encouraged the hope that progress might be accelerated by taking the lead in foreign and defence matters (Buller 2001: 226).

Beyond its role in the creation of a new European defence architecture, the Blair government was equally decisive in promoting EU diplomatic efforts across a range of important international disputes – particularly the Israeli–Palestinian conflict and a joint initiative with France and Germany in 2007–8 to negotiate with Tehran over Iran's nuclear programme to pre-empt a more aggressive approach by the Bush administration. After a Berlin trilateral in September 2003, there were even rumours of the creation of an 'EU3' – a three-sided directorate of Britain, France and Germany to concert policy in key areas of EU diplomacy – but in the end nothing came of the proposal after the protests of less influential member states (*Guardian*, 15 January, 18 February 2004). Nevertheless, it was indicative of the distance that Britain had travelled that it strongly supported clauses in the abortive European Constitution to create a European foreign minister supported by what was effectively an EU diplomatic service (*Guardian*, 4 October 2003).

New Labour, the Euro, the Constitutional Treaty and other problems

For all its successes in some areas, since 1997 New Labour has been forced to grapple with a number of extremely thorny problems in European policy. EMU undoubtedly presented the greatest challenge to its aspiration to occupy a leading position in the EU. In practice, the problem arose because a moderately pro-Euro Prime Minister was afraid of alienating a hostile public opinion and press. He was equally anxious to avoid conflict with his increasingly sceptical Chancellor, given Brown's broader efforts to restrict the economic competence of EU institutions and his blunt refusal to surrender any national powers over taxation and social security. In Opposition, Labour adopted an 'all options open' position regarding the Euro in order to evade the need for a definite decision (Carter 2003). Although the 1997 manifesto highlighted the 'formidable obstacles' to entry in the first wave, the decision to remain outside the Euro-zone was not taken until October 1997, but to consolidate his control further Brown devised 'five economic tests' to be passed before the government recommended entry – allegedly devised on the back of an envelope in a taxi!

To indicate a commitment to eventual membership, the Treasury established a Euro Preparation Unit and a Managed Transition Plan but the outcome of the massive Treasury study of the five economic tests was never in doubt. In June 2003, the Treasury assessment thus concluded that Britain had 'made real progress towards meeting the five economic tests' but a 'decision to join now would not be in the national economic interest' (Cm 5776 2003: 3–6). This represented a major political victory for Brown rather than an economic test of convergence, but it effectively neutralised the issue for the foreseeable future. Although this meant Labour's exclusion from Euro-zone decision-making processes, the greater buoyancy of the British economy compared with Euro-zone competitors after 1997 served to reduce the distinction between members and non-members, and this allowed the Labour government to remain at the centre of economic debates. Notwithstanding these compensations, however, the failure to join the euro represented a defining moment in the Blair government's relations with the EU and a significant blow to his credibility when claiming leadership within Europe.

Table 5.4   Labour's 'Five Economic Tests' for EMU membership

1. Is there a sustainable convergence between Britain's business cycles/economic structures and the economies of the Euro-zone to enable it to live comfortably with the Euro interest rates on a permanent basis?

2. The new currency system should have sufficient flexibility to be able to respond to economic problems.

3. Membership of the single currency should have a favourable impact on long-term investment in Britain.

4. The competitive position of the financial services industry, especially the City of London wholesale markets, must benefit from membership.

5. EMU membership must promote higher growth, stability and a lasting increase in employment.

Source: HM Treasury, Cm 5776, *UK Membership of the Single Currency: an Assessment of the Five Economic Tests*, June 2003, p.1.

New Labour's second major problem concerned the need for a new European constitution outlining intergovernmental arrangements appropriate for a Community of 27 states making new and different demands on EU structures and competences. This problem arose when the Nice summit in December 2000 appointed a convention under the former French President Giscard d'Estaing to draft an EU constitution which would subsume and expand existing EU treaties, while overhauling decision-making structures, institutions and procedures in the light of its expansion from 12 members in 1993 to 25 by May 2004. The British position was one of active participation, but the overall approach was essentially minimalist and intergovernmental, and the Blair government successfully mounted a fierce defence of what it defined as 'red line' issues on which it would not yield. These included powers over electorally sensitive issues such as taxation, social security, immigration and asylum. Given widespread public opposition to ratification, however, the Blair government was extremely fortunate that the overwhelming rejection of the constitutional treaty by French and Dutch voters in May and June 2005 effectively absolved it of the pledge to hold a potentially hazardous referendum on the subject. After this, Blair repeatedly pressed the EU to abandon any ambitious plans to revive the constitution and to settle on what he preferred to describe as an 'amending treaty', consolidating necessary changes to existing agreements but without the need for a referendum; a view shared by the newly elected French president, Nicolas Sarkozy – a supposed 'Blairophile'. After thwarting German efforts to revive the treaty, at his last EU Council in June 2007 Blair once again set out the non-negotiable British 'red lines' which avoided almost any transfer of power from Britain to the EU and he defended them against ferocious attack (Seldon 2008: 569, 527). In so doing, the referendum issue was finally kicked into touch, although his successor experienced constant pressure from the Conservative Opposition on the question throughout the passage of the EU (Amendment) Bill which ratified the Lisbon Treaty in June 2008.

The third perennial issue to confront New Labour concerned the size of Britain's budget contribution. To British fury the issue re-emerged at an extraordinarily acrimonious EU Council in Brussels in October 2002, which ended with Chirac and Blair trading personal insults (Seldon 2007: 126). Another extremely rancorous European Council in June 2005 opened once again with demands for a reduction of some 25 billion ECUs – effectively wiping out Margaret Thatcher's rebate – but this was deftly rebuffed by Blair's argument that even with a rebate of some £3 billion a year in the early 2000s, Britain still made a contribution to the EU budget two-and-a-half-times as large as that of France between 1995 and 2005. Without the rebate, Britain's contribution would have been 15 times the size of France (M. Smith 2006: 168). In retaliation for this attack, Blair insisted that the rebate could be negotiated only when discussions were concluded on CAP reform, which was currently consuming 40 per cent of the EU budget to produce less than 2 per cent of its total output.

Although this ill-tempered summit ended without agreement, Blair was sufficiently anxious to reach a settlement that he ignored the Treasury's vigorous opposition to agreement without radical CAP reform and the issue was finally resolved in December 2005. Britain conceded £7.1 billion spread over seven years, ostensibly because the principal exponent of enlargement could not politically or morally refuse to provide the money necessary to pay for it. Anyway, given the complicated manner in which the rebate was calculated, even this concession meant a rise in the gross value of the British rebate in the years ahead – albeit less than under previous arrangements. In return, Blair accepted the promise of a fundamental review of all EU spending, including CAP, by 2009 – by which time Chirac's retirement would make progress more likely. In the interim, in April 2007 the Treasury finally abandoned its rearguard action against Blair's deal for financing EU enlargement in return for cooperative action to combat VAT fraud on mobile phones and computer chips; an outcome which reduced Thatcher's rebate by another £1 billion a year (*Guardian*, 4 April 2007). The issue will remain a running sore in Anglo-EU relations for some years ahead.

The final problem which emerged in acute form during Blair's last government raised fundamental questions about the entire basis of British foreign policy. It has long been a favoured British conceit to pose as a power uniquely capable of reconciling the interests of Europe and the US. Like Callaghan, Thatcher and Major, Blair consistently emphasised Britain's role as 'the bridge between the US and Europe' in a changing global system (Carr 2001: 226). As he told the Associated Press luncheon in December 1998, to maximise British influence:

> means realising once and for all that Britain does not have to choose between being strong with the US, or strong with Europe; it means having the confidence that we can be both. Indeed, that Britain must be both; that we are stronger with the US because of our strength in Europe; that we are stronger in Europe because of our strength with the US. We have deluded ourselves for too long with the false choice between the US and Europe. (www.fco.gov.uk)

Blair rejoiced in his role as the interlocutor between the Atlantic and European spheres. In the immediate aftermath of 9/11, he emerged as Europe's self-appointed spokesman to give substance to this favoured 'bridge' metaphor and he scored some notable victories in repairing US–EU relations after the tensions of the Iraq war, as, for example, in December 2003 when he brokered a deal in which Washington accepted an independent EU military force and 'planning cell' in return for guarantees that NATO would remain the dominant defence structure in Western Europe (*Guardian*, 12 December 2003). In the event, however, his pro-Americanism and anxiety to curb any overreaction to 9/11 fundamentally undermined Blair's much-vaunted role as a transatlantic intermediary. As Gerhard Schroeder, the German Chancellor, observed contemptuously, the problem with Blair's bridge was that the traffic always seemed to be moving in one direction (Riddell 2005: 368, 372).

Against this background, William Wallace argues that while ministers still cling to the illusion that Britain commands a uniquely pivotal position between the EU and US, recent experiences should have prompted a fundamental reappraisal of British foreign policy priorities to decide where Britain's principal interests lay (Wallace 2005). For many observers, there can only be one answer to this dilemma given a variety of strong forces pushing the United States away from Europe while increasingly thrusting Britain towards it (Niblett 2007). Conversely, other commentators endorse Blair's own position (enunciated at the Lord Mayor's Banquet in November 1999) to the effect that this represents a 'false choice' on the grounds that 'we are listened to more closely in Washington if we are leading in Europe. And we have more

weight in Europe if we are listened to in Washington' (www.fco.gov.
uk). From this perspective, Blair dismissed even the tensions engendered
by the Iraq war with the argument that what Europe and the United
States shared was 'of oceanic depths compared to the shallow water of
any present discord' (www.number-10.gov.uk). Unshaken by European
criticism of his stand in Iraq, Blair declared unrepentantly in his
Mansion House speech in November 2004:

> We have a unique role to play. Call it a bridge, a two lane
> motorway, a pivot or call it a damn high wire, which is how it often
> feels: our job is to keep our sights firmly on both sides of the
> Atlantic, use the good old British characteristics of commonsense
> and make the argument. In doing so we are not subverting our
> country either into an American poodle or a European munici-
> pality, we are advancing the British national interest in a changed
> world in the early 21st century. (www.number-10.gov.uk)

This was scarcely a novel proposition, but, as Driver and Martell argue,
the avoidance of choice represents an inherently unstable position
which is increasingly likely to draw criticism from both international-
ists and Europhiles alike (Driver and Martell 2006: 172).

When considered as a whole, the record of the Blair governments on
Europe was unquestionably mixed. Despite significant failures, some
argue that 'in important areas and in important respects there were
clear policy successes' (Bache and Nugent 2007: 535). According to his
biographer, Blair remained 'utterly sincere about his intention to make
Britain a leading nation in the European Union and at the heart of the
debate about its future'. But in pursuit of this goal he achieved only a
very partial success, although he would undoubtedly have been more
successful if he had Angela Merkel and Nicolas Sarkozy work with
rather than Gerhard Schroeder and Jacques Chirac (Seldon 2008: 527).
Despite Blair's skill in making suitably reassuring *communautaire*
noises, however, as in so many other aspects of his record, the critics
argue the rhetoric did not match the policy reality. As such, the Blair
years are often portrayed as just one more 'missed opportunity' in the
history of Anglo-European relations (Smith 2005).

Gordon Brown and selective Europeanism since 2007

When Labour came to office in 1997, Gordon Brown had been one of
its more committed pro-Europeans since the mid-1980s when this had
been an extremely unpopular position within the party (Peston 2005:

181). Yet, while there was always 'a pro-European integrationist strand to his DNA', during his Chancellorship this enthusiasm became increasingly qualified because of fundamental doubts about the EU's fitness for the challenge facing Europe in the future (O'Donnell and Whitman, 2007). According to Sir Stephen Wall, the UK Permanent Representative to the EU from 1995 until 2000, part of the explanation for this scepticism lies in the fact that when Brown 'thinks of Britain he thinks global, but he doesn't necessarily see Europe as part of the solution in the way that Blair did' (Lunn, Miller and Swift 2008: 65). On this basis, there seemed little reason to expect any radical change in EU policy under a Brown premiership.

This was certainly the case with regard to the future of the constitutional treaty. In October 2007, Brown's call for an end to the EU obsession with prolonged inward-looking debate about institutional and constitutional concerns and to focus on the creation of a liberalised anti-protectionist market deeply frustrated other member states (*Guardian*, 18 October 2007). Having failed with these pleas, the Prime Minister infuriated some of his fellow leaders by arriving in Lisbon too late to witness the ceremony celebrating the signature of the modified EU 'reform' treaty in December 2007; a scheduling 'oversight' widely interpreted as a calculated snub and a further sign of Britain's semi-detached position. Worse still, in the wake of the Irish referendum rejecting the new constitutional treaty in June 2008, Britain jubilantly led the way in rejecting Franco-German plans for an Irish 'opt out', on the grounds that the treaty required unanimous acceptance by all 27 members. After this, the central theme of British rhetoric returned to the need for the EU to turn away from irrelevant institutional reforms to address issues of concern to ordinary citizens. Despite Brown's attempted EU charm offensive two months later, this negative image was compounded by his failure to visit the European Commission for the first eight months of his premiership, while his invitation to Sarkozy and Merkel for trilateral talks in London on the financial crisis in February 2008, without reference to the opinions of the EU as a whole, only added further insult to injury (*Guardian*, 22 February 2008).

As Chancellor of the Exchequer for a decade after 1997, it was inevitable that Gordon Brown's most constructive impact upon the EU should have been in the economic sphere. In a keynote speech at the Mansion House on 22 June 2005 entitled 'Global Britain, Global Europe; a Presidency foundered on pro-European Realism', Brown outlined his key themes as Chancellor and Prime Minister (www.hm-treasury.gov.uk/press57.05). As a committed opponent of excessive EU federalism and ambitious schemes for constitutional advance, he has consistently argued in favour of a 'pro-European realism' on intergovernmental lines. He has been equally critical of the dominant 'social model' while advocating greater labour market flexibility on the grounds that 'flexibility matched by fairness is essential to deliver a Europe of full employment and opportunity for all'. Above all, a central theme of his long Chancellorship was his repeated criticism of the inward-looking protectionist tendencies of the EU and the need to respond more effectively to the challenge of globalisation. To enable Europe to become a 'flexible, reforming, open and globally-orientated Europe', Brown consistently supported the Lisbon Agenda by advocating a fundamental rebalancing of the EU budget away from its backward-looking priorities on agriculture and regional policy in favour of R&D, science, skills and infrastructure to enhance competitiveness and support the knowledge-based growth industries of the future. At the same time, he has advocated radical structural reform to complete the single market, particularly by removing state subsidies, by creating a proactive competition policy and by reducing the burden of regulation on business and finance. In pursuing these goals, the Brown government was inevitably going to find itself in conflict with its European partners but, as he told a conference of business leaders in London in January 2008, the EU must move forward 'not just an internal single market that looks inwards but the driving force of the new fast changing global market place ... competing on and prosperous because of its skills, its innovation and its creative talents' (www. number10.gov.uk).

Beyond the economic sphere, Brown has also been relatively successful in using the EU to promote causes close to his political heart, such as the environmental agenda, the fight against global poverty, African development and the Middle East peace process (see Chapter 8). From necessity rather than choice, he was also prominent in efforts to lead EU responses to the severe financial and liquidity crisis following the 'credit crunch' of 2008–9 during which he attempted to rally member states behind a three-point 'Brown Plan' to stabilise the global financial system, restore confidence and create a 'new financial architecture' to replace the entire Bretton Woods system; an initiative which soon put him on a collision course with France, Germany, Poland and others who opposed the idea of a massive fiscal stimulus to achieve global reflation until Obama brokered a deal on tough new regulations to give 'capitalism a conscience' (*Guardian*, 16 October 2008; 2 April 2009).

The Brown government was more successful in reinforcing its *communautaire* credentials when building on the Blair legacy in the field of foreign and defence policy. In the decade after the St Malo declaration, the EU launched more than twenty civilian and military missions on three continents. Although largely small-scale policing missions, among the more high-profile peacekeeping operations were Operation Artemis in the Congo, Operation Concordia in Macedonia and Operation Althea in Bosnia. Undoubtedly the most impressive demonstration of the EU's nascent nation-building capability came in December 2007, when it was agreed 'to send a clear message to Kosovo' by dispatching 1800 police, judges and administrators to the region to carry it towards full statehood (*Guardian*, 15 December 2007). In response to hints from the newly elected French President, that he was ready to return to NATO's military command if the EU increased its capability to deploy troops for crisis management, at a two-day summit at Arsenal's Emirates Stadium in March 2008 Brown and Sarkozy forged an 'entente formidable' which carried Anglo-French relations to a post-war zenith as they agreed to regular bilateral contacts to institutionalise the relationship and coordinate policy positions. In return for British support for his plans for a military capability supporting a more active EU foreign and security policy, Sarkozy announced the deployment of more French troops in Afghanistan, cooperation to develop the EU military capabilities (particularly its carrier and strategic lift operations), re-entry to NATO's military wing after over 40 years' absence and a common policy on global issues such as UN reform, financial regulation, climate change and trade. As Sarkozy summed up his new approach: 'It is not simply a matter of a one night stand. I believe we can go into the next day breakfast as well' (*Guardian*, 20, 28 March 2008).

These developments paved the way for agreement on the 'Sarkozy Plan' in July 2008 to enable the EU to act independently of the US and NATO. As the failure of several key European NATO members to deploy troops in Afghanistan and Iraq had become a repeated source of Anglo-American complaint about unequal burden-sharing, the Sarkozy proposals only aggravated transatlantic tensions. As the British Defence Secretary warned, NATO–EU relations were 'plagued by mistrust and unhealthy competition'. 'Without US support, NATO has no future', Des Browne declared in the Commons in March 2008. 'But US support depends on NATO becoming more capable, deployable and flexible and on the European allies contributing more' (*Guardian*, 20 March 2008). Following the Defence Secretary's lead, in July 2008 Miliband attempt to square the circle by reaffirming that NATO was the cornerstone of Western defence while insisting that there was 'a genuine role for the EU in conflict prevention and crisis management' (such as in training Palestinian police in the West Bank) and that Europe needed 'to be better at using their hard power', given that there were over two million troops in 27 EU member states but only 100,000 of them were equipped to fight (*Guardian*, 2 July 2008). As a demonstration of this proposition, by December 2008 Britain was leading the first EU naval task force in an anti-piracy operation off the Horn of Africa in parallel with a NATO deployment (*Guardian*, 8 December 2008).

New Labour and the EU: continuity and change

After 12 years of New Labour government, Britain had repositioned itself as more of a mainstream policy actor and less as an 'awkward' partner than at any time since its accession to the EEC in January 1973. In large part, this is because enlargement has incorporated recent accession states that are both more 'difficult' to deal with as partners and more sympathetic to Britain's Atlanticist and anti-federalist positions. Yet, beneath the obvious change in tone and style employed by the Labour governments since 1997, the continuities with the ambivalence of the past remain more striking than the differences. At one level, this is reflected in the 'pick and mix' attitude of governments of both parties towards EU initiatives since the 1970s. In this context, New Labour shared with its Conservative predecessors an enthusiasm for CAP reform, EU enlargement, completion of the single European market, promotion of wealth and employment through deregulation, the elimination of waste and corruption and the need for a more outward-looking Europe committed to trade liberalisation and foreign policy cooperation. Conversely, where crucial issues of national interest were at stake, governments of both parties had shown no compunction about the use of 'opt outs' and non-negotiable 'red lines'. In this respect, the Blair and Brown governments have been no less vigorous than Thatcher and Major in asserting British interests, even when this left them in a minority of one. Ultimately, however, this bipartisan preference for selective engagement has less to do with ideological convergence or an inherent temperamental 'awkwardness' in the British political psyche than with situational constraints.

The first of these stems from the fact that Britain's late entry into Europe meant that most of the architecture of Community rules, norms and structures had been devised by continental Europeans pursuing markedly different national interests. A central theme of Blair's European discourse, therefore, was that (as he put it in 2001) in future 'we must get in on the ground floor of decision-making so that the decisions are ones we are happy with' (Daddow 2007: 589). A second key factor in explaining continuity in European policy over the past three decades is that New Labour, like its predecessors, has been constrained by a hostile press and public opinion which it has been extremely reluctant to confront or to educate to the realities of European interdependence (Daddow 2007). The origins of this problem date back to the mid-1960s but although Blair was supposedly a pro-European leader anxious to play a key role in EU deliberations he preferred not to grasp the domestic political nettle, despite a Demos report (Demos 2007) in August 1997 indicating that three-quarters of the public considered themselves ill-informed about the EU (Buller 2001: 228). As a result, there was overwhelming electoral hostility to the European constitution (although only 6 per cent of voters claimed to be aware of its contents), while opposition to membership of the Euro-zone reached 71 per cent by January 2009 (*Guardian*, 2 January 2009). Most striking of all, since the late Major years 45–50 per cent of the British electorate have regularly declared a desire to leave the EU altogether (Riddell 2005: 380). For the majority of Britons, therefore, 'Europe' is perceived as a hostile 'other' across the Channel seeking to subvert a distinctive British national identity beneath an allegedly oppressive torrent of regulations covering everything from the limitation of the working week to the straightening of cucumbers.

Confronted by these constraints, the general trajectory of all British governments since 1973 has been one of moving from an initially pragmatic approach towards European policy in its early stages, via increasingly reluctant cooperation through to obstructionism in key policy areas towards their later stages. Blair paid the ultimate price for this balancing act when Chancellor Merkel stymied his hopes of becoming the first EU president with the damning verdict that his track record was 'not so good' because 'he made a lot of fine speeches about Europe but, essentially, stood on the sidelines when it came to concrete steps forward' (*Guardian*, 20 February 2008). Although his successor regularly repeated the mantra that 'European Union membership is good for Britain and British membership is good for Europe', there is little evidence to suggest that the foreseeable future will witness any fundamental change in the historical trend (www.number10.gov.uk).

Chapter 6

The Problems of Conventional Defence

British military power: reacting to economic decline or adjusting to change?

Much of the debate about defence policy since 1945 has been dominated by a well-established orthodoxy which emphasises the increasing gulf between Britain's overseas obligations and its defensive capabilities. As Lawrence Freedman puts it:

> the history of British defence policy is of an attempt to reconcile the mismatch between resources and commitments. The reconciliation is often achieved temporarily but it never seems to last. The inexorable rise in equipment costs pushes up the price of defence while the economy refuses to generate the extra funds necessary to keep pace. (Freedman 1983: 62)

When approached from this perspective, the problem with Britain's defence policy is easily explained – successive governments have been guilty of pursuing two totally incompatible goals by seeking to extend Britain's military activism in a variety of global trouble-spots while simultaneously reducing the financial and economic resources devoted to this objective. Furthermore, as the next chapter demonstrates, the overriding Cold War priority upon 'deterrence' against the threat from the Warsaw Pact helped foster the optimistic, if largely mistaken, belief that greater reliance on nuclear weapons would not only protect Britain's security but also more effectively balance resources with obligations while guaranteeing its great power status on the cheap. Instead, the critics argue, the pursuit of the nuclear chimera has unnecessarily diverted scarce resources away from conventional forces and the requirements of more limited out-of-area operations (Carver 1983: 89).

Some commentators carry this indictment even further to argue that rather than simply coinciding with economic decline, the heavy burden of defence spending has been a significant cause of that decline since

1945 because 'when a choice had to be made between economic growth and Britain's status as a world power', successive governments 'chose the latter' (Chalmers 1985: 3, ch. 6; Coates 1994: 192–201). One obvious problem with staking Britain's defensive future on complex high-technology weapons is that development costs have spiralled upwards well above the rate of retail inflation. The average jet engine in the early post-war years required three times as many man-hours and machine tools to produce as its pre-war piston predecessor, while the price tag for a new bomber increased from £16,000 to £77,600 by the early 1950s. This problem only increased in scale as technology advanced. As Defence Secretary during the 1960s, Denis Healey thus recalled the price of a naval frigate doubled, Army equipment quadrupled and military aircraft increased tenfold in price (Healey 1989: 255). Moreover, this problem was not confined exclusively to high-technology weapons systems. As Healey's 1965 Defence White Paper lamented, the cost of an armoured regiment was predicted to double between 1963 and 1968 (in real terms), an artillery regiment would treble in price while the cost of an infantry battalion was expected to increase sixfold (Bartlett 1972: 67, 173). Little wonder that defence absorbed over 20 per cent of total public expenditure until 1957 and over 10 per cent until after the end of the Cold War (Baylis 1989: 143).

Beyond the financial and manpower costs of maintaining a large conventional military force, this level of defence effort demanded a substantial diversion of resources away from heavy engineering, electronics, shipbuilding, vehicle and metal production, with a consequently adverse effect upon Britain's export success. Such problems were reinforced by the fact that defence contractors locked into intimate stable relationships with the MoD were under less pressure to adopt new technologies and more efficient patterns of labour use than those engaged in the highly competitive civilian sector, with the result that it retarded necessary structural adjustments, slowed investment, distorted the concept of what constituted technological advance and ultimately ended in the 'mummification' of the UK's industrial structure (Coates 1994: 196; Kaldor 1980: 115). Another consequence of high military spending has been that a larger share of national R&D has been devoted to military production than in any other major industrial power except the United States. Indeed, in 1956 some 40 per cent of all professionally qualified scientists and engineers engaged in R&D were working on defence projects and nearly two-thirds of the research done by private industry was on defence contracts (Sked 1987: 33). Little wonder that Duncan Sandys' Defence White Paper in 1957 had focused heavily on this burden as a justification for major cuts (Cmnd 124 1957: paras 6–7). During the 1960s, Sir Solly Zuckerman, Wilson's

Chief Scientific Adviser, was equally alarmed by the fact that two decades after the end of the Second World War defence still absorbed 1.4 million workers, around a fifth of Britain's scientists and engineers and nearly two-fifths of its expenditure on R&D.

On the other hand, however, it could be argued that the contraction of Britain's defence expenditure has had an adverse effect upon the domestic economy since a large section of British industry was dependent for commercial survival upon MoD contracts for warships, planes and military equipment. As Michael Dockrill points out, in 1946 Britain boasted 23 major airframe and nine aero-engine manufacturers. By 1974 continuous defence cutbacks had reduced the number to six and one respectively and by 1977 four of the former were merged under public ownership (Dockrill 1988: 128). By 1981, the UK's military budget still absorbed the output of 39 per cent of Britain's aerospace industry, 30 per cent of its shipbuilding production and 29 per cent of its electronics and telecommunications output (Fine and Harris 1985: 246). Four years later, its purchase of £8.5 billion worth of goods and services in British industry directly or indirectly accounted for 400,000 jobs (Cmnd 9763-I 1986). By creating guaranteed markets, the military order book has thus unquestionably served to provide a sheltered haven for sections of manufacturing industry in an otherwise increasingly hostile economic environment (Coates 1994: 193–5). Furthermore, sceptics who question the proposition that high military expenditure has handicapped the British economy also argue that it has produced many positive spin-offs which have been beneficial to product and process innovation in the field of civilian production. Finally, the sceptics point out that arms exports contribute very substantially to Britain's visible balance of trade, although even here David Coates argues that, as a quarter of total R&D is devoted to defence but only 3.5 per cent of visible exports come from the same source, 'it is hard to escape the conclusion that the UK is now a net *importer* of civilian manufactured goods – in part at least, because it is also a net *exporter* of armaments' (Coates 1994: 200).

While the debate about the impact of high military expenditure on Britain's post-war economic performance is finely balanced, this has not been the only important factor in shaping defence budgets, strategies and priorities. One contributory cause of the disequilibrium between commitments and resources has been the technological revolution prompted by the superpower arms race; a competition which often rendered new weapons systems obsolescent almost before they came into operational service, and this increased still further the pressure on already severely overstretched defence budgets. Another important non-economic factor constraining post-war defence policy has been the endemic failure to coordinate foreign policy with defence resources and capabilities. As former Defence Secretary John Nott (1981–83) acknowledged in October 1987, 'No British Prime Minister since the 1960s has been sufficiently devoted to international strategy to think of defence policy within the broader vision of the international system and Britain's place in it' (Coles 2000: 45, 48–9). This has been a chronic problem throughout the post-war era.

For 20 years after Indian independence in August 1947, Britain's strategic and defence arrangements were never adequately related to the timetable of decolonisation or the realities of its power 'East of Suez', with the result that traditional patterns of thought prevented efforts to limit the scope of its overseas military role – at least until economic crisis left absolutely no alternative (Darby 1973: 327). More importantly, the major contraction in British forces over the past 50 or 60 years has rarely been correlated with the level of military activism abroad. In 1953, the armed forces numbered 865,000 – the highest figure since post-war demobilisation. By 2008, the official requirement had fallen to a meagre 102,000, despite a higher level of military activism than at any time since the Korean War. Little wonder that Lord Bramall, a former Chief of the Defence Staff, protested in the House of Lords in 2007 that 'over the past three years or so there has been no coherent or joined up foreign and defence policy in which military force could be deployed and operate with complete confidence about the real aim of the operation nor about how the broad strategy . . . would develop in the future' (HL Deb 22 November 2007: c.955).

Critics claim this disjuncture between ends and means has resulted from a chronic lack of clarity in government policy; a problem which stems from the fundamental fact that reactive short-term crisis economy measures have too often been allowed to determine policy without reference to the broader requirements of external policy. As C.J. Bartlett argued almost 40 years ago, 'British defence policy since 1945 presents a confusing and bewildering picture. Major changes of direction or emphasis have occurred at least ten times between 1945 and 1970 – an average of one every two and a half years' (Bartlett 1972: xi). Bartlett was writing on the eve of another major defence review and, since that time, there have been many similar exercises driven by financial stringency rather than grand strategy. Finance was the driving force behind Churchill's orders to the Chiefs of Staff to produce a 'Global Strategy Paper' in 1952. The same is true of Duncan Sandys's 1957 Defence White Paper, the Wilson government's decision to withdraw from 'East of Suez' in 1967–68, its emergency 1974 Defence Review, Heath's secret Defence Studies Working Party report in 1973, John Nott's White Paper on *The Way Forward* in June 1981, John Major's *Options*

Table 6.1   Outline chronology: defence policy since 1945

November 1946	Peacetime National Service introduced for 18 months
January 1947	Ministry of Defence Act unsuccessfully attempts to centralise defence organisation under a single Minister of Defence
March 1947	British troops withdraw from Egypt to the Suez Canal zone
March 1948	Britain joins Brussels Treaty Organisation
April 1949	North Atlantic Treaty signed by the five Brussels Treaty powers plus the US, Canada, Iceland, Norway, Denmark, Italy and Portugal (joined by Greece and Turkey in 1951)
June 1950	North Korean invasion of South Korea; small British contingent deployed in July; National Service extended to two years
September 1950	Labour government announces £3600 million rearmament programme over next three years; increased to £4700 million in January 1951
January 1952	Churchill government reduces rearmament budget.
July 1952	Cabinet approves the Chiefs of Staff 'Global Strategy Paper' as the basis for British defence policy in the next decade
June 1956	Eden launches review to adjust Britain's defence programme to its economic circumstances
November 1956	Anglo-French invasion of the Suez Canal zone
April 1957	Duncan Sandys's Defence White Paper
July 1958	Anglo-American invasion of Jordan and Lebanon
July 1961	British military intervention to prevent Iraqi invasion of Kuwait
December 1962	British forces suppress Brunei rebellion
July 1963	Ministry of Defence established
November 1964	Healey launches defence review
April 1965	TSR-2 fighter aircraft cancelled as the prelude to further cuts
July 1967	Britain to withdraw from 'East of Suez' by mid-1970s

Table 6.1   Outline chronology: defence policy since 1945 – *continued*

January 1968	'East of Suez' withdrawal advanced to late 1971
August 1969	British troops intervene in Northern Ireland to restore order
April 1972	Ministry of Defence establishes Procurement Executive
December 1974	Publication of Labour Defence review for the next 10 years
March 1977	Britain agrees to spend an additional 3 per cent p.a. over five years on NATO forces
June 1981	John Nott's Defence White Paper, The Way Forward
April–June 1982	Falklands War
July 1984	Heseltine publishes proposals for radical reform of the MoD structure
June 1990	NATO ministers discuss future more 'political' role at Turnberry conference
July 1990	Tom King's Defence White Paper, Options for Change; British Army of the Rhine to be scaled down
Jan-Feb 1991	The Gulf War ejects Iraq forces from Kuwait
July 1998	Blair government publishes Strategic Defence Review
March–June 1999	NATO air strikes to prevent Serbian 'ethnic cleansing' in Kosovo
April 1999	Blair's Chicago speech outlines the case for 'liberal intervention'
Oct–Nov 2001	Military action deposes the Taliban regime in Afghanistan
July 2002	A New Chapter adapts Strategic Defence Review to new threats after 9/11
March–May 2003	Iraq War
October 2003	Delivering Security in a Changing World published
July 2007	MOD announces £3.9 billion order for two new aircraft carriers
December 2007	British troops hand over to Iraqi forces in Basra
March 2008	National Security Strategy published
June 2009	Revised National Security Strategy published
August 2009	British death toll in Afghanistan rises to over 200

for Change in July 1990, and many lesser exercises. Yet, ironically, while each has prompted some marginal changes to existing programmes, none of this effort produced major savings. More to the point, many would argue that it did little fundamentally to disturb the basic framework of assumptions and aspirations within which defence policy is formulated – far less has it prompted any significant revaluation of the appropriate role Britain should play in a changing world.

This narrative of economic determinism has not gone unchallenged. An alternative interpretation suggests that, far from being a helpless reactive victim of the vagaries of poor economic performance, defence policy has been subject to a process of continuous, rational and proactive adjustment to ever-changing conditions, challenges and circumstances. As Tony McGrew argues, British defence policy since the Second World War should be seen as 'a story of incremental adaptation to a new international politico-military order – the story of a former hegemonic power reluctantly coming to terms with the new position in the global hierarchy' (McGrew 1988: 107). Or, as David Greenwood puts it, Britain's defence effort in the post-war period has not simply contracted; rather it has been periodically 'reshaped' to meet new needs and threats to British security at an international level – a 'reshaping' and 'adjustment' which produced armed forces superior in quality to anything achieved in the recent past and a process which has necessarily accelerated in pace since the collapse of the Warsaw Pact (Greenwood 1977: 189–91). A similar interpretation lies at the heart of R.E. Jones's discussion of 'transformation' in British external policy (Jones 1974).

In this context, Michael Dockrill has a point when he argues that it is something of an exaggeration to speak of 'decline' when Britain has consistently spent an average 5–6 per cent of GNP on defence between 1945 and 1985; a proportion much higher than any of its European NATO allies and which has enabled it to retain fourth or fifth position in the global military league table into the twenty-first century (Dockrill 1988: 125–6). Moreover, most of these 'readjustments' were decided calmly rather than as panic reactions to major crises and none was undertaken without much heart-searching. From this perspective, then, the declining size of Britain's armed forces since the late 1940s can be plausibly presented as a continuous adaptation to a world configuration which has changed out of all recognition over the past 65 years; a process which continues into the twenty-first century as British forces are increasingly engaged in 'liberal intervention' and 'Responsibility to Protect' roles (see Chapter 8). As General Sir Richard Dannatt, the outspoken Chief of the General Staff (2006–9), explained in June 2008, the role of the British Army over the next two decades will be to provide long-term support for unstable and 'failed' states rather than preparing for large-scale wars. Echoing the central theme of the National Security Strategy published in March 2008, he envisaged 'permanent cadres of stabilisation specialists' including civilian police, judges, administrators and emergency services personnel ready to be deployed to conflict zones around the world, supported by a complementary multidisciplinary military force capable of fighting alongside local troops in areas where civil agencies were unable to operate (*Guardian*, 13 June 2008).

Disillusioned hopes of military power with reduced expenditure, 1945–57

In the immediate aftermath of the war, the Attlee governments confronted in the starkest terms the extremely delicate dilemma of how to fund its many and varied overseas commitments with depleted revenues, while both reconstructing a war-torn nation and implementing an ambitious domestic programme intended to usher in the 'New Jerusalem' of full employment and comprehensive welfare for all. In these difficult circumstances, the Treasury informed the Services in 1946 that future Defence Estimates should be based on the assumption that Britain would not be involved in a major war for five years, and in 1947 an annual ceiling of £600 million was imposed on defence expenditure (increased to £780 million for 1950–51). This injunction led to a rapid fall in defence expenditure in the first two years of peace, while the armed forces continued to contract until the middle of 1950. Annual defence expenditure, which reached a wartime peak of over £5 billion in 1944, had fallen to £750 million by 1948–49 and further reductions were clearly planned (Cairncross 1987: 212).

The North Korean invasion of the South on 25 June 1950 put an end to all hopes of reducing defence expenditure. It also compounded Britain's economic difficulties and strained its armed forces to the limit. Although Britain contributed a token military force with substantial air and naval support, its principal response to the Korean War was to increase its defence budget for 1951–53 from the planned £2,300 million to £3,600 million over three years. This, Attlee declared, was 'the maximum we can do . . . without resorting to the drastic expedients of the war economy' (Cairncross 1987: 218). Under pressure from the Chiefs of Staff and Washington, however, in January 1951 planned expenditure was now doubled to a staggering £4,700 million over three years – an increase from 8 per cent to 14 per cent of GNP. Peacetime conscription was also extended from 18 months to two years.

This grossly over-ambitious programme was always well beyond the capabilities of Britain's fragile economy – not least because it required industrial production to more than double in the first year and then to double again in the next two – with a particular burden upon the metal and engineering industries, which accounted for 40 per cent of total British exports. According to this plan, by 1954 the arms industry would employ over one million workers and account for 10 per cent of the nation's industrial output (compared with 2.5 per cent in 1950). To make matters worse, informal US assurances that they would 'pick up the cheque' for at least some of this expenditure were not fulfilled. As a result, by the end of 1951, the economy showed alarming signs of inflationary overheating as defence contractors competed for skilled labour, machine tools and raw materials, while the heavy burden on the engineering and metal industries meant that the balance of payments plunged alarmingly from a healthy surplus of £307 million in 1950 to a deficit of £369 million in the following year (Cairncross 1987: 214–17, 222–5).

Returned to office as Prime Minister in 1951, Churchill immediately recognised the urgent need to reconcile what he called 'the twin but the divergent objectives of financial solvency and military security' (Wallace 1970: 193). As Anthony Eden's review of 'Britain's Overseas Obligations' in June 1952 asserted, 'the essence of a sound foreign policy is to ensure that a country's strength is equal to its obligations. If this is not the case, then either the obligations must be reduced to the level at which resources are available to support them, or a greater share of the country's resources must be devoted to their support.' In language which would become increasingly familiar to later policy-makers, he concluded that it was now 'becoming clear that rigorous maintenance of the presently accepted policies of Her Majesty's Government at home and abroad is placing a burden on the country's economy which is beyond the resources of the country to meet' (Bartlett 1972: 79). Four months later, Rab Butler stated the problem more bluntly in Cabinet when he declared: 'we are attempting to do too much' (Thorpe 2004: 363). Confronted by an economic crisis caused by Labour's rearmament programme, the incoming Conservative government thus acted swiftly to cut defence expenditure while spreading it over a longer period. Churchill also ordered the Chiefs of Staff to review British strategy to suggest possible economies in defence expenditure. These deliberations produced the celebrated 'Review of Defence Policy and Global Strategy' in 1952.

The Chiefs of Staff 'Global Strategy' paper was a botched compromise designed to protect the position of each of the Services. Its central proposition was that global war would probably result in a massive

Table 6.2   Defence expenditure, 1946-55 (in £ millions)

	Defence expenditure: current prices	Defence expenditure: constant prices (1980)	% total government expenditure	% of GDP (at market prices)
1946	1,575	26,605	33.9	15.8
1947	939	14,120	22.0	8.8
1948	754	11,344	16.5	6.4
1949	790	11,363	15.7	6.7
1950	863	11,302	17.3	9.1
1951	1,315	15,326	22.9	10.5
1952	1,651	17,757	25.9	10.1
1953	1,719	18,094	25.6	9.4
1954	1,680	17,177	25.1	8.2
1955	1,567	15,389	22.1	7.9

Source: Baylis (1989: 141, 143).

nuclear exchange in which the RAF's strategic nuclear bomber force would play the major role, while so-called 'tactical' nuclear weapons of one kiloton (equivalent to 1000 tons of TNT) deployed in West Germany would significantly reduce the manpower costs of British defence. As this reliance on the V-bomber force left both the Army and Navy vulnerable to substantial cuts, the Service Chiefs agreed that the final document should assert that a nuclear war would be followed by months of 'broken-backed' conventional warfare in which the other services would be engaged in mopping up and destroying the enemy. To achieve security, therefore, Britain needed to possess both atomic weapons and sufficient conventional capability to hold a Soviet advance in Western Europe. In the event, Churchill declared himself well satisfied with the strategy paper, but it offered few opportunities for savings because this highly conservative document simply superimposed a nuclear capability upon an overextended conventional force strategy at a time when British troops were already heavily engaged in security operations in Kenya, British Guiana and Cyprus, as well as fulfilling their BAOR duties in West Germany.

When Eden succeeded Churchill as Prime Minister in April 1955, he was already convinced that, unless defence spending and commitments were brought under much firmer control, the country faced economic disaster. Above all, as defence purchases had more than tripled since 1950 it was clear they were injuring engineering exports, the balance of payments and sterling, as well as retarding industrial re-equipment, while the deployment of 72,000 Service personnel outside the UK was costing £150 million a year. He was equally concerned that, although military manpower had declined from a peak of 3,033,000 in 1947 to only 957,000 by 1954, expenditure had risen sharply from £930 million to £1,551 million in the same period: an increase from 8.4 per cent to 9.1 per cent of GDP. As the Defence White Paper of 1956 explained, while Britain must remain a world power it could not afford both nuclear and balanced conventional forces. The Defence Estimates were thus stabilised at £1,535 million for FY1956/57, but these cuts were not implemented before the Suez crisis, and further pressure from the Services persuaded the Minister to abandon a programme of sweeping defence retrenchment in favour of more modest savings.

Duncan Sandys and the defence White Paper of 1957

Harold Macmillan succeeded to the premiership in January 1957 with strong views on defence expenditure. In his first speech as Prime Minister, he promised that 'no vested interest, however strong, and no traditions, however good', would obstruct the government's reassessment of defence policy. Two months earlier, while still Chancellor, Macmillan had warned Anthony Head, the Minister of Defence, that Britain faced the most difficult economic crisis in its recent history and needed to cut out 'all preparations for global war that we can without losing our power to influence world affairs or alienating our essential allies'. When Head failed to deliver, Macmillan appointed Duncan Sandys as Ministry of Defence in January 1957 with a specific mandate to secure 'a substantial reduction in expenditure and manpower' in Britain's armed forces.

Sandys was precisely the man for the job. He enjoyed the advantage of massively enhanced powers and the guaranteed support of a Prime Minister 'determined . . . make [his] position as strong as it must be' (Horne 1989, II: 47, 50, 245). He was also an arrogant and abrasively forceful politician who ignored and alienated his Chiefs of Staff and infuriated many of his officials, but he knew how to get his own way. Ruthless, unscrupulous in his methods and extremely devious, he aroused much real animosity within the defence establishment and some real hatred. Perhaps Sir Gerald Templer, the Chief of the General Staff, encapsulated the mood best when he declared after one confrontation: 'Duncan, you're so bloody crooked, that if you swallowed a nail, you'd shit a corkscrew!' (Healey 1989: 257). Nevertheless, after two months of frenetic activity and many ill-tempered meetings with the Service Chiefs, he prevailed in forcing through the main outlines of a defence plan described in the ensuing White Paper as 'the biggest change in military policy ever made in normal times' (Cmnd 124 1957: para. 67). Moreover, he did so despite widespread and well justified fears that this was primarily a cost-cutting exercise without reference to the nature of 'deterrence', the demands a future global war would make upon conventional forces or the impact of such cuts upon world opinion (Navias 1996: 223).

The Sandys White Paper entitled *Defence: Outline of Future Policy* (Cmnd 124) was published on 4 April 1957. It was the seventh review of defence policy undertaken in the 11 years since the end of the war, but it was regarded at the time as by far the most radical. In many respects, however, the document merely echoed an established official orthodoxy about nuclear deterrence current since the early 1950s. But at its heart was the need for urgent retrenchment to save £300 million because, as the White Paper grimly recorded, Britain spent a higher proportion of its National Income on defence than any other European NATO ally but it had the lowest rate of internal investment. In these circumstances, the document noted bluntly:

> Britain's influence in the world depends first and foremost on the health of her internal economy and the success of the export trade. Without these, military power cannot in the long run be supported. It is therefore in the true interests of defence that the claims of military expenditure should be considered in conjunction with the need to maintain the country's financial and economic strength. (Cmnd 124 1957: para. 7)

To the fury of Service Chiefs, these financial motivations were carefully obscured beneath a thin strategic veneer and bland assurances that Britain would maintain its obligations and influence with a smaller expenditure.

Three closely related themes dominated the strategic foundations of the White Paper. Firstly, the nature of the defence challenge had fundamentally changed since Korea, as the immediate danger of global war had been replaced by the need to prepare for 'the "long haul"'. Secondly, the White Paper argued that advances in military technology – particularly thermonuclear warheads and missiles – 'must fundamentally alter the whole basis of military planning', and the most cost-effective method of guaranteeing Britain's security was for it to possess 'an appreciable element of nuclear deterrent power of her own' – and by this Macmillan meant 'sufficient weapons to provide a deterrent influence independent of the United States' (Navias 1996: 229).

The final theme was that after such a radical reassessment 'a certain amount of disturbance was unavoidable' (Cmnd 124 1957: para. 67). What this meant in practice was that this reorientation of priorities was to be achieved at the direct expense of conventional forces, whose future role was to 'play their part with the forces of Allied countries in deterring and resisting aggression' and to 'defend British colonies . . . against local attack and undertake limited operation in overseas emergencies'. As surface-to-air missiles progressively superseded manned aircraft, large cuts could be made in Fighter Command. Similarly, nuclear weaponry permitted a substantial reduction in conventional land forces – particularly as Sandys contemptuously dismissed talk of post-nuclear holocaust 'broken-backed warfare' as utterly implausible given the likely devastation from the first thermonuclear strike. This opened the way for a cut in Army manpower, from 690,000 to 375,000, by abolishing the financial, political and electoral incubus of conscription after 1962. The future emphasis would thus be on better equipped, more mobile forces supported by tactical nuclear weapons to compensate for the reduction in Army manpower.

In this fashion, it was hoped that defence expenditure could be reduced by £180 million to £1,420 million in 1957/8 – from 10 per cent to 7 per cent of GNP by 1962. But beyond simply cutting costs, Sandys's Defence White Paper represented the first real attempt to overcome the post-war equivocation within the defence establishment as it clung to the past, while slowly adjusting its strategic thinking to the existence of qualitatively different weapons and methods of warfare. The results of Sandys's reforms were mixed but generally disappointing. Within the projected five-year period, the number of service personnel was drastically reduced from 702,000 to 423,000 and expenditure as a percentage of GNP did fall by 1964 (Dockrill 1988: 151). But these cuts were not accompanied by any reduction in commitments. On the contrary, Sandys's insistence that Britain should adhere to its existing defence obligations in the Middle and Far East soon revealed the 1957 Defence Review as a far less radical exercise than it appeared on the surface. In essence, Britain was still trying to remain a world-class nuclear and military power – a mini-superpower – but with more limited resources than at any time since the early 1930s.

The basic principles of the 1957 Defence White Paper did not remain unchallenged for long, and by 1959 even Sandys was sceptical about the validity of its analysis. From the outset there were doubts about the value of the tactical nuclear weapons around which much of the strategy was constructed – not least because they were still in short supply and almost entirely under American control. More important, the Service Chiefs had warned throughout that nuclear weapons were of little relevance to regional low-intensity conflicts and Sandys's projected manpower levels were simply insufficient to maintain Britain's numerous overseas responsibilities. This lesson was brutally driven home in 1960 by NATO criticism of the reduction in Britain's contingent to only 49,000 men and by crises in Kuwait, Jordan, Saudi Arabia, Kenya, Uganda, Tanganyika, Indonesia and Berlin, which found Britain so undermanned and overstretched that it was compelled to recall reservists and take powers to retain the last National Servicemen to bring existing units up to fighting strength. Indicative of the speed of this disillusionment was the fact that the 1960 Defence White Paper explicitly stated nuclear power 'is only one component of the deterrent . . . conventionally armed forces are a necessary complement to nuclear armaments' (Navias 1996: 233). By 1962–63, therefore, it was clear that Britain had reached a crossroads: it must either radically reduce its global commitments or sharply increase its defence expenditure.

The Wilson governments and the retreat from 'East of Suez'

The Labour governments of 1964–70 entered office with a strong commitment to nuclear weapons and a global role. Wilson's emotional commitment to a British presence 'East of Suez' was also further reinforced by the needs of the 'special relationship' and his secret deal with President Johnson through which he hoped to avert a politically catastrophic currency devaluation in return for a continued military presence in the Far East and the Indian Ocean (see p. 86). Wilson was strongly supported by his Defence minister, Denis Healey, one of the few Labour politicians with a genuine interest in the subject, and whose tenure of the post from 1964 until 1970 was the longest since its creation in 1945. Yet, while Healey shared Wilson's belief in the importance of the role East of Suez, he also described the defence budget as 'a runaway train' which needed to be brought under control. To achieve this goal, in November 1964 the MoD was ordered to reduce the annual defence budget to £2,000 million per annum (at 1964 prices) until 1969–70; a reduction from 8.3 per cent of GNP under the Conservatives to 6 per cent (Bartlett 1972: 170).

This was never going to be an easy task, given the combination of rapidly rising inflation in the weapons procurement sector and the desperate need for an extensive modernisation of Britain's overstretched and under-equipped armed forces. Moreover, while Healey was constantly under pressure from the Treasury to reduce spending, he believed 'no government should cut a military capability without cutting the political commitment which made that capability necessary' and, as the Foreign Office regarded 'every commitment as an invaluable pearl without price', the Defence Minister found himself having 'to fight a war on two fronts' (Healey 1989: 256). In these difficult circumstances, Healey's initial response was simply to defer the supply of new equipment and warships, cancel the new CVA01-class carriers and axe failing prestige projects like the ill-fated TSR-2 strike and reconnaissance aircraft (April 1965) while replacing them with cheaper off-the-shelf US alternatives. As the economic crisis deepened, however, the government was forced to embark upon a more fundamental reappraisal of its overseas obligations – a reassessment which almost inevitably focused upon its position 'East of Suez'.

Such a review was long overdue. Twenty years after the end of the Second World War, Britain still retained a global network of bases in the Far East at Singapore and Hong Kong; in the Middle East at Aden; in southern Africa at Simonstown; and in the Mediterranean in Malta, Libya and Cyprus. In 1965, it had 55,000 military personnel stationed east of Suez at a cost of £317 million per annum – some 15 per cent of the total defence budget of £2,120 million. The problem, as Phillip Darby explains, was that 'the protection of India was part of an ingrained pattern of thought. It was above politics . . . It was the touchstone to which policy must return: the ultimate justification for a defensive system which spanned half the world' (Darby 1973: 1). Yet, while it followed logically that Britain needed to command the gateways to the Indian Ocean when it possessed a global empire, its withdrawal from India and subsequent evacuation of Suez in 1954 implied the need for a major redefinition of Britain's defence posture, to accord with the more limited requirements of the post-imperial order – but no such strategic reassessment ever took place, largely because successive governments failed to relate decisions about defence to the other strands of external policy. As a result, overseas commitments remained broadly constant while capability progressively declined.

This state of denial could not continue indefinitely in the absence of sustained economic growth. Healey's Defence White Paper in February 1966 emphasised Britain's 'overstretched' military capabilities and the need to reduce the defence budget, but it did not indicate that any drastic changes were planned (Cmnd 2901: 1966). The severe retrenchment in all public expenditure following the economic crisis of July 1966 was a significant watershed marking the beginning of the end for Britain's presence 'East of Suez' – particularly as it coincided with the sobering effects of the costly 'Confrontation' with Indonesia over

Malaysia. Against a background of gathering economic crisis, the Supplementary Defence White Paper in July 1967 put the final nail in the coffin by announcing a 50 per cent cut in strength in the Far East by 1971 and the complete withdrawal of all forces from East of Suez between 1975 and 1977. The RAF, Royal Navy and air transport were also to be cut back severely so that by 1970 manpower would be reduced by 75,000 and the Defence Estimates would be £300 million lower. In an effort to put a brave face on it, the Prime Minister declared on 27 July 1967, 'What we shall maintain is not a military presence but the military capability based on the ability to get there to fulfil our remaining commitments' (Bartlett 1972: 221).

The 1967 Defence White Paper proclaimed that it was the culmination of almost three years' work on 'a major review of defence, revising Britain's overseas policy, formulating the role of military power to support it, and planning the forces required to carry out this role' (Cmnd 3357 1967: 12). The decisions it contained were reached after much deliberation, with great reluctance and only under acute economic and political pressure. They were also made in the full knowledge that a hasty British retreat would both jeopardise over a £1,000 million worth of foreign investment and create a power vacuum which the Soviets might fill. All these considerations were swept aside, however, by the disaster of devaluation in mid-November 1967. After this, the defence

Table 6.3   Defence expenditure, 1955–79

	Defence expenditure: current prices	Defence expenditure: constant prices (1980)	% total government expenditure	% of GDP (at market prices)
1955	1,567	15,389	22.1	8.2
1960	1,612	12,127	17.1	6.3
1965	2,127	13,151	15.0	5.9
1967	2,427	13,640	14.5	6.0
1968	2,444	12,846	13.3	5.6
1970	2,466	10,770	11.8	4.8
1975	5,177	10,738	10.0	4.9
1978	7,596	10,530	10.5	4.5
1979	9,006	10,723	10.5	4.6

Source: Baylis (1989: 141, 143).

budget was reduced by a further £100 million in FY1967/68, necessitating an acceleration of the schedule for withdrawal and leaving Britain with only small garrisons in Hong Kong, Gibraltar, Belize and the Falkland Islands.

As in the past, these drastic cutbacks did not generate massive savings – not least because of the sudden outbreak of 'the Troubles' in Northern Ireland in 1969 and expensive advances in weapons technology which threatened to increase the defence budget to 11.25 per cent of GNP by the end of the 1970s. As a result, the new Labour government immediately conducted another Defence Review in December 1974, designed to reduce expenditure by £4.75 billion between 1975 and 1985, while the armed forces were scheduled to shed 11 per cent of existing manpower (about 38,000 men) by 1979. Further cuts followed in the Defence White Paper of March 1975, while the severe sterling crisis in 1976 ended Britain's presence in Singapore and Simonstown and forced the closure of the Gan air staging base in the Indian Ocean. The cuts continued until 1977, when the Callaghan government finally succumbed to NATO pressure for an increase of 3 per cent per annum over five years to fund re-equipment and expansion.

The Thatcher governments and 'the Way Forward'

Mrs Thatcher's reputation as policy radical seeking to overthrow a failed consensus in domestic policy was not paralleled by her policy priorities in defence any more than in foreign policy. Thatcher was undoubtedly a vociferous advocate of strong defence, but the inherent contradiction in her broader ideological commitment drastically to reduce public expenditure while maintaining – or even increasing – Britain's defensive capability only compounded the enduring muddle at the heart of the defence debate. On taking office in May 1979, Thatcher informed her first Defence Secretary, Francis Pym, to abandon all thoughts of increased defence expenditure, or a return to a wider overseas role, and to cut £500 million off the defence budget. When he resisted her wishes, she replaced him with a more compliant John Nott in January 1981 with instructions to 're-establish . . . the right balance between . . . resource constraints and our necessary defence requirements'. Soon convinced of the MoD's inefficiency, and confronting a large departmental overspend, Nott decided to embark upon a thorough re-examination of the defence programme rather than a full-blown defence review. Six months later, he produced the famous *The United Kingdom Defence Programme: the Way Forward* (Cmnd 8288-I June 1981).

This document emphasised that change in many areas of the world, combined with the growing Soviet threat, made it 'increasingly necessary for NATO members to look to Western security concerns over a wider field than before and . . . Britain's own needs, outlook and interests give her a special role in efforts of this kind'. The White Paper declared the objective 'in no way rests on a desire to cut the defence effort'. On the contrary, it sought 'to establish how best to exploit a substantial increase, which will enable us to enhance our "front line capability" in very many areas'. Despite this supposed emphasis, however, Nott recognised that without more resources 'something would have to give'. Trident remained pivotal to defence planning, and the Territorial Army and the enhancement of the Army's out-of-area flexibility were both given higher priority while the exigencies of Anglo-American harmony necessitated the reaffirmation of Labour's commitment to extra funding for NATO until 1985–86.

On the other hand, the 1981 Defence Review focused its most severe cuts upon Britain's surface fleet – partly on the political grounds that it was less likely to generate overseas criticism than reductions in the Army and partly because maritime patrol aircraft and nuclear attack submarines were far more effective platforms for hunting Soviet submarines in the 'Greenland–Iceland–United Kingdom choke point' than surface vessels (Dorman 2001: 103). The ageing aircraft carrier *Hermes* was to be scrapped, the mini-carrier *Invincible* was sold to Australia, the number of frigates and destroyers was scheduled to be reduced from 60 to 42, naval manpower was to be cut by between a third and a quarter and there were corresponding reductions in dockyard capacity at Rosyth and Plymouth. Before these proposals could be implemented, however, Argentina's invasion of the Falkland Islands in 1982 demonstrated the importance of large-scale balanced naval support for out-of-area operations, and in so doing bought the Navy a brief, if disastrously misconceived, reprieve at the expense of the coherence of Britain's global strategic defence policy.

Although many in Whitehall believed the principal lesson of the Falklands War was that Nott's Defence Review had been misguided in its conclusions, David Greenwood contends that 'there was very little wrong with the course for British defence chartered in this document' given Conservative priorities. Above all, John Nott was probably correct in seeking to shift attention away from expensive weapons platforms (warships and aircraft), to focus more upon basic weapons and equipment. His problem, however, was that the strategy he defined came under almost intolerable pressure from a combination of sharply rising costs, shrinking budgets and the distorting effects of an expensively burdensome new commitment in the South Atlantic created by

Table 6.4   The funding gap – defence expenditure (£ billions) and manpower
(000s), 1984/5 to 1988/9

	1984/5	1985/6	1986/7	1987/8	1988/9
Expenditure: 1988/9 prices	21.0	21.0	20.3	19.9	19.1
Expenditure: cash	17.1	17.9	18.2	18.9	19.1
Resources required (estimate)	17.4	19.3	20.9	22.7	24.6
% difference between resources required and allocated	2.4	6.6	11.8	17.6	23.6
Manpower: UK regulars	326	323	320	317	312
MOD civilians	174	169	164	143	141

Source: Greenwood (1991: 52, 57).

the Falklands War. As a result, hopes that the White Paper would map out *The Way Forward* towards an 'appropriate and sustainable blueprint for the coming decade' were almost immediately undermined. Thus, while defence expenditure rose by 18 per cent in real terms between 1979 and 1985, Greenwood rightly argues that for the remainder of the Thatcher decade the defence programme was continuously underfunded in relation to demands and that policy was designed largely with the intention of 'keeping up appearances' (Greenwood 1991: 57–8).

To mask this growing 'funding gap' between resources and commitments, under Michael Heseltine's auspices (1983–86), the MoD papered over the cracks with efficiency drives, improved procurement procedures and enhanced management information systems like MINIS (Management Information System for Ministers), but in the end it was compelled to fall back on an incremental process of 'review by stealth' and more traditional techniques of retrenchment which forced all three Services to economise on manning levels, operations, maintenance and even training with live ammunition, while the MoD stretched out existing procurement projects and imposed a moratorium on payments to contractors (Baylis 1989: 79). As Greenwood notes: 'To call this "management" is a perversion of language, and to claim that it reflects "good housekeeping" is a travesty' (Greenwood 1991: 42). As manpower and expenditure fell, it was scarcely surprising that in his first two Defence White Papers in 1986 and 1987 George Younger spoke of the need for 'difficult decisions' regarding future priorities. But for all that, he staunchly avoided any hint of a fundamental reappraisal of defence roles and resources, partly from fear that this would be interpreted as an admission of underfunding and partly because the Nott review had left a 'morbid fear of such exercises among Conservative politicians' (Freedman 1999: 95). Instead, the Thatcher government preferred to shirk bold decisions in favour of 'muddling through and calling it management' (Greenwood 1991: 56).

'Options for Change' in a world turned upside down, 1989–97

The revolutionary events in Eastern Europe in 1989, which culminated with the dissolution of the Soviet Union in December 1991, and the first Treaty on the Limitation of Conventional Forces in Europe fundamentally transformed the environment in which British external policy was formulated. The bipolar tensions of the Cold War which had so decisively shaped British policy objectives for over 40 years were now a thing of the past. In these transformed circumstances, even the NATO Foreign Ministers meeting at Turnberry in June 1990 agreed that the alliance should henceforth play a more political role. These momentous events made demands for the already long overdue defence review almost irresistible. Moreover, the fact that these changes coincided with John Major's succession to the premiership in December 1990 reinforced the perception that this represented a major watershed in British external policy. As many argued, Britain could now belatedly engage in a decisive shift in its defence posture, adjusting to the loss of empire, the removal of the Soviet threat and the weak performance of its economy, in order to adapt to the political realities of the 1990s rather than the geostrategic conditions and illusions of 1945 (Clarke 1992: 111).

In the event, the remarkably hasty Conservative Defence Review, published by Tom King in July 1990, opted for incremental adjustments to the status quo rather than any radical reformulation of defence priorities. Although tantalisingly entitled *Options for Change*, the content suggested more of an emphasis on continuity with the past than transformation – particularly as its underlying objective of achieving 'smaller but better' armed forces was easily derided by critics as 'Options for Cuts' (Freedman 1999: 96). Britain remained committed to its Trident strategic nuclear forces, but the enhanced deterrent was expected to facilitate a further reduction in the active strength of the Services from 310,000 to 255,000 by mid-decade. In particular, in the absence of a Soviet threat, Army manpower would be cut by 40,000 to a total of 116,000, the RAF would be reduced from 24 to 18 squadrons, while the number of frigates and destroyers was scheduled to fall from 48 to 40. In practice, therefore, this Defence Review was little more than a just another Treasury-led 'prospectus for contraction' indiscriminately sharing the pain relatively equally across all three Services. In total, the envisaged 25 per cent cut in the defence budget was more severe than at any time since the end of the Second World War, reducing spending from 5 per cent to 3 per cent of GDP (Greenwood 1991: 63; A. Smith 1996: 277).

The Major government carried on where Thatcher left off with regard to defence policy. In his first White Paper as Defence Secretary in 1992, Malcolm Rifkind emphasised the uncertainty of the future, while adding a cautionary note to the effect that there 'is hardly any type or scale of military provision for which imagination cannot conceive a come-in handy-scenario; and we cannot afford everything . . . The discipline of resource constraint is inescapable' (Cmnd 1981, 1992: 13). A further cost-saving assessment entitled *Frontline First: the Defence Costs Study* followed in 1994 (Greenwood 1991: 63). As a result, the Major years between 1990 and 1997 were characterised largely by declining capabilities as the defence budget (as a percentage of GDP) fell to its lowest point in the twentieth century, while personnel numbers were smaller than they had been at any time since the 1930s, leaving the Armed Forces 'clearly stretched and probably overstretched' (McInnes 1998: 825, 827).

All of this was bad enough, but the real problem during the 1990s was that, while the Major government presided over yet another sharp cutback in the armed forces, it was also unusually active in its deployments. Not only were 20,000 British troops continually tied down in Northern Ireland, but in November 1990 they participated in 'Operation Desert Storm' to liberate Kuwait from Iraqi occupation, and in late 1992 over 2300 troops joined a humanitarian mission to Bosnia as a prelude to a further deployment to guarantee the ceasefire in 1994. Ultimately, there was nothing new about this unstable combination of the force contraction and military activism. On the contrary, it was the inevitable outcome of an unsustainable bipartisan desire to enjoy all the benefits of a world role without having to pay for it. But, as the Blair government pointed out soon after coming to office in May 1997, since 1990 defence expenditure had fallen by 23 per cent in real terms to 3.5 per cent of GDP, the lowest level since the 1930s, while the forces had been reduced by nearly a third from 315,000 to a meagre 215,000. In these circumstances, a series of largely unexpected operational challenges had created 'excessive and unsustainable pressures' which Labour intended to rectify (Cm 3999, 1998: Foreword). Ironically, contrary to the rhetoric, these demands would become substantially greater during Blair's premiership, as New Labour abandoned the party's traditional anti-militarism and set off on a course that ultimately resulted in it 'resorting to force with a remarkable degree of frequency' (Williams 2005: 25).

New Labour and hopes of delivering security in a changing world

The Blair government entered office in May 1997 with a manifesto commitment to conduct a comprehensive review of defence and security policy. The result was the Strategic Defence Review (SDR) published in July 1998. This document drew on the work of a complex range of working groups and an extremely broad range of consultations (Gummett 2000: 270). Inevitably, it contained some superficial elements of continuity with the past – particularly its emphasis upon nuclear weapons, NATO, the pivotal importance of Anglo-American relations and the quest for defence economies (Lilleker 2000: 230). Yet, beneath the surface, there was much substance in the claims of the Defence Secretary, George Robertson, that this was a 'radical' document which would lead to a 'fundamental reshaping of our forces' (Cm 3999, 1998: paras 2–3).

One obvious novelty was that the review explicitly claimed to be 'foreign policy-led', as opposed to the Treasury-inspired cuts imposed by the Thatcher and Major governments – although some commentators were highly critical of this claim, on the grounds that 'foreign policy may determine priorities but it is the reality of costs and budgets that determine how far down the descending order of priorities capability can extend' (Pugh 2006). The SDR was predicated on the premise that there would be no significant reduction in defence capabilities because the end of the Cold War had not created a more peaceful or harmonious international environment. On the contrary, it dwelt upon the fundamentally different nature of the threat to national security from ethnic conflict, drugs and environmental issues, although the Defence Select Committee complained that it said relatively little about 'asymmetric threats' from terrorism and the use of chemical and biological weapons. The central point, however, was the SDR recognised clearly that as a member of the UN Security Council, NATO and the EU, and as a major trading nation, Britain simply could not stand aside from international problems. As a result, the review was focused on 'the use of armed force as much as the more traditional questions of budgets, procurement and the distribution of resources' (Freedman 2007: 618).

This preoccupation reflected Blair's deeply personal aspiration to make Britain 'a force for good in the world', rather than simply a state driven by narrow self-interest; a theme which conformed well with the government's early emphasis on an 'ethical dimension' to foreign policy and Blair's Chicago speech in April 1999 outlining the circumstances in which the international community had a right to intervene in humanitarian crises (see Chapter 8). To translate good intentions into a military reality on the ground, the SDR argued that, while the armed forces needed to be able to conduct a full range of operations from warmaking to peace-supporting, in future there would be less requirement for heavy armaments, combat aircraft and frigates but a far greater need for an expeditionary capability to enable British forces to intervene flexibly in overseas trouble-spots at short notice. Throughout, the document stressed that its purpose was not to cut resources, but rather 'to create a rebalanced and more flexible force structure capable of meeting our future defence and security needs more effectively'.

These themes had been contained in Malcolm Rifkind's 1992 and 1993 Defence White Papers but they were carried much further under the Blair governments. As flexibility and global reach implied the need for extra sealift and airlift capability, the SDR's reorientation of priorities strengthened the Navy's case for new carriers to act as floating airbases capable of projecting power offshore rather than simply to fulfil their traditional role as expensive centrepieces of large maritime battle groups. The SDR also advocated the need for greater inter-Service cooperation and a Rapid Reaction Force. Another novelty of the review was its emphasis upon 'defence diplomacy', which required the armed forces to undertake a broader range of non-operational roles in support of conflict prevention, education and training, security building, the promotion of good governance and supporting UK defence exports.

In some respects, subsequent White Papers can be seen as extensions and refinements of the SDR's conclusions in the light of evolving events. In the aftermath of 9/11 the government produced the *Strategic Defence Review: A New Chapter* in July 2002 to update and revise key areas with regard to the new threat from international terrorism and 'asymmetric warfare' while underlining the expeditionary nature of future forces and the need to plan for a wider geographical deployment than previously envisaged (Cm 5566, 2002). This significant reorientation of Britain's defence posture was extended still further in December 2003 with the publication of another long-awaited Defence White

Paper entitled *Delivering Security in a Changing World* (Cm 6269, 2004). Again, the emphasis was on the need for 'capabilities to meet a much wider range of expeditionary tasks, at a greater range from the UK and at an ever increasing tempo', but this time on a scale far greater than envisaged in the SDR and more systematically analysed than in the *New Chapter* in order to encompass proactive engagement in multiple, concurrent, small- to medium-scale operations involving a variety of roles ranging from conflict prevention, peace support to counter-terrorism and counter-proliferation operations.

In this respect, this evolutionary document reflected the same priorities as NATO's 'New Strategic Concept' and it mirrored the emerging US security paradigm prepared for what the Bush administration described as 'the Long War'. In both of these documents, the priority had shifted towards a flexible response to regional crises and pre-emptive military action against 'rogue states' and paramilitary opponents. In the US case, this meant cutting back on heavy weapons and achieving 'global reach' by directing more resources into Special Operations, the US Marine Corps's expeditionary capability, and conventional strike and stand-off capabilities (Rogers 2006: 651–2). The 2003 White Paper reflected a similar emphasis upon a 'rebalancing' of forces towards a more flexible but higher intensity expeditionary capability, on the assumption that large-scale operations would still be conducted under the auspices of the US or NATO. Nevertheless, as most likely new enemies would not possess bombers, combat aircraft or tanks, Britain would need fewer such platforms but a far greater stock of lighter, more mobile high-technology weapons systems to deliver against the stated future goal of 'speed, precision, agility, deployability, reach and sustainability'. As the emphasis was no longer on quantity as a measure of capability, the White Paper promised the most sweeping changes since the Cold War.

These practical implications were spelled out in full in July 2004 with the publication of yet another 'additional chapter' to the White Paper, which included substantial cuts in RAF squadrons and bases, the loss of a quarter of the Army's Challenger 2 battle tanks, one-fifth of the Royal Navy's ships, 20,000 jobs (including four infantry battalions) and some of its Lynx helicopter capability (Cm 6041-I, 2003: 8). Despite the economic turmoil brought about by the 'credit crunch' and the ensuing liquidity crisis, the broad strategic thrust outlined in the *Defence Framework* in April 2009 remains largely unchanged in its fundamentals. As Defence Secretary John Hutton told an IPPR conference on national security in April 2009, Britain remained committed to its 'vital' nuclear deterrent, but the armed forces needed to follow the US example and embark on 'a rebalancing of investment in technology, equipment and people to meet the challenge of irregular warfare'. To this end, he emphasised the possibility of radically increasing the size of the SAS and SBS, which had 'massively' contributed to operational success in Afghanistan and Iraq (*Guardian*, 28 April 2009).

Too many commitments, too little money? Defence funding since 1997

Despite the promise of a single-minded defence-led reorientation of policy priorities, financial constraints soon resurrected many of the traditional endemic problems created by a long-term lack of consistency and 'joined-up' thinking in defence policy. As a proportion of GDP, defence expenditure over the period 1997/98 to 2006/07 remained fairly stable at around 2.5 per cent after a long period of sustained decline from a high point of 5.4 per cent in 1984. In near cash terms, the defence budget has risen from £20.9 billion in 1997/98 to £31.5 billion in 2006/07 before reaching a peak of £38 billion announced in the Budget in April 2009. This represented a 2.1 per cent average annual increase in real terms, but as the financial burden has been inflated in recent years by the rapidly escalating costs of military operations and an even faster rise in the cost of defence equipment, which has doubled over the past decade, critics argued that this level of funding was simply insufficient to meet the far higher level of military demands placed on the armed forces. As a result, the ostensible increase in funding had actually led to significant cutbacks and shortfalls in capability. It is certainly true that the defence sector is the only major area of public expenditure that has declined as a proportion of the total Budget, while other areas like health have seen an increase of 36 per cent in real terms in their Departmental Expenditure Limits (DEL) since 2002/03.

In addition to the MoD's annual departmental budget, the cost of operations in Afghanistan and Iraq are reported in Supplementary Estimates and paid directly from the Treasury Reserve. This has been essential given the rapidly rising cost of these deployments. In FY 2006/07 the Afghan campaign cost £770 million and Iraq added over another £1 billion. In the following year, the total cost of these operations almost doubled to more than £3 billion, and in FY2008/09 the figure continued to soar upwards to more than £4.5 billion – a year-on-year increase of over 50 per cent – largely explained by the need to fulfil promises of better equipment for troops on the ground, including £700 million for more heavily armoured vehicles to withstand roadside bombs as well as more helicopters and better communications. In total, between 2001/02 and 2008/09, the Treasury's Reserve contributed over

Table 6.5   Total defence expenditure: 2000/01 to 2007/08 (£ million)

	Voted Estimate	Out-turn	Variation	% change in Estimate over previous year	As % of GDP
2000/01	23,610	23,538	-72	-	2.4
2001/02	32,458	33,060	+604	+37.5	2.6
2002/03	35,653	34,651	-1002	+9.8	2.6
2003/04	30,087	29,337	-749	-15.6	2.6
2004/05	33,659	32,641	-1019	+11.9	2.5
2005/06	31,502	30,603	-829	-6.4	2.5
2006/07	33,746	31,454	-2292	+7.1	2.4
2007/08	33,630	33,076	-116	-0.3	2.4

Source: MoD, *Annual Report and Accounts, vol. 1: Annual Performance Report*, various years.

£13 billion to cover operational costs, of which Iraq claimed £7.882 billion and Afghanistan absorbed the remaining £5.383 billion. It is anticipated that the cost of the Afghan campaign will increase by a further 30 per cent in 2009/10 and the MoD must now bear the full cost of UORs (Urgent Operational Requirements) previously divided equally with the Treasury (*Guardian*, 3 July 2009).

Notwithstanding the financial pressures on the MoD during Gordon Brown's Chancellorship, as Table 6.5 demonstrates, the outcome of the Comprehensive Spending Review in July 2007 was ostensibly favourable in that it proposed an average annual real increase in the defence budget of 1.5 per cent over three years rising to £36.9 billion by 2010/11. But as this supposedly average annual real-terms increase took no account of the fact that inflation in defence equipment was at least 3 per cent (and possibly in excess of 5 per cent) higher than the retail price index, critics argued the defence budget was actually scheduled to suffer a significant decrease in real terms over the CSR cycle (Select Committee on Defence, HC 107 2009: para. 174). Even a leaked internal MoD document conceded that the real cash increase was actually only 0.6 per cent for 2008/09 (*Guardian*, 18 February 2008). As Admiral Lord Boyce, CDS during the Iraq invasion, declared in a highly critical speech in the House of Lords in November 2007, 'the smoke and mirrors work of the government, and in particular the Treasury, actually means that the core defence programme has had no

Table 6.6   The Comprehensive Spending Review settlement, 2006/07 to
2010/11: Departmental Expenditure Limit (DEL) in £ millions

	2007–08	2008–09	2009–10	2010–11
Resource budget	32,618	33,602	35,165	36,702
Capital budget	7404	7871	8187	8871
Total DEL	32,579	34,034	35,342	36,890
Of which near cash	29,411	30,763	31,921	33,628

Sources: Ministry of Defence: *Annual Report and Accounts, 2007-08*, HC
850-I, July 2008, p. 211; Cm 7098 *Government Expenditure Plans 2007/08*,
July 2009.

effective budget rise at all' (HL Deb 22 November 2007: c. 932). A
year later, the highly respected Royal United Services Institute (RUSI)
estimated that the defence equipment budget was £15 billion short of
what was required (Clarke 2008).

Within only three years of the brave new world outlined in the 2003
Defence White Paper, therefore, the heavy cost of operations in
Afghanistan and Iraq, the prior commitment to upgrade Trident and
the additional burden of two new giant aircraft carriers provoked a
bitter row between the Ministry of Defence and Service chiefs versus
the Treasury over the CSR recommendations to slice £4.5 billion off an
already overcommitted defence budget over the next three years – the
heaviest cuts since the end of the Cold War – and a total of £15 billion
over the next decade (Hastings 2008). This retrenchment included further efforts to reduce the fleet from 103 to a mere 50 vessels by 2027
(with particularly heavy cuts in minesweepers, patrol ships and auxiliary vessels) and the reduction in RAF bases and Tornado squadrons.
Among the other proposed casualties were the third tranche of the
much-criticised Eurofighter (Typhoon) project and a halving of orders
for the delayed Type 42 destroyer (down from twelve to six) and the
Astute-class nuclear-powered submarine (four of the planned eight),
while the Nimrod reconnaissance aircraft and the £14 billion Future
Rapid Effect System (FRES) battlefield vehicle projects were both to be
cut or delayed (*Guardian*, 4 December 2007, 18 February 2008, 20
June 2009).

This debilitating conflict between the MoD and Treasury over finance
has been overlaid by an equally fundamental inability to choose between
spending priorities – in particular, the relative claims of those
demanding more essential low-tech kit for troops on the ground versus

those advocating more investment in costly high-technology prestige projects. After years of official disfavour, the Blair government's new focus on the need for a substantially enhanced expeditionary capability meant that by 2007 aircraft carriers were once again hailed by Defence ministers as a means to give Britain 'a powerful navy for the future; which is entirely right because we are a large player on the world scene' (*Guardian*, 17 February and 26 July 2007). It was thus announced that Britain would construct two gigantic 65,000 tonne Queen Elizabeth-class aircraft carriers at a cost of £3.9 billion while simultaneously upgrading Trident. These would enter service in 2012 and 2015 and would each be equipped with 40 US Joint Strike Fighters at a cost of another £12 billion. The construction of the two largest warships ever deployed by the Royal Navy, armed with extremely expensive advanced American F-35 multiple-role aircraft at a cost of $104 million (£59 million) each, will give Britain a global reach capability into the mid-2060s to a degree it has not possessed since the early 1970s. But, as Paul Rogers points out, the total cost of the complete naval package will amount to a minimum of £16 billion and, in conjunction with the upgrading of Trident, these costs 'will dominate defence procurement in the next two decades or more and . . . will make it very difficult for a future government to diverge from that approach unless it is to entertain a massive and costly programme of cancellations' (Rogers 2006: 652).

When signing the contract for these vessels in July 2008, the Defence Secretary, Des Browne, insisted they were 'affordable expenditure' which would provide 'world-class capabilities' without jeopardising other aspects of defence expenditure (*Guardian*, 4 July 2008). The practical reality has proved rather different. The Defence Select Committee has repeatedly opposed the carrier construction programme in the hope of stabilising the MoD budget while questioning the future role of aircraft carriers, given suspicions that the project was based on 'political' rather than defence needs (*Guardian*, 27 March 2008). It has also expressed 'deep concern' that the commitment to build four new Trident submarines and two carriers would reduce the resources available for troops in Afghanistan suffering from a chronic shortage of vital low-tech equipment, such as helicopters and more heavily armoured ground transport to replace the aged Warrior, Scimitar and Spartan armoured vehicles so vulnerable to roadside bombs (*Guardian*, 20 January 2009).

An even more outspoken public contribution to this debate was provided by General Sir Richard Dannatt, the head of the Army, in May 2009. In a speech at Chatham House, he warned the government about the excessive pressures on troops deployed in Afghanistan and Iraq, while describing the defence budget as 'unbalanced' and 'heavily skewed' towards high-tech expensive platforms wholly irrelevant both to present conflicts and the Army's future roles in intervention and stabilisation operations. As only 10 per cent of the existing defence equipment programme was being spent on the Army he declared:

> We have an absolute obligation to understand their needs and to provide [British troops] with the tools and training to do the job, and not squander our increasingly scarce resources on those things that are not relevant to today's and tomorrow's absolute requirements. . . . History will not judge our decision-making kindly if we duck the difficult decision and just muddle through. We are at the crossroads. . . . we are in an era of persistent conflict. Iraq and Afghanistan are not aberrations; they are signposts to the future. We risk becoming irrelevant if we do not adapt right across the board. (*Guardian*, 16 May 2009)

Assailed by unprecedented public criticism from serving, as well as retired Service Chiefs for these politically embarrassing deficiencies, in December 2008 the government postponed the carrier project for two years in order to give priority to the needs of front-line troops who were to receive an additional £635 million for Urgent Operational Requirements in FY2009/10 (*Guardian* 10 December 2008). In his second budget as Chancellor in April 2009, however, Alistair Darling foreshadowed severe cuts in public expenditure to fill the gaping £175 billion 'black hole' in the public finances created by the Brown government's reflationary response towards the severe financial crisis in 2008–9. Among the likely targets for both major parties, the Navy's two new carriers appeared to be extremely vulnerable to the axe, along with the third tranche of Eurofighters, Astute-class submarines, Type-42 destroyers, the A400M transporter and even the Trident replacement programme; a threat which prompted the heads of the largest defence contractors to launch a public campaign in September 2009 to avert draconian cuts in the forthcoming defence review (*Guardian*, 2, 16 September 2009).

Blair, Brown and the crisis of military overstretch

At the Labour Party conference in 1999, Robin Cook, Blair's first Foreign Secretary, boasted that 'no other nation has a higher proportion of its armed forces active on peacekeeping measures around the globe' (Lilleker 2000: 229). This claim was well justified, given the fact that Britain's armed forces have been deployed on contingent operations overseas more times and in greater numbers than under any other Prime Minister since the end of the Second World War. Indeed, according to the MoD's Annual Report and Accounts, in April 2008 British forces were deployed in no fewer than 30 countries or regions across the globe, from Afghanistan and Ascension Island to Sierra Leone, Sudan and the Yemen (MoD, HC 850 I–II 2008: 29). What the Foreign Secretary carefully refrained from mentioning, however, was either the damaging cumulative impact of these commitments on the forces or the heavy financial and opportunity costs involved in these deployments. Yet the reality is, that during the first decade of the twenty-first century, the already well-established problem of 'mission overstretch' reached crisis proportions. Worse still, the Blair government's readiness to commit British forces to such operations has imposed enormous pressures on existing manpower, recruitment and retention levels – not to mention the goodwill of the armed forces and their leadership.

During Blair's premiership, British troops were deployed in five high-profile conflicts spanning almost the entire period, along with a number of smaller operations such as peacekeeping in Cyprus. Worse still, in the case of Kosovo, Afghanistan and Iraq, deployments intended initially to be short-term limited interventions degenerated into protracted and highly demanding commitments. As Defence Planning Assumptions have consistently been exceeded since 2002, these demands have taken a heavy toll on the Services and in the final years of the Blair government the terms and conditions of service became a major issue in the political and public consciousness. This was not least because former Service Chiefs (and even many senior serving officers) have been highly outspoken in their condemnation of the government's neglect of the welfare of its Service personnel – to the extent that Gordon Brown intervened personally, as Prime Minister, to ensure that Sir Richard Dannatt, the Chief of the General Staff, did not automatically succeed to the position of Chief of the Defence Staff because of his vociferous criticism of government policy on Service conditions and defence funding (*Sunday Times*, 15 June 2008).

The House of Commons Defence Select Committee has been equally forthright in its criticism of military overstretch. Despite the SDR's recognition of the need to 'break the vicious circle' of undermanning and the overstretch inherited from the Conservatives, in March 2005 the Committee concluded the sheer intensity of British troop deployment around the world was 'utterly unsustainable' (Cm 3999, 1998: Foreword; *Guardian*, 17 March 2005). Two years later, the Service Chiefs told the Committee that Britain needed to decide whether it wished to continue its existing world role (and fund it adequately) or adopt a more modest posture. 'It is quite clear we are operating beyond the bounds of the Planning Assumptions we were set', Air Chief Marshal Sir Jock Stirrup, the serving Chief of the Defence Staff, told the Committee. 'We are very stretched at the moment.' In contrast, the Permanent Under-Secretary and the Minister preferred the phrase 'stretched but not overstretched' (*Guardian*, 7 March 2007; Select Committee on Defence, HC 57 2006: paras 37, 63). Yet, according to a secret memorandum leaked to the *Daily Telegraph*, General Dannatt warned the government in July 2007 that Britain was perilously short of troops. 'We now have almost no capability to react to the unexpected', he declared on the eve of the Treasury's Comprehensive Spending Review, while reinforcements for Iraq and Afghanistan were 'now almost non-existent' having already called up 600 reservists (*Daily Telegraph*, 21 July 2007). In its Annual Report published in the same month, even the MoD conceded publicly that since 2002 deployments in Afghanistan and Iraq had meant the forces were operating 'significantly beyond the level they were resourced and structured to sustain' (*Guardian*, 24 July 2007). On this basis, the Select Committee caustically observed that, whether stretched or overstretched, 'What is certain is that they are operating in challenging conditions in insufficient numbers and without all the equipment they need' and that, while sustainable in the short-term, 'the current level of deployments poses a significant risk to the MoD achieving success in its military objectives' (Select Committee on Defence, HC 57 2006: paras 63, 66–7).

Pressures of this sort have had a substantial impact upon military recruitment, retention and attrition rates. In fairness, the haemorrhaging of experienced personnel (particularly those with specialist skills) is not a new phenomenon, but during the Blair–Brown governments it became a problem of chronic proportions. In 2003, Britain's armed forces numbered 205,000. Two years later, they were 3000 below their planned strength of 191,000. By November 2007, the manpower deficit had doubled to 6,730; a worrying trend given that more than 5,000 officers and men had left the Services in the preceding three months and another 2,000 applications were awaiting approval (*Guardian*, 23 November 2007) By January 2009, the shortfall had risen to 4,000 against a reduced official requirement of 101,800 personnel at a time when the CDS was repeatedly arguing that the Army needed at least 130,000 men to fulfil its existing functions effectively (*Guardian*, 22 January 2009). The Defence Select Committee has repeatedly expressed grave concern about the effect of this 'high operational tempo and stretch' upon attrition rates among skilled personnel and it has identified the existence of 30 'pinch point' specialist trades in the Army suffering chronic manpower shortages. Equally depressing was the fact that 38 per cent of recruits did not complete the first training course (Select Committee on Defence HC 424 2008: para. 36).

The impact of these trends upon operational effectiveness on the ground has been substantial. At its peak in 1999, around 47 per cent of all military personnel were committed to operations, more than double the level considered to be acceptable under the 'Harmony Guidelines' (defining the minimum time between operations). This had obvious negative implications for efficiency and the Army's ability to train 'to fight the "next war" which could present entirely different challenges' (Select Committee on Defence, HC 57 2006: para 61). Towards the end of 2000, this figure had fallen to some 27 per cent, as the contingents in Bosnia and Kosovo fell from a peak of 22,000 to 5,500 and the Northern Ireland garrison was reduced from a peak of 27,000 to 14,000 by 2000. British forces remained so stretched, however, that only a further substantial reduction in the Northern Ireland contingent in July 2004 permitted participation in a small humanitarian mission to the Darfur region of Sudan. Not until the end of the 38-year Northern Ireland deployment in August 2007, was it possible to reduce the number of soldiers exceeding 'Harmony Guidelines' to 10 per cent. Despite this relative easing of the situation, however, the number of units with 'serious or critical weaknesses' rose from over 30 per cent in 2005/06 to 39 per cent during 2006/07. By July 2008, this figure had risen to 49 per cent (MoD *Annual Report and Accounts*, HC 57: para. 16 and HC 61: para. 47; HC 424: 65; HC 850: para. 17). In March 2007, the Cabinet Office 'Capability Review' thus concluded:

> The current level of sustained operational commitments puts at risk the Department's ability to prepare for potential further missions. Striking a balance between short-term operational activity and long-term capability development will become increasingly challenging and will require the MoD leadership team to unite in taking tough prioritisation and resource allocation decisions. (Cabinet Office 2007c: section 3)

Beyond high casualty rates and increasingly long deployments away from families, a variety of other Service issues have compounded the sense of grievance. One such issue has been the shortage of vital kit and equipment for troops in combat zones, culminating in claims that at least 2,000 British troops had been deprived of essential body armour during the Iraq War because of poor planning by the MoD, while chemical/biological suits were in extremely short supply during the invasion – despite the fact that the war was justified partly by Saddam Hussein's alleged possession of such weapons. Other vital equipment arrived too late to be used, while many others complained about the poor quality of desert boots and the shortage of appropriate camouflage kit (*Guardian*, 12 December 2003; 19 December 2006). There was also a chorus of well-founded and repeated criticism about the severe shortage of medium- and heavy-lift helicopter support needed to evacuate wounded troops and to reduce troop vulnerability to roadside bombs; a shortfall blamed directly on Gordon Brown's decision to cut the helicopter budget by £1.4 billion in 2004 (Select Committee on Defence, HC 434 July 2009). Even more depressing was the revelation that after much fierce criticism about unacceptable delays in replacing vulnerable troop transport with new and more heavily armoured Vector and Mastiff vehicles, they performed so badly in Afghanistan that they were withdrawn from service early in 2009 because of what the Defence Secretary described as 'mechanical and technical issues' – not least that the wheels just kept falling off (*Guardian*, 30 March, 15 May 2009).

These grievances have been compounded by a variety of other pressing personnel issues, including the poor standard of Service accommodation, while in June 2008, General Dannatt publicly compared Army basic pay unfavourably with that of trainee traffic wardens (*Guardian*, 6 June 2008, 20 January 2009). The Defence Select Committee has been equally scathing about the 'truly reprehensible' failings of the Joint Personnel Administration, which have an 'impact upon several areas essential to service personnel satisfaction with life' (MoD Annual Report, HC 214 2009: para. 10). Other sources of frustration include the quality of health care for injured troops, compensation for death and injury, and government's efforts to prevent Coroners at military inquests from condemning the MoD's failure to supply adequate equipment as 'an unforgivable breach of trust between soldiers and those who govern them' for which they should 'hang their heads in shame' (*Guardian*, 12 April, 18 October 2008).

These increasing pressures on an overstretched military capability inevitably took their toll upon morale, and surveys of satisfaction levels with Service life record a high, and increasing, incidence of discontent. In an internal MoD document entitled 'Chief of General Staff's Briefing Report' compiled in May 2007 (leaked to the *Sunday Telegraph* in November 2007), Dannatt warned the MoD that soldiers were feeling 'devalued, angry and suffering from Iraq fatigue' and that continued undermanning and high operational demands in Iraq and Afghanistan were 'mortgaging the goodwill of our people' because 'the tank of goodwill now runs on vapour' (*Sunday Telegraph*, 21 July and 18 November 2007). These concerns were echoed simultaneously in a ferocious and unprecedented attack upon the government's parsimony in the House of Lords delivered by five former Chiefs of the Defence Staff, during which Lord Boyce talked of the Prime Minister's 'contempt' for the Armed Forces, while Lord Guthrie denounced Brown as 'the most unsympathetic Chancellor of the Exchequer, as far as defence was concerned, and . . . the only senior Cabinet minister who avoided coming to the Ministry of Defence to be briefed by our staff about our problems'. He also defended serving officers like Stirrup and Dannatt for speaking out publicly about underfunding because, while unconstitutional, it was indicative of the fact that they were 'at the end of their tether' (HL Deb 22 November 2007: c.120, 952, 961; *Guardian*, 23 November 2007).

This resentment prompted renewed interest in the idea of a 'military covenant' – the contract between the nation and service personnel and their families who make personal sacrifices in return for fair treatment and commensurate terms and conditions of service. As Demos, the New Labour think-tank, noted in November 2007, this relationship has been 'damaged almost beyond repair. (Edwards and Forster 2007: 13). Its recommendation for a new 'civil–military compact' echoed a theme first raised publicly by the newly formed British Armed Forces Federation three months earlier when launching a stinging attack on the government for not honouring the military covenant, which it declared a 'dead letter'. In the following month, the Royal British Legion launched its 'Honour the Covenant' campaign as the theme of the 2007 Poppy appeal (*Guardian*, 15 August 2007).

These attacks were neither unchallenged nor unheeded by government. In November 2007, the Prime Minister responded to charges of underfunding and neglect by pointing out that Labour had spent far more on defence than the Conservatives, but this was tactfully accompanied by a pledge to introduce a new military covenant. In the following months, 14 new initiatives on Service welfare and the terms and conditions of engagement were announced, including plans for a £20 million scheme to enable Service personnel to obtain low-cost shared equity loans to help them get a foot on the housing ladder at preferential rates, along with a variety of other reforms to improve health, education, housing and remuneration for Service personnel and their families. In addition, the MoD ring-fenced the £550 million from the sale of the Chelsea Barracks to improve the often substandard quality of Service accommodation, while in March 2008 the Prime Minister announced a £15,000 bonus for personnel who served for eight years (*Guardian*, 20 March 2008). These efforts culminated in a White Paper on *The Nation's Commitment* in May 2008 announcing a wide-ranging package of 40 measures designed to ameliorate some of the disadvantages of Service life, along with plans to introduce a Veterans Day, to encourage more cadet forces in schools and to include the role of the armed services in the citizenship agenda (Cm 7424, 2008). In April 2009, DEFRA (Department for Environment, Food and Rural Affairs), also instructed local authorities to give priority in specially adapted social housing to the 400 veterans already seriously injured on active service in Afghanistan and Iraq (*Guardian*, 10 April 2009).

Expenditure priorities and the failures of defence procurement

Problems with defence procurement were one of the major problem areas identified in the *Strategic Defence Review* in 1998 – and with very good reason. There are many dimensions to this problem, but almost all touch upon crucial issues. For example, as discussed above, there is an increasingly fundamental conflict between the Labour government's emphasis upon the need for well-trained highly mobile forces equipped with relatively low-tech kit and their equally firm commitment to costly prestige projects such as Trident, new aircraft carriers and Type-42 destroyers. As these increasingly expensive weapons platforms must be paid for out of a limited defence budget, this requires either a substantial increase in defence spending or a contraction in the overall defence effort and, despite Blair's explicit pledge that 'the investment required to maintain [Trident] will not come at the expense of the conventional capabilities the Armed Forces need', the Defence Select Committee noted sceptically that because expenditure on Trident was part of the broader defence budget there was no guarantee that conventional defence would not suffer – particularly without additional funding to cover the on-going running costs as well as the initial procurement (Cm 6994, 2006: 5; Select Committee on Defence, HC 225-I 2007: para. 148).

Another major source of problems stems from the long-term tendency towards what the Defence Select Committee has described as the MoD's culture of 'institutional over–optimism' with regard to budgets and completion times on major development programmes – and with good reason, given the long catalogue of prestige projects blighted by technical problems, massive cost overruns, severe time-into-service delays and lack of a commercial future; failures which depressingly reveal the weakness of the British avionics industry, the higher than average rate of inflation in armaments projects and the difficulties confronting procurement policy (Select Committee on Defence, HC 214 2009: para. 44). Although the SDR promised remedial action, the Defence Select Committee has been highly critical of the organisational reforms introduced in 1998–99. The performance of the new Defence

Procurement Agency has been described as 'woeful', while its 'Smart Acquisition' strategy (introduced in 1998 and renamed in 2000) designed to deliver more projects to time and budget has been portrayed as ridiculous given an average delay of 18 months for the in-service delivery of large defence contracts, while three of the biggest delayed BAe projects accounted for an overspend of almost £3 billion by 2004 (Select Committee on Defence, HC 528 2000; *Guardian*, 28 July 2004).

Perhaps the most notorious of these is the Eurofighter (Typhoon), which was originally conceived in the early 1980s as the fourth-generation strike fighter but, after becoming bogged down in disputes over specification and cost, the 'world's first supersonic white elephant' was not scheduled to become fully operational until 2009 – by which time the initial estimated cost to Britain of £7 billion had risen to £19 billion (*Guardian*, 14 July 2008; Rogers 2006: 657). Similar problems confronted the development of Britain's nuclear Astute-class attack submarine, the Type 42 destroyer (two years late and at £6.46 billion some £1.5 billion over budget), the Nimrod patrol aircraft and the Army's biggest ever equipment programme, the Future Rapid Effect System, currently projected to cost £14 billion but which has already been condemned as 'a fiasco' and 'a sorry story of indecision, changing requirements and delays' largely due to MoD failings (Select Committee on Defence, HC 107 2009: para. 95). Little wonder the PAC criticised the MoD's 'systematic weakness' in its procurement procedures and insisted that it should 'change the culture among its own staff to the industry from one of a "conspiracy of optimism" to one of greater realism' (*Guardian*, 22 July 2008).

Beyond spectacular failures of this sort, the post-war history of weapons procurement in Britain is littered with many other astonishing examples of error, poor management and wasted public money, such as the £422 million spent on eight special operations Chinook helicopters ordered in 1995, without contracts specifying suitable airworthiness standards. Despite much expensive tinkering, they were still not fit for purpose 13 years after ordering, prompting the chair of the PAC to describe the whole affair as 'a gold standard procurement "cock-up"' (*Guardian*, 4 June 2008). Despite assurances from the MoD that important lessons had been learned from these failures, within a year of signing the contract for two new aircraft carriers, a leaked document revealed that the estimated cost had already increased by 28 per cent from £3.9 billion to £5 billion (*Guardian*, 1 July 2009). By this juncture, a highly critical report by Bernard Gray, an official who conducted the SDR, concluded that, on average, new equipment arrived five years later and cost 40 per cent more than first estimated; a situation he described as 'a mystery, wrapped in an enigma, shrouded in an acronym'. He attributed the problem to the fact that there were 'too many types of equipment being ordered for too large a range of tasks at too high a specification' (*Guardian*, 2 September 2009).

Conventional defence forces since 1945: plus ça change . . .

In the 65 years since the end of the Second World War, a great many changes have taken place in Britain's armed forces and their intended role, the nature of their capability and the threats they are designed to counter. In 1948, the defence budget consumed 7.1 per cent of GNP, rising to a peak of 9.8 per cent in 1952. By 1964, it had fallen to below 6 per cent for the first time and between 1969 and the 1980s it remained constant at above 4 per cent. In the 2009 budget, defence was allocated £38 billion out of a total budget of £671 billion, some 5.6 per cent of the total. Notwithstanding relatively modest fluctuations in real-terms defence expenditure since the late 1950s, there has been an inexorable downward trend in the percentage of GDP devoted to these activities, while manpower in the Services has fallen equally dramatically from 847,000 in 1948 to under 500,000 for the first time in 1961 before its gradual decline to 315,000 by the time Margaret Thatcher became Prime Minister in 1979. When New Labour came to power in 1997 there were 218,700 Service personnel but, despite plans to the increase Army recruitment by up to 3,000, by January 2009 the establishment figure was still 4,000 below the official target of 101,800 (Cm 5412, 2002: 24). *Guardian*, 9 November 2007; Cm 7098, 2008: 173) Although Britain's formal overseas commitments have undoubtedly declined greatly since 1945, they have not contracted as rapidly as its Armed Forces.

For all the changes, the continuities with the recent past are even more striking. First, as Table 6.7 illustrates, since the Second World War the UK has directed a greater percentage of its GDP into military expenditure than any other major industrial power except the United States. Despite these high levels of expenditure, however, military overstretch has been a perennial problem throughout this period. In 1950, Britain struggled to field just two battalions in Korea when the Services contained over 700,000 men. Forty years later, Britain's ability to contribute two armoured brigades to the Allied coalition in the Gulf War was made possible only by drafting in troops from other units and by removing every serviceable Challenger tank from Germany – and even then the government was forced to go cap in hand to its allies, begging

Table 6.7   Comparative military expenditure as a percentage of
GDP, 1950–2006

	1950	1955	1960	1965	1970	1975	1980	1990	2000	2006
USA	5.1	10.2	9.0	7.6	8.0	5.9	5.6	5.3	3.1	4.0
UK	6.6	8.2	6.5	5.9	4.8	4.9	5.1	3.9	2.4	2.6
France	5.5	6.4	6.5	5.2	4.2	3.8	4.0	3.4	2.5	2.4
Germany	4.4	4.1	4.0	4.3	3.3	3.6	3.3	2.8	1.5	1.3
Australia	3.0	3.8	2.7	3.4	3.5	2.8	2.7	2.0	1.8	1.9
Canada	2.6	6.3	4.2	2.9	2.4	1.9	1.8	2.0	1.1	1.2
Japan	-	1.8	1.1	0.9	0.8	1.0	1.0	0.9	1.0	1.0

Sources: Chalmers (1985: 13); SIPRI *Yearbook, World Armaments and Disarmament 1992*, Table 7.A3; SIPRI Military Expenditure Database.

for spare ordnance. Little wonder that during the 2003 Iraq War, poorly equipped British troops were so persistent in their importuning of superior American kit that they became known as the 'borrowers'.

A second obvious area of continuity has been the persistent illusion shared by governments of both parties that it is possible to produce ever greater quantities of defence with progressively less money; a miracle of near-biblical proportions founded partly on their faith in the deterrent effect of nuclear weapons and partly a consequence of simple wishful thinking – particularly in a sector in which the cost of weapons systems doubles every decade (Hartley 2006: 679). Indeed, if anything, financial stringency has often resulted in short-term savings being achieved at an extremely high longer-term price, as in the case of the closure of the RAF's state-of-the-art Defence Aviation Repair Agency (DARA) facility in 2005 to save £500 million over 10 years, only then to be forced to raid the Conflict Prevention Fund in March 2008 to subsidise the cost of aircraft servicing with private contractors (*Guardian*, 10 March 2008)

By the mid-1960s, it was already becoming apparent that Britain was fighting a losing battle in its struggle to maintain a global military posture without committing the financial resources needed to match its ambition. Although poor economic performance clearly played a major role in this process, British policymakers did not give up without a fight. On the contrary, according to the Stockholm International Peace Research Institute (SIPRI) even in 2007 Britain was still ranked as the second-highest military spender behind the US when measured in terms of market exchange rate, and fifth behind the US, China, Russia and India, on the basis of purchasing power parity. Either way, it was still devoting around 2.5 per cent of its GDP and 5.5 per cent of total public expenditure to defence and by FY2010/11 the defence budget will be 11 per cent higher than in 1997 when New Labour came into office – the longest period of sustained growth since the 1980s. Even after the next long-anticipated Defence Review, Britain will still remain a major military force with a future aggregate capability superior to that of any other US ally (Chalmers 2008).

The ultimate tragedy is that these increased resources do not provide the capability to fulfil existing commitments, and most analysts, politicians and Service Chiefs doubt whether the armed forces can sustain their current level of operational tempo into the future without severe damage to effectiveness, capabilities and morale. Yet, notwithstanding all the evidence to the contrary, the MoD's four-year Defence Plan for 2008–12 (Cm 7385, 2008) unrepentantly declared that the UK is 'committed to a high tempo of operations and will remain so throughout the period covered by this Plan' (Cm 7385, 2008: para 21). For all the brave talk of new approaches and 'effects-based operations', the critical issue for the defence establishment into the twenty-first century remains precisely the same as it has been ever since 1945 – how Britain can either maintain or radically redefine its defence capabilities, roles and commitments to bring them into balance within an increasingly stretched defence budget at a time when equipment costs are increasing exponentially and the international environment remains in a state of rapid and unpredictable flux.

What is certain is that the next Defence Review (announced in July 2009) will be confronted by diametrically opposing views on future priorities. On one hand, those like Dannatt argue strongly for a focus on the campaign in Afghanistan: 'We must have what we absolutely need in the short-term and limit our ambitions for the medium– and long-term to what we can afford', he declared in his final speech as Chief of the General Staff (*Guardian*, 29 August 2009). Conversely, many others believe the review must be driven by a tightly defined and genuinely national view of security rather than simply the short-term needs of Afghanistan or to justify the upgrading of Trident (Strachan 2008). Above all, it must address the question of what sort of defence the nation wants and how to provide the resources necessary to deliver against its current 'vision, aims and objectives' outlined in the 'Defence Framework' published in April 2009. As the IPPR 'Commission on National Security in the 21st Century' argued in June 2009: 'Fundamental choices are necessary. The attempt to maintain the full spectrum of conventional combat capabilities at the current scale has produced acute strains on resources and, increasingly, on operational effectiveness. It cannot be sustained' (IPPR 2009). In this context, the Brown government's current insistence that the forthcoming Defence Review would focus specifically on Service needs but that Trident modernisation and the two aircraft carriers would be excluded from its deliberations suggests that its final report will please neither side in the debate – far less is it likely to resolve the fundamental long-term dilemma confronting defence planners concerning the nature of Britain's role in the world in the next decade (*Guardian*, 8 July 2009).

Chapter 7

Britain and the Bomb: The Quest for a Nuclear Deterrent

The history of Britain's pursuit of an independent nuclear deterrent provides an illuminating insight into both the vigour of its commitment to continued great power status and the reasons why it has increasingly struggled to defend that position. It also says much about the centrality of the Anglo-American relationship to British external policy – not least because after 1958 what British policymakers liked to call their 'independent deterrent' was almost entirely dependent upon the goodwill of the United States for the increasingly complex missile delivery systems capable of launching warheads constructed in Britain but closely following US designs. Although this defence linkage might be more accurately presented as simple dependency rather than a partnership, it has permitted a medium-sized state with an overextended foreign and defence policy to maintain a great-power-by-proxy status on the cheap. On this basis, John Dumbrell rightly argues that since 1958 Britain's privileged access to US technology combined with the intimate intermeshing of intelligence services under the UKUSA Agreement of 1947 has 'formed the essence and beating heart of the Cold War "special relationship" in that it was different in kind from that of the United States relationship with other states' (Dumbrell 2001: 124). Yet, while nuclear defence has been one of the most intimate areas of cooperation, it also needs to be recognised that early post-war relations were characterised by considerable tensions and conflicting objectives over the issue. Indeed, Britain's determination to develop an independent nuclear weapons programme of its own during and immediately after the Second World War was to a considerable degree driven by profound mistrust of both Washington's motives and its reliability as an ally in an uncertain post-war world, and these anxieties continued to be echoed well into the later years of the twentieth century.

Wartime collaboration and US betrayal

For diplomatic reasons, British policymakers never rebutted the claim in the official US report on the Manhattan Project that the UK contribution was in 'no sense vital' to the construction of the atomic bomb and that the 'date of final success need not have been delayed a single day' without it. (Lee 2006). Yet, as Margaret Gowing demonstrates conclusively, the reality was that without

> the brilliant scientific work done in Britain in the early part of the war, by refugee scientists, the Second World War would almost certainly have ended before an atomic bomb was dropped. It had been the cogency and clarity of the British Maud Report in 1940–41 which had persuaded the Americans of the practical possibility of an atomic bomb and the urgency of making one. (Gowing 1974: 1–2)

After the success of Cockcroft and Walton in splitting the atom at the Cavendish Laboratory in Cambridge in 1932, understanding of the process of nuclear fission and the chain reaction created by the bombardment of an atom of Uranium 235 was rapidly refined in British laboratories. By remarkable coincidence, these revolutionary findings were published by Niels Bohr on 1 September 1939, the day that Hitler launched the invasion of Poland. At this juncture, physicists in Britain and the United States concluded that whatever its long-term importance, this discovery would make no practical contribution to the Second World War. In March 1940, however, Otto Frisch and Rudolf Peierls, two refugee physicists working at Birmingham University, produced a crucial memorandum on the 'Properties of a Radioactive Super-Bomb' which explained precisely how a rapid chain reaction using one kilo of metallic U235 could create an atomic blast equivalent to several thousand tons of dynamite; a scientific breakthrough turned into a practical reality by the Maud Committee report in July 1941 (Gowing 1964: 41).

From the outset, there was much anxiety in Whitehall about the possible involvement of the United States in the development of this revolutionary new technology. The question first arose over whether it would be better to build the necessary vast plant and facilities in Britain, with all the risks of being bombed and where manpower was very scarce, or in North America, where American scientists had made little progress until the Maud Report galvanised the US government into establishing what became the huge Manhattan Project; an act of scientific generosity Peter Hennessy has described as 'almost certainly the most important British gift to the USA' it has ever bestowed (Hennessy 1993: 264). Initially, ministers were extremely reluctant to build the full-scale plant

Table 7.1   Outline chronology: Britain and nuclear weapons

August 1943	Quebec Agreement between Churchill and Roosevelt agrees to nuclear cooperation after the war
September 1944	Hyde Park Agreement reiterates commitment
August 1945	US drops the first atomic bombs on Hiroshima and Nagasaki
November 1945	Truman confirms post-war collaboration in Washington Agreement
August 1946	McMahon Act prohibits the disclosure of nuclear information with any foreign power
January 1947	Cabinet Committee orders secret production of an independent British atomic weapon
January 1948	Britain surrenders the right to be consulted before the use of the atomic bomb
July 1948	US B-29 bombers return to Britain; with a nuclear capability from 1949
August 1949	Soviets detonate their first atomic bomb
December 1950	V-bombers ordered for the RAF
October 1952	First successful British atomic test
November 1952	US test its first hydrogen bomb
July 1954	Cabinet agrees to build a British hydrogen bomb
April 1957	Duncan Sandys's Defence White Paper places heavy reliance on nuclear weapon
May 1957	Britain announces successful testing of its first hydrogen bomb
October 1957	Soviets launch Sputnik satellite; Eisenhower assures Macmillan the McMahon Act will be amended
July 1958	McMahon Act repealed; technological cooperation resumes Ⅲ➡

Table 7.1   Outline chronology: Britain and nuclear weapons – *continued*

March 1960	Macmillan negotiates purchase of US Skybolt missile after the cancellation of Blue Streak; first Aldermaston March organised by the Campaign for Nuclear Disarmament
December 1962	Nassau Conference; Macmillan negotiates purchase of Polaris
August 1963	Britain signs Partial Test Ban Treaty prohibiting nuclear tests in atmosphere, outer space and underwater
January 1967	Britain signs Outer Space Treaty banning the development of weapons in outer space
July 1968	Britain signs Non-Proliferation Treaty
April 1973	Heath government agrees to Polaris improvement programme – the ill-fated Chevaline project
January 1979	President Carter offers Britain the Trident missile system
July 1980	Thatcher government agrees to purchase Trident I (C4) from the US
March 1982	Purchase of Trident II (D5) agreed on extremely favourable terms
January 1984	US Cruise missiles deployed in United Kingdom amidst much protest
June 1988	Labour leader, Neil Kinnock, initiates a move away from the party's commitment to unilateral nuclear disarmament
October 2004	Secret understanding for Britain to participate in the Bush administration's Missile Defence System in Europe
December 2006	Blair government agrees to upgrade and modernise Trident in collaboration with the US

in North America for fear that who ever possessed such a plant would be able to dictate terms to the rest of the world. 'However much I may trust my neighbour and depend on him,' one minister wrote, 'I am very much averse to putting myself completely at his mercy. I would therefore *not* press the Americans to undertake the work' (Gowing 1981: 124). These apprehensions were given substance by the fact that at this stage of the war the US was still neutral and British ministers feared it might return to isolationism after the Second World War just as it had after the First. The British Cabinet were also concerned about American secrecy and security – rather ironic in view of later revelations about British atomic spies working for the Soviet Union.

For all these reasons, when Roosevelt wrote to Churchill in October 1941 proposing the joint development of nuclear weapons, Churchill's belated response adopted a coolly superior tone which accepted a mutual exchange of information – but within relatively narrow limits. Two months later, the Japanese attack on Pearl Harbor brought the United States into the war and within six months its nuclear programme had already far outstripped the British effort; the beginning of a vast technological and infrastructural gap which increased greatly over the next two or three decades. Indeed, by August 1943, the US was sufficiently far ahead that Churchill was forced to employ his most persuasive wiles to cajole Roosevelt into signing the Quebec Agreement enabling Britain to participate in the Manhattan Project. The agreement also contained provisions specifying that neither party would use the bomb or disclose any information about it except by mutual consent and that the distribution of any post-war industrial or commercial benefits would be settled by mutual agreement. After this, almost all Britain's nuclear physicists joined the US Manhattan Project constructing the atomic bomb at Los Alamos, but the harsh reality was that Britain was now effectively demoted to the status of America's junior partner in the nuclear project. Nevertheless, when Churchill and Roosevelt met in September 1944 at Hyde Park, Roosevelt's home in upper New York State, they agreed that full atomic collaboration should be continued after the defeat of Japan. On this basis, Churchill declared naively: 'Our association with the United States must be permanent. I have no fear that they will maltreat or cheat us' (Gowing 1964: 439–45).

Unfortunately, no one else in Washington knew of the existence of this agreement until after Roosevelt's death because it was filed under its 'Tube Alloys' codename and thus a junior official sent it to the Navy Department, rather than to the State Department, in the belief that the title referred to a naval component (Hennessy 1993: 266). Worse still, Roosevelt's successor insisted that because this crucial Anglo-American understanding had not been approved by Congress it was not binding on future administrations. In consequence, the United States revoked its agreements on post-war cooperation despite Truman's own signature on a further Washington Agreement reaffirming the principle of 'all-round collaboration' on nuclear matters in November 1945 (Gowing 1974: 100–1). The final desperate blow to British hopes was delivered by Senator McMahon's Atomic Energy Act in August 1946, which made the communication of classified atomic information to any foreign power punishable by life imprisonment or death.

This American volte face on nuclear collaboration was the product of a number of factors. Firstly, the United States inevitably wanted to retain their technological monopoly over the civil and military applications. Secondly, Britain suffered because Truman was under the influence of the strongly anti-British General Groves, the army engineer responsible for the Manhattan Project, and it had no counter-lobby to promote its interests in Washington where there was already growing impatience with an impoverished ally whose affairs appeared increasingly to be of only marginal relevance to US interests. Finally, US lack of sympathy for Britain was reinforced by the election of a supposedly 'socialist' Labour government and doubts about British security; fears soon amply confirmed by the arrest of Alan Nunn May in March 1946 and Klaus Fuchs in February 1950 on charges of spying for the Soviet Union. Such revelations had a cumulatively negative effect on the American propensity to share its nuclear secrets with London. Even more frustrating for British policymakers was that in January 1948 they were compelled to surrender the clause in the Quebec Agreement which affirmed that neither partner could use the atomic bomb without the other's consent. As a result, therefore, Britain risked annihilation in retaliation for an American strike on the Soviet Union without even being first informed or consulted – and this was no mere theoretical possibility in 1950, as President Truman considered the use of atomic weapons to achieve strategic advantage during the Korean War.

The Attlee government and the independent nuclear deterrent

Although the McMahon Act was regarded as a great betrayal, the Labour government had already decided to build its own independent nuclear deterrent in the immediate aftermath of the war. In December 1945, the 'Tube Alloys' project was transferred to the Ministry of Supply and Attlee established a small and highly secret Cabinet Committee known as GEN 75 to consider the nuclear programme. At a crucial meeting in October 1946, Hugh Dalton and Stafford Cripps, the Chancellor and President of the Board of Trade, began by expressing their opposition to the project on the grounds that Britain needed to conserve its resources for domestic reconstruction. At this critical moment, Bevin appeared and, when Attlee summarised the discussion, the Foreign Secretary replied decisively: 'No, Prime Minister that won't do at all. We have *got* to have this', adding bluntly: 'I don't mind for myself, but I don't want any other Foreign Secretary of this country to be talked at, or to, by the Secretary of State of the United States as I have just had in my discussions with Mr Byrnes. We have got to have this thing over here, whatever it costs, . . . We've got to have the bloody Union Jack flying on top of it' (Bullock 1983: 352). The final decision was taken on 8 January 1947 when Bevin again reasserted that 'We could not afford to acquiesce in an American monopoly on this new development' (Pelling1984: 126). In a manner which set a precedent for all subsequent nuclear deliberations, the decision was not announced to Parliament until 12 May 1948, and throughout the Cabinet as a whole played no part in the process – not least because Attlee did not believe that all his ministers could be trusted with the information (Mackintosh 1968: 496). Furthermore, although the Attlee government spent over £100 million on the programme, much of this expenditure was concealed from Parliament by submerging the costs in other departmental estimates.

Three factors interacted to turn this momentous policy departure into what Sir Michael Quinlan, a former Permanent Secretary at the Ministry of Defence, later described as 'an "of course" decision' (Hennessy 2007: 329). First, at a symbolic level, there was an extremely broad consensus that Britain's prestige and status as a great power depended on the possession of this awesome weapon of mass destruction, simply because anything capable of killing 130,000 people and obliterating more than 80 per cent of Hiroshima would inexorably transform the world's military balance forever. In this context, the initial decision was not prompted by an immediate military threat but rather it arose from 'a fundamentalist and instinctive feeling that Britain must possess so climacteric a weapon' (Gowing 1981: 129). As Sir Frank Cooper (an Air Ministry official at the time and later Permanent Secretary at the MoD) conceded:

> I don't think it ever occurred to anybody that we should not have it. We were a great power, we were a great scientific nation. We were a great industrial nation, quite natural that we should have a nuclear weapon. It did not seem terribly expensive at the time. It wasn't some great analytical, heavily thought out decision which you read about in the textbooks. As with most things, it was taken out of one's guts rather than out of one's head. (Beach and Gurr 1999: 21)

Precisely the same conviction, that an independent deterrent would preserve Britain's status on the 'top table', influenced the thinking of the

Conservative government after 1951. As Churchill had insisted, 'we could not expect to maintain influence as a world power unless we possess the most up to date nuclear weapons' (Reynolds 1991: 182). In this sense, as Sir Michael Quinlan argues, the policy 'grew out of national identity, not out of [national] interest' and much of the subsequent debate involved finding 'a set of rationales to clothe that gut decision' (Hennessy 2007: 328–9). In retrospect, it could be argued that by obscuring Britain's changed status in the world, the development of nuclear weapons was simply one more costly down-payment towards the 'price of victory' the country paid after the Second World War. But as Lord Cherwell (Churchill's scientific adviser) explained bluntly at the time, 'If we are unable to make the bomb ourselves, and have to rely entirely on the United States for this vital weapon, we shall sink to the rank of a second-class nation, only permitted to supply auxiliary troops, like the native levies who are allowed small arms but not artillery' (Gowing 1981: 131).

A second key factor in the decision to build an independent nuclear weapon related to the strategic doctrine of deterrence at the core of Britain's Cold War defence policy. Clement Attlee was a reluctant Cold Warrior who refused to accept what he disparagingly described as 'the strategy of despair' concerning Soviet intentions, but as he noted phleg-matically in August 1945: 'The answer to an atomic bomb on London is an atomic bomb on another great city' (Hennessy 2007: 137). Indeed, as early as April 1946 the Joint Technical Warfare Committee had prepared for the Chiefs of Staff a detailed plan for atomic attacks on 67 Soviet cities (containing 88 per cent of its population) even before the decision was taken to build a British atomic bomb (Lewis 1988: 228–30). The purpose of the independent British bomb, therefore, was not simply to dispel the suspicion that Britain had ceased to be a great power, but also to enhance the effectiveness of deterrence against a very real Soviet threat by being capable, in the last resort, to deliver a 'bigger bang for the buck'.

The third reason for Britain's determination to build a nuclear weapon concerned the nature of its relationship with the United States. In part, the problem was that there was no formal US commitment to European defence but this concern was compounded by grave doubts as to whether Washington could be trusted to mobilise its nuclear arsenal to protect British and European interests in isolation from a direct threat to the United States itself. In the crucial GEN 75 discussion in October 1946, Peter Hennessy rightly emphasises that it was not the Soviet threat that dominated the discussions but rather it was '*America* that Bevin bangs on about – as he was to again on the day the bomb was given the specific go-ahead . . . General Groves and Senator McMahon, not Stalin and Molotov were the reasons for that' (Hennessy 1993: 268). As Attlee later recalled when describing the secret decision to develop the atomic bomb, 'We had to hold up our position vis-à-vis the Americans. We couldn't allow ourselves to be wholly in their hands, and their position wasn't awfully clear always. At that time we had to bear in mind that there was always the possibility of their withdrawing and becoming isolationists once again' (Williams 1961: 118–19). Indeed, even after 1948–49 when the Cold War was in full swing and the military threat seemed far more menacing, doubts still persisted about US willingness to use nuclear retaliation in defence of other nations. National prudence thus dictated a British deterrent as an alternative to complete dependence on Washington's commitment to European defence; a concern about the declining credibility of the American nuclear umbrella which remained potent into the last years of the Warsaw Pact (see Cameron 1983: 113; Hill-Norton 1983: 128).

Although the McMahon Act undoubtedly hampered Britain's ability to compete in the nuclear arms race, it still conducted its first atomic test on the Monte Bello Islands off the coast of North West Australia in October 1952. In its wake, Churchill assured the Commons that the mere existence of an independent nuclear deterrent (in the form of 10-kiloton Blue Danube free-fall bombs carried by the V-bomber force) would demonstrate Britain's technical capability, reaffirm its status as a great (if not super) power and substantially enhance Washington's perception of its value as an ally; an outcome likely both to encourage a closer interchange of information and enable Whitehall to play a larger role in steering US policy in directions which suited British interests (Gowing 1974: I, 115). The same logic applied to the decision of the Chiefs of Staff in 1954 to support the development of an independent hydrogen bomb 1500 times more powerful than the Nagasaki bomb on the grounds that 'it would be dangerous if the United States were to retain their present monopoly since we would be denied any right to influence the policy in the use of these weapons' (Ovendale 1994: 104).

Churchill and the hydrogen bomb

A month after the successful British A-bomb test, the Americans exploded the world's first hydrogen bomb. Deeply impressed by the impact of this new generation of thermonuclear weapons, Churchill ordered the Chiefs of Staff to undertake a major review to consider the implications of this advance for British strategy and to suggest where economies in defence expenditure could be made. The resulting Global Strategy Paper in 1952 has been described as 'the most influential British defence paper of the post-war period' – and not just for British strategic thinking but also for that of the United States and NATO

(Rosecrance 1968: 159). This document was strongly influenced by the opinions of Sir John Slessor, Chief of the Air Staff and a firm believer in the war-winning capabilities of long-range bomber forces carrying atomic bombs. As the Chiefs of Staff acknowledged, as there was no effective defence against atomic attack, the only safe strategy was effective deterrence based on the certainty that any Russian attack would trigger 'immediate and crushing atomic retaliation'. Moreover, the uncertainty created by having two centres of nuclear decision-making within the NATO alliance (in Washington and London) would thus deter Soviet aggression because it would be certain that Britain would act in defence of Western Europe even if the United States did not (Gowing 1981: 440–3).

The potency of this logic for developing a British hydrogen bomb was reinforced less than a year after the American thermonuclear test when the Soviet Union tested its own H-bomb on 12 August 1953. When the Strath Committee estimated that 10 Soviet 10-megaton H-bombs dropped on Britain would kill 12 million and seriously injure a further 4 million (nearly a third of the population) even *before* radioactive fallout spread across the country, the sheer destructive power of such weapons convinced the Churchill government in July 1954 that it must proceed with Britain's own hydrogen bomb. 'We must do it', Churchill told Lord Plowden, the new chairman of the Atomic Energy Authority, 'it is the price we pay to sit at the top table' (Beach and Gurr 1999: 30). More to the point, the H-bomb was expected to enhance security while allowing a reduction in the heavy financial burden of conventional defence. As Churchill explained to the Canadian Prime Minister in June 1954, Britain needed the H-bomb because 'firstly . . . it was necessary in order to belong "to the club" and, secondly . . . [because] . . . possessing effective deterrence was the only sure way of preventing war. Moreover, if we had it, the Americans would respect our intervention in world affairs far more than if we did not' (Arnold 2001: 54). The proposition that Britain must 'possess the means of waging war with the most up-to-date nuclear weapons' was wholeheartedly endorsed by the Chiefs of Staff (Baylis 1984: 163).

Macmillan was equally convinced. As Chancellor of the Exchequer, he had noted despairingly in November 1955 that in future 'we must rely on the power of the nuclear deterrent or we must throw up the sponge' (Horne 1989, II: 50). As Prime Minister, Macmillan appointed Duncan Sandys as Minister of Defence with a mandate to secure substantial reductions in the cost of Britain's armed forces by doing precisely this, and his famous White Paper in April 1957 proposed a far greater reliance on Britain's nuclear arsenal at the direct expense of conventional forces on the grounds that 'the only existing safeguard against major aggression is the power to threaten retaliation with nuclear weapons' (Cmnd 124 1957). Soon afterwards, it was announced that Britain had successfully tested three air-dropped 1-megaton hydrogen bombs on Christmas Island in May–June 1957. In reality, evidence from the US archives released in 1992 indicates that this was a carefully contrived fraud – the product of a series of large enhanced fission bombs rather than a thermonuclear fusion device – and that it was not until November 1957 (with US technical assistance) that Britain successfully tested its first megaton thermonuclear bomb – 75 times more powerful than the atomic device Britain had tested only five years earlier (*Independent*, 15 October 1992; Hennessy 2007: 581).

Great power status – but at a price

Ironically, the triumphant culmination of Britain's H-bomb programme represented the end of the truly 'independent' phase of its nuclear history. By this juncture, it was painfully apparent that Britain did not possess the technological, economic or financial resources necessary to compete with the superpowers in a rapidly escalating nuclear arms race. As a corollary, it was recognised more clearly than ever before that the restoration of transatlantic collaboration was absolutely essential for the maintenance of Britain's future security, as well as its international status. Churchill's meeting in Bermuda with the newly elected Eisenhower, in December 1953 represented 'a small but significant step' towards this goal but Macmillan was far more successful in pursuit of what he called 'the great prize' of unrestricted Anglo-American nuclear cooperation (Horne 1989, II: 36). At the Bermuda conference in March 1957, Macmillan and Eisenhower agreed to the stationing of 60 American Thor IRBMs on British soil under a 'dual key' arrangement which ensured both powers approved their use before they could be activated.

The successful Soviet launch of its Sputnik satellite in October 1957 aroused near-panic in Washington about its possible military applications, and the ensuing shock injected a new urgency into US efforts to restore good relations with Britain. In the same month, Eisenhower promised Macmillan that he would persuade Congress to restore the full exchange of nuclear information. In July 1958, the McMahon Act was finally repealed, while an 'Agreement for Cooperation on the Uses of Atomic Energy for Mutual Defence Purposes' led to technical exchanges which became the cornerstone of the UK nuclear defence programme. Unfortunately, this interchange depressingly highlighted how far Britain had fallen behind its rivals; a revelation that persuaded Whitehall to abandon their own efforts and adopt the American design for the hydrogen bomb, which eventually came into service in 1961 (Simpson 1983: 142–9). As John Baylis argues, this was 'the most important manifestation of the return to a close partnership' and 'without doubt one of the most important peacetime agreements ever arrived at between the two countries' (Baylis 1984: 88, 90). Last renewed in 2004, the agreement runs until 2014.

After 1958, technological failure and escalating financial costs consolidated the logic of Britain's position as a privileged but increasingly dependent nuclear client of the United States. In that year, Britain began to import the enriched uranium and tritium essential as fuel for nuclear explosions and it was not until 1976 that the latter began to be produced in Scotland. Far more importantly, in February 1960 the Cabinet decided to cancel production of Blue Streak, Britain's own IRBM, on the grounds that it was not only prohibitively expensive but also technologically obsolete. This delivered a shattering blow to British confidence and raised worrying questions about its ability to remain a nuclear power during a period of rapid technological innovation (Macmillan 1972: 252–3). Against this background, closer cooperation with the United States was increasingly embraced by policymakers as the only reliable means of maintaining an effective deterrent into the next generation without jeopardising spending on other aspects of defence or even on the welfare state itself. This watershed decision marked the beginning of Britain's reliance upon the United States for its supposedly 'independent' nuclear deterrent, but, as John Young argues, the decision represented the only viable solution to Macmillan's 'problem of being poor and powerful at the same time' (Young 1997: 174).

Macmillan's response to the cancellation of Blue Streak was to secure Eisenhower's agreement to replace it with the American-built Skybolt air-to-ground ballistic missile which could be fired by Vulcan bombers at a distance from the target; a stand-off capability which enabled the otherwise vulnerable V-bomber force to remain in operation until the late 1960s despite rapid improvements in Soviet ABM defences. The Skybolt technical agreement was signed in September 1960 and, in exchange, Britain provided a Scottish base for the US Polaris submarine fleet at Holy Loch. This undoubtedly represented an extremely attractive financial deal for Britain – at least until the US Defense Department cancelled Skybolt without any consultation in November 1962 because of heavy cost overruns, technical difficulties and its increasing vulnerability to Soviet countermeasures. This made good sense from an American strategical and technical perspective, but it left Britain with no means of delivering its nuclear warheads against enemy targets and appeared to confirm Whitehall suspicions that the US was deliberately trying to squeeze Britain out of the nuclear club.

On the other side of the Atlantic, US officials were equally suspicious of the British outcry about the cancellation of Skybolt, believing it was being cynically exploited to distract public attention from the Macmillan government's increasing domestic unpopularity. Certainly, the Prime Minister seized his opportunity with alacrity when he met Kennedy at Nassau in the Bahamas on 18–21 December 1961 for 'one of the great confrontations in the history of Anglo-American relations' (Nunnerly 1972: 149). After an emotional opening declaration invoking the memory of Britain's war dead, its long struggle for freedom and resolute stand as an ally of the United States, Sir Philip Zulueta, Macmillan's private secretary, recalled: 'there was not a dry eye in the house!' (Beach and Gurr 1999: 37). After this manipulative exercise in emotional blackmail, Macmillan warned the President that unless the United States provided Britain with a replacement for Skybolt its continued adherence to NATO would be in jeopardy and an agonising reappraisal of all Britain's foreign and defence plans would be inevitable (Horne 1989, II: 433). The discussions were frank, often stormy and vigorously contested on both sides but the fervour of the Prime Minister's pleas, combined with the fear that Britain might abandon NATO, persuaded Kennedy to provide Britain with Polaris submarine-launched intermediate ballistic missiles for a projected five British-built nuclear submarines to enter service in the late 1960s. This represented a massive victory for Macmillan, who acquired a virtually undetectable state-of-the-art deterrent at a massively lower cost than would have been the case if Britain had persisted with its own missile system. The capital cost of Polaris for Britain was £350 million, with annual operating costs by the early 1970s of £32 million. Beyond the question of value for money, Britain's possession of Polaris guaranteed a place at the 'top table' during the nuclear test ban negotiations in 1963. Indirectly it also ensured de Gaulle's veto of Britain's first application to join the EEC a month after the Nassau conference (see Chapter 5).

Although a spectacular diplomatic victory, some critics argued that it was achieved only by effectively undermining Britain's claim to possess an 'independent' deterrent given the stipulation that prior agreement from the United States was required before it could be used. In practice, however, paragraph 8 of the Nassau Agreement secured Britain's right to use Polaris unilaterally in cases 'where Her Majesty's Government may decide that supreme national interests are at stake' (Ponting 1989: 86). In 1963, Britain also gained access to the US underground nuclear testing site in Nevada and it continued to use these facilities until Clinton briefly rescinded the privilege during John Major's premiership. For all the benefits conferred by Macmillan's triumph, the fact remains that the Nassau Agreement demonstrated unambiguously the degree to which the advanced technology and complex manufacturing facilities needed to compete in the nuclear arms race made it virtually impossible for Britain to afford its own missile development programme without making unacceptable and unsustainable sacrifices. For British policy-makers at the time, however, the independence of their nuclear deterrent mattered far less than its existence and destructive capability.

Trying (and failing) to keep up with the superpowers

As Chapter 4 illustrates, Anglo-American relations declined rapidly after the departure of Macmillan and Kennedy. Tensions emerged immediately over the question of a NATO Multilateral Force (MLF), which Under-Secretary of State George Ball was keen to foist upon a Conservative government under Sir Alec Douglas-Home that proved equally determined to resist any effort to merge its nuclear forces into a broader MLF. Indeed, Lord Mountbatten, the Chief of the Defence Staff, declared it was 'the greatest piece of military nonsense he had come across in 50 years' (Twigge and Scott 2000: 188). Nevertheless, fears of political isolation if the US pressed on without them persuaded the Conservative government that the best course was to modify the scheme into something more acceptable in the hope that delay would ultimately sink the entire project; a strategy pursued with equal determination by the incoming Labour government after October 1964, by which time Washington had effectively lost interest in its own proposal.

When Harold Wilson's Labour government came into office in 1964, it did so after a major intra-party rift over nuclear disarmament during which Hugh Gaitskell's leadership suffered a humiliating defeat at the Labour Party conference in 1960. Although Wilson had united the party after succeeding Gaitskell in 1963, the Labour manifesto still called for the 'renegotiation of the Nassau agreement' and Wilson gave the vague impression that Labour would scrap Polaris if elected. As he declared dismissively in Labour's 1964 manifesto, Polaris 'will not be British, it will not be independent and it will not deter'. In practice, however, both Wilson and Healey, his Defence Secretary, were convinced of the importance of maintaining Britain's nuclear deterrent – particularly as £310 million had already been spent or committed and one submarine was nearly ready for commissioning. They also recognised that Macmillan had obtained an extremely good financial deal at Nassau. Moreover, to drive home the need for such weapons, on the day before the British general election Khrushchev had been deposed as Soviet leader and the Chinese exploded their own atomic bomb; both pungent reminders of global threats at a time when memories of the Cuban missile crisis were still fresh. As a result, the Labour government decided merely to cancel one of the five nuclear submarines the Conservatives had ordered, while it actually produced more warheads than its predecessor had planned (Beach and Gurr 1999: 41).

Polaris more than lived up to expectations coming into service on schedule and cheaper than anticipated – words rarely associated with British weapons procurement programmes at any time. The first Polaris patrol took place in 1967, and in 1969 the nation's nuclear strike responsibilities were formally transferred from the RAF to the Royal Navy. Yet, even before the first Polaris submarine had been commissioned, the Wilson government began to contemplate an enhancement for the missile to overcome improvements in Soviet ABM technology. Afraid that this might make Polaris obsolete, a Cabinet committee consisting of Wilson, George Brown, James Callaghan and Denis Healey resolved from the outset that they would not seek an American solution in the form of its new and highly sophisticated Poseidon missile. Instead, the Labour government decided to enhance the existing Polaris warhead by equipping it with a new front end which was manoeuvrable in space and contained decoys to improve both penetration rates and the size of its destructive footprint. The decision to authorise full-scale development of Chevaline fell to the Labour government re-elected in February 1974.

The Chevaline programme was afflicted by such chronic technical and managerial problems from the outset that Healey later regarded it as one of the major mistakes of his Chancellorship not to have cancelled the project after returning to office in 1974 (Healey 1989: 313). He had every reason for alarm, given that the initial estimated cost of £240 million over ten years eventually overran its budget by some £750 million, while it took eight years to bring Chevaline into service and it was not fully operational until the autumn of 1982. Although Chevaline theoretically enabled Polaris to be deployed into the 1980s, therefore, by this stage the submarines were noisy and vulnerable to substantially improved Soviet anti-submarine warfare technology, the regular replacement of internal systems was becoming increasingly expensive and the discovery of problems with the cooling system on the nuclear reactors in 1990 suggested that an operational life of 25 years might be an optimistic assessment for at least some of these vessels (McInnes 1991: 68). When Callaghan became Prime Minister in 1976, therefore, he was faced with the need for a fundamental decision about a possible successor for the Polaris SLBM when the four *Resolution*-class submarines became obsolete in the early 1990s – particularly as it would take an estimated 10 years to build replacements.

Labour's manifesto, in both the February and October 1974 general elections, had pledged that the party would not proceed with a new generation of nuclear weapons, but these pledges were swiftly brushed aside by the small informal ad hoc subcommittee of ministers whose existence was kept secret from the rest of the Cabinet to neutralise the opposition of anti-nuclear ministers led by Michael Foot. After the Chevaline fiasco, the option of independent maintenance for Britain's ageing Polaris fleet and missiles was distinctly unattractive on both cost and technological grounds. While it was agreed that a new submarine-based system should be acquired, therefore, there was considerable debate over the choice between either Trident (the MoD's preferred option) or the new American Cruise missile launched from ordinary nuclear-powered submarines (as the FCO preferred). In the event, beyond tentatively sounding President Carter about the possibility of acquiring Trident, the defeat of the Labour government in May 1979 ensured that the decision would not be made by Jim Callaghan – although, significantly, before he left office he prepared a confidential memorandum for Margaret Thatcher on his government's deliberations and he authorised officials to show the new government his confidential papers on the subject (Callaghan 1988: 552–7; Healey 1989: 456).

The Thatcher government and the purchase of Trident

Margaret Thatcher entered office in May 1979 convinced that nuclear weapons had prevented a catastrophic conflagration in Europe since 1945 and she was 'utterly determined' to 'maintain a credible deterrent into an uncertain future' (Thatcher 1993: 247). Like the Callaghan government, the Conservative Cabinet immediately rejected the retention of Polaris in new nuclear-powered submarines on the grounds that Britain would no longer be at the cutting edge of nuclear weapons technology, the missiles would be increasingly vulnerable to the risk of total system failure and maintenance costs would be far higher without US government involvement. Anyway, memories of Chevaline provided a bitter lesson about the dangers of operating independently with unfamiliar technology. In some respects, the US Cruise missile represented an attractive alternative given a range of around 2,000 miles and terrain-following radar which enabled them to fly below enemy air defences. But, as a ground-launched missile, it would be vulnerable to a Soviet first strike and it depended upon US satellites for accurate targeting in space. Anyway, it was argued, the large US investment in Cruise missiles guaranteed a correspondingly substantial Soviet defensive effort to counter the large number of missiles the Americans were expected to deploy. As a result, the far smaller number in the British nuclear arsenal would probably be totally overwhelmed by such defences – thereby reducing (or even nullifying) the credibility of its deterrent.

Given these problems, the Thatcher government decided to purchase the far more expensive and more complex Trident missile system. As a submarine-based platform, Trident was almost undetectable and invulnerable; its 4,000-mile missile range and the great precision provided by its MIRV (multiple independently targetable re-entry vehicle) capability, allowing each warhead to be guided on to a separate target as it re-entered the atmosphere, made it more cost-effective because fewer missiles were required than with Cruise. It also involved little technical risk because it enjoyed the full support of the US government and it reaffirmed the special defence link with Washington while ensuring commonality of systems. It was also the cheapest system available, projected at the time to cost only 3 per cent of the defence budget over 20 years and 6 per cent of the equipment budget (Coker 1987: 29). From this perspective, therefore, Trident had much to offer in terms of national prestige, destructive capability and cost-effectiveness. As the 1981 Defence Review concluded, 'Trident remains by far the best way . . . of modernising this crucial element of our capability' and 'no alternative application of defence resources could approach this as real deterrent insurance' (Cmnd 8288-I, 1981: para. 10).

On 6 December 1979, Thatcher's MISC 7 Cabinet committee made the key decisions. The full Cabinet were not informed of the decision to purchase Trident until several weeks later on the morning before the public announcement (McInnes 1986: 12). But in practice, few frontbench politicians challenged the need for an updated deterrent given the Soviet invasion of Afghanistan on Christmas Day 1979 and its rapid introduction of new weapons systems threatening NATO's ability to withstand a full-scale conventional assault on Europe. On 2 June 1980, the final agreement enabled Britain to purchase Trident I (designated C4) at a cost of between £4.5 and £5 billion. Britain would also pay a 5 per cent surcharge on the cost of the missiles, staff the Rapier Air Defence Systems defending USAF bases in Britain and extend the US lease on their base at Diego Garcia to offset R&D costs (Thatcher 1993: 245–6). Overall, the agreement appeared very favourable to the United Kingdom and 'provided a reaffirmation that the "special relationship" was after all alive and well in the early 1980s' (Baylis 1984: 183).

Unfortunately, in October 1981, the Reagan administration's commitment to a rapid increase in American military power led to the early replacement of Trident I with a new version called Trident II (D5). This was at least a generation ahead of the previous model and two generations ahead of Polaris, given its more powerful warhead load of up to

10 highly accurate MIRV warheads. Thatcher later claimed that her government engaged in 'plenty of hard bargaining' with Washington over the terms, but in reality it had little choice but to accept the new system because, although more sophisticated than Britain needed, the danger of continuing alone with an effectively obsolete system was unthinkable. As a sweetener, the Thatcher government negotiated an even more favourable price of $116 million as its share of R&D costs and the agreement overall was on more advantageous terms than for the purchase of Trident I (Thatcher 1993: 249). In the event, the cost of the programme increased from the 1980 estimate of between £4.5 and £5 billion to £9.38 billion by 1990 (Greenwood 1991: 79).

Beyond the inevitable technical problems afflicting the programme, the biggest threat to Trident was that by 1991 the international environment had changed dramatically in the wake of the collapse of the Soviet Union and the dissolution of the Warsaw Pact as an offensive military alliance. One obvious consequence of the formal end of the Cold War and the removal of the Soviet threat was that it effectively removed the traditional rationale for Trident. Yet, by the time John Major became Prime Minister in November 1990, much of the investment had already been committed or spent and the first Trident submarine was scheduled to enter service at the end of 1994. As a result, the Major government's only real adaptation to the collapse of the Warsaw Pact was the withdrawal from service of its stock of US tactical nuclear artillery warheads, the Lance system and the RAF's sub-strategic WE-177 freefall nuclear bombs. In November 1993, it also pledged that Britain's nuclear force would not carry the maximum number of warheads and that greater reliance would be placed upon Trident for sub-strategic minimalist strikes as well as the fulfilment of its maximalist strategic deterrent role. By the end of the century, therefore, Britain's nuclear deterrent consisted of one nuclear-powered submarine on station at all times, carrying a combination of UK-manufactured 100-kiloton warheads each eight times more powerful than the Hiroshima bomb (equivalent to 100,000 tons of high explosive) plus tactical warheads of around one kiloton for use in unspecified limited circumstances.

New Labour and the upgrading of Trident

Since its formation, the Labour Party has contained within its ranks a strong Gladstonian tradition of internationalism and pacifist inclinations. These tendencies were particularly marked in Opposition after electoral defeat in 1979; a trend which culminated in the infamous 1983 general election manifesto, memorably denounced by Gerald

Kaufman as 'the longest suicide note in history'. Among other things, this lengthy document committed a future Labour government to unilateral nuclear disarmament, the closure of all US bases on British territory, the termination of agreements to upgrade the UK's nuclear weaponry and the nationalisation of the armaments industry. Even as late as the 1992, the manifesto commitment to abolish Trident remained the centrepiece of Labour's defence programme and the Conservatives inevitably exploited it as proof their opponents were 'weak on defence' (Freedman 1999). It was, thus, a central part of New Labour's 'modernisation' project to shed this damaging image by asserting that a Blair government would not only retain Trident but would also be prepared to use it. At the same time, to placate party activists, Blair reaffirmed the commitment to multilateral disarmament on a 'something-for-something' basis as part of a general desire to reassert Britain's position as 'a leading force for change in the world' (Labour Party 1996)

Once in office, the 1998 Strategic Defence Review promised 'a rigorous re-examination of deterrence requirements' to ensure 'the minimum necessary to deter any threat to our vital interests'; a posture which allowed the reduction in the number of warheads by a third (from 300 to 200) and by half in the number of Trident missiles carried on each submarine (from 98 to 48); a 70 per cent reduction in explosive power since the 1970s (Cm 3999, 1998: 18). At this juncture, the government celebrated the fact that Britain's nuclear arsenal of 195 warheads accounted for only 1.4 per cent of the world total of 13,470 – well behind the US, Russia, China, France and Israel (IISS 2003: 228). While the rhetoric of minimum deterrence and disarmament might have appeased some traditionalist Labour supporters, it soon became apparent that the Blair government regarded nuclear weapons as a badge of great power status, and to lose this emblem would be to abandon its chosen role in world affairs.

The most obvious example of the Blair government's commitment to the nuclear option concerns its decision to upgrade Trident in 2006–07. Although the 2005 Labour election manifesto had committed the party simply to retain the nuclear deterrent, in July 2006 Tony Blair and Gordon Brown both declared that Britain needed to renew its ageing Trident weapons system, at a cost of between £15 and £25 billion, because the existing submarines were reaching the end of their 20–25-year operational life and the length of the procurement process made it is necessary to act quickly in order to possess a viable deterrent by 2020, when Trident finally became obsolete. By mid-November 2006, Blair told the Cabinet that they needed agreement before he left office, while the Defence Secretary, Des Browne, began a series of bilaterals with key Cabinet colleagues before the publication of the government's White Paper on the subject (*Guardian*, 17 and 24 November 2006).

In the Foreword to this glossy 40-page White Paper on *The Future of the United Kingdom's Nuclear Deterrent* published on 4 December 2006, Tony Blair acknowledged that the world had changed radically but the need for nuclear weapons remained as strong as ever. In part, this was because 'some of the old realities remain' given that many major states, which currently posed no threat, still retained large nuclear arsenals and had no plans to renounce them. In the absence of an agreement to disarm multilaterally, 'we cannot be sure that a major nuclear threat to our vital interests will not emerge over the longer term'. More important, the statement noted: 'We cannot predict the way the world will look into 30 or 50 years time.' Among the new threats outlined in the White Paper were regional 'rogue powers' like Iran and North Korea developing nuclear weapons for the first time and the need 'to deter countries which might in the future seek to sponsor nuclear terrorism from their soil. We must assume that the global struggle in which we are engaged today between moderation and extremism will continue for a generation or more.' On this basis, the Prime Minister declared that 'an independent British nuclear deterrent is an essential part of our insurance against the uncertainties and risks of the future' (Cm 6994 2006: 1)

On these foundations, the government announced its intention to maintain its deterrent beyond the life of the existing *Vanguard*-class submarines with a new generation of state-of-the-art vessels while extending the life of the Trident D5 missile in order to ensure 'no aggressor can escalate a crisis beyond UK control'. In this manner, vital interests would be safeguarded while Britain's nuclear stockpile would be the 'minimum necessary' to achieve the task – and this involved a further 20 per cent cut in operationally available warheads to provide an example for others to follow towards 'a peaceful, fairer and safer world without nuclear weapons'. The document also stressed that the intention was simply to 'deter and prevent nuclear blackmail and acts of aggression' and that Britain 'would only consider using nuclear weapons in self-defence (including the defence of our NATO allies) and even then only in extreme circumstances'. Emphasising that HMS *Vanguard* would go out of service in 2022 (followed by a second submarine in 2024), the Prime Minister warned that the decision was urgently needed to avoid a future break in deterrent protection – particularly as it was estimated that it would take 17 years before the first operational patrol.

The financial costs of this programme were described as 'substantial', but the government asserted its belief that this represented the only safe strategy to adopt. As Blair declared when opening the Commons debate in December 2006, 'Our independent nuclear deterrent is the ultimate insurance' in an era of 'unpredictable but rapid change' because one could not mortgage future national security on the hope that others will disarm. The total cost of procurement was estimated at between £15 and £20 billion at 2006/07 prices. This included £11–14 billion for the four submarine option, with £2–3 billion for replacement warheads and another £2–3 billion for the necessary infrastructure, most of the cost being paid in the period 2010–17. In addition, annual running costs were officially estimated at around £1.5 billion (at 2006/07 prices) or 6 per cent of the defence budget for 25 years – a figure which soon rose to £70 billion over 25 years. As a comparative measure, the Trident system was priced at £14.5 billion.

The decision to upgrade Trident in a post-Cold War environment remains highly controversial. For its defenders, the purpose of the British nuclear deterrent remains unchanged – 'to minimise the prospect of the United Kingdom being attacked by mass destruction weapons' and that its purpose lies 'not in its actual use but in its nature as the ultimate "stalemate weapon"' (Lewis 2006). Other supporters, like James Arbuthnot, the Conservative chair of the Defence Select Committee, employed a modified version of Churchill's 'top table' argument to contend that without Trident, Britain's permanent seat on the United Nations Security Council might be in jeopardy (*Guardian*, 19 January 2009). On the other hand, critics counter that while Britain's nuclear deterrent acquired a totemic significance during the Cold War, today it serves simply as a very expensive 'comfort blanket' which 'in some unexplained way is expected to shield us from unspecified dangers in an unpredictable world'. As such, this massively disproportionate capability is to be retained, without any serious consideration of either the changed geostrategic context or any real cost–benefit analysis of the considerable monetary and opportunity costs in terms of conventional procurements fore,gone and the heavy political costs involved in such a high level of dependence on the United States. Conversely, by renouncing its nuclear capability, critics argue that Britain could give a lead towards disarmament, help restore the viability of the NPT and regain its own foreign policy autonomy while both increasing its status in the world community and enhancing the effectiveness of Britain's conventional expeditionary capability (MccGwire 2006; Select Committee on Defence, HC 225-I March 2007: paras 100, 126–7). Another important line of criticism concerns the cost. According to some, the lifetime cost of the new system could be over twice that estimated because of hidden running costs, which might amount to 5–6 per cent of the annual defence budget over the full 25 years' life of the project, and both the Defence Select Committee and the National Audit Office have expressed concern about the vagueness of some crucial aspects of the total budget. Similarly, initial Greenpeace estimates of the lifetime cost at £76 billion were later increased to £100 billion (*Guardian* 7, 13–14 March 2007; Select Committee on Defence, HC 225-I March 2007: paras 153–4).

Beyond these entrenched battle lines, another school of thought argues that the government has not yet published sufficient information about international obligations, strategic considerations, the options available, and opportunity costs to justify firm conclusions one way or the other (Quinlan 2006). On these grounds, the Defence Select Committee has regularly criticised the government's failure adequately to explain 'the purpose and continued relevance of nuclear deterrence'. Not only was it concerned that Trident 'could serve no useful or practical purpose' in countering the 'most pressing threat' of all posed by international terrorism, but it was also sceptical about its impact on Britain's international status and warned that decisions must be taken on the basis of 'strategic defence needs' alone rather than because of the number of jobs created or the commercial needs of shipbuilding firms which might benefit from the contracts (Select Committee on Defence, HC 986 June 2006: para. 88: HC 304 December 2006: para. 8).

Far more vocal opposition emerged from the Labour backbenches where discontented former ministers, like Charles Clarke, condemned the decision as 'an expensive new weapon to fight the last war' (*Guardian*, 29 November 2006). Although the government always expected a substantial backbench rebellion, in mid-March 2007 3 junior ministers resigned over the issue and no fewer than 95 Labour MPs voted against the government on the question of deferring a decision, while 87 voted against the renewal of the Trident nuclear submarines – one of the largest rebellions since 1997 and the third time in which the votes of the Conservative Opposition saved the government's policy – as it had over Iraq in 2003 and school trusts in March 2006. Passions were not cooled either on the day after the rebellion when the *Guardian* revealed that (despite previous government denials) the Trident upgrade was already under way on a new firing device to make it more effective in terms of power, impact and radioactive fallout (*Guardian*, 14 March 2007). Further evidence, that the programme had already begun before formal parliamentary approval had been given, was provided by the massive upgrading of facilities at Aldermaston AWE in one of the largest construction projects ever undertaken in Britain (Select Committee on Defence, HC 304 2007: 146–7). In the event, by June 2009, concern about the damaging effects of Britain's £175 billion public debt prompted ministers to review the decision on

Trident modernisation while the Conservative Opposition declared that the Trident replacement must pass a proper 'value-for-money-test' (*Guardian*, 11 September 2009).

The US connection and the 'son of Star Wars'

Membership of the nuclear club has proved an expensive business. By some estimates, by the late 1980s it had probably absorbed between £40 billion and £50 billion in total (Hennessy 2003: 45). Yet, in stark contrast to the history of conventional weapons system development, since the late 1950s Britain's extraordinarily close nuclear relationship with the United States has enabled it to acquire highly complex weapons systems at a relatively low cost. The capital cost of Polaris for Britain finally proved to be £350 million, with annual operating costs by the early 1970s of £32 million; a figure which averaged 6–7 per cent of the total defence budget. Similarly, the total capital cost of the four-submarine Trident force was around £12.2 billion at 1995/6 prices (or £15.2 billion at 2004/5 prices). Annual running costs are currently estimated at around £700 million and, even if the continuing expenditure of the AWE is included, the total cost amounts to just under 4 per cent of the UK defence budget or 2.5 per cent of GDP (Hartley 2006: 677–8).

Even if these costs can be dismissed as relatively modest, given the complexity of the technology obtained in return, Britain's heavy dependence on the United States for its nuclear weapons has imposed a relatively heavy diplomatic and military price, as demonstrated by the Blair government's commitment to support George W. Bush's revival of Reagan's 'Son of Star Wars' scheme. This highly controversial action was announced by Defence Secretary Geoff Hoon in November 2002 at the Foreign Policy Centre, a New Labour think-tank, in which he declared that 'developing the capacity to defend against the threat of ballistic missile attack is in the interest of the UK, just as much as it is in the interest of the US' (*Guardian*, 13 November 2002). Two months later, the government announced the United States would use the Fylingdales radar station in Yorkshire as the first step towards a deeper British involvement in the Bush administration's Missile Defence System, which intended to use sophisticated space-bound technology to detect and destroy incoming missiles fired by 'rogue' states. While the computer upgrading at Fylingdales will be undertaken at American expense, the interceptor rocket will be paid for by Britain. Nevertheless, Hoon declared, Britain's involvement was 'an invaluable extra insurance against the development of a still uncertain but potentially catastrophic threat to the citizens of this country.'

The announcement provoked widespread criticism. Peter Kilfoyle, a former Labour Defence Minister, attacked the government for supporting any 'crackpot notion' put forward by the 'ideologues in Washington', while he castigated the Minister for his 'slavish devotion to the American policy in this area which adds further to global destabilisation' (*Guardian*, 16 January 2003). Senior officials at the FCO and MOD also accurately warned that this action could provoke a new arms race, while more than 200 Labour and Liberal Democrat MPs expressed their concern at the proposal. Despite these warnings, and an alarming deterioration in Anglo-Russian relations as a direct result (see p. 290), by October 2004 it emerged that a secret memorandum of understanding had been signed earlier in the month committing Britain to participation in the US missile interceptor system (*Guardian*, 29 October 2004). Further concern about the degree of US leverage conferred by Britain's nuclear dependency was expressed in the outcry following the sale of a majority shareholding in the Aldermaston AWE (which manufactures Trident warheads) to the US-owned Jacobs Engineering and Lockheed Martin in December 2008 (*Guardian*, 20 December 2008). Given the nature of the Anglo-American relationship in the twenty-first century and the logic which underpins Britain's strong defence commitment to Washington, the situation is unlikely to change in the foreseeable future.

Chapter 8

New Labour, the 'Ethical Dimension' and 'Liberal Intervention'

Labour's commitment to an 'ethical dimension' in British foreign policy

The broad outlines of the Labour government's external policy since 1997 have reflected a high degree of continuity with its predecessors in many key respects. The Anglo-American alliance remained pivotal throughout its period in office despite the need to deal with three US administrations of very different political persuasions. Like its predecessors, the Blair and Brown governments sought to evade the issue of whether Britain inclined principally towards a European or an Atlanticist orientation by denying the existence of any inherent conflict between these two identities. On the contrary, as the 2001 election manifesto noted, 'if Britain is stronger in Europe, it will be stronger in the rest of the world. We reject the view of those who say we must choose between Europe and the USA' (Labour Party 2001: 38). Within the EU, Britain employed a far more *communautaire* style of language than its predecessors but the record has not been fundamentally different from that of John Major's 'pick and mix' approach that embraced only those parts of the European project which promoted British interests and did not conflict with its primary attachment to Washington. Continuity was also the order of the day in the defence and security sphere. Trident remained central to British defence planning and is to be updated in a post-Cold War environment to defend against unspecified future threats, while NATO was reaffirmed as the central building block of Britain's engagement in world affairs – at least in part to dispel US fears that an emerging European defence architecture would marginalise its position in Western defence. As a leaked secret briefing document for US Defence Secretary William Cohen noted, Britain 'remains our closest partner in political, security and intelligence matters . . . Beyond Europe there are few apparent differences between the stated foreign policy goals of Labour and its Conservative predecessor' (*Guardian*, 29 November 1999).

Yet, for all the continuities with a past defined by Cold War threats and tensions, in one crucial respect foreign policy under Tony Blair did appear to represent a radical departure from the 'doctrine of benign inactivity' he inherited from Major (Blair 2006: 10). Exploiting the opportunities provided by an initially more benign international environment, New Labour trumpeted its intention to introduce a fundamental change in both the tone and direction of external policy by placing a far greater emphasis upon the role of 'values', 'moral responsibility', 'dialogue' and 'partnership'. In this respect, some claim that after 1997, British foreign policy witnessed a qualitative shift away from the narrowly pragmatic realist orientation of the past. In place of the previous Conservative government's emphasis upon sovereignty, national interest and non-intervention in the internal affairs of other states – however morally reprehensible they might be – New Labour promised an 'ethical dimension' to external policy with all this implied for the defence of human rights around the world and the compelling obligations it imposed upon the international community with regard to arms control, climate change and international development. Above all, the importance of values came to be associated with the responsibility of the international community as a whole to intervene where necessary to avert humanitarian disasters. As Baroness Symons, Parliamentary Under-Secretary at the FCO, explained in a speech on 'New Government, New Foreign Policy' soon after entering office, 'while British interests may stay the same, British foreign policy has changed. The new government in Britain has a clear plan about how it intends to shape British foreign policy and indeed to shape the world in which Britain lives' (www.fco.gov.uk).

Despite Blair's later highly 'presidential' style of foreign policy-making, much of the early impetus behind this radical change in direction can be attributed to Robin Cook. Under his influence, the Labour manifesto of May 1997 promised a completely new and more internationalist approach to foreign policy. More importantly, on 12 May 1997, just 10 days after becoming Foreign Secretary, he launched the FCO's first formal 'Mission Statement', amid great fanfare, at a public ceremony. In his opening speech, Cook declared this document 'sets out a new direction in foreign policy' intended to carry the FCO beyond 'managing crisis intervention' to focus on 'the delivery of a long-term strategy'. The objective, he declared, was 'to make Britain once again a force for good in the world' with a sincere 'national interest in the promotion of its values and confidence in our identity'. The FCO Mission was thus intended to supply 'an ethical content to foreign policy' which recognised that 'the national interest cannot be defined only by a narrow realpolitik':

The Labour government does not accept that political values can be left behind when we check in our passports to travel on diplomatic business. Our foreign policy must have an ethical dimension and must support the demands of other peoples for the democratic rights on which we insist for ourselves. The Labour government will put human rights at the heart of our foreign policy. (www. guardian.co.uk)

This recognition of the impact of globalisation was closely related to another New Labour theme concerning the increasing interconnectedness of the foreign and domestic arenas. As the Foreign Office Mission Statement conceded, 'modern world foreign policy is not divorced from domestic policy but a central part of any political programme. In order to achieve our goals for the people of Britain we need a foreign strategy that supports the same goals' (www.guardian.co.uk). Or, as Blair later put it, 'Idealism becomes realpolitik' (Blair 2007: 90). As the Permanent Under-Secretary at the FCO at the time later recalled, this was precisely the sort of statement of detailed foreign policy objectives that had been missing in the past (Coles 2000: 192).

Three weeks later, the Foreign Secretary's speech on 'The Guiding Principles of British Foreign Policy' to the assembled Diplomatic Corps declared: 'Diplomacy now encompasses the fundamentals of the lives of our people, their jobs, their beliefs of right and wrong, even the quality of the air they breathe' (Lawler 2000: 296). These themes were taken up by the Prime Minister in his annual foreign policy speech at the Lord Mayor's banquet on 10 November 1997, when he spoke of the need for 'a clear definition of national purpose, not just what we want for Britain itself, but the direction of the world and how it deals with the outside world'. Above all, the Prime Minister argued, foreign policy 'should not be seen as some self-contained part of government in a box marked "abroad" or "foreigners". It should complement and reflect on domestic goals. It should be part of our mission of national renewal' (www.number10.gov.uk).

As Cook had given little indication in Opposition that he was specifically concerned about the application of moral principles to UK foreign policy, his motives have prompted some speculation. One obvious explanation is that he genuinely believed it the right thing to do, as a left-winger within Blair's party and a passionate internationalist who believed in the need for a strong international community to preserve peace and transcend national boundaries in pursuit of multilateral solutions to increasingly interconnected global problems. As he told the Foreign Affairs Select Committee, he saw himself as a 'realist with principles' and an 'ethical dimension' to external policy was merely part of

Table 8.1 Robin Cook and the FCO 'Mission Statement', 12 May 1997

The Mission of the Foreign & Commonwealth Office is to promote the national interest of the United Kingdom and to contribute to a strong world community. We shall pursue that Mission to secure for Britain four benefits through our foreign policy:

- *Security.* We shall ensure the security of the United Kingdom and the Dependent Territories and peace for our people by promoting international stability, fostering our defence alliances and promoting arms control actively.
- *Prosperity.* We shall make maximum use of our overseas posts to promote trade abroad and boost jobs at home.
- *Quality of Life.* We shall work with others to protect the world's environment and to counter the menace of drugs, terrorism and crime.
- *Mutual Respect.* We shall work through our international forums and bilateral relationships to spread the values of human rights, civil liberties and democracy which we demand for ourselves.

To secure these benefits for the United Kingdom we shall conduct a global foreign policy with the following strategic aims:

- To make the United Kingdom a leading player in a Europe of independent nation states;
- To strengthen the Commonwealth and to improve the prosperity of its members and cooperation between its members;
- To use the status of the United Kingdom at the United Nations to secure more effective international action to keep the peace of the world and to combat poverty in the world;
- To foster a people's democracy through services to British citizens abroad and by increasing respect and goodwill for Britain among the peoples of the world drawing on the assets of the British Council and the BBC World Service;
- To strengthen our relationships in all regions of the world.

The government will seek to secure these strategic aims over the five years of this Parliament . . .

Source: ww.fco.gov.uk/directory/dynpage.asp.page=26: Cm 3903, FCO *Departmental Report*, 1998 (London: TSO, 1998).

this complex mixture (Wickham-Jones 2000a: 29). An alternative explanation advanced by John Kampfner is that his ethical initiative was essentially an intra-party political development. Cook was frankly unhappy at being appointed shadow Foreign Secretary in Blair's front-bench reshuffle in 1994 because he feared being 'sidelined' within the domestic economic arena. The sudden launch of his 'ethical dimension', therefore, was arguably designed to reinforce his left-wing credentials, raise his profile within the party and so 'stamp his own identity on the government quickly after the election' in order to capture the political imagination – but with little consideration for the long-term policy implications of those commitments (Kampfner 1999: 129; Wickham Jones 2000b: 106–10). A third possibility is that this hint of morality was designed to appeal to party loyalists, deeply unhappy about Labour's retention of nuclear weapons, while suggesting a genuinely innovative approach to a broader electorate eager for change after the failures of a Conservative government mired in a range of scandals encompassing everything, from its financial support for the construction of the Pergau dam in Malaysia in return for the purchase of British arms to the squalid revelations attending the Matrix Churchill affair (see p. 226). Whatever the precise motivations behind Cook's commitment to an 'ethical dimension', it created a benchmark against which the record of the Labour governments would be judged.

New Labour and human rights abroad

In its 1997 election manifesto, Labour declared that it wanted 'Britain to be respected . . . for the integrity with which it conducts its foreign relations' by making 'the protection and promotion of human rights a central part of our foreign policy' (Labour Party 1997: 37–9). In reality, Douglas Hurd, as Foreign Secretary between 1989 and 1995, had first established a human rights policy unit at the FCO and introduced human rights training for diplomats, but the Major government demonstrated considerable reluctance to tackle this issue or to rise to its challenge. In contrast, the controversial fourth objective outlined in the FCO Mission Statement was a commitment to 'work through our international forums and bilateral relationships to spread the values of human rights, civil liberties and democracy which we demand for ourselves'. Henceforth, Cook declared, human rights would be 'at the heart of our foreign policy'.

To give substance to these heady aspirations, in July 1997 the Foreign Secretary announced 12 policies designed to implement this new commitment. He also championed the establishment of an International Criminal Court and International War Crimes Tribunal on the former Yugoslavia to arrest and punish war criminals; a commitment still actively pursued when Britain warned Croatia that if it did not hand over a prominent war criminal to the Tribunal it would block its imminent negotiations on EU entry in March 2005, the conviction of the first British soldier for war crimes in September 2006 and reflected more recently in the fivefold increase in screening for war crimes by the Border and Immigration Agency in 2008–09 (*Guardian*, 7 March 2005, 6 July 2009). Having introduced new tighter criteria for British arms exports, the Labour government used its presidency of the EU in 1998 to introduce a European code on arms exports to 'ensure that human rights remain a key factor in the EU's relations with the rest of the world'. It also introduced an Annual Report on Human Rights to improve the transparency of government policy in this area and, in the pages of which, the FCO repeatedly boasts of its achievements on everything from action against child abduction and forced marriages to the denunciation of some of the world's worst abusers of human rights. Throughout, however, the approach was to promote dialogue and partnership rather than provoke confrontation. 'We have emphatically not sought to lecture or hector', Cook declared at the Mansion House in April 1998. 'We have instead built genuine partnerships that make a practical difference in improving the observance of human rights' (www.fco.gov.uk). Or, as he once humourously defended the idea of a 'Third Way' in external policy, it was a posture located somewhere between 'the row and the kow tow' (Lawler 2000: 291).

For all the rhetoric and genuine advances, the Labour government's record on human rights was mixed, at best. It was also characterised by the application of some appalling double standards. A Spanish request for the extradition of ex-president Augusto Pinochet of Chile to stand trial for the torture and murder of Spanish citizens placed the British government in a very delicate position, particularly as the House of Lords ruled that the former head of state was not protected by sovereign immunity. In the event, after much equivocation, the Home Secretary, Jack Straw, finally allowed the supposedly frail Pinochet to return to Chile after a period of luxurious house arrest in Britain. Conversely, refugees, fleeing from systematic rape, starvation and massacre at the hands of government-sponsored militia in the Darfur region of Sudan, were less fortunate when deported from Britain in 2007, despite repeated warnings from refugee charities that they faced torture and death when they were returned to the regime in Khartoum. Refused asylum seekers from the Democratic Republic of the Congo fared no better in 2009 (*Guardian*, 29 March 2007, 28 May 2009). Human rights were not a major preoccupation either, when the FCO repeatedly ignored High Court rulings authorising 2000 British citizens to return to the Chagos Islands in the Indian Ocean from which they were expelled to make way for a US military base and suspected CIA torture centre; a flagrant breach of their legal rights which the High Court condemned as outrageous and repugnant. According to the controversial Chief Prosecutor at the International Criminal Court, the 'complex agenda' of the Brown government has also helped prevent the arrest of the Sudanese president for crimes against humanity in Darfur (*Guardian*, 25 May 2009).

These individual anomalies were symptomatic of more fundamental problems with the Blair government's 'rather inconsistent' record on human rights (Mepham 2007: 68). The most obvious indictment relates to the manner in which Britain's commitment to the 'global war on terror' has fundamentally compromised its defence of human rights. In the interests of Anglo-American unity, the Blair government aided the 'extraordinary rendition' of alleged terrorists to torture centres in Pakistan, Morocco, Diego Garcia and elsewhere and condoned their subsequent detention at Guantanamo Bay without access to trial or lawyers with barely a quibble – even when this involved the violation of the rights of British subjects. Equally damaging evidence emerged about the many substantive breaches of the European Convention on Human Rights, relating to the death and torture of civilians at the hands of British forces in Iraq, and the government's deliberate suppression of evidence·on these cases from the independent inquiry (*Guardian*, 4 April 2006, 28 March 2008, 7 July 2009). Worse still, during 2008–09 there was irrefutable evidence that the British intelligence services had directly colluded in the torture of various British terrorist suspects at interrogation centres in Egypt, Bangladesh and Pakistan, with the knowledge of ministers and in almost certain violation of international law (*Guardian*, 10 March, 1 June 2009).

Another major source of inconsistency in approach towards rights-violating governments abroad, appears to be directly related to the extent to which Britain's commercial interests were at stake. The Labour government consistently denied the existence of any tension between trade and the defence of human rights because, as Robin Cook put it in 1997, the UK is 'better able to trade with countries that are stable and free' (Miller 2000: 197). More to the point, it was argued that by acting through organisations like the China–Britain Business Council, UK firms would themselves act as agents of political change (Breslin 2004). While there may be a grain of truth in such a proposition, this can easily translate into self-serving hollow cant. In particular, the Select Committee on Foreign Affairs repeatedly criticised the fact that until June 2007 the FCO Minister of State responsible for human rights was also formally designated as its Minister for Trade; a combination of portfolios which 'sometimes stand in sharp contradiction' (HC 269 2006: para.8; HC 574 2006: para.7). In response, the government blandly refuted any such suggestion, claiming 'there is no trade-off between a robust policy on human rights and trade promotion. It is not the case that any commercial relationship stops the government from speaking frankly on issues of concern' (Cm 6774, 2006: para.5).

For its critics, British policy towards powerful human rights abusers like China, does not substantiate this claim. On the contrary, despite an appalling human rights record, Cook's 'quiet diplomacy' during his January 1998 visit to the PRC set the tone for the Labour government's assiduous efforts to strengthen bilateral relations in the hope of significant commercial benefits. In his speech reviewing 'The First Year' at the Mansion House in April 1998, Cook thus proclaimed China to be a shining example of Labour's success in opening a dialogue on this vexed subject. In contrast, critics contend that Labour's policy towards China tended to be 'all carrot and no stick', given its marked reluctance at both the national and European level, to apply a heavy-handed approach on this sensitive issue (Bourne and Cini 2000: 181). Indeed, after Beijing expressed its anger at the practice, in 1998 the Blair government ended the practice of supporting the UN Commission on Human Rights resolution condemning China's record (Coates and Krieger 2004: 17–18). For similar reasons, during State visits to London in 1999 and 2001, 'Free Tibet' and other anti-Chinese protesters were carefully suppressed to avoid offending the visiting delegation. Perhaps the most spectacular act of hypocrisy came in January 2004, when the government offered to endorse a more rigorous EU code on arms sales in return for Franco-German support for British efforts to lift the EU embargo on arms sales to China introduced after the Tiananmen Square massacre in 1989 (*Guardian*, 15 January 2004).

This studied equivocation has been the subject of widespread criticism. As the Foreign Affairs Select Committee declared in its assessment of the FCO's 2006 report on the subject, the 'Human Rights Dialogue' strategy with Beijing was 'still failing to make substantial progress' (HC 269 2007: para.116). By July 2008, having despaired of any 'significant results', the Committee recommended the abandonment of the dialogue strategy altogether unless something was achieved by 2009 (HC 533 2008: para. 103–12). The FCO remained undaunted. Miliband thus continued to urge China to open up politically as well as economically, while rejecting a boycott of the Beijing Olympics, supposedly in order to engage China in world affairs as a force for progress. Significantly, this anodyne rhetoric obscured the fact that Gordon Brown's visit to China in January 2008 ended with the signature of a $60 billion (£30.6 billion) trade deal and an understanding allowing British companies to participate in the construction of a series of new eco-cities (*Guardian*, 19 January, 29 February 2008). In these circumstances, it was scarcely surprising that in spite of a severe crackdown on unrest in Tibet in March 2008 and against domestic dissent prior to the Olympics, the

Human Rights Annual Report 2008 blandly reported that the FCO would 'continue to share our experience of reform and to make the case for it'. There was no hint of any planned change in strategy (Cm 7557 2009: 128).

After Tony Blair's visit to Colonel Gaddafi in March 2004 (following its agreement to destroy all chemical, nuclear and biological weapons), Britain was accused of turning a blind eye to human rights abuses in the country to protect BP's massive investment in Libya's vast and under-explored oil and gas reserves; an allegation apparently substantiated by the Brown government's efforts to accelerate the ratification of a Prisoner Transfer Agreement to enable the repatriation of the terminally ill Libyan intelligence agent accused of bombing the Pan-Am aircraft over Lockerbie in return for Libyan signature of a £500 million oil deal with BP (*Guardian*, 19 August, 5 September 2009). Until relatively recently, the same criticism could be levelled against British policy towards Iran. Although the Foreign Affairs Committee described Iran's human rights record as 'shocking and . . . deteriorating', as Davina Miller demonstrates, recent history suggests that 'human rights have been sacrificed in order to effect engagement' (Cm 7557, 2009: 144; Select Committee on Foreign Affairs HC 533 2008: 122; Miller 2000: 199). Junior Foreign Office minister Derek Fatchett undoubtedly had a point when he argued in 1999 that 'if we do not engage with the Iranians then we cannot hope to influence their thinking or behaviour', but such logic is chillingly reminiscent of Blair's failed justification for supporting US action in Afghanistan and Iraq and, as Miller argues, the objective of '"encouraging moderation" can come close to offering an apologia for the regime' (Miller 2000: 199). Not until 2008 did the official posture become more robust in protesting about human rights abuses and 'false promises', although in the absence of any practicable alternative, the FCO was forced to concede that 'the most significant impact we can have is to ensure that international attention remains focused on the human rights environment in Iran' (Cm 7557, 2009: 143–4).

While Iran suggests that there were limits to British patience, to take seriously the claim that human rights were 'at the heart of our foreign policy' some degree of consistency is necessary in the application of this policy. The reality, however, is that the abuse of human rights has been consistently treated less seriously when perpetrated by a major state with oil, markets for British exports or other forms of economic muscle. In particular, when these considerations are reinforced by the export needs of the British arms industry, human rights have always taken a back seat. As the Annual Report on weapons-related exports in 2006 recorded, the government approved export licences to 19 of the

20 states identified by the FCO as 'countries of concern' because of their record in abusing human rights (*Guardian*, 21 June 2008). Like China, Saudi Arabia has a human rights record denounced by the Foreign Affairs Committee in 2008 as 'one of the worst in the world', but criticism has consistently been muted by the fact that it is also the largest purchaser of British arms and a valuable ally in the 'war against terror'. As the Foreign Affairs Select Committee noted sceptically: 'We accept there is a balance to be struck in any relationship with a strategic ally, but we do not see how the government's current policies are presenting sufficient incentives to the Saudi regime to curtail its most severe abuses.' Israel, Colombia and Russia are in the same category as China and Saudi Arabia (HC 533, 2008: para. 167). In contrast, the FCO has had no compunction about occupying the moral high ground to condemn countries like Burma and Zimbabwe where there is little fear of adverse commercial consequences.

While it is easy to criticise the failure of the Labour government's preferred strategy of 'dialogue' and 'partnership', in practical terms it needs to be recognised that very few other options exist short of economic sanctions and armed intervention. But less easy to excuse is New Labour's reluctance to challenge some of the worst human rights abusers because of commercial, diplomatic or security considerations. Moreover, while the Brown premiership began by separating responsibility for trade promotion from human rights within the FCO ministerial team, this scarcely resolved the underlying conflict given that the first of three 'Essential Services' listed in its new strategy statement, *Better World, Better Britain* (Cm 7398, 2008) is 'support for the British economy'. In striking contrast, human rights were conspicuously downgraded in the 2006 White Paper *Active Diplomacy for a Changing World* in which they were mentioned almost as an afterthought in the context of the FCO's role in 'promoting sustainable development and poverty reduction underpinned by human rights, democracy, good governance and protection of the environment' (Cm 6762, 2006: 35). Two years later, human rights had been deleted altogether from *Better World, Better Britain* (Cm 7398, 2008).

New Labour, ethics and arms exports

Although the idea of an 'ethical dimension' would come back to haunt the Blair government with regard to arms exports, three contextual points should be recognised from the outset. Firstly, suspicion of the arms trade and the 'merchants of death' had been deeply rooted in Labour politics since the party's formation and explicit commitments to its control had been prominent in its 1983 manifesto, Neil Kinnock's comprehensive Labour Party Policy Review in 1989 and the statement entitled *Looking to the Future* published in the following year. It was only with the advent of Tony Blair's leadership in 1994 that New Labour's efforts to shed the negative imagery of the past encouraged it publicly to acknowledge 'that the British defence industry is integral to Britain's overall industrial base and of vital importance to the nation's economic performance . . . Labour will support our defence industry as an economic and strategic asset' (Wickham-Jones 2000b: 98–9). Secondly, the Blair government entered office with a confused, and potentially contradictory, set of pledges on the arms issue. On one hand, the 1997 manifesto pledged to prohibit arms exports 'to regimes that might use them for internal repression or international aggression'. On the other hand, this commitment was carefully qualified by the statement that 'we support a strong UK defence industry which is a strategic part of our industrial base as well as our defence effort' (Labour Party 1997). Finally, Thatcher was an evangelical salesman for British arms abroad, and the trade became a prominent political issue during the scandal surrounding the Conservative government's handling of the Matrix Churchill affair and the ensuing Scott inquiry into 'Arms-to-Iraq', when it was revealed that the Thatcher government had been informed about the proposed export of parts for a 'super-gun' to Iraq but had cynically chosen to allow the prosecution of executives from the machine tool company for breaking the arms embargo, while ruthlessly concealing its own complicity behind a cloak of government secrecy and Public Interest Immunity 'gagging orders'; an astonishing perversion of justice exposed only when Alan Clark, a former Defence minister, admitted in court that the government had been 'economical with the *actualité*' (J. Campbell 2008: 652–62).

Robin Cook had led Labour's attack on the basis of the Scott Report, accusing the government of turning 'a blind eye' to exports which breached its own arms embargo and for misleading Parliament about the prosecution of Matrix Churchill. In February 1997, while still in Opposition, Cook announced eight policy pledges designed to create tighter guidelines for British arms manufacture and export. In fairness, some rapid progress was achieved in this direction. In May 1997, Cook announced the UK would implement the ban on all forms of anti-personnel landmines, and Britain was among the first to destroy stocks when the Ottawa Treaty came into force in March 1999. In July 1997, Labour announced new criteria to ensure a 'responsible arms trade' under which export licences would not be issued if 'the arguments for doing so are outweighed by the need to comply with the UK's international obligations and commitments, or by concern that the goods might be used in internal repression or international aggression, or by the risks to regional stability'. At the same time, it implemented its ban on the export of torture equipment and introduced an Annual Report on arms and other strategic exports to improve official transparency and accountability. In 2002 it also passed the Export Control Act revising the institutional and legal framework for the regulation of arms transfers while formalising cooperation between the FCO, DTI, MoD and DfID on the subject in order to inject human rights, conflict prevention and sustainable development criteria into decisions about arms sales (Lunn, Miller and Smith 2008: 76). Furthermore, during the British presidency of the EU in 1998, it persuaded member states to adopt a new code regulating arms sale, although French opposition ensured it was rather weaker than Britain intended.

While an ostensibly impressive list of achievements, closer examination of the record suggests that the reality fell considerably short of the rhetoric. In part, this was because superficially bold pledges often obscured the mere incremental extension of existing policies. In other cases, Labour pledges were simply beyond the power of Britain to institute alone or they were heavily qualified by conditions which effectively negated the stated objective. For example, restrictions on exports that might be used aggressively against neighbouring states or domestic dissent were significantly watered down with the caveat that equipment needed for the 'legitimate' protection of the country's security forces was exempt – and this was still further diluted with the remarkable qualification that 'a purely theoretical possibility that the items concerned might be used in the future against another State will not of itself lead to a licence being refused' (FCO, DTI and MoD 1999: 3–5). The EU code was equally flawed in that it was not legally binding, it had little requirement for transparency and, as Neil Cooper argues, it was 'as much about making it easier for European defence companies to export in the future as it is about developing the building blocks with which to make arms sales more ethical'. Even real achievements, such as the prohibition on landmines, are dismissed by some commentators as 'little more than a totemic displacement activity, which has the effect of obscuring the continued attempt to maximise arms sales and so avoiding debate about the real economic and security benefits to be derived from such sales'. As the Trade and Industry Select Committee concluded in 1998, the new British criteria 'represented a rather less radical break with past policy than is sometimes represented to be the case' (Cooper 2000: 151).

An important constraint upon Labour's ability to deliver against its promises has been the commercial and political clout of the British arms industry, which had grown considerably under the Conservatives

given Thatcher's active personal support both for sales and for the provision of export credits which effectively subsidised the industry with
public money (J. Campbell 2008: 343). From the outset, Cook's FCO
confronted persistent obstruction from a powerful alliance consisting of
Downing Street, the DTI, MoD and major arms manufacturers like
British Aerospace (BAe) over the degree to which 'ethical' concerns
should be allowed to override the commercial interests of the British
defence industry and the needs of domestic employment. This preoccupation was scarcely surprising, given the fact that when Labour came to
power, in 1997, the UK was the world's second largest exporter of
defence equipment, supplying a quarter (22 per cent) of the world
market. It also had the second largest defence-industrial base as a percentage of GDP, employing 345,000 people, providing 3 per cent of
manufacturing output and exporting some 40 per cent of that production to 140 countries in every part of the world at a value of $4.7 bil-
lion (Select Committee on Defence HC 255 1999: para 2). By 2007/08,
Britain had briefly risen to first place in the arms export league tables
accounting for a third of all worldwide military exports at a value of
$19 billion – albeit a figure artificially inflated by an exceptionally large
Saudi contract for 72 Eurofighters. Nevertheless, in the preceding five
years, Britain's total export sales amounted to $53 billion; sufficient to
enable it to retain second place behind the United States ($63 billion)
but significantly ahead of its closest rival, Russia ($33 billion)
(*Guardian*, 21 June 2008).

In view of the scale of this contribution to the national economy, it is
scarcely surprising that commercial priorities prevailed over the FCO's
purely 'ethical' objectives, just as they had under their Conservative
predecessors (Pythian 2000: 287–308; Cooper 2000: 147–67). Cook
was keenly aware of this conflict of departmental objectives. When
launching his stricter criteria for arms exports in February 1997, he
explicitly emphasised that Britain had 'a right to maintain our competitive edge in this market, but we must also accept responsibility to
ensure that the arms trade is regulated' (Wickham-Jones 2000b: 98–9).
In office, however, his new guidelines on export licences in July 1997
were accompanied by an explicit requirement that 'full weight' should
be given to the 'potential effect on the UK's economic, financial and
commercial interests' and its 'relations with the recipient country'. This
stipulation effectively drove a coach and horses through the superficially bold headline commitment. Indeed, it is indicative of the importance of these sales that, since the end of the Cold War, the government
has permitted the MoD's Defence Export Services Organisation
(DESO) to use the UK intelligence services, particularly MI6, GCHQ
and the Defence Intelligence Staff, to support the export efforts of pri-

vate British arms manufacturers by providing secret intelligence on the negotiating positions of rival manufacturers (Dover 2007).

In these circumstances, it is scarcely surprising that the flow of armaments from British manufacturers scarcely faltered after 1997 – particularly as the FCO's new criteria were not applied retrospectively. As a result, the Indonesian regime acquired already-ordered Hawk jet aircraft, armoured vehicles and water cannon within months of Cook taking office. As Indonesia had been banned from purchasing weapons in the United States and Belgium because of its appalling human rights record, this feeble collapse was rapidly interpreted as proof that 'ethical' concerns were mere rhetoric; a plausible interpretation after British-supplied armoured vehicles had been used in the invasion of East Timor in 1975 and to crush student protests in 1996. Critics were even more disappointed when the distinction between equipment to be used in repression and that needed for 'legitimate' defence permitted the export of 81 armoured combat vehicles to Indonesia in 1997–98 at a cost of £185 million, only to see them deployed in May 1998 to suppress street riots in Jakarta in which hundreds died, while its Hawk jets were used to intimidate East Timor in July 1999. To add insult to injury, in June 2003 Indonesia responded to warnings not to use British arms to violate human rights by deploying Scorpion light tanks to crush separatist discontent in Aceh. By this stage, Indonesia had become the acid test for the sincerity of Labour's commitment to an 'ethical dimension'.

Notwithstanding these political embarrassments, Cook triumphantly assured the Labour Party conference in October 1997 that 'Britain is leading again by cleaning out the arms trade . . . We have put in place tougher criteria that are biting and are delivering our policies' (Wickham-Jones 2000a: 12). Only after being confronted with incontrovertible evidence to the contrary did Britain abandon the pretence over Indonesia, but by then the crimes against humanity had been perpetrated. In the interim, the value of British arms exports to Indonesia had risen from £2 million in 2000 to over £40 million by 2002 (*Guardian*, 29 June and 2 July 2003). Little wonder that human rights groups challenged the legality of this trade with Indonesia (and Israel) in December 2003 or that the Commons Committee regulating these exports complained in 2007 that, while the Export Control Act (2002) provided 'a sound legislative basis for controlling and regulating the UK's strategic exports', its 'gaps and shortcomings' were sufficiently substantial to require urgent legislative amendment (Strategic Export Controls Committee, HC 117 2007: para.6).

Beyond difficulties over Indonesia, the Blair government's claim to an 'ethical dimension' suffered a further self-inflicted blow when it lifted its arms embargo on Pakistan in July 2000, only 10 months after imposing it on a military regime which had overthrown the democratically elected government. This decision initially prompted Indian protests, but with hypocritical even-handedness it was later revealed that the FCO had concealed the Foreign Secretary's active role in promoting a £1 billion sale of Hawk jets to India (*Guardian*, 6 July 2000, 20 May 2003). Other regimes with poor human rights records to which weapons were exported during these years include Colombia, Saudi Arabia, Sri Lanka, Zimbabwe, Turkey, Nepal and China (*Guardian*, 6 December 2003). Despite government pledges to monitor end-user certificates more carefully to prevent third-party countries from evading strategic export controls, in 2004 another controversy erupted over the export of weapons components for assembly in prohibited countries – particularly as the number of component export licences granted between 1997 and 2004 spiralled upwards from 4,500 to nearly 20,000 and the list of countries (again) included Indonesia, Zimbabwe, Israel, Uganda and Colombia. Britain also supplied vital parts and military helicopters to Burma, despite an EU arms embargo on the country (*Guardian*, 16 July 2007).

The Blair government's active participation in the 'global war on terror' further compromised its 'ethical' position on arms sales. As the Foreign Affairs Select Committee pointed out in its review of the Human Rights Annual Report for 2004, it was somewhat ironic that the main customers for British arms were often both its closest allies in the 'war on terror' and among the worst abusers of human rights. The list included Saudi Arabia (£189.3 million), Malaysia (£97.3 million), Turkey (£42.4 million), Oman (£25.2 million) and the United Arab Emirates (£25 million) (HC 109, 2005: para. 67). In August 2006, the joint Select Committee reviewing Strategic Exports were equally critical in condemning the £22.5 million export of arms to Israel as a breach of the government's own guidelines in that it included components for Apache combat helicopters used by the Israeli Defence Force for extrajudicial assassinations and missile strikes in heavily populated areas, while exported F-15 and F-16 fighter jets were deployed in Israel's aggression against south Lebanon, Gaza and the West Bank (*Guardian*, 3 August 2006). The same countries continue routinely to receive official invitations to the Defence Systems and Equipment International Exhibition in London (*Guardian*, 26 February, 8 June, 11 November 2004).

In some respects, the record on arms control has been no more impressive. For example, while prohibiting all anti-personnel mines initially, the Labour government vigorously opposed a ban on cluster bombs. Despite evidence that 90 per cent of the victims are civilians, the military in Britain and the US were strongly committed to the value of such ordnance and were its largest users (along with Israel), having dropped over five million on Iraq during the Gulf War in 1991 and another two million in the 2003 conflict. As a result, during UN discussions on a conventional weapons treaty in 2003, Britain colluded with the United States to weaken the Ottawa Treaty requirement that belligerents clear unexploded ordnance after a conflict, and in 2006 it again supported US attempts to block UN efforts to extend the Ottawa Treaty to include a prohibition on cluster bombs. After Gordon Brown's personal intervention in the Dublin negotiations, however, the Labour government executed a complete volte face and then enthusiastically signed the international convention banning most types of these weapons at Oslo in December 2008 (*Guardian* 3 December 2008, 30 June 2009).

The arms trade, bribery and the control of international corruption

Concern about the questionable ethics of New Labour's record on arms sales was compounded by revelations about the manner in which this business was conducted. The Blair governments initially demonstrated some commitment to the control of international corruption by passing legislation in 2001 making it a criminal offence to bribe foreign officials to obtain contracts. Yet, beneath the surface, the Blair government had an unambiguously deplorable record in this sphere – again, largely because of the importance of arms sales to the British economy. The problem first emerged in June 2003 when it was revealed that, since the 1970s, the MoD's own Defence Export Services Organisation (DESO) has facilitated the payment of 'special commissions' to foreign officials involved in government-to-government arms contracts in breach of UK law; a practice apparently dating back to DESO's formation in the 1960s when Sir Donald Stokes, a hard-headed businessman, advised Denis Healey that to compete in the global arms market, Britain must employ such methods (*Guardian*, 13 June 2003).

These embarrassing revelations were just the tip of what would become a very large iceberg. The sale of a military air traffic control system to the poverty-stricken and heavily indebted Tanzania in 2001 became the subject of furious controversy when it was alleged that BAe had paid a $12 million 'commission' to secure the contract and that this had been pushed through the Cabinet by the Prime Minister, in face of heated protests and allegations of corruption from Gordon Brown and Clare Short, the International Development Secretary (Cook 2003: 152). In December 2004, another leading British arms manufacturer was accused of paying £16 million into the offshore account of the Indonesian

President's daughter for a contract to supply tanks in 1995–96, a deal which allegedly implicated members of the Major government. In the same month, it was revealed that between 1993 and 2004, BAe Systems made secret payments of $5 million (£2.57 million) to General Pinochet, the former Chilean dictator, to secure arms contracts.

Despite this furore, the Trade Secretary, Patricia Hewitt, overruled her own official advice when she diluted the government's rules curbing corrupt payments to foreign governments allegedly at the behest of the CBI, Rolls-Royce and BAe (*Guardian*, 7, 18 and 23 December 2004). Four months later, the government also ignored widespread opposition to announce the privatisation of the Export Control Organisation of the DTI responsible for ensuring that arms sales did not breach the British code of conduct (*Guardian*, 6 April 2005). Investigations provoked further allegations about corrupt payments by British arms manufacturers to secure contracts in South Africa, the Czech Republic and Romania (*Guardian*, 8 June 2006). But in practice, these were relatively inconsequential events compared with the profoundly damaging revelations in the *Guardian* in October 2002 concerning the so-called Al-Yamamah contract ('the Dove' in Arabic) between the British and Saudi governments, negotiated in two parts in 1985 and 1988 and worth a total of almost £43 billion – the largest arms contract in history.

During the subsequent Serious Fraud Office (SFO) investigation, it was alleged that BAe had inflated the price of the aircraft by 32 per cent in order to make secret 'commission' payments of over £1 billion from a secret slush fund paid through offshore 'shell companies' to Prince Bandar, and other officials acting for the Saudi royal family along with a variety of arms brokers and middlemen (including Thatcher's son who allegedly pocketed between £12 and £20 million); illegal activities in which it was alleged the MoD, DESO (headed by a former BAe executive) and the Paymaster General were all deeply implicated. Worse still, just as SFO investigators were on the brink of accessing key Swiss bank accounts, members of the Saudi royal family apparently warned Blair that he had 10 days to drop the SFO investigation, or the £6 billion deal to supply 72 Typhoon Eurofighters would go to France. At the same time, BAe launched a high-profile publicity campaign warning that the SFO inquiry represented a major threat to British business and to 4500 jobs at home and another 11,500 in Europe (*Guardian*, 14–15 February 2008). In response to this Saudi blackmail, the Prime Minister intervened directly to order the Attorney General to terminate the SFO investigation. While denying that commercial considerations played any part in the decision, the government justified their actions on the convenient pretext of 'national security'. As the Attorney General's statement explained on 14 December 2006:

The Prime Minister and the Foreign and Defence Secretaries have expressed a clear view that continuation of the investigation would cause serious damage to UK-Saudi security, intelligence and diplomatic co-operation, which is likely to have serious negative consequences for the UK public interest in terms of both national security and our highest priority foreign policy objectives in the Middle East. (*Guardian*, 24 September 2005, 28 November, 2 and 15 December 2006)

The Prime Minister's role in these events came under particular scrutiny in the light of two subsequent developments. Firstly, a month after the SFO investigation came to an end, Sir John Scarlett, head of MI6, publicly refuted the government claim that the SFO inquiry threatened national security by jeopardising Anglo-Saudi intelligence and security links. Secondly, the *Guardian* subsequently revealed the Attorney General had twice unsuccessfully attempted to stop Blair interfering in the criminal investigation, only to receive a 'secret and personal' letter from the Prime Minister on 8 December 2006 demanding the investigation be stopped, given the 'extremely difficult and delicate issues' raised (*Guardian*, 22 December 2007; 11 April 2008; www.guardian.co.uk/baefiles). The adverse repercussions were not confined exclusively to the domestic arena. In the wake of the SFO crisis, Britain was severely criticised by the OECD for breaching its 1998 international anti-bribery treaty obligations, while the US Department of Justice began its own investigation in June 2007, forcing the British government initially to refuse to comply with the US request for access to SFO files in breach of the Anglo-US Mutual Legal Assistance Treaty. In the event, the government was conveniently spared further discomfiture when an embarrassing High Court judgment against it was overturned when the House of Lords ruled that the government was legally entitled to terminate the SFO investigation. Although this finally brought the Saudi affair to a close, BAe's activities remained under scrutiny by the US Department of Justice, the OECD and Swiss, Austrian and various other European investigators. For its own part, a now ethically challenged government responded defiantly to these humiliating revelations by introducing a provision in the Constitutional Renewal Bill enabling the Attorney General to block such investigations in future when in the 'national interest' (*Guardian*, 12 April 2008). Significantly, the first ever prosecution of a company for corruptly obtaining contracts abroad did not occur until July 2009 (*Guardian*, 11 July 2009).

For its defenders, BAe was simply playing the game and this was 'business as usual' in a murky area of international commerce. For its critics, however, it was a squalid example of governmental hypocrisy on an almost breathtaking level, which confirmed Robin Cook's acid observation that he never knew Blair ever to make a decision that displeased BAe. But, ultimately, the supreme irony of Labour's 'ethical dimension' is that, while the Prime Minister, the FCO and DfID continually stressed to recipients of British overseas aid that they must deliver 'good governance' by eradicating corruption in the Third World, the Blair government was itself actively colluding in the violation of British and EU laws concerning arms sales in pursuit of domestic commercial advantage. Undoubtedly, a persuasive case could be made in defence of the government's action as a realist response to the world as it currently exists, the needs of a leading British company with global sales in 2006 of £11 billion (equivalent to 1 per cent of UK GDP) and the realities of international power when dealing with the world's largest supplier of oil. But these events made a complete mockery of the pledge to introduce an 'ethical dimension' into British foreign policy.

International development and developing world debt relief

Labour's manifesto in 1997 had proclaimed that 'we have a moral responsibility to help combat global poverty' (Labour Party 1997). This explicit commitment to international aid and development was fulfilled immediately after the election, when the Overseas Development Administration (ODA) was transferred from the FCO and turned into a new Department for International Development (DfID), in much the same way as Harold Wilson had in 1964 when creating the Ministry of Overseas Development. It was the first time that international development had its own separate ministry since 1975 and the first time its minister held Cabinet rank since 1967. More important, as Richard Manning argues, 'the UK's international profile on development issues has probably not been higher since John Maynard Keynes was negotiating the establishment of the World Bank in 1944' (Manning 2007: 553). This marked a stark contrast with the neglect of the issue under Thatcher, who dismissed the Brandt Report and its talk of a 'North–South' dialogue as 'wrong-headed', and under whom aid spending fell 7 per cent in real terms while its share of GNP fell from 0.52 per cent in 1979 to 0.31 per cent a decade later. The Thatcher governments also played a major role in the diversion of the aid budget to fund the economically unviable, and environmentally damaging, Pergau Dam project in Malaysia in 1988 in return for a £1.3 billion order for British defence equipment; one of many blatant abuses of the aid budget in contravention of the 1980 Overseas

Development and Cooperation Act (Thatcher 1993: 168; J. Campbell 2008: 340–4).

One of the key objectives in creating a new government department was to demonstrate that the development agenda was not subordinated to broader foreign policy priorities – and, in particular, to separate the primary focus on poverty reduction from other FCO activities, such as the promotion of trade and arms sales. Indeed, its first Minister, Clare Short, had only accepted the portfolio on these terms, and under her leadership there was a marked increase in the momentum behind British aid policy as it focused far more single-mindedly upon the needs of the world's poorest nations. She also had the advantage of knowing Africa and its leaders as the widow of the much-respected Africa expert, Alex Lyons MP. Over the next decade, an increasingly well-funded DfID established itself as the 'Ministry for sub-Saharan Africa', effectively superseding FCO influence in the region. Although critics argued that DfID's humanitarian focus and reduced access to FCO 'political' expertise produced a rather naive approach to the region and its problems, Clare Short was deeply committed to the independence of the Department and the expansion of its role. Moreover, under her influence DfID successfully shifted the terms of the entire debate away from any conception of aid as charity, and its traditional focus on economic development, to a more strategic conception of aid rooted in specific programmes aimed principally at poverty elimination; a theme which lay at the heart of the International Development and Cooperation Act of 2002 which outlawed the use of aid for any other purpose than poverty reduction and humanitarian relief (Young 2000: 264).

As Table 8.2 demonstrates, Labour's 1997 manifesto was far more explicit about international development than it was with regard to foreign or defence policy. In November 1997, within six months of coming into office, DfID had published the ambitiously titled White Paper, *Eliminating World Poverty: A Challenge for the 21st Century* (Cm 3789) – the first on Britain's overseas aid policy since 1975. This was followed by a second White Paper with the same title in 2000, but this time it was significantly subtitled '*Making Globalisation Work for the Poor*' (Cm 5006). A third White Paper amplifying these themes appeared in 2006. These documents explicitly rejected the traditional practice of 'tied aid', which required the recipient to use the credits to purchase goods from the donor. They also pledged to spend more on development, the importance of human rights and 'good governance' in the elimination of poverty, the promotion of business, trade and investment, the diffusion of new technologies and the relief of the Third World debt burden. In addition, they drew upon the exacting principles agreed in the Rio Declaration on Sustainable Development in 1992,

Table 8.2   Labour manifesto commitments to international development
in 1997

- create a separate new department under a minister of Cabinet rank to
  'bring development issues back into the mainstream of government decision-making';
- 'start to reverse the decline in UK's aid spending'; to work towards
  United Nations target of 0.7 per cent of GNI as aid by 2015;
- 'shift resources towards programmes that help the poorest people in the
  poorest countries'
- promote the interests of the poorest countries during negotiations on the
  Lome Convention as part of a broader strategy of giving developing
  countries 'a fair deal in international trade'
- strive to reduce the debt burden of the world's poorest countries
- rejoin UNESCO.

Source: Labour Party, *New Labour, Because Britain Deserves Better* (1997).

which set a target date of 2015 to achieve a number of Millennium
Development Goals (MDG) that included a reduction of extreme
poverty globally by a half; the reduction in maternal mortality rates by
three-quarters and infant mortality by two-thirds along with universal
access to primary education and a variety of other health reforms
(Young 2000: 259). Ultimately, as the White Paper put it, the objective
was to support policies 'which create sustainable livelihoods for poor
people, promote human development and conserve the environment'
(Cm 3789 1997: 3).

Clare Short enjoyed a good working relationship with Gordon Brown
as Chancellor, and she collaborated closely with him in pressing the
case for more flexible arrangements for debt reduction for the poorest
countries and in managing Britain's relationship with the World Bank.
The Treasury was equally sympathetic towards the Department's
budget, which increased substantially throughout the period after 1997,
notwithstanding the prior pledge to operate within Conservative
spending ceilings. In the Comprehensive Spending Review in July 1998,
the Treasury pledged to increase resources over the next three-year cycle
from £2.3 billion to £3.2 billion; an average annual increase of 8.8 per
cent in real terms. This level of commitment raised the DfID's capacity
for aid provision from 0.26 per cent to 0.3 per cent of Gross National
Income (GNI). By 2004, the figure had risen to 0.4 per cent of GNI,
although the CSR for the next three years made no allowance for any
real increase because of the costs of the 'war on terror'. Nevertheless, in
February 2004, Brown took the radical step of announcing that Britain

Table 8.3   DfID expenditure on aid, debt relief and development, 2001/02 to 2007/08 (in £ millions)

	2001/02	2002/03	2003/04	2004/05	2005/06	2006/07	2007/08
GPEX on development	3477	4153	4714	5178	6612	7592	6027
Excluding debt relief	2917	3335	3939	3862	4348	4778	5952
UK net ODA in Africa	836	698	923	1327	2088	2968	1228
Africa debt relief	236	94	32	396	1200	1794	29
Net ODA Sub-Sahara Africa	798	643	885	1235	2071	2933	1176
Sub-Saharan debt relief	236	94	42	387	1230	1794	29

GPEX = Gross Public Expenditure; ODA = Overseas Development Assistance.

Source: *Statistics on International Development*; *DfID Annual Reports*, 2001/02 to 2007/08.

would meet the UN's aid target of 0.7 per cent of GNI by 2015, and he used this pledge very effectively thereafter to press fellow G7 finance ministers to commit to a massive increase in aid.

Clare Short's resignation from the Cabinet in May 2003 in protest at the Iraq War did not have a particularly adverse effect upon the Department's progress – not least because her forceful personality and unusually long term of six years both set the new department off on the right lines. Moreover, following her departure, it was fortunate that after a short holding operation by Baroness Amos, ministerial turnover has been relatively low. Since this brief interregnum, the DfID's former junior minister, Hilary Benn, became Secretary of State until Gordon Brown's prime ministerial reshuffle in June 2007, when the post went to the Prime Minister's close ally Douglas Alexander. Labour's continued commitment to international development has also been assisted by Brown's emergence as a vocal champion of further support for the Developing World, in terms of health and education, debt cancellation and trade reform after his high-profile tour of Africa in January 2005.

By 2007, the fast-rising overseas aid and development budget had risen to £7 billion. By 2010/11, it is scheduled to reach £9.1 billion.

Gordon Brown was also one of the principal driving forces behind the campaign for debt relief. Again, this issue appeared on the agenda in the late 1980s during John Major's Chancellorship, when he launched a campaign to reduce the debt burden on the world's poorest countries. Nevertheless, as Chancellor and later Prime Minister, Gordon Brown emerged as a far more vigorous advocate prepared to offer strong leadership as part of his broader commitment to social justice. In June 1999, the first signs of progress were achieved when the G8 summit in Cologne announced a $100 billion (£63 million) package of debt relief. Six months later, Britain decided to write off the debts incurred on bilateral loans by 41 of the poorest countries in the world. Although a relatively modest gesture, as it involved a sum of only of £640 million to be realised over a 20-year period, as Brown argued at the time, 'This is a pledge with a purpose, because we want other states to follow our lead' (*Guardian*, 22 December 1999).

In retrospect, 2005 represented a significant milestone in this policy arena. During Britain's presidency of the G7 and EU in 2005, Brown talked of a 'new Marshall Plan for aid, trade and debt relief' for sub-Saharan Africa. In January 2005, he adopted a strong line at the meeting of the 'Paris Group' of creditor nations when encouraging debt moratoria for countries hit by the Indian Ocean tsunami, and later in the month his tour of Africa ended with the pledge to relieve Tanzania of part of its debt to the World Bank as the first instalment of his campaign for the cancellation of over $80 billion owed by the world's 37 most indebted countries to the World Bank and the IMF (*Guardian*, 5 and 14 January 2005). Four months later, Britain adopted an equally strong line when persuading the EU to commit to the UN aid target of 0.7 per cent of GNI by 2015, while Blair announced visits to the US and Russia to persuade them to accept the same agreement at a time when Washington was devoting only 0.16 per cent of GDP to development aid (*Guardian*, 12 March 2005). At the G7 in June, Brown also secured a major advance with the writing off of IMF loans and credits to countries covered by the HIPC initiative. In addition, during the opening months of 2005, the Commission for Africa had also been launched, bringing together African leaders and policymakers with the objective (as Blair explained at the Gleneagles summit in July 2005) of establishing 'the basic elements of a comprehensive package that would right the wrongs of Africa' (www.number10.gov.uk). These deliberations played a major role in shaping British thinking and strategy regarding the pledge to 'Make Poverty History' in the lead-up to the G8 summit at Gleneagles (Commission for Africa, 2005).

Gleneagles represented the culmination of Labour's efforts in this direction. Blair and Brown had resolved to make Africa and climate change the central twin themes of Britain's presidency. It was thus hailed as a major triumph for British diplomacy and moral leadership when eight of the world's richest nations endorsed the UN's Millennium Development Goals by pledging an extra $50 billion (£25.8 billion at 2005 prices) in aid by 2010 as a step towards the achievement of the 0.7 per cent target by 2015. They also agreed to fund the total cancellation of $40 billion of debt owed by 18 of the world's poorest countries to the World Bank, the African Development Bank and the IMF, with the prospect of another 20 being eligible for relief if they met the necessary targets for corruption and structural adjustment. In addition, the summit committed itself to provide universal access to anti-HIV/Aids drugs and treatment for polio, TB and malaria in Africa by 2010; to train a 20,000 strong peacekeeping force and to reduce subsidies and tariffs that inhibited access to world markets for poor nations. Little wonder that in his closing speech on 8 July the Prime Minister declared that 'substantial progress' had been made with regard to international development and that this was 'a clear signal on Africa, not just of intent but of detail propositions for help' (www.number10.gov.uk).

Despite the optimistic rhetoric, the practical results proved rather more disappointing. Firstly, several of the G8 soon began backsliding on commitments, which, in some cases, were only repackaged aid deals already in existence. Secondly, the offer of debt relief was confined only to Heavily Indebted Poor Countries (HIPC) and to obtain this status they needed previously to have adopted the neoliberal policies of the IMF and World Bank, including the privatisation of water and other services which often ended up being sold to companies from donor countries delivering poorer services at higher prices. Finally, the OECD reported in April 2007 that for the first time in a decade, international aid had actually declined by 5.1 per cent in the previous year. Despite these setbacks, however, the British government's mid-term policy review at the end of 2006 showed that its overseas aid had doubled and it had cancelled debts valued at over $70 billion (£36.5 billion). By this juncture, Britain was directing over £1 billion per annum in aid to Africa alone – almost double the £510 million provided by the United States. In 2008/9, financial aid to the poorest countries rose by another 24.1 per cent making Britain one of the few countries on course to reach the UN's 0.7 per cent of GNI target by 2015 (*Guardian*, 31 March 2009; Select Committee on International Development, HC 220-I 2009: para 1.18). In conjunction with the publication of another White Paper (Cm 7656) outlining ambitious plans for aid and development, in July 2009 Brown and Alexander pressed the G8 to agree to the publication of league tables setting out each country's progress towards meeting their Gleneagles commitments, in order to shame the laggards into action, and they played a leading role in committing the G8 to an extra $20 billion (£12.4 billion) to assist agricultural development to enable poor nations to feed themselves rather than rely on wasteful sub-sidised food aid (*Guardian*, 7, 10–11 July 2009).

In the past, the departmental Select Committee has been critical of the DfID's emphasis on 'inputs' (what it spends) rather than 'outcomes' (the effect of its spending) but when considered as a whole, the record of the DfID has been relatively impressive. Although it initially worked in over a hundred countries, the number of aid recipients was reduced by a third by 2009. Nevertheless, according to its 2008 Annual Report it had successfully lifted three million of the world's poorest people out of poverty. While acknowledging that most of the eight MDGs on poverty reduction will not be achieved by 2015, the department's 'Global Action Plan on Malaria' has begun to reduce the million deaths a year from the disease and definite progress had been made on the quest to achieve several of the other MDGs (HC 220-I 2009: para 72). For example, in 2006 Gordon Brown launched a new savings bond to help pay for a doubling of the rate of inoculation for every child in the world, with the Pope symbolically purchasing the first one; an initiative likely to save the lives of five million children by 2015. In March 2008, he announced a joint Anglo-French initiative to send another 16 million African children to school within two years to add to the 41 million school places created since 2000; and in a further effort to put the world back on track to fulfil MDG targets, at an emergency session of the UN called at British behest in September 2008, he launched a global plan to recruit a million doctors, nurses and midwives in poor countries to reduce maternal and infant mortality (*Guardian*, 27 March and 25 September 2008). Having acknowledged the maternal and child mor-tality, MDGs were 'significantly off track', in September 2009 further efforts were made at the UN to push for an end to health 'user fees' in Nepal (where a newborn baby dies every 20 minutes), Burundi, Malawi, Ghana and Sierra Leone (where one in seven mothers die in childbirth). Under the plan, Britain will pledge an extra £200 million to give a lead to other countries and to add to the £6 billion it is already devoting specifically to health in the developing world between 2008 and 2015 (*Guardian*, 12 September 2009). In order to tackle another of the Gleneagles objectives, in April 2007 Brown announced a $75 mil-lion (£37.8 million) package to be spent over 5 years to assist 40 of the world's poorest countries to develop their trading capacity on world markets (*Guardian*, 14 April 2007).

For all the very real achievements, these advances need to be seen in context. UK aid to sub-Saharan Africa accounts for only one-fortieth of what it spends on defence and, as the British economy slumped into recession in 2008/09, the 1997 commitment to 'eliminate world poverty' appears vulnerable to remedial measures designed to reduce public sector debt. But for all that, international development is one of the few areas in which New Labour has achieved a significant level of success with its 'ethical dimension'. As Brown explained shortly before the Hokkaido G8 summit in July 2008: 'Unless we help the poor countries to become more prosperous through education, health and economic development, we will be piling up the problem of global inequality' (*Guardian*, 5 July 2008). Such convictions have provided a unifying theme for his foreign policy throughout.

Climate change and the environmental agenda

The Blair–Brown government's policy on climate change is also directly related to its posture on development and aid. At the Kyoto conference in 1997, John Prescott, the Deputy Prime Minister, played a leading role in drafting the protocol on the reduction of greenhouse gas emissions by the year 2010, and he (and Margaret Beckett) adopted an equally high profile at the follow-up climate change conferences in The Hague, Bonn and Marrakech, and the latter's surprise promotion to the FCO in May 2006 has been interpreted in some quarters as an effort to signal the high priority attached to the issue (Khatri 2007: 587). Climate change was one of the two key themes of the Gleneagles summit in 2005, and it subsequently led to a series of G8 Energy and Environmental ministerial meetings. In April 2007, Britain also raised the issue for the first time at the UN's Security Council to highlight the implications of climate change for international security. It also later became an important theme for Gordon Brown, which he declared 'not just an environmental and economic imperative, but a moral one' (*Guardian*, 30 October 2006). At the Treasury, Brown commissioned the landmark Stern Review on climate change, and in its wake he advocated a stiff EU-wide emissions reduction target and an international carbon emissions trading scheme. Ed Miliband, the world's first Energy and Climate Change minister, was equally emphatic at the European summit in October 2008 in rebuffing the suggestion that the EU should retreat from the bold targets agreed in March 2007 simply because of the severity of the global financial crisis, and in June 2009 he followed this with the publication of the 'Road to Copenhagen' as a rallying cry for international agreement on more ambitious targets to deal with global warming (*Guardian*, 17 October and 8 December 2008, 26 June 2009).

While the record on climate change under the Labour governments is undoubtedly open to criticism, its policy has undeniably been formulated with one eye on global development and social justice, and it has actively taken the lead in promoting concern about the issue among the richer nations. As Brown warned the Labour Party conference, 'tackling climate change must not be the excuse for rich countries to impose a new environmental colonialism sheltering an unsustainable prosperity at the expense of the development of the poor' (O'Donnell and Whitman 2007: 265–6). Although initially slow to honour its financial obligations under the 2001 UN Climate Change Agreement in Bonn, in February 2008 Britain finally agreed a tenfold increase in expenditure (£100 million over five years) on its Environmental Transformation Fund to ameliorate the effect of climate change on the poorest countries. Although this aid has some onerous conditions attached, as Douglas Alexander explained, 'climate change is the defining global social justice issue. If we fail to tackle climate change we risk condemning the world's poorest people to poverty for generations to come.' In an effort to revive stalled talks on the subject, in June 2009 Brown's strong warning that global security depended on agreement at Copenhagen was accompanied by a proposal for rich countries to donate up to $100 billion (£60 billion) a year by 2020 to a fund to which poor countries could apply for financing specific projects to help deal with global warming – a fairly generous offer, but well short of the 1 per cent of GDP suggested by the G77 group of developing nations (*Guardian*, 7 February 2008, 27 June 2009).

The 'Blair doctrine', liberal intervention and the Kosovo campaign

Although the Foreign Office Mission Statement made a brief reference to Britain using its position 'to secure more effective international action to keep the peace of the world', there was nothing new in the idea of Britain intervening abroad for humanitarian purposes. As Denis Healey's 1966 Defence Review noted: 'Recent experience in Africa and elsewhere has shown that our ability to give rapid help to friendly governments, with even small British forces, can prevent large-scale catastrophes. In some parts of the world, the visible presence of British forces of itself is a deterrent to local conflict' (Cmnd 2901 1966: para.18). Yet, while neither the activity not the underlying motivation represented a radical departure, under Tony Blair 'liberal intervention'

reached unprecedented heights and led his government into major conflicts in the Balkans, Afghanistan and Iraq as well as more minor
deployments in East Timor, Sierra Leone and the Democratic Republic
of Congo.

Kosovo was Blair's first real engagement with foreign policy and it
had a profound impact upon both the man and his policy framework.
Among other things, it clarified his thinking on the justification for
intervention to be applied in later cases such as East Timor and Sierra
Leone, and it convinced him of the need to press ahead with the EU
Rapid Reaction Force to provide the capability for military action
where the US had no direct interest (see Chapter 5). But above all, as
his biographer notes, Kosovo left Blair with a strong sense of destiny in
foreign affairs and an unwavering self-belief (Seldon 2005: 407).
During Labour's first months in office, the small province of Kosovo in
southwest Serbia was rapidly descending into a vicious civil war
between the ethnic Albanian majority seeking an independent republic
and Serbian security forces engaged in a vicious counter-insurgency
operation. In the event, the Blair government's neutral stance was
transformed by the sheer brutality of the Serbian offensive in July 1998,
which ended with a million refugees forced from their homes and the
destruction of 200 villages (Bartlett 2000). After these atrocities, British
policy adopted a far more robustly interventionist posture towards
Yugoslavia than its Conservative predecessors had over Bosnia.

The failure of the Rambouillet summit to impose a settlement in
February 1999, and the inability to obtain a UN mandate for intervention (because of Chinese and Russian obstruction), prompted the
Labour government to press for the use of force within a NATO framework. Although high-level NATO air strikes continued from 26 March
until 9 June 1999, they proved singularly ineffective in disrupting the
ethnic cleansing activities of small Serbian paramilitary units and it was
only the threat of ground operations which eventually forced Serb
capitulation. Nevertheless, in language which would subsequently
become far more familiar, Blair defended this intervention in the
Commons on 23 March by declaring that air strikes were morally justified because all possible diplomatic efforts had been exhausted and
there were no other options to prevent crimes against humanity. The
NATO action was thus effectively portrayed as a humanitarian war in
terms which conformed well with the government's earlier rhetoric
about an 'ethical dimension' in foreign policy. Kosovo and Sierra Leone
(see below) were thus, perhaps, the finest hour of liberal intervention.

Not all commentators accept this interpretation. In particular, some
critics argue that, far from being driven by ethical considerations, Blair
simply drifted into the crisis and used the 'moral war' argument as a

retrospective justification to legitimise what might be called 'warlike humanitarianism' (Coates and Krieger 2004: 21). Yet, whatever the original reasons for intervention in Kosovo, Blair's defence of what he described (in Chicago) as a 'just war based not on territorial ambition but on values' was subsequently elevated to the heady status of a 'Blair doctrine'. Adapting 'Third Way' rhetoric about rights and obligations to the international sphere, Blair told the South African Parliament in January 1999:

> Countries have a right to live free from the threat of force. But they also have a responsibility to maintain peace, and not to threaten or attack their neighbours. Otherwise the international community has a responsibility to act ... People say you can't be self appointed guardians of what is right and wrong. True, but when the international community agrees certain objectives and it fails to implement them, those who can act, must. (www.number10.gov.uk)

Blair elaborated these themes in a landmark speech on 'The Doctrine of the International Community' at the Economic Club of Chicago on 22 April 1999: 'Non-interference has long been considered an important principle of international order. And it is not one we would want to jettison too readily', the Prime Minister declared. 'But the principle of non-interference must be qualified in important respects. Acts of genocide can never be a purely internal matter'

> We need to enter a new millennium where dictators know that they cannot get away with ethnic cleansing or repress their people with impunity. We are fighting not for territory but for values. For a new internationalism where the brutal repression of ethnic groups will not be tolerated. For a world where those responsible for such crimes have nowhere to hide. (www.fco.gov.uk)

This speech has been described as 'one of the most theoretical speeches on foreign policy ever given by a British Prime Minister' (Cox and Oliver 2006: 176). Christopher Hill even goes so far as to argue that 'it amounts to a minor revolution against a pragmatic empiricism which has dominated the language of British foreign policy since the days of Cobden, Bright and Gladstone' (Hill 2001: 342). The task of drafting Blair's credo was assigned by the Downing Street chief of staff, Jonathan Powell, to his old friend and former Foreign Office planning staff colleague Professor Lawrence Freedman (Seldon 2005: 398). Freedman had been working on the same questions himself and had devised five criteria for intervention. In his speech, the Prime Minister thus argued that the decision on 'when and whether to intervene' depended on the answer to five key questions.

1. Are we sure of our case?
2. Have all diplomatic options been exhausted?
3. Can military operations be sensibly and prudently undertaken?
4. Is there a will to hold out for the long term?
5. Do we have national interests involved?

Although these were never intended to be 'absolute tests', they supposedly explain why there was no intervention in the vicious Russian campaign in Chechnya, while they did provide a rationale for later interventions in East Timor in 1999, where 300 British troops participated in an Australian-led UN operation to protect against Indonesian attack; in Sierra Leone in May 2000, when 4,500 British troops intervened to restore order and security; and in the Democratic Republic of Congo in 2003, where a small detachment participated in a French-led EU operation. Above all, in the wake of 9/11, Blair's doctrine provided a rationale (of sorts) for Britain's very substantial contribution to a US-led 'coalitions of the willing' in Afghanistan and Iraq. The experience radically transformed the nature of 'liberal intervention' and gravely tarnished the credibility of the doctrine and its principal exponent.

Afghanistan, the Taliban and the 'war on terror'

Once Al Qaida had been identified as the perpetrators of the 9/11 terrorist attacks, it was inevitable that the US would attack their bases in Afghanistan and seek to overturn the Taliban regime which had hosted them. The Prime Minister had no hesitation in committing Britain to the ensuing military campaign because principled nations had a duty to act against those who harboured 'the sworn enemies of everything the civilised world stands for' (*Guardian*, 3 October 2001). The rapid collapse of the Taliban regime on 13 November, after only five weeks' fighting, served to silence Blair's critics and massively boosted his faith in the fundamental rectitude of 'liberal intervention' in this new form.

Five years later, the commander of British forces in Afghanistan declared the scale of fighting to be unparalleled since the Second World War, while the Chiefs of Staff were pressing the government to withdraw British troops from Iraq (which they considered unwinnable) to reinforce their existing detachment of 5,600 troops in Afghanistan where a military victory was still possible (*Guardian*, 29 September, 13 October 2006). In the intervening period, the number of terrorist attacks and British military casualties rose steadily. Even more depressing, opium poppy production increased from 8,000 hectares (producing 135 tonnes) in 2001 (when it was suppressed by the Taliban) to around 165,000 hectares (producing 8,200 tonnes) in 2007 and 2008; an increase in Afghanistan's share of world production from 52 per cent in 1995 to 93 per cent by 2007 (*Guardian*, 29 November 2006, 21 February 2008). Against this gloomy background, after seven years of fighting the US Director of Intelligence in Washington was obliged to confess in February 2008 (*Guardian*, 29 February 2008) that the Karzai government controlled only 30 per cent of the country and the security position in Afghanistan was still deteriorating; a verdict confirmed by the massive intensification of Taliban attacks in the Helmand and Kandahar provinces during the second half of 2008.

Confronted by this escalating challenge, the British government's change of tactics in 2007 reflected the widespread belief among Whitehall planners that outright military victory was no longer an option in Afghanistan, given the remarkable success of Taliban insurgents in adapting their military tactics and their ability to draw upon coffers swollen with soaring opium revenues. The massive scale of the budget deficit in 2009 also played a significant part in Brown's rejection of plans to deploy an additional 2,000 troops in June 2009. British thinking has thus increasingly turned towards a strategy of undermining support for the Taliban by continuing the battle to win 'hearts and minds' through reconstruction (since 2001 it has spent over £600 million in reconstruction), combined with a 'reconciliation' drive to win over lower- and mid-level Taliban who were tired of fighting and to persuade them to renounce violence, and either join the political process or rejoin their tribal communities. At the same time, a parallel plan was developed to employ cash incentives to discourage farmers from engaging in opium production; a 'second best' strategy adopted by the UN in 2009 when it sought to convert Afghan farmers to legal crops with a 'flood of drugs' designed to undermine the market value of opium to discourage production at a time when wheat prices had soared and opium was worth only a fifth of its value in 2001 (*Guardian* 27 February 2007, 26 May 2009). Significantly, the UN's Office on Crime and Drugs reports that production declined by 28 per cent during 2008 alone (*Guardian*, 25 June 2008). Despite this supposed progress, however, in June 2009 US forces formally abandoned efforts to eradicate opium cultivation on the grounds that they were ineffective.

Unfortunately, while military victory may be impossible, this alternative strategy appears to offer little ground for optimism about an early disengagement, although since the election of Obama the emergence of a 'new realism' has at least produced greater convergence in Anglo-

American strategy. Launching his new vision for South Asia in March 2009, President Obama spoke of the need for a comprehensive regional solution embracing both Afghanistan and Pakistan. This strategy consists of a 'military surge' to accelerate the training of Afghan security forces to defeat the Taliban combined with a 'civilian surge' designed to promote socio-economic development and win hearts and minds. Significantly, this clarification of the new administration's thinking was accompanied by its adoption of a far more modest strategic objective simply 'to disrupt, dismantle and defeat Al Qaida in Pakistan and Afghanistan and to prevent their return to either country in the future' (*Guardian*, 27 March 2009). After his visit to Afghanistan and Pakistan in April 2009, the Prime Minister announced a correspondingly dramatic reduction in UK strategic objectives. Put simply, the stated purpose of Britain's presence in Afghanistan today is no longer to create a Western-style liberal democracy but simply to turn a failing state into a functioning entity 'able to handle its security and deliver basic services to the people' (*Guardian*, 30 April 2009).

Unfortunately, even if Anglo-American strategy is fully coordinated, major problems still remain. The outgoing UK ambassador to Kabul recently condemned the naïve 'hangover of misplaced optimism' which still shrouded the operation, but the sheer scale of the challenge defies easy solution (Grey 2009: 61). As a DfID report (in conjunction with the World Bank) concluded in 2008, it would take at least 20 years and over £1 billion invested in the Afghan infrastructure to eradicate the opium and even this rather sobering calculation appears excessively optimistic given estimates of the opium crop's value, which varied in 2007 between an IMF figure of $1 billion (£515 million) and the official US calculation of $4 billion (*Guardian*, 6 and 21 February 2008). Despite the deployment of more and more troop reinforcements and the expenditure of ever greater amounts of public money, after eight years of military engagement Taliban forces still control large areas of the south and east and are increasingly making progress in the north and west against NATO forces, which are tied down in nearly impossible circumstances with little prospect of an early (far less easy) withdrawal. Indeed, despite the supposed success of Operation 'Panthers Claw', during the second half of 2009, the intensity of the fighting and the British death toll both reached an alarming new peak while calls for more 'boots on the ground' continued unabated. As Bob Ainsworth, the Defence Secretary, conceded in September 2009, British troops were a long way from defeating a 'resilient enemy' in Afghanistan, but military failure could not be contemplated because it would have 'profound consequences for our national security' and 'undermine the NATO alliance' (*Guardian*, 16 September 2009).

What began as a supposedly brief exercise in 'liberal intervention' has thus turned into a running sore which, as Gordon Brown conceded in December 2007, was likely to require British troops to remain in the country for at least another decade (*Guardian*, 10 December 2007). Although the opinion polls during 2009 indicated increasing electoral concern about the loss of over 200 British troops and many billions in expenditure, in public the Brown government remained unwavering. As the Prime Minister explained: 'There is a chain of terror that runs from the mountains and towns of Afghanistan to the streets of Britain. Our resolution to complete the work we have started is undiminished' (*Guardian*, 11 July, 10 September 2009).

Saddam Hussein, Operation Desert Fox and the Iraq War

The Blair government inherited the problem of Iraq and its persistent obstruction of the UN inspection regime searching for Weapons of Mass Destruction (WMD). Although critics often argue that Blair's default setting was to 'go with the Americans' over everything, this should not obscure the degree to which Blair was genuinely outraged by Saddam Hussein's 'detestable, brutal, repressive' regime and the threat he believed it posed to international peace and stability (Kampfner 2003: 350; Bluth 2004: 876). Blair's moral repugnance and propensity to act was demonstrated by his enthusiastic support for 'Operation Desert Fox' in December 1998, when four days of aerial bombardment of Iraqi installations was designed to degrade Saddam Hussein's capability to construct WMDs and to demonstrate forcefully the consequences of violating international obligations and obstructing the UN weapons inspectors. Given these convictions, it is not surprising that when Bush informed him on 6 April 2002 that the US intended to remove Saddam Hussein from power, Blair had little hesitation in committing Britain to support the action; particularly given an interdepartmental briefing document a month earlier which argued that only military action to achieve regime change was capable of delivering the objectives of British policy (Bluth 2004: 874–7). After all that had happened since the Gulf War in 1991, for Blair there was barely a decision to make other than to follow the US lead (Danchev 2007: 46–8)

On 21 March 2003, the 30-nation US-led coalition, including a British contingent of 48,000 troops, launched a pre-emptive military action against Iraq designed to destroy its WMD capability and to secure regime change. The military operation was short and ostensibly successful. By 1 May, major combat operations had come to an end as

George Bush triumphantly declared 'Mission Accomplished'. But euphoria at the ease of victory was rapidly dissipated by increasingly insistent calls for an adequate justification for the war. Firstly, Iraq's collapse into chaos, anarchy and incipient civil war came as a severe blow after assurances that this was a war of liberation to free oppressed people from a vicious tyrant. Secondly, the failure of the Iraq Survey Group to find any WMD fuelled this disillusionment by undermining a central justification for a war which increasingly appeared to have been launched on a false prospectus. The discovery of some 270 mass graves containing more than 300,000 bodies was not in itself sufficient to assuage public resentment at having been duped. Finally, the complete absence of any US planning for post-war reconstruction exposed Blair to much criticism and resulted in an unremitting erosion of public support from the Labour government, its Prime Minister and his policy in Iraq.

Beyond its impact upon the Blair government's popularity, the Iraq War had a number of negative implications for British foreign policy as a whole. Many believed that it wrecked Britain's much proclaimed commitment to multilateralism, the UN and international law – not to mention any lingering recollections of an 'ethical dimension' to its foreign relations. It certainly split NATO to such an extent that the 'coalition of the willing' contained more former Warsaw Pact members than it did its Cold War members, and this divide was bitterly reinforced by Britain's repeated condemnation of NATO allies who failed to deploy combat troops in Afghanistan and Iraq. Britain's leading role in the war equally deeply divided the European Union and poisoned its relations with Germany and France to such a degree that for some time it had an adverse effect upon Britain's influence within the EU (see Chapter 5). The consequences were even more damaging in alienating the bulk of the Islamic world, while contrary to assurances that the invasion would increase the security of the Western democracies, a spate of attacks in May 2003 on Saudi Arabia, Morocco and Israel were followed by terrorist bombings in Madrid in March 2004 and London in July 2005. To make matters worse, Blair's astonishing reluctance to demand an appropriate 'payback' for his unwavering support allowed Bush to abandon his commitment to the Middle East 'peace roadmap' along with the creation of a viable Palestinian state and the need for Israeli withdrawal from Gaza (see p. 99).

The Iraq War tarnished Blair's crusade for 'liberal intervention' even more than it besmirched his personal reputation and political standing. Hollow US assurance that reconstruction had been adequately planned soon proved to be a disastrous deception. Four months after the invasion, the head of the FCO's Iraq policy unit described the country as 'a bloody mess' given the collapse of an infrastructure already severely weakened by 12 years of sanctions. Estimates vary considerably about the number of Iraqi civilian losses since the war ended in 2003. The Iraqi Body Count at the start of 2008 put the figure at an implausibly low 47,668. Conversely, the World Health Organization household survey suggested that as many as 151,000 had perished, while a BMA study published in the *Lancet* estimated as many as 601,027 civilian fatalities (*Guardian*, 10 January 2008). Whatever the true figure, beyond the shattered infrastructure and collapse into violence, the appalling human cost of the operation has undoubtedly dulled enthusiasm for any such future interventions.

Following elections to the Parliamentary National Assembly in December 2005, and a temporary improvement in the security situation, Britain handed over its responsibility for the security of Basra to Iraqi forces in December 2007. But, as the new Iraqi police commander protested, the province was still ravaged by lawlessness and violence, well-armed militias were better equipped than the security forces and the country's infrastructure was still in complete chaos. Even the 4000 British troops who remained in Iraq were effectively besieged by insurgents at their base at Basra airport. While Miliband acknowledged that it was 'not a land of milk and honey', he also insisted the time had come for withdrawal (*Guardian*, 17 December 2007). Only after the success of a major offensive in 2008 did the security situation improve sufficiently to allow the British deployment finally to come to an end in May 2009, leaving only 400 British troops behind to train the Iraqi security force. When assessed as a whole, opinion is inevitably polarised on the operation. Some follow Christoph Bluth in the pragmatic verdict that 'if the reconstruction of Iraq and the establishment of a stable democracy succeed, then the decisions of 2003 will be vindicated' (Bluth 2004: 892). For others, however it was an ignominious end to an arguably disastrous and ill-conceived engagement.

Gordon Brown and the 'Responsibility to Protect'

Britain's engagement in military operations in Afghanistan and Iraq has left a bitter legacy. In his Chicago speech, Blair declared that 'our actions are guided by a more subtle blend of mutual self-interest and moral purpose in defending the values we cherish. In the end, values and interests merge' (www.number10.gov.uk). The supposed blurring of the line between narrow national interest and internationalist values remained a consistent theme in Blair's discourse throughout his premiership, despite the disappointments of Afghanistan and Iraq. In contrast, his critics often argue the doctrine of 'liberal intervention' strayed too far from a clear-sighted pursuit of the national interest in its quixotic desire to spread the universal values of liberty, democracy, the rule of law, human rights and an open society. Burgeoning doubts about 'liberal intervention' thus prompted support for the concept of the 'Responsibility to Protect' (R2P) as an emerging legal norm capable of recasting and re-legitimising the interventionist project, by linking it far more closely to conflict prevention and a broader humanitarian agenda than that espoused by Blair – at least in his later years. This emerging doctrine was formulated by the International Commission on Intervention and State Sovereignty in 2001 to provide an international framework of protection for civilians facing mass atrocities. Endorsed by a UN summit in 2005, R2P imposes a threefold duty on member states to 'prevent', 'react' and 'rebuild' (Brown 2008).

Under Gordon Brown's leadership, Britain has actively participated in these efforts to recast the philosophy underpinning Blair's policy of 'liberal intervention', and this quest has produced significant changes in tone and emphasis. In his first major foreign policy speech at the Mansion House in November 2007, Brown acknowledged that there was 'still a gaping hole in our ability to address the illegitimate threats and use of force against innocent peoples', pointing to the 'shame of the whole world' at its failure to prevent genocide in Rwanda. 'We now rightly recognized our responsibility to protect behind borders where there are crimes against humanity.' But while he spoke of the need for a more 'hard-headed intervention', he also placed the priority on the 'reform of our international rules and institutions' and the need for a new framework to assist reconstruction, peacekeeping, stabilisation and development; a form of words which suggests a greater focus upon pragmatism and non-military action within a clearly defined overarching framework of international rules quite different from Tony Blair's uneasy admixture of idealism about universal values allied to 'hard power', military intervention and the pursuit of regime change (Brown 2008).

Brown has certainly been far more concerned with conflict prevention, resolution and reconstruction than his predecessor, and this has been a central theme of his rhetoric since January 2008, when he first launched a plan for a \$200 million (£102 million) UN crisis prevention and recovery fund to enable it to place judges, police and key civilian experts in global trouble-spots on the grounds that 'there is limited value in military action to end fighting if law and order does not follow'; a coded criticism of Blair, reflecting lessons learned the hard way in Afghanistan and Iraq and applied more successful, in the Congo which did benefit from immediate help with reconstruction (*Guardian*, 21 January 2008). Similar themes have emerged from his subsequent utterances on Afghanistan, Iraq, and the need for an 'economic roadmap for reconstruction' in the Occupied Palestinian Territories. These priorities were enshrined in Brown's National Security Strategy unveiled in March 2008, and given further substance in July 2009 when the new DfID White Paper pledged another £1 billion for aid to countries emerging from conflict (Cm 7656 2009).

This is not to deny Brown's willingness to deploy troops in limited operations, nor to denigrate his notable success in August 2007 when persuading the Bush administration to support a UN Security Council resolution to deploy an international force of 26,000 to the Darfur region of Sudan after 2 million had been displaced and 200,000 killed by government-supported militia (*Guardian*, 1 August 2007). But, in contrast to his enthusiasm for the goals of 'prevention' and 'reconstruction', he has shown little appetite for any new large-scale military intervention in humanitarian crises and has studiously ignored the French foreign minister's proposal to invoke R2P to justify UN intervention in Burma in the wake of Cyclone Nargis in May 2008, on the grounds that the military junta's incompetence and increased repression amounted to a crime against humanity (Brown 2008).

The 'ethical dimension' in retrospect

Neither Robin Cook nor Tony Blair ever promised to deliver 'an ethical foreign policy', and to judge it against that benchmark is unreasonable. Nevertheless, in his speech launching the FCO Mission Statement, Cook declared that it did represent 'the Labour government's contract with the British people on foreign policy' and that these were 'strategic aims ... by which we can measure its success over a full, five-year, Parliament' (www.guardian.co.uk). A decade later, Tony Blair left office still convinced that liberal interventionism represented the essence of his foreign policy (Garton Ash 2007: 633). When an assessment of New Labour's policy is made, however, even at its most charitable, the record can only be described as mixed at best – and at worst it is inconsistent, hypocritical and characterised by precisely the same realpolitik pragmatism as its predecessors. This is certainly true in the case of arms sales, which the Select Committee on International Development identified during the 1998/99 session as 'a litmus test of this government's concern to prevent conflict and inject an ethical dimension into foreign policy' (Lawler 2000: 292). As Neil Cooper concludes, when 'judged only on its own language, Labour's arms sales policy is less ethical than its own policy in the 1980s, less ethical than that of a number of other states, less ethical than the EU code and little different from the ethically challenged approach of its Conservative predecessors' (Cooper 2000: 163). Much the same verdict could be delivered on the defence of human rights, while Britain's engagement in Iraq and Afghanistan appears to have fundamentally undermined Blair's rationale for 'liberal intervention'. Only perhaps in the field of international development, and to a lesser extent climate change, has the record since 1997 represented a qualified success.

The passage of time and the realities of international diplomacy increasingly eroded the credibility of Cook's commitment to an 'ethical dimension'. In 1998, Nicholas Wheeler and Tim Dunne concluded that the 'ethical dimension' really did possess some relevance for an understanding of the 'marked shift' in Labour foreign policy. Two years later, they delivered a much less positive assessment when commenting on the 'growing discrepancy between the moral rhetoric of the Blair government and its subsequent practices' (Wheeler and Dunne 1998: 848–9; Wickham-Jones 2000a: 22). In retrospect, perhaps the venture was fatally flawed from the outset by the government's failure to think the project through sufficiently clearly to construct a conceptual framework capable of deciding the relative priority and consistency of the various principles contained within the Mission Statement. For a radical realist school the indictment goes much further, in so far as New Labour's ostensibly principled idealist rhetoric is dismissed simply as a smokescreen behind which lurked the realpolitik primacy of Britain's long-standing relationship with the United States. As Carne Ross, a senior British diplomat at the UN who resigned over the war in Iraq, later recalled, 'I question whether "values" have not simply become a more palatable and politically correct excuse for realist "business as usual".' When viewed from this perspective, Britain's military engagement in Afghanistan and Iraq is explained largely by a desire to respond to the ideological threat of militant Islam and the increasingly urgent need to secure control over Middle East oil reserves. As such, it is argued the concept of 'humanitarian intervention' is more accurately described as the latest incarnation of old-fashioned imperialism designed to provide 'a legitimate means of imposing western liberal values on those who violated democracy' (Lunn, Miller and Swift 2008: 15–16; Kampfner 1999: 253).

Whatever the motivations for its adoption and the reasons for its failure, Robin Cook's commitment to an 'ethical dimension' proved to be a temporary aberration which enjoyed only a short life as New Labour's 'most favoured soundbite' (Williams 2004: 921). As the Foreign Affairs Committee noted in December 1998, in some quarters there was always much scepticism about the public acknowledgement of an 'ethical dimension' on the grounds that it was either undesirable because foreign policy was always driven by narrowly defined national interest or it was impossible to achieve in practical and consistent terms (Select Committee on Foreign Affairs, HC 100-I, December 1998: para. 5). The Mandarins at the FCO were certainly believed to be unhappy about the entire concept from the outset, prompting the *Economist* to record that throughout the launch ceremony for the new Mission Statement in 1997, Sir John Coles, the Permanent Under-Secretary, 'looked like a man who had shown up for his customary lunch at the Athenaeum Club to find that it had been converted overnight into a heavy-leather-and-chains gay bar'. According to his memoirs, this was a complete misapprehension because 'the general reaction of the Foreign Office, me included, was to welcome so clear a statement of objectives at the outset of the new government' (Coles 2000: 191). But the perception was widespread and it persisted (Jenkins and Sloman 1985: 103–5).

Whatever the truth of the matter, the commitment to an 'ethical dimension' was quietly abandoned. As Foreign Secretary, Jack Straw published two White Papers enunciating the FCO's international priorities and David Miliband launched his own strategy paper entitled *Better World, Better Britain* in April 2008 (see Chapter 9). The content and tone of this blandly brief statement appear to reflect a disillusionment with inflated expectations and a desire to build Britain's external policy on solidly tangible foundations devoid of high-flown language and worthy but unattainable goals. Significantly, 'support for the British economy' was listed as the first of the 'three essential services' provided by the FCO while among the 'policy goals' counter-terrorism, weapons proliferation, conflict prevention and a sustainable environment each appear but human rights and control over arms exports are conspicuous by their absence (www.fco.gov.uk). In the end, therefore, in foreign and defence policy, as in so many areas of domestic strategy, it appears that New Labour has been long on rhetoric and short on the delivery.

Chapter 9

Making Foreign and Defence Policy in a Changing World

The complexity of the foreign policy process in Britain

Over 20 years ago, a distinguished authority on British external policy argued that 'none of the major books that have been written on the policy process over the last 25 years are actually out of date' because 'to characterise the process accurately, we should recognize that British foreign policy-making is a combination of unchanging realities and evolutionary developments in response to certain demands and pressures' (Clarke 1988: 72). There is still much truth in this judgement, as demonstrated by the continued validity of works written 45 years ago, such as Donald Watt's classic discussion of the 'foreign policy-making elite' in Britain and David Vital's distinction between the elite 'central core' operating largely unconstrained by a wider public and the 'surrounding mantle' of ministries sporadically involved in foreign policy (Watt 1965: 1; Vital 1968: 49–50). Yet, in parallel with the evidence of continuity on the fundamentals, powerful forces have precipitated significant changes in nuance, interaction and relationships within a once-established institutional framework. For example, Sir John Coles, the Permanent Under-Secretary at the FCO until 1997, argues the policy process is

> often both complex and messy because the nature of foreign policy today is more complex than it was, because the pace of international events is quicker and the need for response more urgent, because the quantity and diversity of information available to policy makers have greatly increased and because the process is operated by people. (Coles 2000: 83–4)

Other former members of the Diplomatic Service echo these concerns about the 'multilateralisation' of international relations, the 'shorter reaction time and faster turnover for diplomatic decisions' and the increasing volume of work which makes the supposedly heavy burdens of 30 years ago appear 'amazingly relaxed by today's standard' (Bailes 2007: 191, 195).

In understanding the nature and impact of these changes, systemic theory has much to offer by emphasising the influence of the international system in shaping foreign policy and the parameters within which it is formulated. While bilateral relations still remained the norm in the mid-1950s, even then professional diplomats talked anxiously about the accelerating trend towards interdependence and multilateral engagement (Strang 1955: 197). Such was the pace of change that within two decades Britain was paying a subscription to no fewer than 126 international organisations and today it belongs to more international organisations than any other country except France. Britain's international economic policy is strongly influenced by its membership of the EU, WTO, UN, G8, OECD, IMF, the Paris Group and a whole host of other organisations. A similar position exists with regard to defence. To take just one example, by the late 1980s Britain was involved in at least six different overlapping institutions concerned with European defence cooperation alone, and this figure has increased as the EU develops its own foreign, defence and security architecture. Beyond these formal organisational connections, diplomatic understandings and alliances inevitably strongly influence policy – most notably, Britain's ties with the United States, NATO and the EU. In addition, as one of the world's largest economies and a major trading nation, the needs of the export industry play a major role in shaping priorities because (until 9/11 at least) 'the criterion of successful foreign policy [wa]s not physical security but material prosperity' (Martin and Garnett 1997: 3). As discussed in Chapter 8, the al-Yamamah arms deal with Saudi Arabia and BP's investment in Libya demonstrate the degree to which trade and business can influence British policy, just as the FCO's responsibility for promoting British exports has directly influenced attitudes towards states like China even when this conflicts with its own published objectives.

When approached from the perspective of societal and state-centric theory, where the focus is on the influence of domestic politics, society and culture, the policy process has reflected the same combination of continuity and change in recent years. For example, Michael Clarke's verdict that the 'most obvious and unchanging reality' of foreign policymaking in Britain is 'the fact of executive dominance in the foreign policy process' is as true today as it was in 1988 – perhaps even more so. On the other hand, however, Clarke's 'second unchanging reality of foreign policy-making', concerning the manner in which the Cabinet system operates and the ascendancy of the FCO as one of the most senior departments in Whitehall, appears curiously outdated given recent developments (Clarke 1988: 72–3). Today, the position is far more complex given a broader range of governmental and non-governmental policy actors engaged in complex interaction within a more fragmented and 'compartmentalised' policy environment, in which a diverse range of pressures are brought to bear on the formulation, implementation and presentation of external policy.

Arguably, there has never been a clear separation of overseas and domestic policy, if only because the former has always been dependent on economic capacity, but the two are now more closely interwoven than ever before – with the result that the FCO has increasingly lost its monopoly over the conduct of diplomacy as international relations have become more complex and more commercial, requiring different abilities from those possessed by the classic British diplomat. Even in the late 1980s, in one way or another, external relations involved at least 10 different spending ministries plus numerous subordinate agencies and it accounted for 23.9 per cent of all central government expenditure (Clarke 1988: 82). Today the list is even longer. Above all, in the European arena virtually every government department plays a role because almost every problem facing modern government has a European dimension. Under Blair, this led to a 'quiet revolution' in Whitehall as every department began 'mainstreaming' EU affairs with the objective, *inter alia*, of improving bilateral relations with other member states (Bulmer and Burch 2006: 37). In practice, the hub of contemporary European policymaking consists of the Prime Minister's Office, the European Secretariat within the Cabinet Office, the FCO and the UK Permanent Representative to the EU (UKREP). In acknowledgement of the EU's increasing importance, in 2003 the FCO belatedly created the post of Director-General Europe with a seat on the new Foreign Office Board but the proliferation of ministries and agencies dealing directly with the EU through their own specialist European sections has continued to the substantial detriment of the FCO's status and influence within Whitehall. Today, more than half the civil servants working in the Brussels offices of UKREP come from departments other than the Foreign Office (Blair 2002: 78; Dickie 2004: 122).

When foreign policy is conceptualised beyond the narrow confines of formal diplomatic relations and security to encompass a more broad-ranging interrelationship between domestic and external policy in areas as diverse as trade, monetary management, the environment, agriculture, safety regulation and human rights, the number of policy actors has increased even more dramatically in recent years. Among the more remarkable developments has been the increasing incorporation of NGOs and pressure groups into the external policy process, particularly since the arrival of a Labour government in 1997. Among the more successful 'insider groups' today, are Oxfam and the leading aid and development charities with whom both the FCO and DfID have established close relations in pursuit of shared objectives in sub-Saharan Africa and among HIPCs. Similarly, the coalition of NGOs brought together in the International Campaign to Ban Landmines proved useful in achieving government goals at the Ottawa conference and in passing the legislation before the target date of March 1999. It is a measure of this new influence that Robin Cook recruited policy advisers from Amnesty International and Save the Children Fund. He also soon introduced a series of working breakfasts with representatives of the more respectable NGOs, while his successor made it clear to leading groups that his door would always be open to them. Today, such groups are more regularly consulted by ministers over issues such as human rights, climate change and world poverty than ever before.

Beyond the realm of NGOs, some major 'think-tanks', like the Royal United Services Institute (RUSI), Chatham House (the Royal Institute of International Affairs), the International Institute of Strategic Studies (IISS) and the Foreign Policy Centre (created by Robin Cook in 1998), play a part in shaping the intellectual environment within which policy is made, particularly through authoritative publications like the IISS's annual assessment of *The Military Balance* and journals like *International Affairs*. Again, the degree to which such bodies directly influence policy is open to question, but some clearly do, as witnessed by the role of Professor Michael Clarke's International Policy Institute at King's College, London (established 1990) which supplies the MoD, FCO and DfID with expert analysis and risk assessments on security issues (Dickie 2004: 1986). On the other hand, however, the deeply rooted FCO culture of treating policymaking as an insular activity has, traditionally, tended to exclude NGOs and think-tanks from the inner workings of the decision-making process for fear that their active involvement 'may make the policy process less controllable' (Coles 2000: 155).

Media influence is also often exaggerated, but it does play some role in shaping foreign policy – not least through the manner in which it presents world crises and diplomatic issues to the electorate, particularly when screening emotive television pictures of civil wars, famines and disasters. As Foreign Secretary Douglas Hurd put it in January 1993: 'Like it or not, television images are what forces foreign policy-makers to give one of the current 25 crises in the world greater priority' (Dickie 2004: 213). At a more routine level, the media can be influential in shaping the background context within which citizens interpret international news. For example, the remorseless Euro-scepticism of the tabloid press has imposed significant constraints upon the government's freedom of manoeuvre in Anglo–EU relations since the late 1960s given its conspicuous reluctance to either educate the British electorate about the benefits of membership or to confront media hostility (see Chapter 5). For all the subtle changes which have marginally opened up the foreign policy process over the past half-century, however, the fundamental fact remains that this is essentially a closed arena dominated by a narrow core executive consisting of Prime Minister, Foreign Secretary, Chancellor of the Exchequer and Defence Minister. Around them a second concentric circle contains the other directly interested government departments like DfID, Business and Energy, the intelligence services, the Chief of the Defence Staff and his Service Chiefs. Beyond these official participants lies an outer concentric circle in which various pressure groups, lobbies, think-tanks and the media vie for attention as they seek to influence policy outcomes.

Executive dominance in the formulation of foreign policy

The formal constitutional responsibility for conducting British foreign policy rests with the Secretary of State for Foreign Affairs, but in practice it is a responsibility shared with the Prime Minister and this can create tensions – as demonstrated by the strained relations between Eden and Macmillan (1955), Wilson and George Brown (1966–68) and Thatcher and both Francis Pym (1982–83) and Geoffrey Howe (1983–89). The degree to which Prime Ministers interest themselves directly in the management of foreign affairs has varied considerably. Attlee allowed Bevin considerable autonomy on the grounds that 'You don't keep a dog and bark yourself – and Ernie was a very good dog' (Bullock 1983: 75). Wilson trusted Callaghan and left him alone to conduct policy between 1974 and 1976, and John Major adopted a far lighter touch than his predecessor because of a more collegial leadership style and a close personal relationship with his Foreign Secretary, although like Attlee and Wilson he still actively involved himself in foreign policy where necessary. With these limited exceptions, however, most Prime Ministers have been deeply immersed in external relations since Lloyd George was first accused of subverting the traditional role of the Foreign Office between 1916 and 1922. Indeed, Eden, Macmillan, Home and Callaghan had all been Foreign Secretary before becoming Prime Minister, Heath had been a Foreign Office Minister, Wilson was Labour's Opposition front-bench spokesman on the subject, and even John Major had spent three uncomfortable months at the Foreign Office.

In recent years, Prime Ministers have tended to intervene without any great experience in foreign affairs. Thatcher knew little about the subject and apparently cared less before she became Prime Minister (Clark 1993: 219). Nevertheless, while she briefly deferred to the superior experience of her first much-respected Foreign Secretary, Lord Carrington, after his resignation in 1982 she became increasingly assertive when dealing with Francis Pym's open defiance of her policy directives, while her relationship with Geoffrey Howe rapidly deteriorated over the European question and he ended his tenure at the FCO as 'little more than her bag carrier, entrusted with the tiresome detail of diplomacy' (J. Campbell 2008: 254). In order to strengthen her direct personal control, Thatcher brought in Charles Powell as her omnipresent special adviser and general 'fixer' and he eventually emerged as 'effectively her real Foreign Secretary' (J. Campbell 2008: 601). Although Thatcher was not attracted by the idea of a Prime Minister's Department as an alternative institutional source of foreign policy along the lines of the National Security Council in Washington, Powell was supported by specialist advisers like Sir Anthony Parsons and Sir Percy Cradock. In addition, trusted friends like Cecil Parkinson, Nicholas Ridley and Lord Hugh Thomas provided an ideologically aligned source of advice on foreign policy in much the same way as Sir Alan Walters supplied her with economic advice to counter the mistrusted official opinion at the Treasury.

Blair built enthusiastically on the foundations laid by Thatcher. He had equally little experience or obvious interest in foreign affairs before becoming Prime Minister, but Kosovo created a self-belief which soon encouraged his complete domination of foreign affairs to the detriment of the FCO and the Cabinet as a whole. From the outset, Blair talked approvingly of a 'command and control' model of government and this soon provoked allegations that he was a 'control freak' exercising 'powers that would make Stalin blush' as he turned the Cabinet into a rubber stamp for quasi-presidential ambitions (Allen 2003). The replacement of Robin Cook at the FCO by the internationally inexperienced Jack Straw, and his subsequent appointment of a political lightweight like Margaret Beckett to the FCO in May 2006 (to the department's frustration and fury) provided another clear indication of Blair's ambition to dominate foreign policy unconstrained by an assertive or knowledgeable Foreign Secretary.

To achieve this goal, Blair seconded two top diplomats, Sir David Manning and Sir Stephen Wall, each with his own staff, to advise him personally on policy, while 'sound' men were appointed to key positions abroad. Like Thatcher, Blair preferred to work through small ad hoc groups composed of trusted officials, ministers and advisers rather than with the Cabinet as a whole. Known as the 'denocracy' because it met in Blair's 'den' at Downing Street, these informal groupings of senior ministers and confidants formed the nucleus of the foreign policymaking process throughout the Blair premiership (Seldon 2005: 692). For the sake of appearances, small ministerial War Cabinets were established to coordinate military operations but the real strategic decision-making core consisted of his relevant special advisers, the Foreign, Defence and Cabinet Secretaries, the heads of the JIC, MI6 and MI5 and the Chief of the Defence Staff (Seldon 2005: 499, 580). As Clare Short later put it, 'decision-making was sucked out of the Foreign Office' as the power increasingly came to reside in a 'small unelected entourage' of advisers like Powell, Campbell and Manning (*Guardian*, 18 June 2003; Sampson, 2004, 144).

While this concentration of control accelerated the speed of decision-making and shortened the lines of communication, as the Butler Report on the intelligence failures associated with the Iraq War suggests, the informality of these meetings without proper minutes circulated to the broader Cabinet precluded any opportunity for informed collective decision and judgement, while briefing papers carefully prepared by officials were too often ignored. Ministers were thus not unnaturally concerned about the excessively 'informal nature of the government's decision-making process', which 'concentrated detailed knowledge and effective decision-making in fewer minds at the top' while depriving the rest of the Cabinet of both information and the opportunity for influence (Butler 2004: paras 606–11). In this respect, the UK's decision to invade Iraq in 2003 provides an outstanding example of the manner in which prime ministerial manipulation of prerogatives, electoral popularity and information enabled him to 'structure the choices faced by the effective veto players – the Commons, the Parliamentary Labour Party and the Cabinet – so that Blair's preferred option was seen as preferable' (O'Malley 2007: 10). Although Iraq was apparently raised at 28 Cabinet meetings in the eight months leading up to intervention on 22 May 2003, therefore, challenges to Blair's policy were rendered nugatory by skilful Prime Ministerial manoeuvres which effectively stifled any genuine debate about the invasion until it was too late (Cook 2003: 135–6; Short 2005: 149–51, 180–8). 'Things were not decided properly,' Clare Short subsequently protested, 'no records, and no papers, in the Prime Minister's study – all informal with a small group of people' while the Cabinet received nothing but 'mere updates' (*Guardian*, 18 June 2003). Indeed, according to David Blunkett, ministers received so little information from Cabinet meetings that Gordon Brown questioned the value of his attendance at all because he learned more from the media (Blunkett 2006).

While bitter wrangling over Britain's participation in the invasion of Iraq in 2003 highlights the reality of prime ministerial ascendancy, this was by no means unprecedented. On the contrary, many key foreign and defence policy decisions since the Second World War have been made without Cabinet approval – or (at times) without even their knowledge. The Attlee government's initial decision to launch an independent nuclear weapons programme and its agreement to provide airbases for US nuclear forces in Britain both fall into this latter category. Among other outstanding examples are Eden's ill-fated conspiracy to engage in military action over Suez, Wilson's deal with the Johnson administration to support sterling in return for a presence East of Suez, the Callaghan government's decision to upgrade Polaris and conduct secret underground nuclear tests in 1977 and Thatcher's agreement to purchase Trident, to prohibit trade union membership at GCHQ and to allow US planes to attack Libya from British bases. When viewed against this background, Blair's highly personal role in the decisions leading up to the Iraq War merely highlights the long-term divergence between the Cabinet's theoretical position at the apex of the executive decision-making structure and the practical reality which suggests that it plays an increasingly marginal role in such deliberations even at a strategic level.

While the modern Prime Minister enjoys a number of positional advantages with regard to foreign affairs, the case should not be exaggerated. Today, arguments about 'Prime Ministerial government' and a British 'presidency' are generally dismissed as excessively simplistic in that they misleadingly focus on the theoretical sources of power while understating the practical constraints upon the exercise of those powers. Yet, while leadership styles differ, for a variety of reasons, over the past few decades the Prime Minister has increasingly been compelled to act as the principal representative and final arbiter of foreign policy by virtue of their position as head of government. Firstly, the growth in summitry has inevitably focused attention on heads of government meeting to resolve urgent or pressing problems. In addition, the EU necessitates twice-yearly meetings of the European Council and various intergovernmental conferences, while membership of a whole host of other international organisations implies similar obligations with regard to G8, NATO, WTO and the Commonwealth. Beyond these high-profile jamborees, routine bilateral meetings with visiting foreign leaders and overseas trips occupy much of the Prime Minister's time. Even in the 1970s, Harold Wilson estimated that he had an average of one heads of government meeting every seven weeks and three or four meetings with foreign dignitaries each week – and they all involved a detailed briefing, often in several parts. These demands have increased exponentially as modern diplomacy continues to expand beyond traditional great power relations to encompass a far broader range of activities from trade and economic cooperation through defence and security to aid, cultural relations and environmental concerns (Wilson 1976: 120–1).

A second factor which has propelled the Prime Minister to the forefront in international affairs, relates to the media's need to present complex issues and stories in accessible terms; a problem partially overcome through an increasing 'personalisation' of politics in which the status of the Prime Minister becomes magnified into the physical embodiment of Britain's policy position. Thirdly, for domestic political reasons Prime Ministers invariably welcome this opportunity to stride the world stage as international statesmen in order to differentiate themselves in the electoral mind from Opposition leaders, who are mere party politicians. At a personal level, they also often relish the glamour and adulation of such meetings when shrouded in an appropriate aura of dignity and prestige. Finally, summit meetings between heads of government often produce constructive results – as demonstrated by their success in breaking through the impasse in EC–EU relations at the Copenhagen meeting in 1982, Fontainebleau in 1984, Luxembourg in 1985 and Madrid in 1989. For all these reasons, therefore, Harold Macmillan was correct when he told the Commons half a century ago that Prime Ministerial involvement in foreign affairs 'is no longer a matter of choice but a matter of fact' (James 1992: 138).

In sharp contrast to the dominance of the Prime Ministerial axis with the Foreign and Defence Secretary, as Simon James points out, 'other ministers do not get much of a look-in on foreign affairs' (James 1992: 141). Under Margaret Thatcher's leadership, the strengthening of the policy advice at No 10 was paralleled by a substantial diminution in the opportunities for collective deliberation and influence through a systematic reduction in the number of Cabinet meetings, ad hoc Cabinet Committees and Cabinet papers issued for information to ministers. After 1997, Blair's reform of Cabinet procedure along lines established by Thatcher deprived it of much of what little influence it still possessed. More important, during weekly Cabinet meetings which occasionally lasted as little as 45 minutes, the traditional agenda of pressing issues was replaced by a number of increasingly perfunctory presentations offering ministers a tour d'horizon updating them on a few major lines of policy and firefighting measures. At the same time, the influence of special policy advisers operating within Downing Street increased dramatically as did their numbers – from 38 in 1997 to 74 by July 2000 – by which time Blair had established a 'Prime Minister's Department' in all but name, at the direct expense of the traditionally expert role of the FCO.

The rise of the Downing Street special adviser has had important implications for the locus of decision-making in the policy process. The longer Charles Powell remained in post, the more his personal Euro-scepticism brought out the worst of Thatcher's anti-German, anti-Community prejudices and his perceived indispensability enabled him to compose her highly controversial Bruges speech without FCO input. Similarly, Blair's Chicago speech in 1999 was drafted by his own foreign policy advisers without consulting the FCO and the final result came as an unpleasant shock to its senior legal advisers (Hill 2001: 344). Blair's appointment of his personal friend Lord Levy also gravely alarmed FCO Arabists, who suspected this influential envoy saw the Middle East problem too much through Israeli eyes and was far too fond of promoting their interests. Under such influences, it is perhaps not surprising that Blair ignored both Foreign Office advice and the fury of his own parliamentary party when he joined Bush in lending his personally disastrous support to the Israeli invasion of Lebanon in 2006.

Declining collective Cabinet influence has been paralleled by the diminishing role of the once important Defence and Overseas Policy Committee (DOPC), formed from the merger of the separate Defence and Foreign Affairs Committees in 1963. Although initially the principal Cabinet forum for considering these issues at a detailed level, by the end of the century it met infrequently, was dominated by the Prime Minister, Chancellor, Foreign and Defence Secretary and was so heavily overloaded with business that it had ceased to fulfil a useful policy function. To remedy this situation and improve efficiency, on 23 July 2007 Gordon Brown announced a 'strengthening' of the Cabinet Committee system designed to reduced the number of committees while creating more cross-cutting bodies 'recast . . . to focus on the government's priorities'. Within this structure the DOPC was replaced with a new National Security, International Relations and Development Committee (NSID), fulfilling similar functions but with a far wider range of more relevant new subcommittees. The new structure also contains a ministerial Committee on Security and Intelligence (CSI) which operates in parallel with the Joint Intelligence Committee (see Tables 9.1 and 9.4). As in the previous structure, where the DOPC delegated most European decisions to the ministerial subcommittee on European affairs (E)DOP under the chairmanship of the Foreign Secretary, detailed decisions on European affairs now occur in the reconstituted NSID(EU).

Who makes British defence policy?

The Ministry of Defence is a relatively recent creation in British administrative history. The idea of a unified defence administration was first

Table 9.1   Cabinet Secretariats and Cabinet Committees on foreign and defence policy, 2009

Cabinet Secretariat. Three of the seven secretariats are currently related to external policy. These are:

- European and Global Issues Secretariat
- Foreign and Defence Policy Secretariat: 'to support the Prime Minister and Cabinet in driving the coherence, quality and development of foreign and defence policy across departments'
- China Task Force: created November 2003 'to deepen relations, foster mutual understanding, and further co-operation between the UK and China'.

Ministerial Committees of the Cabinet (since July 2007).
National Security, International Relations and Development Committee (NSID). Its terms of reference require it 'to consider issues relating to national security and the government's international, European and international development policies'. This is serviced by a number of subcommittees:

- NSID (EU) European Affairs.
- NSID (NS) National Security.
- NSID (OD) Overseas and Defence (with subcommittees).

Sub-committees of the Overseas and Defence Sub-Committee of the NSID:
- NSID(OD)(A) Africa
- NSID (OD)(T) Trade
- NSID (OD)(PSR) Protective Security and Resilience.
- NSID (OD)(E) Tackling Extremism.

Ministerial Committee on Security and Intelligence (CSI) exists 'to review policy on security and the intelligence services'.

Sources: www.number10.gov.uk/page12595; Cabinet Office, *A List of Cabinet Committees* and *A Guide to Cabinet and Cabinet Committee Business*, November 2008, www.cabinetoffice.gov.uk.

proposed formally in 1890, but inter-Service rivalry and a lack of political will prevented action until Churchill combined the posts of Prime Minister and Minister of Defence in 1940 (Philpott 1996). The chief weakness in the early post-war structure was the inability of ministers to impose coherence on the three separate Service ministries and this lack of authority was exacerbated by the fact that between 1951 and 1964 there were no fewer than nine Conservative Ministers of Defence. In July 1963, however, the Conservative government announced its intention to create a unified Ministry of Defence able 'to strike a correct balance between commitments, resources and the roles of the Services' (Darby 1973: 39). On this basis, the War Office, Air Ministry, Admiralty and Ministry of Aviation were amalgamated into a massively more powerful and centralised Ministry of Defence in 1964 under a single Secretary of State authorised to decide 'all major matters of defence policy affecting the size, shape, organisation and disposition of the Armed Forces and their weapons'. Fortuitously, Denis Healey's long period at the MoD between 1964 and 1970 enabled him to consolidate these reforms and to subordinate the Services to civilian control (Bartlett 1972: 131–2).

Although the modern MoD came into existence in 1964, it changed out of all recognition during the next half-century. As Denis Healey recalled:

> When I took over [in 1964], I became directly responsible for 458,000 servicemen and women and 406,000 civil servants, scattered all over the world from Washington to Oslo, from Malta to Hong Kong. In the sixties the government owned the military nuclear installations, the naval dockyards, and the ordnance factories ... The manpower working on these defence contracts were probably another million. No other minister had management problems on this scale (Healey 1989: 255).

In stark contrast, by April 2008 Britain's trained military strength had been reduced to a meagre 179,300 and its civilian staff accounted for only 92,500 (Cm 7098, 2008: 23; MoD HC 850, 2008: 12). Moreover, its Atomic Weapons Establishments had been privatised along with its naval dockyards, ordnance factories and the Ministry's defence research arm, while many other civilian functions were 'hived off' to separate agencies as part of the Thatcher government's sweeping public sector reforms. John Nott shifted the balance of influence still further in favour of civilian officials at the expense of his military advisers, while Michael Heseltine produced an even more seismic shift in power. Heseltine had been appointed to impose greater coherence on management structures and more discipline upon budgetary processes within a sprawling ministry riven with inter-Service competition. In March 1984, his radical reorganisation of the MoD abolished the separate junior ministers for each Service, while depriving the three Service Chiefs of their right to attend the DOPC. This was, henceforth, to be addressed only by the Chief of the Defence Staff, who was elevated to the position of principal military adviser with the authority to submit an independent point of view rather than serving merely as spokesman for the other services (A. Smith 1996: 265–8).

The policy community which surrounds the MoD has traditionally been the preserve of a far smaller number of 'insider' policy actors than those revolving around the FCO, and they operate within a closed and highly secretive policy arena surrounded by high barriers to entry. Like foreign affairs, most post-war Prime Ministers have shared Anthony Eden's belief that 'Defence is very much a Prime Minister's special subject' (Wallace 1975: 124). For this reason, the core of the defence policy community centres upon the axis between Prime Minister and the Secretary of State for Defence. Beyond this necessarily close relationship, the principal actors are the Foreign Secretary and the Chancellor who controls the budgetary purse-strings through the CSR process. As discussed in Chapter 7, this narrow ministerial grouping has traditionally dominated nuclear weapons policy and although Churchill initially consulted the Cabinet on the issue, it was 'the first and last time that a British Cabinet was allowed to take the decision on a new generation of nuclear weapon' and he did not repeat the experiment when resolving to build a hydrogen bomb (Hennessy 1986: 135). Indeed, all Prime Ministers except Churchill, Macmillan and Blair have imposed a strict prohibition on any Cabinet discussion of nuclear weapons. On non-nuclear defence policy, Cabinet debate is more frequent, but even here the outcome is invariably heavily influenced by the conclusions of the DOPC and the dominant ministerial axis.

Beyond this narrow ministerial conclave, supported by their special policy advisers and the Chief of the Defence Staff, defence is a policy community most notable for the influence of powerful vested interests. Perhaps the most obvious interest group in this respect are the armed forces themselves, whose professional expertise has traditionally conferred considerable authority upon their views when negotiating with government – albeit perhaps a declining asset given the recent spate of outspoken public criticism of government policy from the Chief of the Defence Staff and the Chief of the General Staff. Even more importantly, the defence contractors represent a classic example of the privileged 'insider' interest able to exert massive influence over its client department. Little has changed since 1964, when William Snyder's classic study of defence policymaking concluded that the 'industry's influence on defence policies is widespread' and so pervasive that it was 'virtually impossible to detail with any precision' (Snyder 1964: 102). The MoD currently spends 95 per cent of its equipment budget with British firms, supporting some 700,000 jobs in the UK, and the ministry's procurement arm absorbs 45 per cent of the UK's aerospace output and 20 per cent of its electronics production (Hennessy 1990: 415). It also runs its own Defence Industrial Strategy (DIS) to support Britain's 'defence industrial structure' in the belief that the country must retain the capability to meet its own defence needs. To this end, in 2005 the MoD adopted a 'Through Life Capability Management' strategy under which the same contractor builds, repairs and upgrades weapons systems throughout their operational life to ensure continuity of work (Cm 6697, 2005: 90–4). It has also been extremely active in promoting mergers to spread the available defence contracts among fewer but larger and more profitable companies. In 2007, the order for two new aircraft carriers was tied to such a deal, while BAe Systems and the VT Group created an MoD-sponsored joint-venture to supply fleet support services to the Royal Navy (*Guardian*, 27 March 2007).

Although the idea of a military-industrial complex has less relevance to Britain than the United States, the closed and highly secretive nature of the defence policy community has aroused some concern – not least because 'insiders' like the Services, defence contractors and trade bodies, like the Defence Manufacturers Association and the Defence Industries Council, have a greater mutual interest in the maintenance of the policy community's stability than in necessarily resolving funda- mental problems if this were likely to engender internal disruption and conflict. For this reason, the Defence Select Committee has consistently warned about the dangerously close – even 'incestuous' – relationship between MoD officials and defence suppliers; allegations regularly fuelled by revelations about the industry's privileged access to MoD buildings and senior officials, and the 'revolving door' which enables MoD officials to take up posts in the defence industries (and vice versa). For example, the first head of DESO was recruited from BAe, while one of the company's principal lobbyists was formerly private secretary to Alan Clark, the Defence Procurement Minister (1989–92). The Defence Select Committee has equally regularly suggested that the MoD's intimate connection with a small number of contractors has impeded its willingness to tackle the dismal catalogue of time-into-ser- vice delays, cost overruns and poor management which has afflicted defence procurement over many years (see Chapter 6).

Outside the magic circle: who is excluded from the policy process?

Almost as important as knowing who is involved in the policy process, is an understanding of who is excluded from it within a democratic system. One key institution which has a severely circumscribed role is the British Parliament because it has traditionally lacked information and has been constrained by official secrecy, strict parliamentary disci- pline and a fundamental lack of interest among the vast majority of

MPs. During an international crisis, MPs do occasionally get the opportunity to influence policy by expressing the national mood – as, for
example, the dramatic debate over the Falklands invasion (the first
Saturday session since the Second World War), over 'ethnic cleansing'
in the Balkans and the plight of the Kurds in northern Iraq. Given the
marked decline in back-bench discipline since 1972, government MPs
also have the power to withhold their votes from policies of which they
disapprove – but even here parliamentary rebellions are of limited effectiveness when confronting a determined executive, as demonstrated by
Blair's support for the war in Iraq despite facing the largest parliamentary rebellion since the repeal of the Corn Laws in the 1840s, and he
was no more constrained by Labour back-bench opposition when
obstructing international calls for a ceasefire after the Israeli invasion of
Lebanon in 2006. Although ostensibly the House of Commons Register
of All-Party Groups suggests there is no shortage of interest in overseas
affairs (with no fewer than 149 country and 58 subject groups devoted
to these issues), such groups generally have very little influence.
Moreover, notwithstanding the extraordinary influence of the back-
bench Falkland Islands Committee and a few others, the reality is that
government has equally little to fear from the vast majority of these
bodies. Indeed, according to one authoritative estimate, only around 5
per cent of MPs are actually interested in foreign affairs and even fewer
express an interest in defence policy (Clarke 1992: 118–20).

While MPs exercise very little influence on the floor of the House of
Commons, in the specialist departmental Select Committees established
in June 1979 they have been increasingly active in scrutinising the conduct of external policy and the objectives behind it, and with the benefit
of hindsight it is clear that Michael Clarke was unduly pessimistic when
he declared in 1988 that 'these committees have not lived up to their
early promise' (Clarke 1988: 75–6). Today, both the Defence and
Foreign Affairs Committees command great respect for their energy,
independence and tenacity when producing unanimous reports often
highly critical of policy failures – despite the fact that a majority of
members are drawn from the government's own benches. Moreover, stability of membership and regularity of attendance has enabled these
committees to accumulate a sufficient body of expertise that they can at
last exercise informed judgements on government policies and the accuracy and candour of official answers. The impact of the departmental
select committees should not be exaggerated. They have limited powers,
there is no guarantee that the reports will be debated and ministers are
under no obligation to act on their recommendations. The influence of
the FAC has also been impaired by its overlap with the relatively presti-
gious European Scrutiny Committee (established in 1974), while a

similar struggle with the Intelligence and Security Committee has been fuelled by the latter's privileged access to secret intelligence not available to the FAC; a bone of contention which arose over Sierra Leone, Kosovo and Iraq. Nevertheless, for all the caveats, these Select Committees do enable Parliament to fulfil its primary function of scrutinising the work of the executive and calling it to account publicly for its actions.

Public opinion has traditionally been regarded as an even more marginal influence upon the content and conduct of foreign and defence policy. As William Wallace argued in his authoritative study of the foreign policy process in 1975, while 'no government can afford to ignore the domestic content of foreign policy', only 'a very small section' of 'informed opinion' in Parliament, the press, universities and sections of business and finance are interested in these issues. In contrast, 'mass opinion' is typically characterised as 'relatively uninterested and uninvolved in foreign policy issues' and a high level of official secrecy ensures they remain that way (Wallace 1975: 88). There are obviously exceptions to this general proposition. In 1956, public opinion mobilised strongly in protest against the Suez invasion. In the late 1950s and early 1960s, CND successfully attracted much support for its cross-party (even anti-party) 'Ban the Bomb' campaign and Easter marches from AWE Aldermaston, while the Vietnam War provoked huge demonstrations outside the US Embassy in Grosvenor Square. More recent examples can be found in the apparent public support for the Jubilee 2000 'Drop the Debt' and the 2005 'Make Poverty History' campaigns, while the 'Stop the War' coalition opposing military intervention in Iraq mobilised up to a million protesters on the streets of Britain under the banner 'Not in my Name' in 2003. Notwithstanding these exceptions (and the fact that the significant fall in Labour's vote in 2005 is often attributed to popular hostility to the Iraq war), foreign and defence policy has traditionally been an extremely low salience electoral issue with a correspondingly negligible impact on the outcome of most general elections. Even the politically controversial question of Europe failed to arouse much electoral passion, as the Conservatives under William Hague found to their cost during the 2001 election campaign (Geddes 2002: 149–53).

Executive 'overload' and the problems of priorities

The process of making British foreign and defence policy in recent years has been radically transformed by massive enhancements in the speed of international travel and communications. Ernest Bevin rarely needed to leave the country while Foreign Secretary, but Margaret Thatcher made no fewer than 95 visits to more than 50 countries during her first two terms as Prime Minister between 1979 and 1987, while Blair made 38 flights covering 40,000 miles to attend 54 meetings with various foreign leaders in order to mobilise support for the 'coalition of the willing' about to invade Afghanistan during the eight weeks after 9/11 (Clarke 1992: 96; Seldon 2005: 498). Yet the increasing demands on a Prime Minister's time also limits their ability to intervene on anything other than a sporadic basis and this can have deleterious effects upon the overall coherence of external policy. As Thatcher's foreign policy adviser, Sir Percy Cradock recalls that she saw foreign policy 'not as a continuum ... but rather as a series of the separate problems with obtainable solutions, or even as a zero sum game, which Britain had to win' (Cradock 1997: 22). From his experience as her private secretary, Sir John Coles also found that 'one of the most persistent questions was: "what's the next thing?" Some piece of business had just been transacted, some decision taken, and the Prime Ministerial mind wanted to know what the next practical thing was which had to be settled. Not much reaching for an overall policy concept there' (Coles 2000: 49).

In practice, the demands of modern government are often inimical to coherent long-term policy planning even for the minister specifically charged with the responsibility. According to Lord Strang, even in the mid-1950s the Foreign Secretary and his senior officials were 'chronically overworked' and the burden has increased exponentially since that relatively relaxed era (Strang 1955: 196). George Brown looked back on 'the fantastic tempo' of his period at the Foreign Office during the 1960s and considered it 'the toughest, yet the most exciting, period of my political career' (Brown 1971: 159). Twenty years later, Sir Geoffrey Howe recalls that during his 'six years at the Foreign Office I took home, to work through overnight while others slept, no less than 24 tonnes of paper: three boxes a night, six nights a week, 40 weeks a year. Six o'clock was my normal time for getting up. My average bedtime was about four hours earlier' (Howe 1995: 568). During this period he also clocked up over 700,000 miles on official travel to 75 countries (Clarke 1992: 96). Pressures of this sort are compounded still further by the relatively rapid rotation of ministers. Although the average post-war tenure of 31 months at the Foreign Office is significantly longer than the 21 months of Defence ministers, this is a short time in which to master the complexities of such a vast portfolio and this fact alone impairs policy effectiveness among ministers often without previous expertise in the field, who are soon overwhelmed by the burden of paperwork, foreign travel and the claims of the media.

The problem of ministerial 'overload' is more alarming because senior officials are equally afflicted with such burdens – particularly as a legacy of the Thatcherite obsession with 'the cult of managerialism' compels senior officials to devote precious time to such matters at the expense of policy, while strategic thinking is demoted still further down the hierarchy of priorities or abdicated to more junior staff. As Sir John Coles recalls: 'As Permanent Under-Secretary at the Foreign Office I struggled to fulfil my responsibility, described in the Department's Annual Reports to Parliament, "for providing advice on all aspects of foreign policy to the Foreign Secretary" precisely because my second declared responsibility "for the management of the FCO . . . and the Diplomatic Service" assumed such large dimensions' (Coles 2000: 31). Alyson Bailes, an experienced former ambassador, also highlights the need for 'more time to *think* about what is going on' because the speed of communication tended 'to prioritise tactical over strategic thinking, articulacy over grasp and expression over substance' (Bailes 2007: 195). Since 1997, these pressures have undoubtedly increased substantially given New Labour's embrace of the Thatcherite enthusiasm for private sector management methods, operational efficiency and 'delivery'. Worse still, these demands have been compounded by New Labour's obsession with 'spin' to manage the presentation of government policy in the media; a priority carried so far that to some insiders 'it sometimes seemed that presentation drove policy, that the need to describe, explain and defend influenced, almost dictated, the very substance of policy' (Coles 2000: 31). Work and time pressures of this sort lie at the heart of the related problem of long-term planning in an uncertain world.

The problems of long-term planning and 'horizon-scanning'

Soon after Robin Cook became Foreign Secretary in May 1997, he inaugurated the 'Foresight' initiative designed to modernise the FCO and Diplomatic Service to meet the challenges of the decades ahead (Dickie 2004: vii). One of the key findings to emerge from the largest survey ever conducted within the civil service was that staff believed the FCO possessed many strengths, but at the top of the list of its self-perceived weaknesses was its capacity for long-term strategic planning, followed by planning for worst-case scenarios, recognising failure and learning by mistakes, setting and following priorities, and meeting and reallocating resources to meet those new priorities. This was scarcely a new problem. Phillip Darby contends that one of the main reasons there was no reappraisal of British defence commitments East of Suez after Indian independence was because the Foreign Office culture contained such 'an inbuilt prejudice against forward planning' that there was no desk specifically responsible for this function until Bevin established the Permanent Under-Secretary's Committee (PUSC) in 1949 – and even that was hampered by the pressures of day-to-day work and a lack of a permanent staff (Darby 1973: 16–17). This judgement is a little harsh. As part of Eden's Foreign Office reforms in 1943, a Research Analyst's Department was established to consider long-term problems and this subsequently evolved into the largest department dealing with political affairs, with a staff of 80 experienced officials. It also became 'the envy of many Western foreign ministries because there [was] nothing comparable to it in any other capital'. In 1964, a Policy Planning Staff was also created to produce strategic advice, although its effectiveness was undermined by ministerial perceptions that its output was 'worthy' but 'disconnected from the here and now', earning it the reputation of being 'the Blue Sky Department'.

In the light of the conclusions of the Foresight initiative, Sir Michael Jay embarked upon a radical institutional reorganisation soon after he succeeded as Permanent Under-Secretary in January 2002. The Policy Planning Department was abolished to make way for a Directorate for Strategy and Innovation (DSI) intended to provide 'fresh, strategic thinking on current, long-term and cross-cutting issues and to make an influential contribution to policy formulation'. In addition, the old Board of Management and the Policy Advisory Board were both replaced by a new joint body within the DSI with a high-powered staff of 25, while a Director's Committee brought together all departmental heads to comment on papers prepared by the DSI. At the same time, a new Finance and Strategy Group emerged to enable ministers and their special advisers to be more closely involved with the assessment of priorities and the allocation of resources. Another innovation designed to increase the scope for new ideas was the 'Policy Net' which enabled the FCO to use state-of-the-art information technology to canvass the views of diplomatic staff around the world – 'Thinking with 1,000 brains' as it became known (Dickie 2004: 109–15).

Notwithstanding all these reforms, critics might argue that institutional and structural reform is of tangential significance until fundamental unanswered questions are resolved about whether Britain has an essentially global, transatlantic or European orientation; when the government remains profoundly ambivalent about Britain's relationship with a wider and deepening European Union; when it struggles to find an appropriate level of defence and security it can realistically afford; and when its priority upon the needs of business and trade often conflicts sharply with the fundamental purposes of British foreign policy itself. Almost two decades ago, Michael Clarke argued that the malaise created by this failure to choose decisively between alternative paths (in the hope of keeping every option open) had a seriously debilitating effect upon British external policy. At the end of the first decade of the twenty-first century, Clarke's judgement remains as pertinent as ever. 'The policy system can react to the immediate manifestations of such issues but it cannot establish meaningful priorities within a context it barely comprehends' (Clarke 1992: 112).

Redefining the role of the FCO within a challenging Whitehall environment

Questions about the sort of organisational structure needed for effective long-term policy planning raise equally fundamental issues about the precise role and purpose of the FCO in a policy environment very different from that of only a generation ago. Because other Whitehall departments no longer turn to the Foreign Office as their essential first port of call whenever an international – and particularly European – issue arises, the Foresight planners recognised the need for a 'step change in expertise' to broaden and deepen the range of skills the Diplomatic Service could offer to its clients beyond a traditional knowledge of difficult languages and foreign countries. One immediate response was to deploy more specialists in topical subject areas like disarmament, environmental problems, population pressures, international crime, trade and terrorism in the hope of increasing its relevance and value to other Whitehall departments by providing an overarching perspective beyond the capability of more narrowly focused departments. In consequence, the relative prestige and importance of functional units dealing with cross-national-cross-departmental issues has risen markedly in recent years, at the expense of the traditional geographical departments dealing with specific countries or areas. In practice, however, efforts to redefine the FCO's role in a changing policy process went well beyond a review of service provision.

One of the DSI's first tasks was to help restore morale by tackling the 'vision thing'. This required a 10-year Strategic Plan setting out long-term priority areas and the necessary structure to make best use of FCO resources in achieving these goals. To this end, no fewer than 104 Ambassadors, 46 High Commissioners from Commonwealth countries, and various senior envoys and officials gathered for a two-day conference in London in January 2003 to contribute to this plan. The need for such an exercise was deeply felt. As PUS at the FCO until 1997, Sir John Coles became convinced that it was 'the lack of strategy or "vision" which weakens British foreign policy, the absence of a single overarching concept or design, an "Idea of Britain" which would inform more detailed objectives and the day-to-day thrust of diplomatic activity'. This craving for a fresh definition of Britain's purpose in the world was particularly felt at a time when George Bush's promise of a 'New Global Order' failed to materialise in a world characterised instead by flux and profound uncertainty (Coles 2000: 44).

The idea of an explicit public statement of purpose had been the driving force behind Robin Cook's FCO Mission Statement in May 1997 and his successor embraced the concept with enthusiasm. In December 2003, a White Paper entitled *UK International Priorities: A Strategy for the FCO* was proudly proclaimed as the first White Paper on the subject in the 221-year history of the Foreign Office. Its objective was to outline the UK's strategic priorities in the emerging international system and the FCO's role in pursuing them (Cm 6052, 2003: 16). In the event, the document received a cool reception, not least because it 'smacked too much of a blend of wish list and public relations exercise on a grander scale than . . . Robin Cook's mission statement' (Cm 6052 2003; Dickie 2004: 110). In March 2006, it was superseded by a revised version entitled *Active Diplomacy for a Changing World*, with objectives adjusted to changing circumstances – with particular reference to energy issues, migration and illegal immigration. This document set out no fewer than nine international strategic priorities defining the government's 'active and strategic' response to 'the forces of globalisation – and the globalisation of threats'; a list to which Margaret Beckett added a tenth objective in June 2006 (Cm 6762, 2006: 4).

When David Miliband succeeded as Foreign Secretary in June 2007, he immediately launched a review of these strategic priorities. This study concluded that a new statement was required to achieve greater clarity and a closer alignment between resources and priorities. The result was *Better World, Better Britain*. Published in April 2008, this was a direct lineal descendant of Jack Straw's earlier efforts but repackaged within a new streamlined framework to create a modern FCO 'clear about its role' and able to focus its effort where it would make the most difference (see Table 9.3). How far his attempt to 'make foreign policy by blueprint' has contributed to efficiency, effectiveness or the more accurate measurement of performance has been the subject of considerable scepticism within the Foreign Affairs Select Committee.

Despite the implicit suggestion of novelty, the objectives in Miliband's statement reflected a high level of continuity with the past. For example, trade promotion was already an important function in the early 1930s (Tilley and Gaselee 1933: ch. X). By the mid-1950s, a third of all FCO work was commercial or financial and this focus has intensified still further in recent years (Strang 1955: 39); a fact reflected in

Table 9.2   The UK's international strategic priorities, 2006

- Making the world safe from global terrorism and weapons of mass destruction
- Reducing the harm to the UK from international crime, including drug trafficking, people smuggling and money laundering
- Preventing and resolving conflicts in a strong international system
- Building an effective and globally competitive EU in a secure neighbourhood
- Supporting the UK economy and business through an open and expanding global economy, science and innovation and secure energy supplies
- Promoting sustainable development and poverty reduction underpinned by human rights, democracy, good governance and protection of the environment
- Managing migration and combating illegal immigration
- Delivering high quality support to British nationals abroad, in normal times and in crises
- Ensuring the security and good governance of the UK's Overseas Territories
- Achieve climate security by promoting a faster transition to a sustainable, low carbon global economy (added by Margaret Beckett in June 2006).

Source: Cm 6762, *Active Diplomacy for a Changing World: the UK's International Priorities*, March 2006.

its rise from the fifth of ten departmental international priorities in 2006 to the first of three 'essential services' two years later. The need to improve the FCO's effectiveness in export promotion emerged from the Foresight exercise and culminated in 1998–99 with the creation of British Trade International – later UK Trade & Investment (UKTI) – which brought together the trade development and export promotion arms of the Foreign Office and DTI under a single chief executive in the hope of improving British export performance. From a network of 150 offices in over a hundred markets overseas, its 1500 staff support exporters with advice on foreign markets, assist their attendance at trade shows and exhibitions, and arrange sector-specific missions to promote British business. By June 2009, more than 7500 companies have benefited from UKTI support, generating around £2.5 billion in exports (www.fco.gov.uk).

At the other end of the spectrum, the FCO plays an important role in 'public diplomacy'; a function closely associated with Joseph Nye's

Table 9.3   Better World, Better Britain, April 2008

... from climate change to health pandemics, the UK's national security and prosperity depends on how we work with other nations.

This requires a modern and effective Foreign & Commonwealth Office that is clear about its role and focuses effort on where we will make the most difference.

We break our work down into three parts:

1. Global network
A unique and flexible global network of staff, embassies and offices around the world serves all of UK government. We will continue to shift resources to Asia and the Middle East to better deliver [sic] our goals and services and to reflect global economic and political trends.

2. Essential services
We help to deliver three essential services:
- Support the British economy
- Support British nationals abroad
- Support managed migration for Britain

3. Policy goals
We have four policy goals to focus our work:
- Counter terrorism and weapons proliferation, and their causes
- Prevent and resolve conflict
- Promote a low carbon, high growth, global economy
- Develop effective international institutions, above all the UN and the EU

Source: Better World, Better Britain, April 2008, www.fco.gov.uk/en/fco-in-action/strategy.

concept of 'soft power' which involves the 'ability to influence the behaviour of others to get the outcomes you want ... without the tangible threats or payoffs' associated with the exercise of 'hard power' (Nye 2002: 2–3; HC 903, 2006). There is nothing new about the projection of Britain's image abroad to promote positive impressions and to counteract the stock outdated picture of Britain which the media tends to perpetuate. Nevertheless, while significant strides had been taken in this field prior to 1997, Robin Cook took the initiative by projecting an image of a modernising foreign policy more in touch with its own people and he strongly supported the 'cool Britannia' image-making of the new Foreign Policy Centre (Hill 2001: 345). After two disappointing reviews (by Lords Wilton and Carter) had concluded that these efforts suffered from poor coordination, however, a reformed Public Diplomacy Board was established in 2005 to monitor the effectiveness of a new three- to five-year public diplomacy strategy. Despite these setbacks, the National Security Strategy in 2008 continues to emphasise the belief 'that encouraging a more positive attitude to the United Kingdom across the world will bring lasting benefits not just to our prosperity but to our security' (Cm 7291, 2008: para. 2.4)

At a day-to-day level, 'transformational' or 'public diplomacy' is pursued through a variety of channels, ranging from the Foreign Office's Chevening Scholarship programme bringing overseas students and future decision-makers to Britain to study through to the supply of vast quantities of publications for distribution via overseas missions. By the turn of the century, the first Foreign Office interactive CD-ROM was launched, along with an FCO blog and online website which has 25,000 documents downloaded each week, while the FCO's British Satellite News provides independent TV footage to over 500 overseas broadcasters along with several hundred hours of radio in various languages (www.fco.gov.uk; Coles 2000: 145). Beyond these official efforts, public diplomacy is pursued through FCO-sponsored non-governmental organisations like the British Council and the BBC World Service despite concerns that governmental involvement might damage the perceived independence and impartiality upon which public diplomacy ultimately depends for its success.

The British Council was established in 1934 to 'promote abroad a wider appreciation of British culture and civilisation' (Donaldson 1984: 1–2). With representatives in 109 countries promoting British values, the British Council is too valuable an asset for the government to ignore and in 2007/08 FCO funding reached £194 million. Similarly, the FCO's conviction that the English language is Britain's 'cheapest diplomatic asset' sustains its funding of the BBC World Service (at a cost of £225 million in 2007/08) in return for which it broadcasts 734 hours a week in English and 42 other languages to a regular audience of at least 120 million people (Clarke 1992: 69–70; Cm 6052, 2003: 7). In 1991, the BBC also launched its international television unit broadcasting in English to 18 million viewers worldwide and, in 2008, it introduced a Farsi-Persian satellite TV news channel with FCO funding, much to the irritation of the Iranian regime (www.fco.gov.uk).

Despite the vigour of these efforts to promote British trade and values abroad, there was little new in the objectives outlined in New Labour White Papers to bolster morale by redefining the FCO's raison d'être within a changing policy process. Underlying their bland description of services and objectives in these White Papers, however, there are some indications that a more imaginative vision of the FCO's future added value role is emerging. As David Miliband told an assembly of Ambassadors in London in March 2008:

The traditional roles of the Foreign Office are still needed. Political reporting, sound analysis, and close contact with the foreign governments will remain at the core of our work. We will continue to provide the platform overseas for other government departments . . . But we need to adapt to external changes . . . In an age when . . . every department is developing a foreign perspective, and where interaction with foreign governments can often be directly between ministers rather than via the diplomatic machinery, we must be clearer about our added value. I believe added value comes in three core competencies. First, we should understand foreign countries interests, power structures and culture better than anyone else. Second, we should have unparalleled networks that enable us to influence the country's position from the bottom as well as the top down. Third, while other departments focus on the single issue and have a single policy tool, the Foreign Office should have the overview of how to prosecute cross-departmental priorities. We should develop a global reputation for being the generator of new ideas to global problems. We should see ourselves as a central department, using our global network to interface with other countries. (www.fco.gov.uk)

Sceptics will no doubt dismiss these efforts to define a 'vision' and 'mission' for the FCO as symptomatic of what one former ambassador describes as a government enthusiasm for the 'belated and half-hearted imitation of the private sector' implemented with 'leftover and second-best . . . advisers and equipment' (Bailes 2007: 197). Less jaundiced observers will question whether these core competencies are sufficient to stake out a clearly differentiated future role for the FCO capable of justifying its continued position in Whitehall's Premier league. But at the very least, Miliband's thinking appears to suggest that the problem of how to add value within a competitive policy environment is being addressed in a manner which accepts Jack Straw's guiding principle that 'we should not do what others can do better. Our aim is to facilitate and guide their international activity' (Cm 6052, 2003: 3).

 ## Reviewing Britain's overseas representation

One core purpose of the FCO will always be to represent British interests overseas. Between 1964 and 1977, however, its effectiveness in fulfilling this function was the subject of no fewer than three detailed reviews – plus Harold Wilson's mysterious secret assessment in 1966 which ended with all copies of the report being destroyed (Coles 2000:

70–1). In February 1964, the Plowden Report concluded that Britain should maintain 'a high degree of worldwide influence' because without it 'national and international interest and objectives will suffer'. As a result of its recommendations, the Foreign Overseas Trade Service and Diplomatic Service (and later the Commonwealth Relations Office) were amalgamated into the Foreign and Commonwealth Office. Plowden also prioritised the commercial function (Cmnd 2276, 1964). In 1968–69, Sir Val Duncan conducted another review which placed even greater emphasis on export promotion, prompting one critic to quip that the committee believed a diplomat was a man who goes abroad to sell washing machines for his country (Theakston 2000: 121). Most controversial of all was Duncan's division of the world into two parts – 'areas of concentration' for British diplomacy (Europe, North America, Japan and Australia) and the remaining 'outer area' where diplomatic missions were to be selectively located to save between 5 per cent and 10 per cent of overseas expenditure. Needless to say, the report was greeted with hostility at the Foreign Office and even the Cabinet blanched at its austere distinction between 'areas of concentration' and the rest of the world, and the incoming Conservative administration quietly shelved the report (Cmnd 4107, 1969; Coles 2000: 70–1).

In 1976–77, a third review of overseas representation was attempted by Sir Kenneth Berrill and the Central Policy Review Staff (CPRS) in the Cabinet Office. Its report endorsed earlier views that British interests would suffer unless it maintained a diplomatic presence equivalent to that of the other major powers of the second-order, but it also proposed a radical reduction in the size of the Diplomatic Service, which it accused of being elitist, overstaffed, extravagant and unnecessarily obsessed with 'perfectionism'. Like its predecessors, the CPRS advocated the need for more trade experts to promote exports at the expense of generalist diplomats while proposing the closure of 50 overseas missions and the abolition of the British Council (Cmnd 7308, 1977). Again, the main thrust of the report was rejected by the Callaghan government and there has been no formal review since the CPRS study, although a leaked private consultant's report in 2005 comprehensively condemned the FCO's 'generalist' ethos, amateurish senior leadership, its risk-averse blame-shifting culture and severe over-staffing (*Guardian*, 4 August 2005).

In the absence of any systematic redefinition of functions or priorities, Conservative governments between 1979 and 1997 simply allowed the FCO's assets to wither under its indifference as it was relegated to the role of 'scapegoat department for bureaucracy-baiters in the eighties' (Hennessy 1990: 407). Between 1981 and 1987, FCO expenditure was

Table 9.4   FCO expenditure baseline and additions, 2007/08 to 2010/11 (£ millions)

	2007/08 baseline	2008/09	2009/10	2010/11
Total DEL	1581	+99	+125	+123
Of which: the British Council share	193	+3	+8	+4
Of which: the BBC External Services share	246	+19	+26	+25

Source: fco.gov.uk.

cut by 4 per cent and manpower by 9 per cent – economies particularly damaging to overseas posts concerned with cultural diplomacy and the projection of Britain's image abroad. The World Service and British Council also suffered significant cuts (Clarke 1992: 70). Gordon Brown's National Asset Register, detailing the FCO's possession of £991 million in property and £132 million in furniture and equipment, was also intended as a prelude to a raid by the Treasury, but this time the attack fizzled out (Sampson 2004: 138).

Ironically, the FCO's problem is that it has never been a big spender in Whitehall terms. In 2007/8 it spent only £1.925 billion and employed around 6,000 London-based staff, with another 10,000 locally recruited overseas (Cm 6052, 2003: 7; Cm 7398, 2008). By any measure, therefore, the central administration of Britain's foreign relations remains 'a very cost-effective business' (Clarke 1992: 78). But, as some 80 per cent of its expenditure is on personnel, it has proved difficult to economise without significantly restricting the scope of its activity. While governments have shied away from radical reform of Britain's overseas representation, therefore, they have achieved much the same effect by stealth. In 1970 there were 273 overseas Embassies and High Commissions. After 30 years of repeated demands for economy, by 2003 the number of overseas posts had fallen to 233 before a modest expansion to 260 in 145 countries in 2008. Under the terms of the Comprehensive Spending Review settlement (2007), the department's core budget is scheduled to fall to £1.7 billion by 2010/11 and this again can only be to the detriment of its ability to deliver against strategic objectives (FCO 2007).

A much too Diplomatic Service? Defending the national interest

Questions about the quality of the FCO's representation of British interests are not confined simply to the cost and efficiency of its overseas embassies. One of the most damaging criticisms in recent years has focused on the underlying culture and ethos of modern diplomacy. Above all, the FCO stands accused of being insufficiently tenacious in defending the national interest through an overdeveloped preference for compromise and negotiation which critics regard as tantamount to an 'appeasement' mentality. When combined with its perceived elitism and social superiority, this indictment has left it vulnerable to vilification across the entire political spectrum and still further reduced its status within the Whitehall community.

During the 1970s, Brian Sedgemore, a Labour left-wing MP, condemned the Foreign Office's 'Vichy mentality' while Joe Haines (Harold Wilson's press secretary) alleged that 'the Foreign Office prepares new orchestrations of 'I surrender, dear' to every demand or démarche made to it' (Hennessy 1990: 400; Theakston 2000: 112). After his experience as Foreign Secretary, David Owen also complained that 'the culture of diplomacy elevates splitting the difference into an art form'. Over Europe in particular, he recalled they 'clashed, sometimes violently' because 'they were intelligent people but they never had the tenacity to fight for British interests in the same way as the French diplomats fight at every level for France'. According to Owen, the FCO's only redeeming feature was that a new 'less effete and more realistic' generation of Foreign Office officials had emerged who were 'more robust in protecting British interests in the 1990s than they ever were in the 1970s' (Owen 1991: 246, 264–5).

Margaret Thatcher did not agree. She made no secret of her belief that the FCO was filled with craven 'appeasers' unwilling to uphold British interests – particularly in Europe. Thatcher despised Francis Pym for being a 'quitter' who surrendered to his department's timidity over the Falklands crisis (Young 1989: 272). Reflecting on her mistake in appointing Geoffrey Howe to the post in 1983, she also revealingly complained that

> he fell under the spell of the Foreign Office where compromise and negotiation were ends in themselves. . . . In his new department he fell into the habits which the Foreign Office seem to cultivate – a reluctance to subordinate diplomatic tactics to the national interest and an insatiable appetite for nuances and conditions which can blur the clearest vision. (Thatcher 1993: 309)

It was precisely this suspicion of the mealy-mouthed equivocation of professional diplomats which led her to recruit Charles Powell as her principal foreign affairs adviser and it was a measure of her mistrust that she increasingly travelled abroad with no FCO presence at all, supported only by the indispensable Powell and Bernard Ingham, her Press Secretary. As Norman Tebbit, one of Thatcher's most pugnacious ministerial allies, encapsulated the leadership view during the 1980s: 'the Ministry of Agriculture looks after farmers; the Foreign Office looks after foreigners' (Clarke 1992: 107). Endemic suspicions of this sort represent a significant constraint upon the FCO's ability to regain its former position as the principal source of expertise, advice and policy to British governments of either complexion.

Reforming the composition and career structure: the Foresight initiative

The Foreign Office emerged in 1782 as one of two of the great modern departments along with the Home Office and it remained a stronghold of aristocracy well into the twentieth century until the Bevin–Eden White Paper on *Proposals for the Reform of the Foreign Service* in January 1943 amalgamated the Foreign Office, the Diplomatic Service, the Commercial Diplomatic Service and the consular service, and opened recruitment to a more representative and diverse range of social backgrounds and specialisms. While dismissing 'overstated' criticisms that the Diplomatic Service was too elitist, the White Paper conceded that 'Every member of our Foreign Service should be in the fullest sense representative of our whole nation, of every class and section of the community' (Cmnd 6420 1943: paras 2–3). Despite Bevin's pivotal role in drafting the Eden White Paper, his biographer argues that his innate institutional conservatism ensured that he did little to widen recruitment (Bullock 1983: 101). As Labour governments during the 1960s and 1970s were no more ambitious in their efforts to create a more representative Foreign Service, it retained a strongly aristocratic 'Old Etonian' air well into the post-war era. Even in 1998, the 7 per cent of the population attending independent public schools provided 61 per cent of the senior intake, while Oxbridge supplied 65 per cent of its recruits (Theakston 2000: 119). In stark contrast, women were not even allowed to apply to the administrative grade of the Diplomatic Service until 1943, and as late as 1972 they were still required to resign when they married. The first female ambassador was not appointed until 1976, and the first married woman to occupy such a post was not appointed until 1987.

Discontent within the Foreign Office had been festering for some time among younger ambitious diplomats having to mark time for years because of the slow progress of promotion, the excessively hierarchical structure for policymaking and outmoded means of communication. Robin Cook came to the Foreign Office in May 1997, deeply suspicious of its 'stuffy' elitist culture and determined to broaden the recruitment profile of its senior ranks. In 1997, women represented 36 per cent of the FCO's London-based staff but only 3.4 per cent held positions in the senior grades and none of the 21 Under Secretaries was female. By 2003, the proportion of women in senior positions had risen to 20 per cent – and 20 of these were now heads of overseas missions, as were 7 of the 21 Under Secretaries. Similarly, ethnic minorities had been conspicuous by their absence at senior levels prior to 1997, with only one representative among the 433 officials in the top four grades of the 'senior management structure'. By 2003, ethnic minorities accounted for only 6 per cent of total staff but 2 per cent were in the senior ranks of the service. The first ambassador from an ethnic minority was appointed in 2004 (Cm 6052, 2003: 59). Although scarcely a revolutionary advance, steady progress has been made towards the objective outlined in Jack Straw's 2006 White Paper to the effect that 'The FCO will best represent modern Britain to others by resembling modern Britain itself' (Cm 6762, 2006: 5). It still has a long way to go, however, before it matches the DfID's outstanding success in achieving an acceptable gender balance in its senior ranks, its ability to recruit top-level staff from the World Bank and elsewhere, and the coherence of its structures for cascading the Department's goals into the 'Delivery Plans' of each of its Directors: an organisational superiority reflected in the fact that the DfID was the only government ministry to be rated as 'strong' in the Cabinet Office's first round of 'Capability Reviews' in March 2007 (Cabinet Office 2007a).

The role of the intelligence services

Although official secrecy makes it difficult to assess its real contribution, John Dickie argues that 'on many occasions the shaping of policy is determined much more by the intelligence dimension than the political or ethical dimension' (Dickie 2004: 103). There may be some truth in this proposition, but revelations about the abuse of intelligence to justify military intervention in Iraq should not distort the picture. Intelligence has a significant role to play, but it is not the crucial factor driving all foreign policy – or even Blair's decisions over Iraq. Indeed, as Lady Manningham-Buller, the former head of MI5, revealed, her organisation and the JIC had repeatedly warned that the invasion of Iraq would increase the domestic threat from terrorism by breeding resentment within the Muslim community, but the government ploughed on regardless (*Guardian*, 11 July 2009). Nevertheless, intelligence undoubtedly makes an important input and, since the Second World War, it has been an area of extremely close Anglo-American cooperation in which Britain has traditionally possessed considerable leverage; the more so since 9/11, given its more extensive sources in Pakistan, its greater diplomatic experience within the Muslim world as a whole and the acknowledged leadership of GCHQ in the interception of confidential signals intelligence (sigint) with its 7000 experts fluent in 67 languages – including a far larger proportion of Arabic and Farsi speakers than its US counterparts.

As Table 9.5 illustrates, the British intelligence community consists of an interlocking web of organisations and committees covering all aspects of the work, from espionage abroad, to homeland security. Although this output permeates all aspects of policymaking in complex ways, the central link in the chain is the Joint Intelligence Committee, which conveys intelligence and early warnings into the policy process via weekly 'Red Book' threat assessments. Although it does not give advice, during crises it typically meets several times a day to produce revised assessments of fast-moving situations (Coles 2000: 92; Cradock 1997: 41).

Since 9/11, the intelligence services have inevitably occupied a position of centrality unparalleled since the darkest days of the Cold War; a new status reflected in the creation of a Cabinet Committee on International Terrorism (now the Committee on Security and Intelligence) and the appointment of a Security and Intelligence Coordinator within the Cabinet Office. Spending on intelligence has increased at a correspondingly rapid rate in recent years (see Table 9.6). In 2002/03, the combined intelligence budget was £893 million. By 2007/08, it had increased by 55 per cent to £1.63 billion. In addition, funding has significantly increased for related tasks such as an extra £1.2 million to improve the BBC Monitoring Service coverage of Islamic broadcasts. Although this escalating expenditure is justified by the increased perceived terrorist threat since 9/11 and 7/7, additional funds have also been needed to support MI5's efforts to strengthen its counter-espionage arm to combat what Jonathan Evans, the head of MI5, recently described as the 'unreconstructed attempts by Russia, China, and others to spy on us' at a time when best estimates suggested 'that at least twenty foreign intelligence services are currently operating in the UK against UK interests' (*Guardian*, 9 July 2008).

Table 9.5   The intelligence community in Britain

The Security Service (MI5). Established in 1909. The UK's principal counter-intelligence organisation and (since the Security Service Act 1996) supports the police in defeating serious crime. Employs around 3,000 staff with plans for 4,000 by 2010/11 by which time its budget will be £3.5 billion.

Secret Intelligence Service (MI6). Established in 1909 to collect secret foreign intelligence for the Foreign Secretary. The Intelligence Services Act 1994 placed it on a statutory basis for the first time. Employs around 2,300.

Government Communications Headquarters (GCHQ). Established in 1919 as the Government Code & Cypher School, it became GCHQ in 1946; located at Cheltenham since 1952. Responsible for coding/decoding and monitoring signal intelligence from all sources including satellites and listening posts. Employs around 7,000.

Defence Intelligence Staff (DIS). Established in 1964 from the amalgamation of the three Service intelligence staffs and the civilian Joint Intelligence Bureau. Now part of the MoD to provide assessments of military threats. Regulated by the Investigatory Powers Act 2000. Estimated manpower 4,600.

Joint Terrorism Analysis Centre (JTAC). Established 2003 to coordinate the dissemination and analysis of all-source intelligence matter. A multi-agency body including the MoD, MI5, MI6, GCHQ, DIS, FCO, Home Office and the Police.

Joint Intelligence Committee. Located in the Cabinet Office to provide intelligence assessments and to scrutinise the work of other agencies. Membership includes FCO, MoD, Home Office, DTI, DfID, Treasury, Cabinet Office and the heads of all the intelligence agencies. Chaired by the Permanent Secretary (Intelligence, Security and Resilience).

Parliamentary Intelligence and Security Committee (ISC). Established by the Intelligence Services Act (1994) to conduct parliamentary oversights of the Security Services.

National Criminal Intelligence Service (NCIS). Established 1992 to collect and analyse intelligence on serious, organised and transnational crime. Employs 900.

BBC Monitoring Service. Located at Caversham Park, near Reading. Since 1939 this produces daily assessments of nuanced shifts in foreign reporting for the FCO Research Analysts Department. Currently monitors 3,000 sources in over a hundred languages in 150 countries around the clock. Employs 370.

Sources: Cabinet Office, *The National Intelligence Machinery*, November 2006, (London: Cabinet Office); Dickie (2004): 204. BBC Monitoring, *Review of the Year, 2008/09*.

Table 9.6　Funding the intelligence services, 2004/05 to 2007/08
(in £ millions)

	2004/05	2005/06	2006/07	2007/08
The Single Intelligence Account (SIA) covers the expenditure of MI5, MI6 and GCHQ. DIS is funded by the MoD and the JTAC is jointly funded				
Resource budget	1,126.6	1,266.0	1,336.0	1,391.8
Capital budget	150.8	231.8	232.4	238.0
Total	1,277.4	1,497.8	1,568.4	1,629.8

Source: Cabinet Office, *National Intelligence Machinery*, November 2006, p.7.

Chapter 10

Conclusion: The Challenge of an Uncertain Future

The changing international environment after 1945

In reviewing the history of British foreign and defence policy since the end of the Second World War, it is impossible to avoid one particularly striking paradox. On one hand, there has been a remarkable degree of continuity in policy and priorities since Anthony Eden and Ernest Bevin laid the foundations for a post-war foreign policy consensus in the 1940s. On the other hand, the international environment within which this bipartisan policy has been applied has changed out of all recognition. During a period of only 65 years, the world has witnessed the collapse of the wartime Allied alliance; the consolidation of Soviet control over much of Eastern Europe; the outbreak of the Cold War; periodic threats that this would turn into a 'Hot War' over Korea, Berlin and Cuba; a period of marked East–West détente; the outbreak of a 'Second Cold War'; the emergence of Mikhail Gorbachev's dramatic reform programme in the mid-1980s; the even more spectacular collapse of communism in Eastern Europe; the formal end of the Cold War; the end of the Warsaw Pact as an aggressive alliance and the final dissolution of the Soviet Union, leaving the United States as a single superpower in an increasingly multi-polar world.

Beyond these remarkable developments in East–West relations, during the same period the nature of the international environment has been radically transformed by the collapse of the Bretton Woods economic system established in 1945, the rise of Communist China into an economic and military superpower; the dissolution of the great European empires, the transition of these former colonies to independence across much of Africa and Asia, and the proliferation of nuclear weapons beyond the control of the superpowers to states like Israel and Pakistan. Closer to home, the once fiercely independent states of Europe have increasingly pooled their sovereignty within a rapidly evolving European Union, currently consisting of 27 states operating a broad range of common policies and competences under a relatively high level of supranational control. At the same time, the dramatic rise of Islamic consciousness in large parts of the world after the Iranian revolution in 1979 has fundamentally transformed the balance of power in the Middle East and much of Asia. Above all, the traumatic events of 9/11 have had a truly seismic impact on perceptions of international security. Ever since, the seemingly omnipresent threat of international terrorism in its many guises has remained at the top of the international agenda. As Blair told the US Congress in July 2003, 9/11 'changed the world'.

Continuity and change in British policy

Continuity in broad policy objectives does not mean that Britain has remained aloof from these global developments, or immune to their effects. On the contrary, its own position on the world stage has also changed out of all recognition. Britain no longer possesses a global empire and the Commonwealth of Nations has proved a bitter disappointment to those who expected it to act as a surrogate empire loyally enhancing the diplomatic authority of the 'Mother Country' in the council chambers of the world. Britain's ability to exert 'hard power' in a military sense has also been vastly diminished since the 1940s. It no longer possesses a global network of strategic bases from which to project its power around the world and the once dominant Royal Navy has been so reduced in size that it does not possess the capability to launch major out-of-area operations without great exertion – as demonstrated by the ramshackle nature of the naval task force which recaptured the Falkland Islands in 1982 – and an armada well beyond its capability today. Although the professionalism and prowess of its armed forces are arguably still second to none, their existing strength is but a fraction of what it was in the late 1940s, while operations in Afghanistan and Iraq have revealed severe deficiencies in both the quality and quantity of equipment as well as the Defence Planning Assumptions about necessary manpower levels in the first decade of the twenty-first century.

Many of these problems stem directly from Britain's relatively indifferent economic performance since 1945 and the chronic strategic misalignment between ambitions and resources. Ironically, the two world wars which still play such a pivotal role in defining Britain's own self-image for its citizens (or at least those born before 1960) were the root cause of much of its undoing. While Britain emerged from these global conflicts as a victorious power, to paraphrase Churchill's verdict on the Great War, in retrospect it appears that victory was achieved at such a high price as to be almost indistinguishable from defeat. Put simply,

Britain lost nearly 15 per cent of its total assets in the First World War and 28 per cent of what remained in the Second. The long-term damage inflicted by these sacrifices cannot be overstated and its impact has pervaded every aspects of public policy in the second half of the twentieth century. Yet, although such problems made it increasingly difficult to maintain the nation's former position in the world, policy continuity has remained the order of the day throughout the post-war era.

More remarkable is that the revolution in international affairs created by the end of the Cold War barely caused a ripple on the surface of British external policy – beyond Thatcher's outrage at the idea of German reunification. Confronted by an uncertain future, Britain has opted for incremental adjustments to the status quo rather than radical revision. As David Sanders argues, this approach reflected the triumph of the FCO's realist conception of international affairs which assumes that because the nation-state can never be sure that it is safe from attack, the overriding priority must be upon external security. When viewed through the lens of realism, it is easy to see why the end of the Cold War made very little difference to Britain's international role or its defence posture. One arch-enemy, the Soviet Union, had disappeared but another might appear at any moment. In these circumstances, it was better to cling to an old and trusted ally like the United States and the resources provided by an independent deterrent, a privileged relationship with the US and a permanent seat on the UN Security Council than to trust to luck (Sanders 1990: 301). As Margaret Thatcher recalled after surveying the wreckage of the old order, 'the "new world order" was turning out to be a dangerous and uncertain place in which the conservative virtues of hardened Cold Warriors were again in demand' (Thatcher 1993: 770).

This preference for continuity and cautious pragmatism soon appeared to be vindicated by the Russian response to US plans to build a missile defence system in Poland and the Czech Republic – supposedly against 'rogue' missiles fired by Iran but violently denounced by President Vladimir Putin as a provocative act which threatened 'tremendous changes to the strategic balance in Europe, and to the world's strategic stability'. In retaliation, Putin warned of a new Cold War-style arms race while upgrading Russia's nuclear arsenal with a new ICBM (RS-24) and an improved version of the short-range Iskander missile for use against US silos from the Kalinigrad enclave (*Guardian*, 30 May 2007). While the war of words continued, in December 2008 Putin's successor and close associate, Dmitry Medvedev, announced a massive $95billion defence procurement package for 2009–11 and the revival of the great May Day parades of military hardware in Moscow. Although the election of the Obama administration eased tensions with the US, relations with the outside world remained strained, as demonstrated by official harassment of the British Council in Russia (*Guardian*, 24 December 2008, 18 March, 4 April 2009).

While policy continuity appears surprising, given the kaleidoscopic changes that have taken place in the international environment over the past 20 years, critics dismiss it as just one more 'missed opportunity' to adopt an international role commensurate with Britain's status as a middle-income, middle-sized European power; a failure attributable to the same forces of history and nostalgia which have constrained British foreign policy since the end of the Second World War. There might be some truth in this interpretation, but there is nothing quite like hindsight and the knowledge of precisely how things turned out, to be able to detect 'missed opportunities', mistaken logic and ill-conceived policy responses. To confuse retrospective wisdom with a proper understanding of the contemporary perception of opportunities and constraints, however, is not only fundamentally unjust but also profoundly unhistorical. Nothing more compellingly demonstrates the truth of this proposition than the contemporary dilemma facing British policymakers in the twenty-first century.

A recurrent theme in the utterances of British statesmen over the past decade has been the recognition that the world is in a worrying state of flux. One established order has been destroyed with the collapse of communism and the removal of East–West tensions – and with it has gone the strategy of Mutually Assured Destruction and the prospect of nuclear annihilation. Yet, notwithstanding these dangers, the world order which developed during the Cold War era was at least something which policymakers recognised and understood because the nature and range of threats was predictable. More to the point, by being able to define the enemy and the nature of the threat it was possible to devise strategies to counter that challenge; a happy state of affairs which produced stability in a world in which 'threats-based planning' became the norm. Ultimately, the post-war peace was the product of precisely this nuclear and military stalemate.

The challenge of the unknown: redefining the threat

The challenge confronting foreign policymakers and the defence planners in the first decade of the twenty-first century is far more formidable than at any time covered by this study. As Jack Straw acknowledged when launching the FCO's White Paper on Britain's overseas priorities in March 2006, this was partly because 'the pace of change is remarkable and it shows no obvious sign of slowing down' (www.fco.gov.uk; Cm 6762). But the speed of change matters far more today because the direction in which international relations are moving is also far less predictable and more complex than ever before. As David Shukman noted presciently in 1996, 'from the moment the Berlin Wall fell in November 1989, the first of the old certainties in planning was lost'. After this, it became increasingly clear that the Cold War 'had made way, not for the "New World Order" promised by the first President Bush, but for an era of limitless uncertainty and incalculable dangers' (Shukman 1996: 3–4). The collapse of communism and the devastating impact of 9/11 swept away most of the old familiar land-marks with which policymakers had once navigated their course through difficult diplomatic terrain. In their place, the new international environment is largely uncharted, unpredictable and full of as yet unknown and previously unimagined dangers requiring the application of new and untried policy responses. As an IPPR report on *The New Front Line* (IPPR 2008b) summed it all up in February 2008, 'the world has changed and notions of security that helped protect us in the 20th century are no longer able to protect us in the 21st century'.

Even when considered in the most reassuringly familiar terms of state power and the military balance, the twenty-first century represents a far greater challenge to foreign policymakers than the second half of the twentieth century because radical shifts in the distribution of power will leave it more geographically dispersed than at any time since the early nineteenth century. The pace and magnitude of this transforma-tion can be demonstrated by comparing the conclusions of the US National Intelligence Council's last two four-yearly reviews of global trends. In 2004, the NIC confidently predicted 'continued US domi-nance . . . [because] most major powers have forsaken the idea of bal-ancing the US'. By November 2008, however, the report's title *A Transformed World: Global Trends 2025* indicated a far more pes-simistic assessment of an increasingly fragmented multi-polar world in which the power of China, India and Brazil will increase as a 'less dom-inant' US superpower gradually subsides to the status of the 'first among equals' in a more evenly balanced world (*Guardian*, 21 November 2008).

A far more alarming threat for the future concerns the impact of 'failed' and 'failing' states – particularly when they offer safe havens for terrorists, pirates and transnational criminals. One of the great ironies of the early twenty-first century is that, for the first time in its history, Britain faces greater danger from weak states than from strong ones. According to the IPPR-sponsored Commission on National Security in the 21st Century, an 'arc of instability' stretches across Africa, from oil-rich Nigeria on the west coast, through most of sub-Saharan Africa to drought-stricken Somalia, with its uncontrolled international piracy around the Horn of Africa, into the Gulf region and then on to Central Asia and Pakistan (a state armed with a nuclear arsenal); an area consisting of no fewer than 20 weak or failed states with a total population of 880 million people (*Guardian*, 27 November 2008).

Less easy to predict is the future threat from so-called 'rogue states' intent on developing their own nuclear weapons. Iran has resisted all attempts to curb its uranium enrichment as part of its broader nuclear programme and, in May 2009, it tested a surface-to-surface missile capable of hitting Israel and US bases in the Middle East. Of more immediate concern is North Korea's successful launch of a long-range rocket in April 2009, to be followed a month later by its second successful test of a 10–20 kiloton nuclear weapon. Equally worrying is that it has renounced the armistice ending the Korean War and warned that any effort at naval inspection to prevent the smuggling of nuclear or other WMDs into North Korea would immediately be met with 'a powerful military strike'. Given the volatility of the Pyongyang regime, such fears are likely to increase as the century progresses – particularly given evidence of its military links with the Burmese junta, which has been also recently sought to develop its own nuclear technology by purchasing components form North Korea, Syria and Japan (*Guardian*, 26 May, 22 July 2009).

Beyond the dangers of nuclear proliferation, NATO recently warned that the threat from 'rogue states' engaging in state-sponsored cyberwarfare to shut down the Internet is potentially just as menacing as a missile strike or threats to energy security; an issue of practical concern after a gang of Chinese hackers called Titan Rain (allegedly sponsored by Beijing) entered Pentagon computers in 2008 and stole valuable information on the $300 billion Joint Strike Fighter, putting the entire programme in jeopardy. Russia is also accused of launching a Distributed Denial of Service (D-DOS) attack against both Estonia in 2007 and Georgia in 2008 to coincide with its military advance. Similarly, Israel disabled the Syrian air defence system before attacking its fledgling nuclear facility in September 2007, while North Korea established a state-sponsored cyber-warfare unit in the late 1980s and this was probably responsible for wide-ranging D-DOS attacks on government computers in the US and South Korea in July 2009 which closed some US sites for three days (*Guardian*, 6 March 2008 and 26 June, 9 July 2009). An equally unpredictable but more immediate danger since 9/11 is that posed by Al Qaida and other sources of international terrorism. 'Asymmetric' threats of this sort are undoubtedly the principal preoccupation of foreign policymakers and intelligence agencies around the world and they have forced a redefinition of the entire concept of national security. As Bill Rammell, the Armed Forces minister put it, 'For Britain to be secure, Afghanistan needs to be secure, Pakistan needs to be secure' (*Guardian*, 11 July, 4 August 2009). Such is the price of global interdependence.

Beyond this already formidable spectrum of dangers ranging from international terrorism to 'failed' and 'rogue' states, the twenty-first century is also likely to suffer from the fundamental mismatch between national power and truly global problems, such as the threat of catastrophic financial crisis, climate change and global warming, health pandemics, bio-terrorism, genocide and ethnic cleansing, drug and human trafficking, and resource shortages on an unprecedented scale. Among the most ominous threats, three themes stand out as of particular importance for the next three decades. Firstly, the deepening socio-economic divide between the prosperous 'North' and the poverty-stricken 'South' will leave a privileged elite of well over a billion people benefiting greatly while the remaining six or seven billion are marginalised – with the inevitable result that economically induced mass migration to the developed 'North' is likely to be one of the most challenging problems of the current century. Secondly, the impact of world poverty and population pressures is likely to be severely exacerbated by climate change; a threat described by the updated National Security Strategy (published in June 2009) as an increasing 'driver of global insecurity' because of its effect upon 'large scale migration, water stress, crop failure and food shortages' (www.cabinetoffice. gov.uk). By some estimates, by 2080 another 600 million could be malnourished, 400 million will face malaria and 200 million are likely to lose their homes due to rising sea levels, heavier flooding and intense drought (*Guardian*, 7 February 2008).

The third and final major non-military challenge relates to the competition for scarce natural resources. The most obvious area for concern is the control, supply and pricing of fossil fuels such as oil and gas. As Britain moves from being an energy exporter to a net importer, its vulnerability to supply decisions was highlighted in December 2008 when Russia cut off supplies to the Ukraine, which briefly disrupted supply to other European states. More to the point, in December 2008 President Putin menacingly declared at the height of his conflict over the US missile defence plan that the era of 'cheap gas is surely coming to an end' (*Guardian*, 24 December 2008). This represents a very significant threat at a time when Russia supplies a quarter of Europe's gas, and the Kremlin's security strategy for the period up to 2020 stated explicitly that 'in a competition for [energy] resources, it can't be ruled out that military force could be used for resolving emerging problems'

(*Guardian*, 14 May 2009). Competition is likely to be just as intense to control the supply of water, given UN estimates that by 2080 some 1.8 billion people will be living without sufficient water, while food scarcity is another obvious potential source of conflict, given a predicted 50 per cent increase in demand for food by 2025 (*Guardian*, 7 February 2008).

Devising a strategy for an uncertain world

The multifaceted nature of the threat requires an equally broad-ranging spectrum of policy responses. The purpose of the National Security Strategy published in March 2008 was to outline the government's 'single, overarching strategy bringing together the objectives and plans of all departments, agencies and forces involved in protecting our national security'; a range of responses which covered everything from its commitment to 'a multilateral, rules-based approach to international affairs' through to 'the use of force as a last resort' (Cm 7291 2008). Unfortunately, the extremely diverse, ill-defined and interconnected nature of the threat creates particularly formidable problems for those responsible for long-term defensive planning. Even when confronting a clearly identifiable enemy mobilising known military resources during the Cold War, the problem of prediction was a notoriously dangerous enterprise (Haines 2007). But in a post-Cold War environment, characterised by a wide constellation of unpredictable new threats and uncertainties there is inevitably a strong tendency to cling to established patterns of thinking which have served the national interest well in the past. As Blair put it in the preface to *Active Diplomacy for a Changing World*: 'We cannot predict the future, but we can prepare for it' (Cm 6762, 2006: 3).

The most obvious area in which to prepare is the field of conventional military hardware and capabilities. While eschewing radical departures, the Blair and Brown governments have presided over a reorientation of defence policy in recent years which has responded to the collapse of Soviet power and the Warsaw Pact along lines very similar to those in the United States and NATO's so-called 'New Concept'. As discussed in Chapter 6, this redefinition of likely future demands has theoretically produced a shift in strategy away from expensive large-scale weapons platforms like warships and sophisticated fighter aircraft towards a more mobile flexible expeditionary capability with a high global reach. How far the theory has been applied in practice is open to question. With regard to the absolute scale of the budgetary allocation devoted to defence, its relentless long-term decline as a percentage of GDP means that one major long-term threat is quite simply that the

Table 10.1   National security strategies, structures and reforms since 2001

Strategy:

2002   'New Chapter' added to Strategic Defence Review, setting out the role of the armed forces in counter-terrorism.

2006   First cross-government counter-terrorism strategy, CONTEST, and cross-government counter-proliferation framework.

2008   New strategic framework for the FCO emphasising national security depends on working with other nations; National Security Strategy published in March.

2009   Updated National Security Strategy published outlining measures against cyber-attacks.

Structures:

2001   Conflict Prevention Pools created to improve cooperation between the FCO, MoD and DfID; new Cabinet Office emergency structures established.

2003   Joint Terrorism Analysis Centre brings together expertise from the police, intelligence agencies and 16 government departments.

2006   Serious and Organised Crime Agency established.

2007   Office for Security and Counter-terrorism established to coordinate cross-government counter-terrorist activity; new UK Border Agency established; new Cabinet Committee on National Security, International Relations and Development.

2008   National Risk Register published setting out the assessment of potential risks.

2009   Cyber Security Operations Centre established at GCHQ to combat the threat to Whitehall and corporate computer systems.

Sources: Cm 7291 *The National Security Strategy of the UK: Security in an Interdependent World*, March 2008, pp. 4–5; *Guardian*, 15 and 26 June 2009.

strategic environment will change much faster than the nation's ability to acquire or apply the defensive resources needed to counter new threats. Moreover, while this has always been a theoretical possibility since 1945, it is likely to become a far greater risk in the future given the far more extensive range of demands implied by a wider spectrum of potential threats.

An even greater question mark exists with regard to the expenditure priority attached to this mobile expeditionary capability, relative to the obsession with major high-tech prestige defence projects. If the remarks of General Sir Richard Dannatt as the head of the Army are any guide, then the balance still remains far too 'heavily skewed' in favour of the latter. In May 2009, he thus accused the MoD of 'squander[ing] scarce resources on those things that are not relevant to today's and tomorrow's absolute requirements' while denying British troops on the ground the tools and training to do their job; a doubly mistaken strategy because this failure damaged the effectiveness of British forces in the field and undermined Britain's value to the United States as its principal ally in a troubled world (*Guardian*, 16 May 2009). This condemnation would appear to be wholly justified by the confusion reflected in the National Security Strategy (March 2008), which repeated the pledge to 'shift the overall balance of defence procurement towards support of current operations' while in the same paragraph asserting that it will 'continue to invest for the long term in a broad range of military capabilities – including assets like the two new aircraft carriers and enhanced air defence and antisubmarine warfare capabilities' (Cm 7291, 2008: para. 4.70). Britain thus enters the twenty-first century with the same jumble of conflicting priorities and insufficient resources that has dogged its defence policy since the decision to build the atomic bomb in 1946.

In diplomatic and foreign policy terms, planning for the future looks rather less problematical. One of the central themes of FCO activity during the past decade has been the need for multilateral action to respond effectively to global problems that transcend both national boundaries and old-fashioned calculations about the 'balance of power'. The language of globalisation and 'interdependence' so beloved of New Labour's Third Way politicians has thus been translated into tangible policy outcomes. In his Chicago speech in April 1999, Blair called for a new financial structure because 'the Bretton Woods machinery was set up for a post-war world. The world has moved on' (www.number10.gov.uk). Nine years later, Gordon Brown declared at the JFK Memorial Library in Boston that 'for the first time in human history we have the opportunity to come together around a global covenant, to reframe the international architecture and build a truly global society' (*Guardian*, 19 April 2008). Thereafter, as David Miliband has repeatedly argued, 'our longer term challenge is to adapt and strengthen other multilateral institutions and networks to renew their mandates, reform the way they work, and adapt more quickly to new threats and new opportunities'. Among the proposals designed to give substance to this aspiration, the Foreign Secretary has recently emphasised the importance of finding a new raison d'être for the EU, given that its original mandate to prevent conflict within Western Europe no longer existed. Brown has repeatedly urged that the World Bank should be strengthened to finance poverty elimination or to become a 'Bank for the Environment' funding climate change initiatives. Similarly, the IMF should be reformed to exercise a surveillance role over the global financial system to prevent a repetition of the 'credit crunch' crisis of 2008–09 (www.fco.gov.uk; *Guardian*, 19 April 2009; www.number10.gov.uk).

Another defining theme in the discourse of the Blair–Brown governments had been the importance of cultivating rising powers like China and India and the need to reform international institutions to incorporate these states into existing structures. For example, Brown supports a permanent seat for India, Japan, Brazil and one African state on the UN Security Council, as part of his plan to modernise a whole range of international institutions to make them 'representative of 2008 rather than 1945'. He was also one of the first to call for the creation of the 'G8 Plus Five' to represent Brazil, China, India, Mexico and South Africa prior to the launch of the G20 (*Guardian*, 21 January 2008). At the other end of the threat spectrum, when launching *Active Diplomacy for a Changing World* in March 2006, Jack Straw argued that Labour's 'strongly activist foreign policy' since 1997 had been designed to resolve the problem of weak and failing states and this objective underpinned everything from its central role in Afghanistan and Iraq to the creation of a UN conflict resolution force. As the National Security Strategy put it in 2008, failing states were the subject of 'a wide range of government activity from diplomacy to development to overseas military operations' (Cm 7291, 2008: 83).

Beyond a strictly defensive response to international terrorism, British foreign policymakers have also increasingly emphasised the importance of 'winning the battle of ideas' in order to remove the underlying causes of the threat to Western security. Far from retreating from the Blairite focus on spreading the values of liberty, democracy, human rights and justice after the bitter lessons of Iraq and Afghanistan, in his lecture on the 'New Diplomacy' in July 2007, David Miliband emphasised that this remains high on the FCO agenda. 'Our objective is not domination. It is not to force others to live as we do. In a world as diverse and complex as ours, it is to establish, on however thin a basis, a set of rights and responsibilities, by which we can live side by side. Our aim must be to galvanise all the resources of moderation to block the path of radical extremism' (www.fco.gov.uk). He was even more expansive in a speech on 'The Democratic Imperative' at Oxford, where he argued that the debate about Iraq should not 'obscure our national interest, never mind our moral impulse, in supporting the movement for democracy'. Among other benefits, he observed that in the Middle East this represented 'the best long-term defence against global terrorism and conflict' (*Guardian*, 12 February 2008).

Despite its enthusiasm for the exercise of 'soft power' and the need to win 'the battle of ideas', the Labour governments in the early years of the twenty-first century have not entirely abandoned the idea of 'hard power' – or at least the application of 'harder power' in the form of incentives and sanctions. Despite widespread opposition from other member states, the Blair government supported Turkish accession to the EU as a means of building a bridge to a major Muslim country. But, in return, it was clearly understood that this was directly linked to Turkey's willingness to abolish the death penalty and improve the rights of women and minorities. The Brown government's diplomacy towards Iran and its nuclear ambitions has reflected a similar 'carrot and stick' approach. 'A balanced package of incentives and sanctions are also required to apply pressure', Miliband declared in July 2007. 'Iran has every right to be a secure, rich country. But it doesn't have a right to undermine the stability of its neighbours. That is why we are taking a dual track approach' (www.fco.gov.uk). In the wake of new sanctions on Iran, Gordon Brown used his annual foreign policy speech at the Mansion House in November 2007 to leave 'no doubt about the seriousness of our purpose' when warning that Britain would lead the international campaign against Iran's nuclear programme by calling for new UN sanctions on oil and gas investment (www.number10.gov.uk). In March 2008, Britain was also instrumental in passing Security Council resolution UNSCR 1803 further censuring Iran, while in the same month it combined warnings to Iran that it faced harsher international penalties if it continued with uranium enrichment with renewed promises of international assistance with a nuclear programme for strictly civilian purposes (*Guardian*, 18 March 2009).

Britain's position in the world – the more that changes the more that stays the same

In his thought-provoking book on British foreign policy, John Coles highlights the importance of national self-image and the need for an 'idea of Britain' as a means to describe objectives and activities in a manner which has meaning, not just to the foreign policy elite, but also to the public at home and foreign audiences at the receiving end of that policy. This is an important point, given past difficulties experienced in defining Britain's changing position in the world. While all agree that Britain is manifestly not a 'superpower', it cannot accurately be described as a 'middle power' either – particularly as it still possesses many of the features of a great power, given the size of its economy, the scale of its overseas investments, its established role in the international financial system, its level of military expenditure and role within core international organisations (see Chapter 1). Although Attlee, Macmillan and even Harold Wilson could still speak of Britain as a 'great power' without blushing, as the impact of relative economic decline became increasingly apparent, the language employed to describe Britain's position was forced to change. The Duncan Report on Britain's overseas representation in the late 1960s described the country as 'a major power of the second order'. The Berrill Report in 1977 conceded that, although Britain retained some of the attributes of a great power, it was 'on a par with the three other medium-sized countries in the European Community'. As Foreign Secretary during the early 1990s, Douglas Hurd also described Britain as a 'European power with interests that reach far beyond Europe' while his principal FCO official preferred the phrase 'a major European power with global interests and responsibilities' (Coles 2000: 180).

The problem with labels of this sort is that they describe Britain's location in the international system relative to other states without adequately conveying the precise role, purpose and raison d'être of its foreign and defence policy in a changing world. When Dean Acheson declared so memorably in 1962 that Britain had 'lost an empire and not yet found a role', he touched a raw nerve, precisely because the allegation raised such fundamental issues about national purpose and identity. Margaret Thatcher resolved the problem in her own mind when she assured Bedfordshire Conservatives in April 1982 that 'I believe Britain *has* now found a role. It is in upholding international law and teaching the nations of the world how to live' (J. Campbell 2008: 253). This vision of world leadership, based on Britain's long diplomatic experience and its desire to propagate its essential democratic values around the world, would later underpin New Labour's 'ethical dimension' and its commitment to 'liberal intervention' and R2P. Blair also understood that the 'Acheson barb' (as he called it) had offended British sensibilities so painfully because it hit its target with such accuracy. In a speech at Chatham House in April 1995, Blair talked of Britain as a 'major global player' (Coles 2000: 178). Like every Prime Minister before him since Harold Macmillan, he was also attracted by the idea of Britain acting as a bridge between Europe and the United States. By the time he made his first prime ministerial speech on 'The Principles of Modern British Foreign Policy' in November 1997, however, his thinking had moved on. In terms reminiscent of Harold Macmillan, he conceded that Britain was no longer a military superpower, but it could 'still make its presence felt in the world'. 'With our historical alliances, we can be pivotal. We can be powerful and influence – the nation to whom others listen'. More recently, David

Miliband has abandoned the notion of a 'pivotal power', in favour of Britain being a 'global hub,' but whatever the precise label, in recent years government has at least sought to provide a unifying vision of what it stands for in the world and what it seeks to achieve.

There is no telling what a future Conservative government might do about foreign and defence policy once in office. In Opposition there are indications of change. They have distanced themselves from the major centre-right grouping in the European Parliament and threatened an end to aid for HIPCs in favour of a private-sector-led approach focused on the Commonwealth, as part of a 'root and branch review' of DfID activities. There are also strong suggestions that 'ethical' concerns would be replaced by the pursuit of 'enlightened national interest' and, to this end, human rights issues would no longer be allowed to cloud diplomatic relations. Alongside ominous talk from the Shadow Defence Secretary about the MoD living in a 'new age of austerity' with unspecified cuts in spending, there have also been hints about the abandonment of the Trident modernisation – or at the very least a reduction in the programme from four to three new submarines (*Guardian*, 16, 20–21 July, 16 September 2009). Beneath the rhetorical hubbub, however, if the past tells us anything at all, one thing would appear to be fairly certain. Continuity in the main outlines of policy will remain the order of the day. Plus ça change – the more things change the more they really do seem to stay the same.

Useful Websites for Foreign and Defence Sources

www.cabinet-office.gov.uk	The Cabinet Office
www.number10.gov.uk	Downing Street: the Prime Minister's website
www.europa.eu.int	European Union
www.fco.gov.uk	Foreign and Commonwealth Office
www.fpc.prg.uk	Foreign Policy Centre
www.iiss.org	International Institute for Strategic Studies
www.intelligence.gov.uk	The Intelligence Services
www.mod.gov.uk	Ministry of Defence
www.nato.int	NATO
www.oecd.org	Organisation for Economic Co-operation and Development
www.parliament.gov.uk	Westminster Parliament
www.riia.com	Royal Institute of International Affairs
www.rusi.org	Royal United Services Institute
www.hm-treasury.gov.uk	The Treasury (with links to MoD and FCO issues)
www.wto.int	World Trade Organisation

Bibliography

Primary sources

Command Papers

Cmd 6420 *Proposals for the Reform of the Foreign Service*, January 1943.

Cmnd 124 *Defence: Outline of Future Policy*, April 1957.

Cmnd 2276 *Committee on Overseas Representation*, July 1964 (The Plowden Report).

Cmnd 2592 *Statement on Defence Estimates 1965*, February 1965.

Cmnd 2901 *Statement on Defence Estimates: The Defence Review*, February 1966.

Cmnd 3357 *Supplementary Statement on Defence Policy*, July 1967.

Cmnd 4107 *Review Commission on Overseas Representation*, July 1969 (the Duncan Report).

Cmnd 7308 *The United Kingdom's Overseas Representation*, 1977 (The Berrill Report).

Cmnd 8288-I *United Kingdom Defence Programme: The Way Forward*, June 1981.

Cmnd 8787 *Falkland Islands Review*, 1983 (The Franks Report).

Cmnd 9763-I *Statement on the Defence Estimates, 1986*, July 1986.

Cm 1981 *Statement on Defence Estimates 1992*, July 1992.

Cm 2270 *Defending the Future: Statement on Defence Estimates 1993*, July 1993.

Cm 3789 *Eliminating World Poverty: A Challenge for the 21st-Century*, DfID, 1997.

Cm 3999 *Strategic Defence Review and Supporting Essays*, July 1998.

Cm 5006 *Eliminating World Poverty; Making Globalisation Work for the Poor*, DfID, 2000.

Cm 5412 (2002) *The Government's Expenditure Plans 2002/2003 to 2003/2004*, Ministry of Defence, TSO.

Cm 5566 *The Strategic Defence Review: A New Chapter*, July 2002.

Cm 5776 *UK Membership of the Single Currency: An Assessment of the Five Economic Tests*, June 2003.

Cm 6041-I *Delivering Security in a Changing World: Defence White Paper*, December 2003.

Cm 6052 *United Kingdom International Priorities: A Strategy for the FCO*, December 2003.

Cm 6201 *Public Expenditure: Statistical Analyses 2004*, March 2004.

Cm 6269 *Delivering Security in a Changing World, Future Capabilities*, July 2004.

Cm 6697 *Defence Industrial Strategy*, December 2005.

Cm 6762 *Active Diplomacy for a Changing World; The UK's International Priorities*, March 2006.

Cm 6774 (2006) *Foreign Affairs Committee, Annual Report on Human Rights 2005. Response of the Secretary of State for Foreign and Commonwealth Affairs*. TSO.

Cm 6994 *The Future of the United Kingdom's Nuclear Deterrent*, December 2006.

Cm 7098 *The Government's Expenditure Plans 2007–08.*

Cm 7291 *The National Security Strategy of the United Kingdom: Security in an Interdependent World*, March 2008.

Cm 7385 *Defence Plan, including the Government's Expenditure Plans 2008–2012*, June 2008.

Cm 7398 (2008) *Foreign and Commonwealth Office Departmental Report 1 April 2007–31 March 2008; Better World, Better Britain*, 14 May 2008.

Cm 7424 *The Nation's Commitment: Cross-Government Support to Our Armed Forces, Their Families and Veterans*, 17 July 2008.

Cm 7557 (2009) *Foreign and Commonwealth Office, Annual Report on Human Rights 2008*, 26 March 2009, TSO.

Cm 7656 *Eliminating World Poverty: Building our Common Future*, 6 July 2009.

House of Commons Select Committees and other serial publications: various years

DfID. *Annual Report and Departmental Report.*

FCO. *Foreign & Commonwealth Office Annual Report.*

FCO *Foreign & Commonwealth Office Departmental Report.*

FCO (2008) *Better World, Better Britain*, www.fco.gov.uk.

FCO and DfID *Human Rights Annual Report.*

FCO, DfID, DTI and MoD *Strategic Export Controls: Annual Report.*

HM Treasury *Public Expenditure Statistical Analyses.*

HM Treasury *Main Supply Estimates.*

Ministry of Defence *Annual Report and Accounts.*

Ministry of Defence *Government Expenditure Plans.*

Office of National Statistics *UK National Accounts: The Blue Book.*

Select Committee on Defence: reports

HC 225 (1999–2000) *Strategic Export Controls.*

HC 528 (1999–2000) *Major Procurement Projects*, July 2000.

HC 1241 (2005–06) *UK Operations in Iraq*, March 2006.

HC 986 (2005–06) *The Future of the UK's Strategic Nuclear Deterrent*, June 2006.

HC 57 (2006–07) *Annual Report and Accounts, 2005–6*, December 2006.

HC 304 (2006–07) *The Future of the UK's Strategic Nuclear Deterrent: the Manufacturing and Skills Base*, December 2006.

HC 1633-I (2006–07) *Recruitment and Retention in the Armed Forces*, November 2006.

HC 56 (2006–07) *Defence Procurement*, December 2006.

HC 225-I (2006–07) *The Future of the UK's Strategic Nuclear Deterrent: The White Paper*, March 2007.

HC 117 (2007) *Select Committee on Defence, Strategic Export Controls, 2007 Review*, 7 August 2007.

HC 61 (2007–08) *Ministry of Defence, Annual Report and Accounts, 2006–7*, 20 January 2008.

HC 424 (2007–08) *Recruiting and Retaining Armed Forces Personnel*, July 2008.

HC 885 (2007–08) *Main Estimates, 2008–09*, July 2008.

HC 850 I–II (2008) *Ministry of Defence, Annual Report and Accounts, 2007–2008*, 2008.

HC 214 (2008–09) *Annual Report and Accounts 2007–08*, March 2009.

HC 107 (2008–09) *Defence Equipment 2009*, February 2009.

HC 434 (2008–09) *Helicopter Capability*, 16 July 2009.

Select Committee on Foreign Affairs: reports

HC 100-I *Foreign Policy and Human Rights*, 21 December 1998.

HC 318 (2000–01) *European Enlargement and Nice Follow-Up*, 10 April 2001.

HC 327 (2001–02) *British-US Relations*, 18 December 2001.

HC 813-I (2003–04) *The Decision to go to War in Iraq*, 7 July 2003.

HC 109 (2002–03) *Human Rights Annual Report 2004*, 26 March 2005.

HC 36-I (2005–06) *Foreign Policy Aspects of the War Against Terrorism*, 5 April 2005.

HC 574 (2005–06) *Human Rights Annual Report 2005*, 23 February 2006.

HC 573 (2005–05) *Foreign Policy Aspects of the War Against Terrorism*, 2 July 2006.

HC 903 (2005–06) *Public Diplomacy*, 2006.

HC 269 (2006–07) *Human Rights Annual Report*, 29 April 2007.

HC 254 (2007–08) *Scrutiny of Arms Export Control (2008)*, 17 July 2008.

HC 533 (2007–08) *Human Rights Annual Report 2007*, 1 July 2008.

Select Committee on International Development

HC 220-I (2009) *Department for International Development Annual Report 2008*, 19 January 2009.

Select Committee on the Treasury: reports

HC 187 (2082–3) *The UK and the Euro*, June 2003.

House of Lords Debates, 22 November 2007, col. 932.

Secondary sources: books and articles

Abrahamsen, R. and Williams, P. (2001) 'Ethics and foreign policy: the antinomies of New Labour's "Third Way" in sub-Saharan Africa', *Political Studies*, 49 (2): 249–65.

Adamthwaite, A. (1985) 'Britain and the world 1945–49: the view from the Foreign Office', *International Affairs*, 61 (3): 223–35.

Aldrich, R.J. (1994) 'British intelligence and the Anglo-American "special relationship" during the Cold War', *Contemporary Record*, 8 (2): 133–50.

Aldrich, R.J. (1997) 'OSS, CIA and European Unity: the American Committee on a United Europe, 1948–60', *Diplomacy and Statecraft*, 8 (1): 184–227.

Alexander, P. (2006) 'A tale of two Smiths: the transformation of Commonwealth policy, 1964–70', *Contemporary British History*, 20 (3): 303–21.

Alford, B.W.E. (1996) *Britain in the World Economy since 1880* (London: Longman).

Allen, G (2003) *The Last Prime Minister: Being Honest about the UK Presidency* (London: Imprint Academic).

Amery, J. (1951) *The Life of Joseph Chamberlain*, vol. IV (London: Rupert Hart Davis).

Ansprenger, F. (1989) *The Dissolution of the Colonial Empires* (London: Routledge).

Arnold, L. (2001) *Britain and the H-Bomb* (Basingstoke: Palgrave Macmillan).

Ashton, N. (2002a) '"A rearguard action": Harold Macmillan and the making of British foreign policy, 1957–1963', in Otte, T.G. (ed.), *The Makers of British Foreign Policy: From Pitt to Thatcher* (Basingstoke: Palgrave Macmillan).

Ashton, N. (2002b) *Kennedy, Macmillan and the Cold War* (Basingstoke: Palgrave Macmillan).

Bache, I. and Jordan, A. (2006) 'Britain in Europe and Europe in Britain', in Bache, I. and Jordan, A. (eds), *The Europeanization of British Politics* (Basingstoke: Palgrave Macmillan).

Bache, I. and Nugent, N. (2007) 'Europe', in Seldon, A. (ed.), *Blair's Britain 1997–2007* (Cambridge: Cambridge University Press).

Bailes, A. (2007) 'Reflections on thirty years in the Diplomatic Service', in Johnson, G. (ed.), *The Foreign Office and British Diplomacy in the 20th Century* (London: Routledge).

Baker, K. (1993) *The Turbulent Years: My Life in Politics* (London: Faber).

Bamford, J. (1982) *The Puzzle Palace: America's National Security Agency and its Special Relationship with Britain's GCHQ* (London: Longman).

Barber, J. (1988) 'Southern Africa', in Byrd, P. (ed.), *British Foreign Policy under Thatcher* (Oxford: Philip Allan).

Barker, E. (1983) *The British between the Superpowers, 1945–50* (London: Routledge).

Barnett, C. (1995) *The Lost Victory: British Dreams, British Realities 1945–50* (London: Macmillan).

Bartlett, C.J. (1972) *The Long Retreat: A Short History of British Defence Policy, 1945–70* (London: Macmillan).

Bartlett, C.J. (1992) *'The Special Relationship': A Political History of Anglo-American Relations since 1945*, (London: Longman).

Bartlett, W. (2000) '"Simply the right thing to do": Labour goes to war', in Little, R. and Wickham-Jones, M. (eds), *New Labour's Foreign Policy: A New Morale Crusade* (Manchester: Manchester University Press).

Baylis, J. (ed.) (1977) *British Defence Policy in a Changing World* (London: Macmillan).

Baylis, J. (1982) 'Britain and the Dunkirk Treaty: the origins of NATO', *Journal of Strategic Studies*, 5: 236–47.

Baylis, J. (1983) 'Introduction; defence policy for the 1980s and 1990s', in Baylis, J. (ed.), *Alternative Approaches to British Defence Policy* (London: Macmillan).

Baylis, J. (1984) *Anglo-American Defence Relations, 1939–1984: the Special Relationship*, 2nd edn (London: Macmillan).

Baylis, J. (1986) '"Greenwoodery" and British defence policy', *International Affairs*, 62 (3): 443–57.

Baylis, J. (1989) *British Defence Policy: Striking the Right Balance* (London: Macmillan).

Baylis, J. (ed.) (1997) *Anglo-American Relations since 1939: the Enduring Alliance* (Manchester: Manchester University Press).

Baylis, J. (1999) 'The Development of Britain's Thermonuclear Capability 1954–61: Myth or Reality?', *Contemporary Record*, 8 (1): 159–74.

Beach, H. and Gurr, N. (1999) *Flattering the Passions. Or, the Bomb and Britain's Bid for a World Role* (London: Tauris).

Bell, C. (1973) 'The Special Relationship', in Leifer, M. (ed.), *Constraints and Adjustments in British Foreign Policy* (London: George Allen & Unwin).

Beloff, M. (1966) 'The Special Relationship: an Anglo-American Myth', in Gilbert, M. (ed.), *A Century of Conflict, 1850–1950: Essays for AJP Taylor* (London: Hamish Hamilton).

Benvenuti, A. (2009) 'The Heath government and British defence policy in Southeast Asia at the end of Empire, 1970–71', *Twentieth Century British History*, 20 (1): 53–73.

Best, R.A. (1986) *'Co-operation with Like-Minded Peoples': British Influences on American Security Policy, 1945–49* (New York: Greenwood Press).

Blair, A. (1998) 'Swimming with the tide? Britain and the Maastricht Treaty negotiations on Common, Foreign and Security Policy', *Contemporary British History*, 12 (3): 407–23.

Blair, A. (2002) *Saving the Pound? Britain's Road to Monetary Union* (London: Prentice-Hall).

Blair, T (2006) *Global Alliance for Global Values* (London: Foreign Policy Centre).

Blair, T. (2007) 'A Battle for Global Values', *Foreign Affairs*, 86 (1).

Blank, S. (1979) 'Britain's economic problems: lies and damned lies', in Kramnik, I. (ed.), *Is Britain Dying? Perspectives on the Current Crisis* (Ithaca, NY: Cornell University Press).

Blunkett, D. (2006) *The Blunkett Tapes: My Life in the Bear Pit* (London: Bloomsbury).

Bluth, C. (2004) 'The British road to war: Blair, Bush and the decision to invade Iraq', *International Affairs*, 80 (5): 871–92.

Bourantonis, D. and Magliveras, K. (2002) 'Anglo-American differences over the UN during the Cold War: the Uniting for Peace Resolution', *Contemporary British History*, 16 (2): 59–76.

Bourne, A. and Cini, M. (2000) 'Exporting the Third Way in foreign policy: New Labour, the European Union and human rights policy', in Little, R. and Wickham Jones, M. (eds), *New Labour's Foreign Policy: A New Moral Crusade?* (Manchester: Manchester University Press).

Boyce, G. (2005) *The Falklands War* (Basingstoke: Palgrave Macmillan).

Breslin, S. (2004) 'Beyond diplomacy? UK relations with China since 1997', *British Journal of Politics and International Relations*, 6 (3): 409–25.

Brown, A. (2008) *Reinventing Humanitarian Intervention: Two Cheers for the Responsibility to Protect?*, House of Commons Library Research Paper 08/55.

Brown, G. (1971) *In My Way: The Political Memoirs of Lord George-Brown* (London: Gollancz).

Brown, J. and Louis, W. R. (eds), (1999) *The Oxford History of the British Empire: The Twentieth Century* (Oxford: Oxford University Press).

Buller, J. (1996) 'Foreign and defence policy under Thatcher and Major', in Ludlum, S. and Smith, M. (eds), *Contemporary British Conservatism* (London: Macmillan).

Buller, J. (2001) 'New Labour's foreign and defence policy: external support structures and domestic politics', in Ludlam, S. and Smith, M.J. (eds), *New Labour in Government* (Basingstoke: Palgrave Macmillan).

Bullock, A. (1983) *Ernest Bevin Foreign Secretary, 1945–51* (London: Heinemann).

Bulmer, S. (2000) 'European policy: fresh start or false dawn?', in Coates, D. and Lawler, P. (eds), *New Labour in Power* (Manchester: Manchester University Press).

Bulmer, S. and Burch, M. (2006) 'Central government', in Bache, I. and Jordan, A. (eds), *The Europeanization of British Politics* (Basingstoke: Palgrave Macmillan).

Burk, K. (1995) 'American foreign economic policy and Lend-Lease', in Lane, A. and Temperley, H. (eds), *The Rise and Fall of the Grand Alliance, 1941–45* (London: Macmillan).

Burk, K. and Stokes, M. (eds) (1999) *The United States and the Atlantic Alliance since 1945* (Oxford: Berg).

Butler, D. and Kitzinger, U. (1976) *The 1975 Referendum* (London: Macmillan).

Butler, Lord (2004) *Review of Intelligence on Weapons of Mass Destruction: Report of the Committee of Privy Counsellors* (London: The Stationery Office).

Byrd, P.(ed.) (1988a) *British Foreign Policy under Thatcher* (Oxford: Philip Allan).

Byrd, P. (1988b) 'Defence Policy', in Byrd, P. (ed.), *British Foreign Policy under Thatcher* (Oxford: Philip Allan).

Byrd, P. (ed.) (1991) *British Defence Policy: Thatcher and Beyond* (Oxford: Philip Allan).

Cabinet Office (2006) *The National Intelligence Machinery* (London: The Stationery Office, www.cabinetoffice.gov.uk).

Cabinet Office (2007a) *Capability Review of the Department for International Development* (London: TSO).

Cabinet Office (2007b) *Capability Review of the Foreign and Commonwealth Office: Progress and Next Steps* (London: TSO).

Cabinet Office (2007c) *Capability Review of Ministry of Defence: Progress and Next Steps* (London: TSO).

Cabinet Office (2008) *A Guide to the Cabinet and Cabinet Committees* (London: Cabinet Office).

Cabinet Office (2009) *Capability Review of the Ministry of Defence: Progress and Next Steps* (London: TSO).

Cairncross, A. (1987) *Years of Recovery: British Economic Policy 1945–51* (London: Methuen).

Cairncross, A. (1992) *The British Economy since 1945* (Oxford: Blackwell).

Callaghan, J. (1988) *Time and Chance* (London: Fontana).

Cameron, Lord (1983) 'Alternative strategies: strategy, tactics and new technology', in Baylis, J. (ed.), *Alternative Approaches to British Defence Policy* (London: Macmillan).

Campbell, A. (2008) *The Blair Years* (London: Arrow Books).

Campbell, J. (2008) *Margaret Thatcher, Volume 2: The Iron Lady* (London: Vintage Books).

Camps, M. (1964) *Britain and the European Community, 1955–63* (Oxford: Oxford University Press).

Carr, F. (1990) 'Foreign and defence policy: the impact of Thatcherism', in Savage, S. and Robins, L. (eds), *Public Policy under Thatcher* (London: Macmillan).

Carr, F. (2001) 'Foreign and defence policy' in Savage, S. and Atkinson, R. (eds), *Public Policy under Blair* (Basingstoke: Palgrave Macmillan).

Carrington, Lord (1998) *Reflect on Things Past: The Memoirs of Peter Lord Carrington* (New York: Oxford University Press).

Carter, N. (2003) 'Whither (or wither) the Euro? Labour and the single currency', *Politics*, 23 (1).

Carver, Lord (1982) *A Policy for Peace* (London: Faber).

Carver, Lord (1983) 'Getting defence priorities right', in Baylis, J. (ed.), *Alternative Approaches to British Defence Policy* (London: Macmillan).

Central Statistical Office (1949) *Annual Abstract of Statistics, 1938–48* (London: HMSO).

Chalmers, M. (1985) *Paying for Defence: Military Spending and British Decline* (London: Pluto).

Chalmers, M. (2008) 'A force for influence? Making British defence effective', *RUSI Journal*, 153 (6): 67–82.

Charlton, M. (1989) *The Little Platoon* (Oxford: Basil Blackwell).

Charmley, J. (2007) 'Splendid Isolation to Finest Hour: Britain as a global power 1900–1950', in Johnson, G. (ed.), *The Foreign Office and British Diplomacy in the 20th Century* (London: Routledge).

Clark, A. (1993) *Alan Clark Diaries* (London: Phoenix Paperback).

Clark, I. (1994) *Nuclear Diplomacy and the Special Relationship: Britain's Deterrent and America, 1957–1962* (Oxford: Oxford University Press).

Clarke, M. (1988) 'The policy-making process', in Smith, M. Smith, S. and White, B. (eds), *British Foreign Policy: Tradition, Change and Transformation* (London: Unwin Hyman).

Clarke, M. (1992) *British External Policy-Making in the 1990s* (London: Macmillan).

Clarke, M. (2007) 'Foreign policy', in Seldon, A. (ed.), *Blair's Britain 1997–2007* (Cambridge: Cambridge University Press).

Clarke, M. (2008) 'The overdue Defence Review: old questions, new answers', *RUSI Journal*, 153 (6).

Coates, D. (1994) *The Question of UK Decline: State, Society and Economy* (Hemel Hempstead: Harvester Wheatsheaf).

Coates, D. and Krieger, J. (2004) *Blair's War* (Cambridge: Polity Press).

Coker, C. (1987) *British Defence Policy in the 1990s: A Guide to the Defence Debate* (London: Brassey Defence Publishers).

Coles, J. (2000) *Making Foreign Policy: A Certain Idea of Britain* (London: John Murray).

Coleman, J. (2008) '"What now for Britain?" The State Department's intelligence assessment of the "Special Relationship", 7 February 1968', *Diplomacy and Statecraft*, 19 (2): 350–60.

Coleman, J. (2004) *A 'Special Relationship'? Harold Wilson, Lyndon B. Johnson and Anglo-American Relations 'at the Summit', 1964–68* (Manchester: Manchester University Press).

Coleman, J. (2007) 'Dealing with disillusioned men: the Washington Ambassadorship of Sir Patrick Dean, 1965–69', *Contemporary British History*, 21 (2): 247–70.

Commission for Africa (2005) *Our Common Interest* (London: Penguin).

Cook, R. (1997) *Mission Statement for the Foreign and Commonwealth Office, May 1997*.

Cook, R. (2003) *The Point of Departure* (London: Simon & Schuster).

Cooper, N. (1997) *The Business of Death: Britain's Arms Sales at Home and Abroad* (London: Tauris).

Cooper, N. (2000) 'The pariah agenda and New Labour's ethical arms sales policy', in Little, R. and Wickham-Jones, M. (eds), *New Labour's Foreign Policy: A New Moral Crusade?* (Manchester: Manchester University Press).

Cosgrave, P. (1985a) *Thatcher: The First Term* (London: Bodley Head).

Cosgrave, P. (1985b) *Carrington: A Life and Policy* (London: Dent).

Cox, M. and Oliver, T. (2006) 'Security policy in an insecure world', in Dunleavy, P., Heffeman, R., Cowley, P. and Hay, C. (eds), *Developments in British Politics 8* (Basingstoke: Palgrave Macmillan), pp. 174–92.

Cradock, P. (1997) *In Pursuit of British Interests: Reflections on Foreign Policy under Margaret Thatcher and John Major* (London: John Murray).

Crossman, R. (1976) *The Diaries of a Cabinet Minister: Volume 1, 1964–1966* (New York: Reinhardt and Winston).

Curtis, M. (1995) *The Ambiguities of Power: British Foreign Policy since 1945* (London: Zed Books).

Curtis, M. (2003) *Web of Deceit: Britain's Real Role in the World* (London: Zed Books).

Daddow, O. (2007) 'Playing games with history: Tony Blair's European policy in the press', *British Journal of Politics and International Relations*, 9: 582–98.

Danchev, A (ed.) (1998) *On Specialness: Essays in Anglo-American Relations* (London: Macmillan).

Danchev, A. (2000) 'The Cold War "Special Relationship" revisited', *Diplomacy and Statecraft*, 17 (3): 581–92.

Danchev, A. (2007) '"I'm with you"; Tony Blair and the obligations of alliance', in Lloyd, C., Young, M. and Appy, C. (eds), *Iraq and the Lessons of Vietnam* (New York: Free Press).

Darby, P. (1973) *British Defence Policy East of Suez, 1947–1968* (London: Oxford University Press).

Darwin, J. (1984) 'British decolonisation since 1945: a pattern or a puzzle?', *Journal of Imperial and Commonwealth History*, 12 (2): 187–209.

Darwin, J. (1988) *Britain and Decolonisation: The Retreat from Empire in the Post-War Period* (London: Macmillan).

Darwin, J. (1991) *The End of the British Empire: The Historical Debate* (Oxford: Basil Blackwell).

Dawson, D. and Rosecrance, R.N. (1966) 'Theory and reality in the Anglo-American alliance', *World Politics*, October, 21–51.

Demos (2007) *National Security for the 21st Century* (London: Demos).

Deighton, A. (2001) 'European Union policy', in Seldon, A. (ed.), *The Blair Effect: the Blair Government 1997–2001* (London: Little, Brown).

Denman, R. (1997) *Missed Opportunities: Britain and Europe in the 20th Century* (London: Cassell).

Dewey, P. (1997) *War and Progress: Britain 1914–1945* (London: Longman).

Dickie, J. (1994) *"Special" No More – Anglo-American Relations: Rhetoric and Reality* (London: Weidenfeld & Nicolson).

Dickie, J. (2004) *The New Mandarins: How British Foreign Policy Works* (London: Tauris).

Dilks, D. (1971) *The Diaries of Sir Alexander Cadogan, 1938–45* (London: Cassell).

Dilks, D. (ed.) (1981) *Retreat from Power: Studies in Britain's Foreign Policy of the Twentieth Century*, 2 vols (London: Macmillan).

Dillon, G. M. (1989) *The Falklands, Politics and War* (London: Macmillan).

Dimbleby, D. and Reynolds, D. (1988) *An Ocean Apart: the Relationship between Britain and America in the Twentieth Century* (London: Hodder & Stoughton).

Dixon, R. and Williams, P. (2001) 'Tough on debt, tough on the causes of debt? New Labour's Third Way foreign policy', *British Journal of Politics and International Relations*, 3 (2): 150–72.

Dobson, A. (1986) *US Wartime Aid to Britain, 1940–1946* (London: Routledge).

Dobson, A. (1988) *The Politics of the Anglo-American Economic Special Relationship, 1940–87* (Hassocks, Sussex: Wheatsheaf).

Dobson, A. (1995) *Anglo-American Relations in the 20th Century: Of Friendship, Conflict and the Rise and Decline of the Superpowers* (London: Routledge).

Dockrill, M. (1988) *British Defence since 1945* (Oxford: Blackwell).

Dockrill, M. (1989) 'Britain and the first offshore islands crisis, 1945–55', in Dockrill, M. and Young, J.W. (eds), *British Foreign Policy, 1945–56* (London: Macmillan), pp. 173–96.

Donaldson, F. (1984) *The British Council: The First Fifty Years* (London: Jonathan Cape).

Dorman, A. (2001) 'John Nott and the Royal Navy: 1981 Defence Review revisited', *Contemporary British History*, 15 (2): 98–120.

Douglas-Home, A. (1976) *The Way the Wind Blows: An Autobiography by Lord Home* (London: Collins).

Dover, R. (2007) 'For Queen and company: the role of intelligence in the UK arms trade', *Political Studies*, 55 (4): 693–708.

Driver, S. and Martell, L. (2006) *New Labour*, 2nd edn (Cambridge: Polity Press).

Duke, S. (1987) *United States Defence Bases in the United Kingdom* (London: Macmillan).

Dumbrell, J. (2001) *A Special Relationship: Anglo-American Relations in the Cold War and After* (Basingstoke: Palgrave Macmillan).

Dunne, T. and Wheeler, N. (2000) 'The Blair Doctrine: advancing the Third Way in the world', in Little, R. and Wickham-Jones, M. (eds), *New Labour's Foreign Policy: A New Moral Crusade?* (Manchester: Manchester University Press), pp. 61–76.

Eden, A.(1960) *Full Circle* (London: Cassell).

Edmonds, R. (1986) *Setting the Mould: The United States and Britain, 1945–50* (Oxford: Clarendon Press).

Eisenhower, D. (1963) *The White House Years: Mandate to Change, 1953–1956* (New York: Doubleday).

Edwards, T. and Forster, A. (2007) *Out of Step: The Case for Change in Britain's Armed Forces* (London: Demos).

Feiling, K. (1946) *The Life of Neville Chamberlain* (London: Macmillan).

Fieldhouse, D.K. (1984) 'The Labour Governments and the Empire-Commonwealth, 1945–51', in Ovendale, R. (ed.), *The Foreign Policy of the British Labour Governments 1945–51* (Leicester: Leicester University Press).

Fine, B. and Harris, L. (1985) *The Peculiarities of the British Economy* (London: Lawrence & Wishart).

Floud, R. (1980) 'Britain 1860–1914: a survey', in Floud, R. and McCloskey, J. (eds), *The Economic History of Britain since 1700*, (2 vols, Cambridge: Cambridge University Press).

Foreign & Commonwealth Office (FCO) (2007) *CSR07 Value for Money Programme: Delivery Agreement*, December 2007.

FCO, DTI and MoD (1999) *Second Annual Report on Strategic Export Controls* (London: TSO).

Forster, A. and Blair, A. (2002) *The Making of Britain's European Foreign Policy* (Harlow: Pearson Education).

Forster, A. (2007) 'Breaking the covenant: governance of the British Army in the 21st century', *International Affairs*, 82 (6): 1043–57.

Fox, W.T.R. (1944) *The Superpowers: The United States, Britain and the Soviet Union – Their Responsibility for Peace* (New York: Harcourt Brace).

Franks, O. (1955) *Britain and the Tide of Affairs* (Oxford: Oxford University Press).

Freedman, L. (1980) *Britain and Nuclear Weapons* (London: Macmillan).

Freedman, L. (1983) 'British defence policy after the Falklands', in Baylis, J. (ed.), *Alternative Approaches to British Defence Policy* (London: Macmillan).

Freedman, L. (1988) *Britain and the Falklands War* (Oxford: Blackwell).

Freedman, L. (1991) 'Thatcherism and defence', in Kavanagh, D. and Seldon, A. (eds), *The Thatcher Effect: A Decade of Change* (Oxford: Oxford University Press).

Freedman, L. (1999) *The Politics of Defence 1979–1998* (London: Macmillan).

Freedman, L. (2001) 'Defence', in Seldon, A. (ed.), *The Blair Effect: The Blair Government 1997–2001* (London: Little, Brown).

Freedman, L. (2007) 'Defence', in Seldon, A. (ed.), *Blair's Britain 1997–2007* (Cambridge: Cambridge University Press).

Freedman, L. and Gearson, J. (1999) 'Interdependence and independence: Nassau and the British nuclear deterrent', in Burk, K. and Stokes, M. (eds), *United States and the Atlantic Alliance since 1945* (Oxford: Berg).

Friedberg, A.L. (1988) *The Weary Titan: Britain and the Experience of Relative Decline* (Princeton, NJ: Princeton University Press).

Gallagher, J. (1982) *The Decline, Revival and Fall of the British Empire* (Cambridge: Cambridge University Press).

Garton Ash, T. (2007) 'Commentary', in Seldon, A. (ed.), *Blair's Britain, 1997–2007* (Cambridge: Cambridge University Press).

Geddes, A.(1994) 'Labour and the EC 1973–1993: pro-Europeanism, "Europeanisation" and their implications', *Contemporary British History*, 8 (2): 370–80.

Geddes, A. (2002) 'In Europe, not interested in Europe', in Geddes, A. and Tonge, J. (eds), *Labour's Second Landslide: The British General Election of 2001* (Manchester: Manchester University Press).

George, S. (1998) *An Awkward Partner: Britain in the European Community*, 2nd edn (Oxford: Oxford University Press).

George, S. and Sowemimo, M. (1996) 'Conservative foreign policy towards the European Union', in Ludlum, S.and Smith, M. (eds), *Contemporary British Conservatism* (London: Macmillan), pp. 244–63.

Gilbert, B.B. (1966) *The Evolution of the National Insurance in Great Britain: the Origins of the Welfare State* (London: Michael Joseph).

Gill, S. (ed.) (1988) *Atlantic Relations in the Reagan Era and Beyond* (Brighton: Wheatsheaf).

Goodman, M.I. (2007) '"With a little help from my friends": the Anglo-American atomic intelligence partnership, 1945–1958', *Diplomacy and Statecraft*, 18 (1): 155–83.

Gowing, M. (1964) *Britain and Atomic Energy, 1939–1945* (London: Macmillan).

Gowing, M. (1974) *Independence and Deterrence: Britain and Atomic Energy, 1945–52, volume I* (London: Macmillan).

Gowing, M. (1981) 'Britain, America and the Bomb', in Dilks, D. (ed.), *Retreat from Power: Studies in Britain's Foreign Policy of the Twentieth Century* (London: Macmillan).

Gowing, M. (1986) 'Nuclear Weapons and the "Special Relationship"', in Louis, W.R. and Ball, H. (eds), *'The Special Relationship: Anglo-American Relations since 1945* (Oxford: Clarendon).

Green, E.H.H. (1995) *The Crisis of Conservatism: The Politics, Economics and Ideology of the British Conservative Party, 1880–1914* (London: Routledge).

Green, E.H.H. (2006) *Thatcher* (London: Hodder Arnold).

Greenwood, D. (1976) 'Constraints and choices in the transformation of British defence policy since 1945', *British Journal of International Studies*, 2: 5–26.

Greenwood, D. (1977) 'Defence and national priorities since 1945', in Baylis, J. (ed.), *British Defence Policy in a Changing World* (London: Macmillan), pp. 174–207.

Greenwood, D. (1991) 'Expenditure and management', in Byrd, P. (ed.), *British Defence Policy: Thatcher and Beyond* (Oxford: Philip Allan), pp. 36–66.

Greenwood, S. (1983) 'Return to Dunkirk: the origins of the Anglo-French Treaty of March 1947', *Journal of Strategic Studies*, 6: 49–65.

Greenwood, S. (2000) *Britain and the Cold War 1945–91* (Basingstoke: Palgrave Macmillan).

Greenwood, S. (2002) 'Ernest Bevin: reluctant cold warrior', in Otte, T.G. (ed.), *The Makers of British Foreign Policy: from Pitt to Thatcher* (Basingstoke: Palgrave Macmillan).

Greenwood, S (2003) '"A war we don't want". Another look at the British Labour Government's commitment to Korea, 1950–51', *Contemporary British History*, 17 (4).

Grey, S. (2009) *Operation Snakebite: The Explosive True Story of an Afghan Desert Siege* (London: Viking Books).

Grey, Viscount (1925) *Twenty Five Years, 1892–1916* (London: Frederick Stokes).

Gummett, P. (2000) 'New Labour and defence', in Coates, D. and Lawler, P. (eds), *New Labour in Power* (Manchester: Manchester University Press).

Hahn, P.L. (2000) 'Discord or accommodation? Britain and United States in world affairs, 1945–92', in Leventhal, F.M. and Quinault, R. (eds), *Anglo-American Attitudes; from Revolution to Partnership* (Aldershot: Ashgate), pp. 276–93.

Haines, S. (2007) 'The real strategic environment. A call for long-term thinking on UK defence investment', *RUSI Journal*, 152 (5).

Hancock, W.K. and Gowing M.M. (1949) *British War Economy* (London: HMSO).

Harris, J. (1993) *Private Lives, Public Spirit* (Oxford: Oxford University Press).

Hartley, K. (2006) 'The economics of UK nuclear weapons policy', *International Affairs*, 82 (4): 675–84.

Hastings, M. (2008) 'Sleep-walking towards the precipice: the crisis in British defence policy' *RUSI Journal*, 153 (6).

Hathaway, R.M. (1981) *Ambiguous Partnership: Britain and America, 1944–47* (New York: Columbia University Press).

Healey, D. (1989) *The Time of My Life* (London: Michael Joseph).

Heath, E. (1998) *The Course of My Life: The Autobiography* (London: Hodder & Stoughton).

Henderson, N. (1984) *The Private Office* (London: Weidenfeld & Nicolson).

Henderson, N. (1987) *Channels and Tunnels: Reflections on Britain and Abroad* (London: Weidenfeld & Nicolson).

Henderson, N. (1994) *Mandarin: The Diary of an Ambassador* (London: Weidenfeld & Nicolson).

Hennessy, P (1986) *Cabinet* (Oxford: Blackwell).

Hennessy, P. (1990) *Whitehall* (London: Fontana).

Hennessy, P (1993) *Never Again: Britain 1945–51* (London: Vintage).

Hennessy, P. (2000) *The Prime Minister: The Office and its Holders since 1945* (London: Allen Lane).

Hennessy, P. (2003) *The Secret State: Whitehall and the Cold War* (London: Penguin).

Hennessy, P (2004) *Rulers and Servants of the State: The Blair Style of Government, 1997–2004* (London: Office of Public Management).

Hennessy, P. (2007) *Having It So Good: Britain in the 1950s* (London: Penguin).

Hill, C. (1988) 'The historical background: past and present in British foreign policy', in Smith, M., Smith, S. and White, B. (eds), *British Foreign Policy: Tradition, Change and Transformation* (London: Unwin Hyman).

Hill, C. (2001) 'Foreign policy', in Seldon, A. (ed.), *The Blair Effect: The Blair Government 1997–2001* (London: Little, Brown), pp. 331–54.

Hill, C. (2005) 'Putting the world to rights: Tony Blair's foreign policy mission', in Seldon, A. and Kavanagh, D. (eds), *The Blair Effect 2001–5* (Cambridge: Cambridge University Press).

Hill-Norton, Lord, (1983) 'Return to a national strategy', in Baylis, J. (ed.), *Alternative Approaches to British Defence Policy* (London: Macmillan), pp.117–37.

Hodder-Williams, R. (2000) 'Reforging the "Special Relationship": Blair, Clinton and foreign policy', in Little, R. and Wickham-Jones, M. (eds), *New Labour's Foreign Policy* (Manchester: Manchester University Press), pp. 234–50.

Holden, R. (2002) *The Making of New Labour's European Policy* (Basingstoke: Palgrave Macmillan).

Holland, R.F. (1985) *European Decolonisation, 1918–81: An Introductory Survey* (London: Macmillan).

Holt, A.(2005) 'Lord Home and Anglo-American relations, 1961–1963', *Diplomacy and Statecraft*, 16 (4): 699–722.

Hopkinson, W. (2000) *The Making of British Defence Policy* (London: Stationery Office Books).

Horne, A. (1989) *Macmillan*, 2 vols (London: Macmillan).

Howard, M. (1974) *The Continental Commitment: The Dilemma of British Defence Policy in the Era of Two World Wars* (London: Pelican).

Howarth, J. (2003) 'France, Britain and the Euro-Atlantic crisis', *Survival*, 45 (4): 173–92.

Howe, G. (1995) *Conflict of Loyalty* (London: Macmillan).

Hyam, R. (1976) *Britain's Imperial Century 1815–1914* (London: Batsford).

Inder-Singh, A. (1987) *The Origins of the Partition of India* (Oxford: Oxford University Press).

Ingham, B. (1991) *Kill the Messenger* (London: Fontana).

IPPR Commission on National Security in the 21st Century (2008a) *Shared Destinies: Security in a Globalised World* (London: IPPR).

IPPR Commission on National Security in the 21st Century (2008b) *The New Front Line: Security in a Changing World* (London: IPPR).

IPPR Commission on National Security in the 21st Century (2009) *Shared Responsibilities: A National Security Strategy for the United Kingdom* (London: IPPR).

International Institute for Strategic Studies (IISS) (2003) *The Military Balance 2003–04* (Oxford: Oxford University Press).

James, S. (1992) *British Cabinet Government* (London: Routledge).

Jeffery, K. (1999) 'The Second World War', in Brown, J.M. and Louis, W.R. (eds), *The Oxford History of the British Empire: Volume IV: The 20th Century* (Oxford: Oxford United Press).

Jenkins, P. (1987) *Mrs Thatcher's Revolution: The Ending of the Socialist Era* (London: Jonathan Cape).

Jenkins, S. and Sloman, A. (1985) *With Respect, Ambassador: An Enquiry into the Foreign Office* (London: BBC).

Johnson, G. (2007) 'Introduction: the Foreign Office and British diplomacy in the Twentieth Century', in Johnson, G. (ed.), *The Foreign Office and British Diplomacy in the 20th Century* (London: Routledge).

Joll, J. (1967) *Britain in Europe: Pitt to Churchill 1793–1940* (Oxford: Clarendon Press).

Jones, M. (2003) 'Anglo-American relations after Suez', *Diplomacy and Statecraft*, 14 (1): 49–79.

Jones, R.E. (1974) *British Defence Policy in a Changing World* (London: Longman).

Kaiser, W. (1996) *Using Europe, Abusing the Europeans: Britain and European Integration, 1945–63* (London: Macmillan).

Kaldor, M. (1980) 'Technical change in the defence industry', in Pavitt, K. (ed.), *Technical Innovation and British Economic Performance* (London: Macmillan).

Kampfner, J. (1999) *Robin Cook* (London: Phoenix).

Kampfner, J. (2003) *Blair's Wars* (London: Free Press).

Kavanagh, D. and Morris, P. (1994) *Consensus Politics from Attlee to Major*, 2nd edn (Oxford: Blackwell).

Kavanagh, D. and Seldon, A. (1991) *The Thatcher Effect: A Decade of Change* (Oxford: Oxford University Press).

Kavanagh, D. Richards, D., Smith, M. and Geddes, A. (2006) *British Politics*, 5th edn (Oxford: Oxford University Press).

Kennedy, P. (1976) *The Rise and Fall of British Naval Mastery* (London: Penguin).

Kennedy, P. (1981) *The Realities Behind Diplomacy: Background Influences on British External Policy, 1865–1980* (London: Fontana).

Kennedy, P. (1989) *The Rise and Fall of the Great Powers: Economic Change and Military Conflict from 1500 to 2000* (London: Fontana).

Kent, J. (1993) *British Imperial Strategy and the Origins of the Cold War 1944–49* (Leicester: Leicester University Press).

Kincaid, B. (2008) *The Battle to Reform UK Defence Acquisition* (London: RUSI).

King, A. (1977) *Britain Says Yes: The 1975 Referendum on the Common Market* (Washington, DC: American Enterprise Institute).

King, A. (1998) *New Labour Triumphs: Britain at the Polls* (Chatham, NJ: Chatham House).

Kissinger, H. (1979) *The White House Years* (London: Weidenfeld & Nicolson).

Kissinger, H. (1982a) *Years of Upheaval* (London: Weidenfeld & Nicolson).

Kissinger, H. (1982b) 'Britain and the United States: reflections on a partnership', *International Affairs*, 58 (4).

Kitzinger, U. (1968) *The Second Try: Labour and the EEC* (London: Pergamon).

Kitzinger, U. (1973) *Diplomacy and Persuasion: How Britain Joined the Common Market* (London: Thames & Hudson).

Khatri, K (2007) 'Climate change', in Seldon, A. (ed.), *Blair's Britain 1997–2007* (Cambridge: Cambridge University Press).

Labour Party (1996) *New Labour: New Life for Britain* (London: Labour Party).

Labour Party (1997) *New Labour, Because Britain Deserves Better* (London: Labour Party).

Labour Party (2001) *Ambitions for Britain, The Labour Party Manifesto* (London: Labour Party).

Lapping, B. (1985) *The End of Empire* (London: Paladin).

Lawler, P. (2000) 'New Labour's foreign policy', in Coates, D. and Lawler, P. (eds), *New Labour in Power* (Manchester: Manchester University Press).

Lawson, N. (1992) *The View from Number 11: Memoirs of a Tory Radical* (London: Bantam Press).

Lee, S. (2006) '"In no sense vital and actually not even important". Reality and perception of Britain's contribution to the development of nuclear weapons', *Contemporary British History*, 20 (2): 159–85.

Lewis, J. (1988) *Changing Directions: British Military Planning for Postwar Strategic Defence, 1942–1947* (London: Sherwood Press).

Lewis, J. (2006) 'Nuclear Disarmament versus Peace in the Twenty First Century', *International Affairs*, 82 (4) (June): 667–73.

Lilleker, D. (2000) 'Labour's defence policy: from unilateralism to strategic review', in Little, R. and Wickham-Jones, M. (eds), *New Labour's Foreign Policy: A New Moral Crusade?* (Manchester: Manchester University Press), pp. 218–33.

Little, W. (1988) 'Anglo-Argentine relations and the management of the Falklands Question', in Byrd, P. (ed.), *British Foreign Policy under Thatcher* (Oxford: Philip Allan).

Little, R. and Wickham-Jones, M. (eds) (2000) *New Labour's Foreign Policy: A New Moral Crusade?* (Manchester: Manchester University Press).

Little, R. (2000) 'Conclusions: the ethics and strategy of Labour's Third Way and foreign policy', in Little, R. and Wickham-Jones, M. (eds), *New Labour's Foreign Policy: A New Moral Crusade?* (Manchester: Manchester University Press), pp. 251–63.

Lord, C. (1995) 'Foreign policy', in Catterall, P. (ed.), *Contemporary Britain: An Annual Review of 1994* (London: Institute of Contemporary British History).

Louis, W.R. and Bull, H. (eds) (1986) *The 'Special Relationship': Anglo-American Relations since 1945* (Oxford: Clarendon Press).

Ludlum, S. and Smith, M. (eds) (1996) *Contemporary British Conservatism* (London: Macmillan).

Lundestad, G. (1998) *'Empire' by Integration: United States and European Integration, 1945–1997* (Oxford: Oxford University Press).

Lunn, J., Miller, M. and Swift, B. (2008) *British Foreign Policy since 1997*, House of Commons Library Research Paper 08/56.

Manning, R. (2007) 'Development', in Seldon, A. (ed.), *Blair's Britain 1997–2007* (Cambridge: Cambridge University Press).

Martin, L. and Garnett, J. (1997) *British Foreign Policy: Challenges and Choices for the 21st-Century* (London: Royal Institute of International Affairs/Pinter).

Martin, P. and Brawley, J. (eds) (2000) *Atlantic Politics, Kosovo and NATO's Role* (Basingstoke: Palgrave Macmillan).

McGrew, T. (1988) 'Security and order: the military dimension', in Smith, S. Smith, M. and White, B. (eds), *British Foreign Policy: Tradition, Change and Transformation* (London: Unwin Hyman).

MccGwire, M.(2006) 'Comfort blanket or weapon of war: what is Trident for?', *International Affairs*, 82 (4), July: 627–38.

McInnes, C. (1986) *Trident: The Only Option?* (London: Brassey).

McInnes, C. (1991) 'Trident', in Byrd, P. (ed.), *British Defence Policy: Thatcher and Beyond* (Oxford: Philip Allan).

McInnes, C. (1998) 'Labour's Strategic Defence Review', *International Affairs*, 74 (4), October: 823–45.

McIntyre, W.D. (1998) *British Decolonisation, 1946–1997* (London: Macmillan).

McIntyre, W.D. (1999) 'Commonwealth legacy', in Brown, J. and Louis, W.R. (eds), *The Oxford History of the British Empire: The Twentieth Century* (Oxford: Oxford University Press).

Mackintosh, J.P. (1968) *The British Cabinet* (London: University Paperback).

Macmillan, H. (1966) *Winds of Change, 1914–1939* (London: Macmillan).

Macmillan, H. (1971) *Riding the Storm, 1956–1959* (London: Macmillan).

Macmillan, H. (1972) *Pointing the Way, 1959–1961* (London: Macmillan).

Major, J. (1999) *The Autobiography* (London: HarperCollins).

Makin, G.A. (1983) 'Argentine approaches to the Falklands/Malvinas: was the resort to violence foreseeable?', *International Affairs*, 59 (3): 391–403.

Marsh, S. and Baylis, J. (2006) 'The Anglo-American "Special relationship": the Lazarus of international relations', *Diplomacy and Statecraft*, 17 (1), March: 173–211.

Meacham, J. (2003) *Franklin and Winston: Portrait of a Friendship* (London: Granta).

Mepham, D. (2007) 'Human rights, justice and security', in Held, D. and Mepham, D. (eds), *Progressive Foreign Policy: New Directions for the UK* (London: IPPR), pp. 56–70.

May, A. (1999) *Britain and Europe since 1945* (London: Longman).

Menon, A. (2004) 'From Crisis to Catharsis: European Security and Defence Policy after Iraq', *International Affairs*, 80 (4): 631–48.

Miller, D. (1996) *Export or Die: Britain's Defence Trade with Iran and Iraq* (London: Cassell).

Miller, D. (2000) 'British foreign policy, human rights and Iran', in Little, R. and Wickham-Jones, M. (eds), *New Labour's Foreign Policy: A New Moral Crusade?* (Manchester: Manchester University Press), pp. 186–200.

Ministry of Defence (2009) *Defence Framework: How Defence Works* (London: Stationery Office).

Morgan, K. (1984) *Labour in Power, 1945–51* (Oxford: Oxford University Press).

Nailor, P. (1996) 'The Ministry of Defence, 1959–70', in Smith, P. (ed.), *Government and the Armed Forces in Britain, 1856–1990* (London: Hambledon).

Naughtie, J. (2004) *The Accidental American: Tony Blair and the Presidency* (New York: PublicAffairs).

Navias, M. S. (1996) '"Vested interests and vanished dreams": Duncan Sandys, the Chiefs of Staff and the 1957 White Paper', in Smith, P. (ed.), *Government and the Armed Forces in Britain 1856–1990* (London: Hambledon Press), pp. 217–34.

Nielson, K. (1995) *Britain and the Last Tsar: The Russian Factor in British Politics, 1894–1907* (Oxford: Clarendon).

Newhouse, J. (1989) *The Nuclear Age: from Hiroshima to Star Wars* (London: Michael Joseph).

Niblett, R, (2007) 'Choosing between America and Europe: a new context for British foreign policy', *International Affairs*, 83 (4), July: 627–41.

Nicholas, H.G. (1975) *United States and Britain* (Chicago: Chicago University Press).

Northedge, F.S. (1974) *Descent from Power: British Foreign Policy 1945–73* (London: George Allen & Unwin).

Northedge, F.S. (1976) 'Britain as a second rank power', in Winkler, H. (ed.), *Twentieth Century Britain: National Power and Social Welfare* (New York: New Viewpoints), pp. 243–53.

Nunnerly, D. (1972) *President Kennedy and Britain* (London: Bodley Head).

Nutting, A, (1967) *No End of a Lesson: The Story of Suez* (London: Chatto and Windus).

Nye, J. (2002), *Soft Power: The Means to Success in World Politics* (Oxford: Oxford University Press).

O'Donnell, C.M and Whitman, R.G. (2007) 'European policy under Gordon Brown: perspectives on a future Prime Minister', *International Affairs*, 83 (1): 253–72.

O'Malley, E, (2007) 'Setting choices, controlling outcomes: the operation of prime ministerial influence and the UK's decision to invade Iraq', *British Journal of Politics and International Research,* 9 (1): 1–19.

Otte, T. G. (ed.) (2002a) *The Makers of British Foreign Policy: From Pitt to Thatcher* (Basingstoke: Palgrave Macmillan)

Otte, T. G. (2002b) '"It's what made Britain Great": reflections on British foreign policy from Malpaquet to Maastricht', in Otte, T.G. (ed.), *The Makers of British Foreign Policy: From Pitt to Thatcher* (Basingstoke: Palgrave Macmillan), pp. 1–34.

Otte, T. (2002) '"Floating Downstream"?: Lord Salisbury and British Foreign Policy, 1878–1902', in Otte, T.(ed.), *The Makers of British Foreign Policy: From Pitt to Thatcher* (Basingstoke: Palgrave Macmillan), pp. 98–127.

Ovendale, R, (1984) *The Foreign Policy of the British Labour Governments 1945–51* (Leicester: Leicester University Press).

Ovendale, R. (ed.) (1994) *British Defence Policy since 1945* (Manchester: Manchester University Press).

Ovendale, R. (1996) *Britain, the United States and the Transfer of Power in the Middle East, 1945–1962* (Leicester: Leicester University Press).

Ovendale, R. (1990) 'William Strang and the Permanent Under-Secretary's Committee', in Zametica, J. (ed.), *British Officials and British Foreign Policy, 1945–1950* (Leicester: Leicester University Press), pp. 212–27.

Ovendale, R. (1998) *Anglo-American Relations in the Twentieth Century* (London: Macmillan).

Overy, R. (1999) *The Road to War*, rev., updated edn (Harmondsworth: Penguin).

Owen, N. (1991) '"Responsibility without power". The Attlee government and the end of British rule in India', in Tiratsoo, N. (ed.), *The Attlee Years* (London: Pinter).

Parsons, Sir Anthony (1991) 'Britain and the world', in Kavanagh, D. and Seldon, A. (eds), *The Thatcher Effect: A Decade of Change* (Oxford: Oxford University Press).

Payne, A. (2006) 'Blair, Brown and the Gleneagles agenda: Making Poverty History, or confronting the global politics of unequal development', *International Affairs*, 92 (5): 917–35.

Pearce, R. (1991) *Attlee* (London: Longman).

Peden, G.(1979) *British Rearmament and the Treasury 1932–1939* (Edinburgh: Scottish Academic Press).

Peden, G. (2000) *The Treasury in British Public Policy 1906–1959* (Oxford: Oxford University Press).

Pelling, H. (1984) *The Labour Governments 1945–51* (London: Macmillan).

Peston, R. (2005) *Brown's Britain* (London: Short Books).

Philpott, W. (1996) 'The campaign from Ministry of Defence, 1919–36', in Smith, P. (ed.), *Government and the Armed Forces in Britain, 1856–1990* (London: Hambledon).

Pierre, A.J. (1972) *Nuclear Politics: The British Experience with an Independent Strategic Force* (London: Oxford University Press).

Pimlott, B. (1985) *Hugh Dalton* (London: Macmillan).

Pliatzky, L. (1982) *Getting and Spending: Public Expenditure, Employment and Inflation* (Oxford: Basil Blackwell).

Pollard, S. (1984) *The Wasting of the British Economy* (London: Croom Helm).

Ponting, C. (1989) *Breach of Promise: Labour in Power, 1964–70* (London: Hamish Hamilton).

Porter, B. (1987) *Britain, Europe and the World, 1850–1986: Delusions of Grandeur*, 2nd edn (London: George Allen & Unwin).

Porter, B. (1996) *The Lion's Share: A Short History of British Imperialism 1850–1995* (London: Longman).

Porteous, T. (2005) 'British government policy in sub-Saharan Africa under new Labour', *International Affairs*, 81 (2): 281–97.

Pugh, P. (2006) 'Our unaffordable defence policy: what now?', *RUSI Defence Systems* (www.contention@rusi.org).

Pythian, M. (2000) *The Politics of British Arms sales since 1964* (Manchester: Manchester University Press).

Quinlan, M. (2006) 'The future of United Kingdom nuclear weapons: shaping the debate', *International Affairs*, 82 (4): 627–37.

Renwick, R. (1996) *Fighting with Allies: America and Britain in Peace and War* (London: Macmillan).

Reynolds, D. (1981) *The Creation of the Anglo-American Alliance, 1937–41: Study in Competitive Co-operation* (London: Europa).

Reynolds, D. (1986) 'Roosevelt, Churchill and the wartime Anglo-American alliance, 1935–1945: towards a new synthesis', in Bull, H. and Louis, W.R. (eds), *The Special Relationship: Anglo-American Relations since 1945* (Oxford: Clarendon Press).

Reynolds, D. (1991) *Britannia Overruled: British Policy and World Power in the 20th Century* (Harlow: Longman).

Rhodes, R. (1995) 'From prime ministerial power to core executive', in Rhodes, R.A.W. and Dunleavy, P. (eds), *The Prime Minister, Cabinet and Core Executive* (London: Macmillan).

Riddell, Lord (1933) *Intimate Diary of a Peace Conference and After* (London: Gollancz).

Riddell, P.(2005) 'Europe', in Seldon, A. and Kavanagh, D. (eds), *The Blair Effect 2001–5* (Cambridge: Cambridge University Press).

Roberts, F. (1984) 'Ernest Bevin as Foreign Secretary', in Ovendale, R. (ed.), *The Foreign Policy of the British Labour Governments 1945–51* (Leicester: Leicester University Press).

Rogers, P. (2006) 'Big boats and bigger skimmers: determining Britain's role in the Long War', *International Affairs* 82 (4): 651–65.

Rose, R. (2001) *The Prime Minister in a Shrinking World* (Oxford: Polity).

Rosecrance, R.N. (1968) *Defence of the Realm: British Strategy in the Nuclear Epoch* (New York: Columbia University Press).

Ruane, K. (1995) 'Refusing to pay the price: British foreign policy in pursuit of victory in Vietnam in 1952–54', *English Historical Review*, 150 (453).

Ruane, K. (1996) '"Containing America": Aspects of British Foreign Policy and the Cold War in South East Asia, 1951–54', *Diplomacy and Statecraft*, 7 (1): 141–74.

Ruane, K. and Ellison, J. (2007) 'Managing the Americans: Anthony Eden, Harold Macmillan and the pursuit of "Power by Proxy" in the 1950s', in Johnson, G. (ed.), *The Foreign Office and British Diplomacy in the 20th Century* (London: Routledge), pp. 147–67.

Runciman, W.G. (2004) *Butler and Hutton: Lifting the Lid on the Workings of Power* (London: British Academy).

Sampson, A. (2004) *Who Runs This Place? The Anatomy of Britain in the 21st Century* (London: John Murray).

Sanders, D. (1990) *Losing an Empire, Finding a Role: British Foreign Policy since 1945* (London: Macmillan).

Sanders, D. (1993) 'Foreign and defence policy', in Dunleavy, P., Gamble, A., Holliday, I. and Peele, G. *Developments in British Politics 4* (London: Macmillan).

Savage, S. and Atkinson, R. (eds) (2001) *Public Policy under Blair* (Basingstoke: Palgrave Macmillan).

Savage, S. and Robins, L. (eds) (1990) *Public Policy under Thatcher* (London: Macmillan).

Schlesinger, A.M. Jr. (1965) *A Thousand Days: John F. Kennedy in the White House* (London: Deutsch).

Scott, L. (2006) 'Labour and the bomb: the first 80 years', *International Affairs*, 82 (4): 695–700.

Scott-Smith, G. (2003) '"Her rather ambitious Washington program": Margaret Thatcher's International Visitor Program visit to United States in 1961', *Contemporary British History* 17 (4): pp. 65–86.

Seitz, R. (1998) *Over Here* (London: Weidenfeld & Nicolson).

Seldon, A. (1981) *Churchill's Indian Summer, the Conservative Government 1951–1955* (London: Hodder and Stoughton).

Seldon, A. (ed.) (2001) *The Blair Effect, 1997–2001* (London: Little, Brown).

Seldon, A. and Kavanagh, D. (eds) (2005) *The Blair Effect, 2001–5* (Cambridge: Cambridge University Press).

Seldon, A. (2005) *Blair* (London: The Free Press).

Seldon, A. (ed.) (2007) *Blair's Britain 1997–2007* (Cambridge: Cambridge University Press).

Seldon, A. (2008) *Blair Unbound* (London: Pocket Books).

Self, R. (2006a) *Neville Chamberlain: A Biography* (Aldershot: Ashgate).

Self, R. (2006b) *Britain, America and the War Debt Controversy: The Economic Diplomacy of an Unspecial Relationship, 1917–1941* (London: Routledge).

Self, R. (2007) 'Perception and posture in Anglo-American relations: the War Debt controversy in the "Official Mind", 1919–1940', *International History Review*, 24 (2): 282–312.

Sharp, P.(2002) "British foreign policy under Margaret Thatcher", in Otte, T.G. (ed.), *The Makers of British Foreign Policy: From Pitt to Thatcher* (Basingstoke: Palgrave Macmillan).

Shepherd, R. (1994) *Iain Macleod: A Biography* (London: Pimlico).

Short, C. (2005) *An Honourable Deception? Iraq and the Misuse of Power* (London: Free Press).

Sked, A. (1987) *Britain's Decline: Problems and Perspectives* (Oxford: Blackwell).

Shukman, D. (1996) *Tomorrow's War: The Threat of High-Technology Weapons* (New York: Harcourt).

Simpson, J. (1983) *The Independent Nuclear State: The United States, Britain and the Military Atom* (London: Macmillan).

SIPRI (1992) *Yearbook: World Armaments and Disarmament* (Oxford: Oxford University Press).

SIPRI (2008) *Yearbook: World Armaments and Disarmament* (Oxford: Oxford University Press).

Smith, A. (1996), 'Michael Heseltine and the reorganisation of the Ministry of Defence, 1983–84', in Smith, P. (ed.), *Government and the Armed Forces in Britain, 1856–1990* (London: Hambledon Press).

Smith, G. (1990) *Reagan and Thatcher: The Extraordinary Inside Story of the 'Special Relationship'* (London: Bodley Head).

Smith, J. (2005) 'A missed opportunity? New Labour's European policy 1997–2005', *International Affairs* 81 (4), July: 703–21.

Smith, M. (1988) 'Britain and United States: beyond the "Special Relationship"?', in Byrd, P. (ed.), *British Foreign Policy under Thatcher* (Oxford: Philip Allan), pp. 8–34.

Smith, M. (2006) 'Britain, Europe and the world', in Dunleavy, P., Heffernan, R. Cowley, P. and Hay, C. (eds), *Developments in British Politics 8* (Basingstoke: Palgrave Macmillan).

Smith, P. (ed.) (1996) *Government and the Armed Forces in Britain, 1856–1990* (London: Hambledon Press).

Smith, S. and Smith, M. (1988) 'The analytical background: approaches to the study of British foreign policy', in Smith, M. Smith, S. and White, B. (eds), *British Foreign Policy: Tradition, Change and Transformation* (London: Unwin Hyman).

Snyder, W.P. (1964) *The Politics of British Defense Policy 1945–62* (Ohio: Ohio University Press).

Stoler, M.A. (2007) *Allies in War: Britain and America Against the Axis Powers 1940–45* (London: Hodder Arnold).

Stothard, P. (2003) *Thirty Days: A Month at the Heart of Blair's War* (London: HarperCollins).

Strachan, H. (2008) Campaign plans, war plans and British defence policy', *RUSI Journal*, 153 (6).

Strang, Lord (1955) *The Foreign Office* (London: George Allen & Unwin).

Strang, Lord (1956) *Home and Abroad* (London: Andre Deutsch).

Taylor, P.M. (1989) 'The projection of Britain, 1945–56', in Young, J.W. and Dockrill, M. (eds), *British Foreign Policy 1945–56* (London: Macmillan).

Thatcher, M. (1993) *The Downing Street Years* (London: HarperCollins).

Thatcher, M. (1995) *The Path to Power* (London: HarperCollins).

Thatcher, M.(2002) *Statecraft: Strategies for a Changing World* (London: HarperCollins).

Theakston, K. (2000) 'New Labour and the Foreign Office', in Little, R. and Wickham-Jones, M. (eds), *New Labour's Foreign Policy: A New Moral Crusade?* (Manchester: Manchester University Press).

Thomas, H. (1970) *The Suez Affair* (London: Penguin).

Thorne, C.(1978) *Allies of a Kind: The United States, Great Britain and the War against Japan, 1941–1945* (Oxford: Oxford University Press).

Thorpe, A. (1994) *Britain in the Era of Two World Wars 1914–45* (London: Longman).

Thorpe, D.R. (2004) *Anthony Eden: the Life and Times of Anthony Eden, First Earl of Avon, 1897–1977* (London: Pimlico).

Tilley, J. and Gaselee, S. (1933) *The Foreign Office* (London: Putnam's).

Tomlinson, J. (1990) *Public Policy and the Economy since 1900* (Oxford: Clarendon Press).

Tomlinson, J. (2009) 'Thrice denied: "Declinism" as a recurrent theme in British history in the long 20th-century', *Twentieth Century British History*, 20 (2): 227–51.

Turner, J. (2000) *The Tories and Europe* (Manchester: Manchester University Press).

Twigge, S. and Scott, L., (2000) *Planning Armageddon: Britain, the US and the Command of Nuclear Forces, 1945–1964* (London: Harwood Academic Press).

Urban, G. (1996) *Diplomacy and Disillusion at the Court of Margaret Thatcher: An Insider's View* (London: Tauris).

Vickers, R. (2000) 'Labour's search for a Third Way in foreign policy', in Little, R. and Wickham-Jones, M. (eds), *New Labour's Foreign Policy: A New Moral Crusade?* (Manchester: Manchester University Press), pp. 33–48.

Vital, D. (1968) *The Making of British Foreign Policy* (London: George Allen & Unwin).

Wallace, W. (1970) 'World status without tears', in Bogdanor, V. and Skidelsky, R. (eds), *The Age of Affluence 1951–1964* (London: Macmillan).

Wallace, W. (1975) *The Foreign Policy Process in Britain* (London: Royal Institute of International Affairs).

Wallace, W. (1991) 'Foreign policy and national identity in United Kingdom', *International Affairs*, 67 (1): 70–86.

Wallace, W. (1992) 'British foreign policy after the Cold War', *International Affairs*, 68 (3), July: 235–52.

Wallace, W.(1994) 'Foreign policy', in Kavanagh, D. and Seldon, A. (ed.), *The Major Effect* (London: Macmillan).

Wallace, W. (2005) 'The collapse of British foreign policy', *International Affairs*, 81 (1), January: 53–68.

Wallace, W. and Stockley, N. (1998) *Liberal Democrats and the Third Way* (London: Centre for Reform).

Waltz, K. (1979) *Foreign Policy and Democratic Politics: The American and British Experience* (Boston: Little, Brown).

Warner, G. (1989) 'The Anglo-American Special Relationship', *Diplomatic History*, 13 (4): 479–99.

Warner, G. (1984) 'The Labour Governments and the Unity of Western Europe', in Ovendale, R. (ed.), *The Foreign Policy of the British Labour Governments 1945–51* (Leicester: Leicester University Press).

Watt, D.C. (1965) *Personalities and Policies: Studies in the Formulation of British Foreign Policy in the Twentieth Century* (London: Longman).

Wheeler, N.J. and Dunne, T. (1998) 'Good international citizenship: a Third Way for British foreign policy', *International Affairs*, 74 (4): 847–70.

Wheeler, N.J. and Dunne, T. (2001) 'Blair's Britain: a force for good in the world?', in Light, M. and Smith, K. (eds), *Ethics and Foreign Policy* (Cambridge: Cambridge University Press).

Wickham-Jones, M. (2000a) 'Labour's trajectory in foreign affairs: the moral crusade of a pivotal power?', in Little, R. and Wickham-Jones, M. (eds), *New Labour's Foreign Policy: A New Moral Crusade?* (Manchester: Manchester University Press), pp. 3–32.

Wickham-Jones, M. (2000b) 'Labour party politics and foreign policy', in Little, R. and Wickham-Jones, M. (eds), *New Labour's Foreign Policy: a New Moral Crusade?* (Manchester: Manchester University Press), pp. 93–111.

Widen, J.J. and Colman, J. (2007) 'Lyndon B. Johnson, Alec Douglas-Home, Europe and the NATO Multilateral Force, 1963–64', *Journal of Transatlantic Studies*, 5 (2): 179–98.

Williams, F. (1961) *A Prime Minister Remembers: The War and Post-War Memoirs of the Rt Hon. Earl Attlee* (London: Heinemann).

Williams, G. (1997) '"A matter of regret": Britain, the 1983 Grenada crisis and the Special Relationship', *Twentieth Century British History*, 8.

Williams, P. (2004) 'Who is making UK foreign policy?', *International Affairs* 80 (5): 911–29.

Williams, P. (2005) *British Foreign Policy under New Labour 1997–2005* (Basingstoke: Palgrave Macmillan).

Wilson, H. (1971) *The Labour Government 1964–1970: A Personal Record* (London: Weidenfeld & Nicolson).

Wilson, H. (1976) *The Governance of Britain* (London: Weidenfeld & Nicolson).

Wilson, H. (1979) *Final Term: A Labour Government, 1974–76* (London: Weidenfeld & Nicolson).

Winand, P. (1993) *Eisenhower, Kennedy and United States of Europe* (London: Macmillan).

Wyatt, W. (1998) *The Journals of Woodrow Wyatt, volume 1* (London: Macmillan).

Young, H. (1991) *One of Us: A Biography of Margaret Thatcher*, final edn (London: Macmillan).

Young, H. (1998) *This Blessed Plot: Britain and Europe from Churchill to Blair* (London: Papermac).

Young, J.W. (1993) *Britain and European Unity, 1945–1992* (London: Macmillan).

Young, J.W. (1997) *Britain and the World in the 20th Century* (London: Arnold).

Young, R. (2000) 'New Labour and international development', in Coates, D. and Lawler, P. (eds), *New Labour in Power* (Manchester: Manchester University Press).

Zametica, J. (1990) *British Officials and British Foreign Policy, 1945–1950* (Leicester: Leicester University Press).

Zeigler, P. (1993) *Wilson: The Authorised Biography of Lord Wilson of Rievaulx* (London: Weidenfeld & Nicolson).

Index